Human Rights in the Americas

This interdisciplinary book explores human rights in the Americas from multiple perspectives and fields. Taking 1492 as a point of departure, the text explores Eurocentric historiographies of human rights and offers a more complete understanding of the genealogy of the human rights discourse and its many manifestations in the Americas.

The essays use a variety of approaches to reveal the larger contexts from which they emerge, providing a cross-sectional view of subjects, countries, methodologies, and foci explicitly dedicated toward understanding historical factors and circumstances that have shaped human rights nationally and internationally within the Americas. The chapters explore diverse cultural, philosophical, political, and literary expressions in which human rights discourses circulate across the continent taking into consideration issues such as race, class, gender, genealogy, and nationality. While acknowledging the ongoing centrality of the nation, the volume promotes a shift in the study of the Americas as a dynamic transnational space of conflict, domination, resistance, negotiation, complicity, accommodation, dialogue, and solidarity where individuals, nations, peoples, institutions, and intellectual and political movements share struggles, experiences, and imaginaries.

It will be of interest to all scholars and students of Inter-American studies and those from all disciplines interested in Human Rights.

María Herrera-Sobek is Professor Emerita from the University of California, Santa Barbara where she worked from 1997 to 2019.

Francisco A. Lomelí is Professor Emeritus from the University of California at Santa Barbara and has worked and taught in both the Spanish and Portuguese and Chicana/o Studies Departments since 1978.

Luz Angélica Kirschner is an Assistant Professor in the School of American and Global Studies at South Dakota State University.

Inter-American Research: Contact, Communication, Conflict
Series Editors: Olaf Kaltmeier, Wilfried Raussert,
and Sebastian Thies

The Americas are shaped by a multitude of dynamics which have extensive, conflictive, and at times contradictory consequences for society, culture, politics, and the environment. These processes are embedded within a history of interdependence and mutual observation between North and South which originates in the conquest and simultaneous "invention" of America by European colonial powers.

The series will challenge the ways we think about the Americas, in particular, and the concept of area studies, in general. Put simply, the series perceives the Americas as transversally related, chronotopically entangled, and multiply interconnected. In its critical positioning at the crossroads of area studies and cultural studies, the series aims to push further the postcolonial, postnational, and cross-border turns in recent studies of the Americas toward a model of horizontal dialogue between cultures, areas, and disciplines.

The series pursues the goal to "think the Americas different" and to explore these phenomena from transregional as well as interdisciplinary perspectives.

For more information about this series, please visit https://www.routledge.com/InterAmerican-Research-Contact-Communication-Conflict/book-series/ASHSER-1426.

Entangled Heritages
Postcolonial Perspectives on the Uses of the Past in Latin America
Edited by Olaf Kaltmeier, Mario Rufer

Mobile and Entangled America(s)
Edited by Maryemma Graham and Wilfried Raussert

Practices of Resistance in the Caribbean
Narratives, Aesthetics and Politics
Edited by Wiebke Beushausen, Miriam Brandel, Joseph T. Farquharson, Marius Littschwager, Annika McPherson and Julia Roth

Political Protest and Undocumented Immigrant Youth
(Re-)framing Testimonio
Stefanie Quakernack

Critical Geopolitics of the Polar Regions
An Inter-American Perspective
Dorothea Wehrmann

Sonic Politics
Music and Social Movements in the Americas
Edited by Olaf Kaltmeier and Wilfried Raussert

Human Rights in the America
Edited by María Herrera-Sobek, Francisco A. Lomelí, and Luz Angélica Kirschner

Human Rights in the Americas

Edited by María Herrera-Sobek,
Francisco A. Lomelí, and
Luz Angélica Kirschner

LONDON AND NEW YORK

First published 2021
by Routledge
2 Park Square, Milton Park, Abingdon, Oxon OX14 4RN

and by Routledge
52 Vanderbilt Avenue, New York, NY 10017

Routledge is an imprint of the Taylor & Francis Group, an informa business

© 2021 selection and editorial matter, María Herrera-Sobek, Francisco A. Lomelí, and Luz Angélica Kirschner; individual chapters, the contributors

The right of María Herrera-Sobek, Francisco A. Lomelí, and Luz Angélica Kirschner to be identified as the authors of the editorial material, and of the authors for their individual chapters, has been asserted in accordance with Sections 77 and 78 of the Copyright, Designs and Patents Act 1988.

All rights reserved: No part of this book may be reprinted or reproduced or utilized in any form or by any electronic, mechanical, or other means, now known or hereafter invented, including photocopying and recording, or in any information storage or retrieval system, without permission in writing from the publishers.

Trademark notice: Product or corporate names may be trademarks or registered trademarks and are used only for identification and explanation without intent to infringe.

British Library Cataloguing-in-Publication Data
A catalog record for this book is available from the British Library

Library of Congress Cataloging-in-Publication Data
A catalog record has been requested for this book

ISBN: 9780367636913 (hbk)
ISBN: 9781003120315 (ebk)

Typeset in Times New Roman
by KnowledgeWorks Global Ltd.

To Josef Raab 1960–2019

*Whose commitment to Inter-American
Studies is an inspiration to all of us*

Contents

Preface x
List of illustrations xi
List of contributors xiii
Acknowledgments xviii

Introduction: Human rights in the Americas 1
LUZ ANGÉLICA KIRSCHNER, MARÍA HERRERA-SOBEK,
AND FRANCISCO A. LOMELÍ

PART I
Early origins of human rights 29

1 **Human rights in the Americas: A stony path** 31
 JOSEF RAAB

2 **Constructing rights and empires in the early Americas: The parallel reception histories of Carlos de Sigüenza y Góngora and Cotton Mather** 45
 PHILIPP REISNER

3 **Maps of violence, maps of resistance, or, where is home in the Americas?** 61
 ROLAND WALTER

PART II
Human rights in Central America and the Caribbean 79

4 **Human rights situation in Central America through the lens of literary representations of violence** 81
 XAVER DANIEL HERGENRÖTHER

viii *Contents*

5   Rebellion, repression, reform: U.S. Marines in the
    Dominican Republic   95
    BREANNE ROBERTSON

PART III
Human rights and gender   115

6   Black women writers in the Americas: The struggle
    for human rights in the context of coloniality   117
    ISABEL CALDEIRA

7   Autobiography, fiction, and racial hatred representation
    in Jamaica Kincaid's *See Now Then*   132
    GONÇALO CHOLANT

8   The rebirth of the myth of the American hero and feminism   144
    RITA SANTOS

PART IV
**Human Rights: Mexican Indigenous groups and
Mexican Americans groups**   161

9   Dancing resistance, controlling singing and rights
    to name heritage: Mexican Indigenous autonomy,
    P'urhépecha practices, and United Nations   163
    RUTH HELLIER-TINOCO

10 Carey McWilliams' activism and the democratic
    human rights tradition   181
    MARÍA JOSÉ CANELO

11 The ontogenesis of fear in Héctor Tobar's
    The Barbarian Nurseries   196
    ALEXANDER ULLMAN

PART V
Human rights: Afro-Brazilians and Afro-Latinas/os   209

12 Brazilian *quilombos*: Castaínho and its struggle
    for human rights   211
    WELLINGTON MARINHO DE LIRA

13 *Capá Prieto* and the decolonial Afro-Latin(a/o)
   American imagination   223
   LUZ ANGÉLICA KIRSCHNER

14 "We got Latin soul!": Transbarrio dialogs and Afro-Latin
   identity formation in New York's Puerto Rican community
   during the age of Black Power (1966–1972)   243
   MATTI STEINITZ

PART VI
Human right, animals rights, and posthuman rights   263

15 From racism to speciesism: The question of freedom
   of the other in the works of J. M. Coetzee
   and Jure Detela   265
   MARJETKA GOLEŽ KAUČIČ

16 To be or not to be human: The plasticity of
   posthuman rights   283
   NICOLE SPARLING BARCO

   Index   295

Preface

The volume *Human Rights in the Americas* is part of a larger project related to the comprehensive and interdisciplinary study of the Americas. The sponsoring scholarly organization is the International Association of Inter-American Studies (IAS). Founded in Bielefeld, Germany in 2009, the Executive Committee members consisted of President Josef Raab, from the University of Duisburg-Essen, Germany; Vice President María Herrera-Sobek, from the University of California, Santa Barbara; and Secretary Wilfried Raussert, from the University of Bielefeld. One of the primary objectives of the IAS was to sponsor a biennial international conference on an important theme focusing on the Americas. It was to take place every 2 years and the site was to alternate between Europe and the Americas. The second important goal was to publish a select number of papers from a variety of scholars who represent critical perspectives on Inter-American topics. The present volume, written in English, derives from the papers presented at the conference held at the University of California at Santa Barbara in 2016 on the topic of human rights. The editorial board for this volume consists of three members of the IAS: María Herrera-Sobek from the University of California, Santa Barbara (UCSB), Francisco A. Lomelí also from UCSB, and Luz Angélica Kirschner from South Dakota State University (SDSU).

Illustrations

Figures

5.1 13th Company, 4th Marines traveling with Colonel Joseph Pendleton's column on the road from Monte Cristi to Santiago, 26 June to 6 July, 1916. Official Marine Corps photograph #521541, Marine Corps History Division, Quantico, VA. 100

5.2 U.S. Marines searching Dominican homes for arms. Official Marine corps photograph #5012, Marine Corps History Division, Quantico, VA. 104

5.3 Acting Military Governor, Brigadier General Harry Lee, USMC (first row, far right) and Executive and Military Staffs. Official Marine Corps photograph #530542, Marine Corps History Division, Quantico, VA. 110

9.1 The auditorium for the XLV Artistic Contest of the P'urhépecha People (XLV Concurso artístico de la raza P´urhépecha), October 18, 2016, Zacán, Michoacán, México. The long paper streamers, displaying the colors of rights movement for the P'urhépecha Autonomous Nation and the Supreme Indigenous Council of Michoacán, are strung around the auditorium. Photography by Ruth Hellier. 164

9.2 The insignia and flag of the P'urhépecha Autonomous Nation and the Supreme Indigenous Council of Michoacán is suspended high above the heads of the audience and performers at the Artistic Contest of the P'urhépecha People. Photography by Ruth Hellier. 164

9.3 An ensemble of the Dance of the Old Men (los Viejitos) at The XLV Artistic Contest of the P'urhépecha People (XLV Concurso artístico de la raza P´urhépecha), October 18, 2016, Zacán, Michoacán, México. This group is Tzipikua, Los Viejos Alegres, led by Procopio Cázares Patricio from the Island of Jarácuaro, Lake Pátzcuaro, winners of the 2016 Tata Gervasio López prize. Photography by Ruth Hellier. 165

xii *Illustrations*

9.4 A frame displaying the Dance of the Old Men of Jarácuaro, within the official video for the *pirekua* on the UNESCO website, Intangible Cultural Heritage of Humanity, United Nations Educational, Scientific and Cultural Organization (UNESCO). See www.unesco.org/culture/ich/en/RL/pirekua-traditional-song-of-the-purhepecha. 175

9.5 A frame displaying the Zacán Concurso, within the official video for the *pirekua* on the UNESCO website. See www.unesco.org/culture/ich/en/RL/pirekua-traditional-song-of-the-purhepecha. 176

Table

15.1 Traditional comparison of the human being and the non-human being or animal 267

Contributors

Editors

María Herrera-Sobek is Professor Emerita from the University of California, Santa Barbara where she worked from 1997 to 2019. She also taught at UC Irvine and was a Visiting Professor at Harvard University and Stanford University. At UCSB she served as Associate Vice Chancellor for Diversity, Equity, and Inclusion and Professor of Chicana and Chicano Studies. Her publications include *The Mexican Corrido: A Feminist Analysis; Northward Bound: The Mexican Immigrant Experience in Ballad and Song; Chicano Folklore*; and *Celebrating Latino Folklore: An Encyclopedia of Cultural Traditions* Vol. I, II, and III. She has published numerous articled and edited and coedited several books on literature and folklore. In addition, she has published poetry in journals and book anthologies. Herrera-Sobek has received numerous awards and honors, including Modern Language Association, Division of Chicano and Latino Literature: Distinguished Scholar Award; UCLA Spanish and Portuguese Department: Distinguish Alumna; and 2o Galardón Internacional Luis Leal Hispa/U.S.A. Association.

Francisco A. Lomelí is Professor Emeritus from the University of California at Santa Barbara and has worked and taught in both the Spanish and Portuguese and Chicana/o Studies since 1978. He is a trained Latin Americanist with an expertise in Chicano/a literature, emphasizing literary history and theory of the novel while maintaining an eye on a variety of foci: testimony, barrio poetics, cultural semiotics, Spanglish, and other areas. He has published extensively in both Latin American and Chicano/a topics, including a number of prize-winning reference books such as *Chicano Literature: A Reference Guide, Dictionary of Literary Biography (three volumes), Handbook of Hispanic Cultures in the United States: Literature and Art, Aztlán: Essays on the Chicano Homeland* (including an expanded second edition), *Routledge Handbook of Chicana/o Studies, and Historical Dictionary of U.S. Latino Literature*. He has also written or coauthored such works as *Chicano Perspectives in Literature, Defying* *the Inquisition in Colonial New Mexico: The Life and Writings of Miguel de Quintana, The Writings of Eusebio Chacón, and Other Works.*

Luz Angélica Kirschner is an Assistant Professor in the School of American and Global Studies at South Dakota State University. Located at the intersection of critical race, gender, and ethnic studies, her research focuses on comparative studies from inter-American and Transatlantic Perspectives. She is editor and author of the volume *Expanding Latinidad: An Inter-American Perspective* (2012). Her most recent publications appeared in *The Cambridge History of Latina/o American Literature* (2018), *The Routledge Handbook to the History and Society of the Americas* (2019), and *The Routledge Handbook to the Culture and Media of the Americas* (2020). Kirschner is currently completing her single-authored monograph with the working title "The Persistence of Racialization: Literature, Gender, and Ethnicity."

Contributors

Isabel Caldeira is an Associate Professor of American Studies, at the Faculty of Letters, and Senior Research Fellow of CES, at the University of Coimbra. She teaches American Literature and Culture and Feminist Studies at the graduate and undergraduate levels. Her present research fields are the literatures of the African diaspora with an inter-American, postcolonial and feminist lens. She contributed to *Trans/Oceanic, Trans/American, Trans/lation: Issues in International American Studies* (Cambridge Scholars, 2009), *America Where? 21st Century Transatlantic Views* (Peter Lang, 2012) and *The Edge of One of Many Circles* (Coimbra University Pr., 2018), which she also coedited, and *Companion to Inter-American Studies* (Routledge, 2017). She is the President of the International Association of Inter-American Studies.

Maria José Canelo is an Assistant Professor at the Faculty of Letters and senior researcher at the Center for Social Studies, University of Coimbra. She holds a Ph.D. in American Studies from NYU ("Carey McWilliams and the question of cultural citizenship in the 1940s"). Her latest publications include: "Nations in Review(s): modernist 'little' magazines and the (trans)national imagination," *Comparative Literature Studies* (2018); "Lessons in transnationalism as a framework of knowledge in the critiques of José Martí, Randolph Bourne, Herbert Bolton, and Waldo Frank" (*The Edge of One of Many Circles* 2017). Main interests: citizenship, nationalism, difference, visuality, literary magazines, cultural and literary studies, American and Inter-American Studies.

Gonçalo Cholant holds a Ph.D. in Modern Languages: Culture and Literature by the Faculty of Humanities at the University of Coimbra, an MA (2012) in Feminist Studies (FLUC), Portugal, and a BA (2008) in

English Language and Literature by the Federal University of Pelotas (UFPel), Brazil. His research interests are African American Literature, Caribbean Literature, Autobiography, Women's Writing, Feminist Studies, Representations of Violence, and Trauma.

Marjetka Golež Kaučič is a Research Advisor at the Research Centre of the Slovenian Academy of Sciences and Arts, Institute of Ethnomusicology and Associate Professor at Postgraduate School ZRC SAZU, Ljubljana, Slovenia where she teaches the courses: "Slovenian folk songs and literary poetry - folkloristic and intertextual viewpoints" and "Ecoculture: Studies of animals and nature in folklore, literature and culture." She has published and edited several scholarly monographs as well as a number of articles and papers in Slovenia and abroad ("Zoofolkloristics: first insights towards the new discipline," 2015; *Slovenian Folk Ballad*, 2018).

Ruth Hellier-Tinoco is a Professor and creative artist at the University of California, Santa Barbara, United States, researching and teaching in the areas of critical performance, music, dance and theater studies, cultural history, and feminist studies. Dr. Hellier-Tinoco's research projects focus on representation, power dynamics and the politics and poetics of performance and visual culture in Mexico and on experimental performance-making, embodied vocality, and community and environmental arts. Her publications include *Embodying Mexico: Tourism, Nationalism, and Performance*; *Women Singers in Global Contexts: Music, Biography, Identity*; and *Performing Palimpsest Bodies: Postmemory Theatre Experiments in Mexico*. She held the role of editor of the multidisciplinary journal *Mexican Studies/Estudios Mexicanos* for 5 years.

Xaver Daniel Hergenröther, Mag. Dr. Phil., is university assistant at the Center for Inter-American Studies (CIAS) at the University of Graz. He studied Romance Studies at the Universities of Graz and Bamberg (Cotutelle de thèse) writing his doctoral thesis on the topic "The Reworking Process of the Past in Guatemala after the Civil War. Narration and Factuality in Archive, Literature and New Media." His emphasis in research and teaching in Latin-/Inter-American Studies is on cultural representations of human rights in the Americas, the role of the author/cultural worker in political conflicts, and the creative production of literature/culture in exile.

Wellington Marinho de Lira is a Professor at the Universidade Federal de Pernambuco (UFPE), Recife, Brazil, where he coordinates research and extension projects that have their foundations on the basis of language, culture, and identity. He has held workshops on the Portuguese Language of Brazil and Brazilian culture in several universities abroad, among them: Justus-Liebig Universität in Giessen, Germany; Sheridan College in Toronto, Canada; Metropolitan University of Education Sciences and University of Santiago, both in Chile; Appalachian State

University in Boone, NC, United States; University of Oslo in Norway and Magnitogorsk State University in Russia. His current research is titled *Language Education for Promoting Dignity and Helping Overcome Humiliation: Principles and Practices for Language Teachers.*

Josef Raab was a Professor of North American Studies at the University of Duisburg-Essen. His research interests include Inter-American Studies, ethnicity (especially U.S. Latinas and Latinos), borders, cultural hybridity, and the whole range of U.S. American Literature from the seventeenth to the 21st century. He has also written on U.S. Catholicism, the German presence in the United States, city narratives, television, film, and transnationalism in the Americas. From 2009 to 2018, he served as the Founding President of the International Association of Inter-American Studies.

Philipp Reisner is a Lecturer at the American Studies Department of Heinrich Heine University Düsseldorf. His research interests include early modern Anglo-America, religion in U.S. America, the histories of childhood, education, and music, and contemporary U.S. American Literature. He received his doctorate from Heinrich Heine University Düsseldorf with his dissertation on the New English theologian Cotton Mather (1663–1728) in the context of early modern society. His dissertation with the title *Cotton Mather als Aufklärer. Glaube und Gesellschaft im Neuengland der Frühen Neuzeit* was published in 2012. He is currently working on his habilitation project, which is a structural study of contemporary U.S. American poetry.

Breanne Robertson is an education specialist at the National Archives in Washington D.C. Her research focuses on U.S.-Latin American relations, and the U.S. Marine Corps. Her publications include Investigating Iwo: *The Flag Raisings in Myth, Memory, & Esprit de Corps* (2019) and various essays about cultural diplomacy and representations of race in World War II-era textbooks and mural art. Her current book project, *Good Neighbors in the Good War: Mesoamerican Antiquity in the Art of Hemispheric Defense* considers U.S. artists' appropriation of pre-Columbian themes in relation to President Franklin D. Roosevelt's foreign policy initiatives in Latin America under the Good Neighbor Policy.

Rita Santos is currently a Ph.D. student in Modern Languages: Cultures, Literatures, and Translation at FLUC/CES. Her doctoral dissertation, entitled "Pearl Harbor and 9/11 trauma: understanding the gendered (super) hero mythical narratives," focuses on the mythological construction of "the American hero" in popular culture post-Pearl Harbor and 9/11.

Nicole Sparling Barco is a Professor of World Literature and the director of the Cultural & Global Studies Program at Central Michigan University where she teaches courses on World Literature, Literature of the Americas, African American Literature, Women and Gender Studies, and Genre. She specializes in comparative studies of North and South American cultural production and, more specifically, in the literature of the 20th-century written in English, Spanish, and Portuguese from these regions. Her most recent publications include "Can the Fetus Speak?: Revolutionary Wombs, Body Politics, and Feminist Philosophy" in *New Encounters between Philosophy and Literature II*, a special issue of *Humanities*; and "La ciencia de género según Angélica Gorodischer" in *La ciencia ficción en América Latina: Aproximaciones teóricas al imaginario de la experimentación cultural*, a special issue of *Revista Iberoamericana*

Matti Steinitz is a researcher on Afro-diasporic movements and cultures at the Center for Inter-American Studies (Bielefeld University) with a special interest in transnational flows and networks of solidarity between Black communities in Latin America and the United States. Currently, he is writing his Ph.D. thesis on the impact of Soul music and the Black Power movement in Panama, Brazil, and New York's Puerto Rican community. He is also coordinator of the Black Americas Network, which brings together a broad range of scholars, activists, and artists, whose work is related to cultural and political developments in the African diasporas of the Americas.

Alexander Ullman is a Ph.D. candidate in the Department of English at UC Berkeley who studies race relations and American Literature. He is particularly interested in how sound and ethnicity meet in 20th century literature of the African and Jewish diasporas, specifically through the uses of dialect, translation, and music. He has also written on Jewish writing ranging from medieval piyutim to the work of contemporary Israeli author David Grossman.

Roland Walter is a Full Professor of English, Comparative Literature, and Literary Theory at the Universidade Federal de Pernambuco (UFPE), Recife, Brazil. He is the author of three books, *Magical Realism in Contemporary Chicano Fiction* (1993), *Narrative Identities: (Inter) Cultural In-Betweenness in the Americas* (2003), and *Afro-América: Diálogos Literários na Diáspora Negra das Américas* (2009). Walter has further edited the e-book *As Américas: Encruzilhadas Glocais* (2007) and coedited the books *Narrações da Violência Biótica* (2010) and *Entre Centros e Margens: Literaturas Afrodescendentes da Diáspora* (2014). He has published widely in journals throughout the Americas and Europe on diverse aspects of Inter-American literatures.

Acknowledgments

The editorial board of the volume *Human Rights in the Americas*, composed of María Herrera-Sobek from UCSB, Francisco A. Lomelí from UCSB, and Luz Angélica Krischner from SDSU, expresses their appreciation to numerous institutions and persons that made possible this important volume on human rights in the Americas. We first want to convey our sincere gratitude to the late Josef Raab, the Founding President of the International Association of Inter-American Studies (IAS) for his vision and support throughout the years. Unfortunately, he passed away while we were finalizing the volume. We also want to express our appreciation to Professor Josef Raab's spouse Dr. Melissa Knox-Raab for her support of this project.

We thank the IAS for their monetary and logistical support, including Wilfried Raussert (Bielefeld University, Germany), Ulla Kriebernegg (University of Graz, Austria), Olaf Kaltmeier (Bielefeld University, Germany), and Heidrun Moertl (University of Graz, Austria). We also thank the Center for Inter-American Studies (CIAS) housed at the University of Bielefeld in Germany. Professors Raussert and Kaltmeier were instrumental in reading key samples of the manuscript in order to approve and recommend it for publication. We also express our appreciation for the continuing encouragement and financial support the College of Arts, Humanities and Social Sciences, and the School of American and Global Studies, directed by Dr. Christine Garst-Santos, at SDSU gave to Professor Luz Angélica Kirschner.

We want to acknowledge funding from the UCSB College of Letters and Science Dean's Council chaired by Dean Melvin Oliver. Crucial infrastructural support came from the Chicano Studies Institute. We are grateful to Director Laura Romo and the CSI staff, including Raphaella Nau, Tracey Goss, Candace Pérez, Marselina Ortiz, Kayla Adams, Mariela Aguilar, Gustavo Agredano, and Grace Vega. In addition, we thank the staff from the Chicana and Chicano Studies Department at UCSB, especially Business Officer, Joann Erving and Undergraduate Advisor, Shariq Hashmi.

We graciously offer our heartfelt thanks to the assistance offered organizing the conference to Helena María Viramontes, award-winning author and Professor in the English Department at Cornell University and well-known author and poet, Lucha Corpi. They both participated at a literary panel where they read from their works.

Others who contributed funding for the success of the conference were UCSB Chancellor Henry Yang, the Office of the Executive Vice Chancellor, David Marshal, the Office of Associate Vice Chancellor for Diversity, Equity and Academic Policy, María Herrera-Sobek, and Professor Francisco A. Lomelí. We are very grateful for the support received from the Multicultural Center and its Director, Zaveeni Khan-Marcus; the Office of Equal Opportunity and Discrimination Prevention and its Director, Ricardo Alcaíno, plus the numerous UCSB Departments who generously contributed funding: History, Philosophy, Linguistics, Art and Architecture, Classics, Arts and Film Media Studies, and Chicana/o Studies.

We would also like to thank the following individuals and organizations for permission to reproduce previously published material.

Josef Raab's contribution "Human Rights in the Americas: A Stony Path," contains an excerpt from I, RIGOBERTA MENCHÚ: AN INDIAN WOMAN IN GUATEMALA by Rigoberta Menchú. Translation © Verso 1984 (All rights reserved). Reprinted by permission of the Director of Rights, Verso, Mr. Federico Campagna.

Alexander Ullman's contribution "The Ontogenesis of Fear in Héctor Tobar's The Barbarian Nurseries," contains excerpts from THE BARBARIAN NURSERIES by Héctor Tobar. Copyrights © 2011 by Héctor Tobar. Reprinted by permission of Farrar, Straus and Giroux.

Every effort was made to contact copyright holders for their permission to reprint material in this book. The publishers would be grateful to hear from any copyright holder who is not here acknowledged and will undertake to rectify any errors or omissions in future editions of this book.

Introduction
Human rights in the Americas

Luz Angélica Kirschner, María Herrera-Sobek, and Francisco A. Lomelí

Eurocentric historiographies of human rights commonly posit the *Magna Carta*, the British Revolution and the *Bill of Rights* (1689) the *Declaration of Independence of the United States of America* (1776) as well as the French Revolution and the *Declaration of the Rights of Man and Citizen* (1789) as milestones that paved the way to the development of the human rights discourse. Traditional histories of human rights, José-Manuel Barreto reminds us in "Imperialism and Decolonization as Scenarios of Human Rights History," largely focus on "the relations between the state and society, or between governments and individuals, while putting aside the problematic of the interactions between empires and colonies" (142). In the context of the Americas, this tendency not only marginalizes movements and human rights struggles that arose in the hemisphere as a result of the discovery, conquest, and colonization of Indigenous communities previously unknown to the Spanish conquerors. It also sidelines the commentaries and debates about the validity of the violence deployed during the conquest and the rights of conquest on theological, ethical, and legal grounds that progressed in modern Spain at the School of Salamanca during the 16th and into the 17th centuries long before the emergence of the United States. Similarly, on the one hand, the practice obscures the continuity of struggles of Indigenous, Black, women, children, and other non-gender conforming, non-European, non-Christian, non-white communities in the Americas against colonialism and imperialism since the inception of the hemisphere into global modern history. On the other, it obfuscates the way the antislavery and anti-colonialism movements of the above mentioned constituencies have challenged European notions of the "human." The volume builds on the work of Ana Forcinito, Raúl Marrero Fente, and Kelly McDonough, *Human Rights in Latin America and Iberian Cultures* (2009) and of José-Manuel Barreto, *Human Rights from the Third World Perspective: Critique, History and International Law* (2013). By locating the origins of modern human rights in the conquest of the Americas, *Human Rights in the Americas* is couched much within a decolonial and inter-American perspective and contributes to disseminate the awareness of a marginalized canon and relegated struggles against imperial violence that brought forth modern anti-colonialism and anti-imperialism.

The collection thus advances "historical justice" (Barreto, "Introduction" 22) that often has been absent in customary genealogies of the origins of human rights. After all, the "Columbian Exchange" (Mann 67) has been considered "the worst demographic catastrophe in human history" (68) sequels of which continue to affect life options for peoples in the Western hemisphere.

In "Introducing Human Rights and Literary Forms; Or, The Vehicle and Vocabularies of Human Rights," Sophia A. McClennen and Josef R. Slaughter explain that "the languages of human rights are many—legal, political, economic, cultural, scientific, sentimental, theoretical—even if all the words that constitute them can be found in the same linguistic family" (12). The chapters of this interdisciplinary collection explore diverse cultural, sometimes philosophical, political, and literary expressions, in which human rights discourses circulate across the continent taking into consideration issues such as race, ethnicity, class, gender, genealogy, and at times nationality. *Human Rights in the Americas* additionally avoids the paradigmatic tendency to study the Western hemisphere in two separate and oppositional or binary constructs: Protestant Anglo (read: North) versus Catholic Hispanic (read: South) America. This fixity can contribute to the reproduction of stereotypes and too often pushes into the background regions such as Brazil, Canada, and the Caribbean from historical analysis of the Western hemisphere. This volume similarly contributes to correct this oversight. It equally problematizes the tendency to approach the United States in the American Hemisphere exclusively in terms of empire and imperialism. This method too often obfuscates the internal heterogeneity of the nation and its people. Avoiding a reductionist approach that overlooks the ongoing historical struggles for human rights of minority communities within the United States against colonialism and imperialism, the book highlights the way these constituencies not only have challenged European notions of the "human" but also shaped modern human rights struggles in the hemisphere and the world. While acknowledging the ongoing centrality of the nation, *Human Rights in the Americas* promotes a shift in the study of the continent as a dynamic transnational space of conflict, domination, resistance, negotiation, complicity, accommodation, and solidarity where individuals, nations, peoples, institutions, and intellectual and political movements have shared struggles, experiences, ambivalences, dreams, and imaginaries. By being attentive to voices that continue to struggle against racism, colonialism, and discrimination resulting from persistent colonial structures of domination and power implemented during the occupation and colonization of the hemisphere, the essays disclose some of the varied and complex ways that human rights have been approached and communicated by those who have rights but, often, not necessarily the power to claim them. Yet, the articles simultaneously prove the people's ongoing resolve to address abuses of power and resist neocolonial domination that ensues socioeconomic inequities and political repression. This introduction to *Human Rights in the Americas* does not intend to be exhaustive. In fact, considering the myriad movements and struggles of peoples in the Americas throughout the modern history of the vast continent, it can only be inevitably exclusionary. No single volume can provide a comprehensive overview of this enormous field of study. It does expect, however, to promote a more inclusive, a more global and more complete perspective of the history of human rights that acknowledges the contributions made by non-Western countries and cultures to human rights.

An exercise on collective cultural memory

Eurocentric approaches to human rights "afford little or no significance to the history of the relations between modern empires and colonies or the Third World" (Barreto, "Introduction" 6). Yet, the global sociocultural phenomenon called the Americas has been a frontline in the struggle for human rights since Christopher Columbus by chance encountered the Caribbean islands in 1492. Decolonial scholarship of intellectuals such as Enrique Dussel, Aníbal Quijano, Walter Mignolo, María Lugones, Michel-Rolph Trouillot, Sylvia Wynter, Immanuel Wallerstein, and others have demonstrated how the conquest of the continent and the transformation of the Atlantic Ocean into the center of intersecting or succeeding empires impelled the flow of goods, commodities, diseases, and knowledge at a local and global level. The events also launched the voluntary and involuntary mass migration of populations from all continents responding to the labor demands dictated by the emerging capitalist modern world-economy that the making of the Americas enabled. The "primitive accumulation" of capital that the colonization of the New World instigated not only prompted the emergence of modern racial categories that served as colonial ordering mechanism of the world, but it also enabled the rise of the West. The modern "racial axis" (Quijano, "Coloniality of Power" 181) expediently naturalized relations of exploitation and subordination, superiority and inferiority, refinement, and barbarism between Europeans and non-Europeans in the first European colonies. Delineating and justifying the boundaries corresponding to racialized divisions of labor, the categorized colonial world order of the Americas resulted in the subjugation and minoritization of Indigenous populations, the introduction of plantation slavery for Africans, and the implementation of various forms of forced labor for some mixed race people and peoples from Asia. The hierarchical structure also advanced the subordination, even if uneven, of women of all colors, among others, to warrant the genealogical transmission and preservation of wealth in the hands of a few deserving "white" Europeans (Lugones). The model of racial classification of the world's populations imposed during the subjugation of the New World, and the colonization of the rest of the world in subsequent centuries has survived colonialism in what Quijano has theorized as "coloniality of power" (181) and continues to operate today in the neoliberal rhetoric of the 21st century.

Interestingly, the tendency to exclude events and deliberations, taking place in the context of the conquest and colonization of the Americas from contemporary genealogies of human rights, evokes the theorizations of modernity by German philosophers such as G.W. Friederich Hegel or Jürgen Habermas to mention some. These philosophers posit the refined European condition of modernity as a lineal self-product of the European Renaissance, the European Enlightenment, the French Revolution, or the Industrial Revolution that is isolated from the European imperial history initiated by Spain and Portugal in the hemisphere between the 15th and 17th centuries. A similar approach prevails in terms of the historical enslavement of Africans by modern subjects in the New World, states Sabine Broeck who problematizes the resistance or "ethical avoidance" (105) to "engage with the connection between slavery and modernity's Enlightenment, including its transatlantic history" (102) in the Old Continent. To this day, David Theo Goldberg elucidates, colonialism "is thought to be the history properly speaking not of Europe" (155) since apparently it "has had little or no effect in the making of Europe itself, or of European nation-states" (155) as if the logic of oppression and exploitation implemented in the Americas was not constitutive of "rational" European modernity.

Yet as early as the 1500s on the Island of Hispaniola (today Haiti and the Dominican Republic), the *Taíno* Cacique Hatuey perhaps assumed the earliest use of the language of human rights by Indigenous peoples in the Americas against European oppression. To an important extent, his rebellion reveals how from an early stage the Americas have been "built on dissent" (Raab par. 1). Hatuey, who was eventually burned by the conquerors in 1512 in Cuba, confronted the Spaniards, repelled the imposition of a foreign creed, and mobilized his people to stop the atrocities they encountered at the hands of the invaders and resist their enslavement and that of Africans. The Dominican Friar Antonio de Montesinos similarly criticized the enslavement of the *Taíno* Amerindian people under Spanish rule. His struggle inspired Bartolomé de Las Casas to launch his internal critique of the ethics of colonialism. Las Casas fought the enslavement of Indigenous populations, affirmed their full humanity, improved their legal status, and became an advocate against colonial abuse in the Americas even if in the end the Dominican missionary did not succeed in preventing the progressive enslavement of Indigenous peoples. Recent critiques of Las Casas' evaluation of "the right of the conquest" (Dussel 172), however, identify him as the originator of "the hierarchy of indigeneity over African descent" when the Dominican endorsed African slavery in the Caribbean as a means to prevent the enslavement of Indigenous populations (Arias 35).

Along these lines, questioning Eurocentric approaches to human rights in "Who Speaks for the 'Human' in Human Rights?," Mignolo analyzes the generally overlooked debates led by the Dominican Francisco de Vitoria, who questioned the authority of the Pope to distribute the New World between the Spaniards and the Portuguese (50). Mignolo's study is a case in point that displays how inclusionary approaches to human rights discourses can strengthen the field. Placing in center stage the complex exchanges between empires and colonies that have been absent from European theories of human rights, the scholar argues, among others, that concepts such as "human" and "rights" are creations that instantaneously emerged in the context of "modern colonialism" (48). "Rights" appear, in Mignolo's terms, when "responding to imperial necessity" (49), the humanist Vitoria tackled issues of "property rights" premised on the progressive idea of the rationality (read: humanity) of the, even if "barbaric," communities of the newly found territories (50). As history has shown, however, the humanity that Vitoria conferred to Indigenous communities not only subjected them and Spaniards to the same "natural law of peoples or nations" (Mignolo 51). Natural law would eventually legitimize the right of Spaniards to dispossess Indigenous peoples (read: inferior barbarians) of the "property" that the latter did not perceive as such and, in the end, to the negation of all their rights.

Revealing the complexity of the concepts that shape human rights, which historically have haunted debates on human rights and their application, Mignolo on the one hand points at Vitoria's ethnocentric universalizing move that pretending to "speak for others" assumes the uniform equivalence of "the concept of 'property'" (51) for Spaniards and Indigenous populations. Mignolo's scholarship reveals how Vitoria's initial universalism, far from being neutral, already entails the weight of imperial history through which enlightened Western universality has been promoted and foreshadows the unequal access to rights that are supposed to be universal. Vitoria's intervention introduces complications that remain at the heart of human rights and the humanities, namely, "the entanglement of human rights discourses with atrocities" (McClennen and Schultheis, 5) and the query as to whether the idea of human rights may in itself be "the basis for human rights violations" (4). At the same time, obliquely Vitoria's intellectual move brings to mind the ongoing engagement of human rights organizations with the dilemmas of universalism and relativism, as Domna C. Stanton reminds us, "western and non-western critics have emphasized the abuse of the local as an alibi for human rights violations perpetrated with dictatorial impunity" (67). We need to be aware that the ambivalent status of the universal in human rights discourses has indeed revealed that an indiscriminate "rejection of universalism in the name of cultural particularity" has not been "necessarily emancipatory" (67) in pursuit of human rights claims. As a matter of fact, Hatuey's and Las Casas' struggles along with Mignolo's analysis of Vitoria's argumentations demonstrate how, at the dawn of modernity as it is today, the human rights discourse already proved to be "infinitely adaptable and amenable to the needs of both the powerless and the powerful to legitimize all sorts of grievances" (McClennen and Slaughter 1).

The Haitian Revolution (1791–1804) inspired by the French Revolution and the *Declaration of the Rights of Man* is another notable instance that still has not found the prominent place that it deserves in the collective cultural memory of the genealogy of human rights. Despite the noteworthy interventions of, for instance, the Haitian anthropologist Michel-Rolph Trouillot in *Silencing the Past: Power and the Production of History* (1995) and the academic Sibylle Fischer in *Modernity Disavowed: Haiti and the Cultures of Slavery in the Age of Revolution* (2004), the slave rebellion that led to the independence of the French Caribbean colony, Saint Dominique, from France remains lightly treated in human rights historiographies. Alluding to the banishment of this most significant, even if ambivalent, event of self-liberation in the Age of Revolution from accounts of the history of the West, Sibylle Fischer argues, Eurocentric historical accounts that explicate the "modern world" between 1789 and 1848 use terms such as, "industry," "industrialist," "capitalism," "scientist," "railway," "socialism," "aristocracy," "engineer," and "proletariat" ("Having Hitherto" 360). Historical adumbrations stress the achievements of the United States, French, and British revolutions; however, it fail to include "any concept that would refer us to racial slavery, colonialism, and the political struggles against them" (Fischer 360) as if slavery and colonialism were immaterial in the conflicts of the Age of Revolution. At a historical juncture when major revolutionary documents of the time engaged the "equality of mankind" (Bogues 224), while excluding enslaved Africans from humanity, the Haitian Constitution "reversed the colonial hierarchical status of human beings" (229–230), conferred citizenship to people of African and Native American descent, turning them into legal persons.

Similar to the Haitian Revolution led by Black and African slaves, even the struggles for independence in the Americas need to be understood as anti-imperial enterprises that aimed at destroying the legitimacy of some 300 years of European imperial rule in the hemisphere. It is necessary to remember that the hierarchies established between Europeans and Americans deemed them "inferior or less capable because of their place of birth, race or culture" (Barreto, "Imperialism" 158). The mainly white War for Independence of the United States against British tyranny (1775–1783), more than a decade ahead of the French Revolution, and the *U.S. Declaration of Independence of 1776* stipulated that all men are created equal with certain unalienable rights. This mindset also contributed to fuel and justify the "unfinished revolutions" (Cardenas 25) of independence in most of the Latin American regions as well. This document, which was not the first U.S. rights document (Langlois, 12–13), did not appear out of a vacuum. The document certainly draws on Western political history but similarly needs to be understood as a product that emerged in the context of the steadiness of the unassailable desire for self-emancipation and self-determination exhibited by the *Taino* Cacique Hatuey at an early stage of the conquest that has characterized the struggles for human rights in the continent.

Over 500 years after the conquest and colonization of the Americas, in the context of what migration scholars have called "The Age of Migration" (Castles, de Haas, and Miller 5), many consider Bartolomé de Las Casas as one of the first advocates for universal human rights (Cleary 5) despite his imperfect and controversial legacy. Some view him as "one of the first people in history to advance the idea of *group* rights" (Cardenas 8; emphasis in original), while others advance contentious Francisco de Vitoria as the founder of modern international law (Anghie 152). Celebratory narratives propagate that racism has been overcome and that by now human rights and the "human" are recognized to be self-evident because we live in the post-World War II "Age of Human Rights" that articulated the *Universal Declaration of Human Rights* (UDHR) in 1948. What is usually overlooked in these self-congratulatory accounts is, however, that the horror of the Second World War (1939–1945) and the atrocities of the Jewish Holocaust, which "outraged the conscience of mankind" (Langlois 15), were not the first crises of European modernity. The moral determination that animated people after the Second World War was also present in the early interventions and arguments of the individuals and peoples who, horrified by the capacity of destruction of modern colonization and imperialism, advanced the human rights of Indigenous populations. Just like the UDHR responded to the horrendous obliteration brought about by the Second World War by restoring "the natural law" to accuse members of Nazi Germany of "crimes against humanity" (Langlois 15), the legitimacy of the conquest and the annihilation of Indigenous populations in the Western hemisphere were debated on the basis of the same tradition (Barreto, "Introduction" 20–21).

Concurrently, the history of the Americas displays that the 20th and 21st centuries have not invented mass migration. In the context of the Americas, e.g., just to mention a few, 12 million of enslaved Africans were brought to work on plantations as a result of the slave trade. Approximately half a million Asians from China to Java and Sri Lanka were contracted to work as laborers following the end of Caribbean slavery. Historically thousands of Indigenous communities across the American hemisphere have been dispossessed of their lands and forcibly relocated. The sociopolitical turmoil produced by the fall of the Ottoman Empire in the Balkan, Middle Eastern, and North African countries forced Arabs and Muslims as well as hundreds of thousands of Arab Jews, Ashkenazim, Mizrahim, and Sephardim to escape the deteriorating economic circumstances extant in their lands. Equally, religious and/or racial persecution impelled these people to migrate to the American continent during the second half of the 19th and beginning of the 20th century. An unspecified number of millions of Europeans have migrated to the Western hemisphere throughout its modern history with a strong motivation to succeed in the Americas. And yet, in the context of the globalized neoliberal economic order of the 21st century—which decoloniality intellectuals such as Dussel, Quijano, Mignolo, Trouillot, and Wallerstein regard as the culmination of the Western capitalist enterprise initiated with the conquest of the American hemisphere—ethnic minorities, composed of citizens and noncitizens, as well as migrants and refugees searching for new opportunities, or escaping poverty, conflict, persecution, or environmental disasters are viewed as anomalies worldwide. Since open expressions of racism are considered odious in our "colorblind" globalized world that purportedly has moved beyond the inconveniences of race, old and new minorities (not always the product of migration but of colonialism), political and economic refugees, and migrant communities are, more often than not, perceived as threats to national security. They are perceived as a challenge to the social, cultural, economic, and political cohesion of receiving societies on account of the purported incommensurable otherness not only of their unchallengeable cultures, faiths, religious practices, values, lifestyles, but also attires, languages, and countries of origin. We should remember that in sustaining ideologies of a "borderless world" and "open borders," neoliberal globalization promised economic growth in developing countries and the reduction of global inequality. But the preservation of barriers in rich countries and the one-sided demand for the removal of restrictions in less economically privileged nations has turned the liberalization of flows of commodities, labor, capital, technology into a highly undemocratic, socioeconomically, and geopolitically polarizing process that reduces existence to economic terms and which has resulted in the unprecedented increment of global inequality.

Human rights in the Americas

Not surprisingly, Sophia A. McClennen and Joseph R. Slaughter claim, "the language of human rights is everywhere" (1). Reminiscent of the European conquest of the American hemisphere and Euro-American imperialism, human rights vocabulary is regularly coopted in the name of humanistic Western civilization and enlightened secular progress. The language of human rights is embraced to justify wars as the price to pay for the expansion of democracy, socioeconomic equality, and global human rights, while unsentimental interventionism revokes international and national laws, implements inhuman or humiliating practices, and determines who has no right to human rights and who has the right to have rights. In this sense, this volume also concedes that the struggle for human rights, whether in the form of anti-colonial insurrections, antiracist mobilization, anti-imperial social movements, and artistic articulations, or literary works in diverse genres premised on the urgency of addressing human rights, has never ceased or become less urgent in a continent historically marked by deep inequality and structural discrimination. After all, Suzanne Oboler and Anani Dzidzienyo observe,

> "Freedom" has always had a different meaning for Black and other "people of color" through the Americas when they censure their movements on the streets and in areas where people of white-European descent live; when the hemisphere's indigenous populations know that they take a chance by leaving their towns, villages, or reservations, or when

African Americans, Blacks, Afro-Latinas/os, Afro-Latin Americans, dark skinned mestizos, and people of Asian descent are discriminated against in terms of employment and denied access to political and other institutions in the societies of the Americas. (6)

The United States traditionally is celebrated as a nation of unconditional opportunities built on the labor of immigrants, a melting pot, which welcomes immigrants from all over the world. But the histories that record the trajectories of minority groups and their incorporation into the nation, Vilna Bashi Treitler reminds us, reveal a narrative that rapidly resembles more "a complex contest for resources, one that was from the beginning contextualized in a language that demarked the deserving from the underserving, arranging the humans into unequal ethnic groups" (2). The racialized stratification of immigrants has been controlled by "civilizational discourses, separating the civilized from the uncivilized; that is, the privileged white males from the racialized and gendered populations within and without who were colonized, subjugated, or ripe for conquest" (Kandiyoti 29). After World War II, race discourses underwent important alterations in most of Europe but this was not the case in Britain and the United States. After the victory over Nazi Germany, the victorious nations did not feel compelled to change their racist discourses; in the United States, racist discrimination based on biological racist discourse would have to wait until the Civil Rights Act of 1964 (Grosfoguel et al. 13). As battles over what it means to be "American" rage on and struggles over how the nation's diversity should be conceptualized continue, fears of national division that stress the importance of domestic unity decry the achievements of the civil rights movements of the 1970s that paved the way for the emergence of multiculturalism in the 1980s.

Considering that the founding of the United Nations occurred after World War II at a time when the United States emerged as a military and economic superpower, in the nation human rights "have been characterized by distance and disavowal" (Parikh 380). We need to remember, for instance, that seeking to prevent embarrassing international criticism for the treatment of African Americans as the Nuremberg Trial was underway, the State Department fashioned a definition of "national minority" that led the institution to conclude that "there probably are no national minorities in the United States" (Anderson 82). National minorities were "a European problem, not an American one" (82). During the "American century," human rights have been largely regarded as that "which *others, elsewhere* (almost inevitably victims of the Global South) are in need of, and which—sometimes—Americans deliver unto them, whether in the guise of humanitarian NGOs, religious missionary enterprises, or military interventions" (Parikh 380; emphases in the original). The advocacy for human rights tacitly has evoked "challenges to oppressive regimes abroad" (Soohoo et al. viii), while activists fighting economic and political oppression in the United States have operated with the term "civil rights" to articulate their demands for equality rights (viii).

In this sense, this volume honors the long-standing legacy of human rights advocates that reveal that human rights activism is not foreign to the U.S. intellectual tradition. It means to remember, for instance, that at a time when the humanity and rights of African Americans remained unacknowledged, Frederick Douglass made one of the earliest adoptions of the term "human rights" as he articulated the fundamental rights of enslaved African Americans (Soohoo et al. vii). We acknowledge the Chicanos/as' struggle for human rights and Latina/o legacies of resistance against dehumanizing processes that have been integral to their trajectory in the United States as testified in *The Oxford Encyclopedia of Latinos & Latinas in Contemporary Politics, Law, and Social Movements* edited by Suzanne Oboler and Deena J. González. It not only celebrates inspiring Chicana/o labor leaders and activists such as Dolores Huerta and César Chávez, but also the queer poet philosopher Gloria A. Anzaldúa who gave the world the concept *Borderlands* as an analytical tool to explore the colonization of the mind, and the devastating psychological, spiritual, and physical sequels of colonialism and racism on racialized individuals and peoples. In a hemispheric spirit, in her groundbreaking work *Borderlands/La Frontera: The New Mestiza*, Anzaldúa advocates the awareness of each other's histories and trajectories of oppression to dismantle divisive *Borderlands* and build interethnic and intra-ethnic collaborations of resistance against dehumanization. In the Asian American tradition, for instance, the volume evokes the Filipino American Carlos Bulosan who called for the recognition of Filipinos as human beings, or the former internee Japanese American Yuri Kochiyama who, inspired by Malcolm X's struggle, led a life-long fight for the rights not only of Asian American but also Black, Latino/a, and Native American communities against structural racism. The book praises Anishinabe activist and journalist Winona LaDuke who writes on the devastating consequences of colonialism on Native Americans and advances their right to maintain their cultures, sacred objects and places, and traditions. It commemorates the historian and activist Ronald Takaki who devoted his teaching and scholarship to counter racism; his landmark work *A Different Mirror: A History of Multicultural America*, joining Howard Zinn's labor, reaffirms a multicultural United States that is, among many others, Native American, Jewish, Asian American, and Latino/a. The manuscript also acclaims the politically engaged Hellen Adams Keller, the deafblind intellectual, who brought the human rights of disabled people to the forefront and became one of the most important humanitarians of the 20th century.

More recently, in 2005, Hurricane Katrina in New Orleans, Louisiana, not only accentuated human rights activism but also revealed to the world how African Americans were still lacking "basic human rights" (Anderson 89). After the attacks of September 11, 2001, and the ensuing War on Terror, human rights advocates and social justice groups have sought "to promote and protect rights placed at risk in the name of fighting terrorism" (Patten 287).

Progressive organizations, for instance, challenged the implementation of the PATRIOT Act and longtime anti-immigrant policies that placed noncitizens in general, and Arab and Muslim noncitizens in particular "as outside the realm of rights protections" (295). In more recent years, books by liberal-minded scholars such as *Documenting the Undocumented: Latino/a Narratives and Social Justice in the Era of Operation Gatekeeper* of Marta Caminero-Santangelo reveal how Latino/a writers increasingly express their solidarity with undocumented immigrants.

Moreover, according to Soohoo, the customary divide between "civil rights" and "human rights" characteristic of U.S. jurisprudence has started to erode (198). Globalization and the Internet have enabled progressive conversation on issues such as "the death penalty and the right of privacy" that embrace international human rights standards and consider experience from abroad (198). Human rights work in the United States is multilayered and carried out by educators, artists, musicians, lawyers, Web activists, economists, sociologists, and other activists increasingly making use of social media to organize and protest violence. This is the case of the international activist organization *#BlackLivesMatter* initiated in California in July 2013 to protest the killing of Trayvon Martin in 2012 and George Zimmerman's acquittal 1 year later.

The decentralized nonviolent movement that needs to be understood in the context of the protracted struggle of African Americans against racial injustice and for basic human rights counts a large number of activist women and members of the lesbian, gay, bisexual, transgender, queer, intersexual, and asexual (LGBTQIA+) community.

In the context of the Western hemisphere, the vast military, economic, and cultural presence of the United States has often led observers in the international community to perceive Canada as committed to the rule of law, multilateralism, democracy, and human rights. In Canada itself, there is the tendency to contrast the nation's historical record with that of the United States with the result that it often "leads to the portrayal of the past as devoid of discrimination and oppression, and instead characterizes it by a tradition of inclusion and tolerance" (Miron, "Preface" vii). In reality, Canada also has a history of state-sponsored and legislative discrimination as well as hostility toward immigrants, racialized ethnic minorities (e.g., Indigenous peoples, Chinese-Canadians, Japanese-Canadians, Indo-Canadians, and Blacks), religious minorities (e.g., Jewish refugees fleeing Nazi Germany), and women. More recently, seeking to complicate the nation's self-perception, some Canadian scholars are in the process of rewriting the history of race and Blacks. They point at similarities "between patterns of racial discrimination in Canada and the Southern United States," although a number of Canadian historians still prefer to avoid the analysis of race in the Canadian context (Walker 91). The evolution of human rights has been slow (Lamberston), but Canada has struggled to become a more open society that embraces diversity and where human rights do have an impact on people's life (Miron, "Introduction" 3). As Canada's Indigenous peoples continue to struggle for recognition and survival in the 21st century, however, the low mark of success of Canada's Aboriginal policies, Miller proposes, undermines the myth of moral superiority of Canada in relation to "others, especially their American neighbors" (257).

Moreover, a critical look at Canada's engagement in the Americas, more specifically Latin America, reveals that its interventions have not always been benign. As a member of the Organization of American States (OAS) and thus the inter-American human rights system since 1990, the nation has been often "criticized for its timid membership" (Duhaime 640) as Canada does not adhere to the American Convention on Human Rights, the OAS's central instrument for human rights enforcement. It is true that Ottawa promoted democracy throughout the 1990s (Mace and Thérien 571), but the reality is that Canada has largely sought profit-oriented economic integration based on substantial investment in the area of extractive industries that benefits Canadian investors. Although economic integration can promote democracy, social justice, and human rights, "it can also generate important human rights problems" (Duhaime 654) especially considering that numerous bilateral free trade agreements that Canada has entered with Latin American nations fail to establish a common institutional framework to address human rights and free trade contiguously. Under these circumstances, it is then unsurprising that the ground-breaking 2016 Canadian report by the Justice and Accountability Project (JCAP) has revealed that "Canadian mining companies in Latin America contribute to violence and act with impunity" (Granados Ceja and Jamal par. 3). The 2009 murder of human rights advocate Mariano Abarca over his resistance to a Canadian-run barite mine in his community of Chicomuselo, Chiapas, and the 2019 failure of his son José Luis Abarca to find justice over the murder of his father in the Canadian court system further contribute to demystify the alleged moral superiority of Canada in the Americas. When it comes to Latin America, Canada and the United States "exhibit much more similarity than difference" (Lacroix 721).

In Latin America, human rights violations are historically linked to the experience of colonialism which left in place "ideological systems of subjugation and economic disarray" (Cardenas 25). Governments of the region mostly led by *criollo* (native-born Creole elite of Spanish ancestry) and *mestizo* elites turned to European Enlightenment, the *French Declaration on the Rights of Man and Citizen*, and the *U.S. Constitution* and used the language of equality, liberation, and self-determination. Unfortunately, these intellectuals left unquestioned colonial structures that relegated peoples of Indigenous and African descent and women of all colors to the margins of the liberal republics, and privileged landowners. Political elites of the young nations adopted the racialist ideology of unifying *mestizaje* that promotes

Introduction 13

democratic racial and cultural mixing of Indigenous, African, and European subjects while promoting *blanqueamiento* (whitening), a process of "racial improvement" ideal of which is the Western European subject and culture. The *mestizalo* credo similarly pushed to the margins communities with heritages from the Middle East, Eastern Europe, and non-Catholic traditions that historically have belonged to the sociocultural landscape of the region (Kirschner 19–28). Similarly, m*estizaje* has failed "to acknowledge Asians bodies" (López 127), presence, and contributions despite Asians were also enslaved and share "a common trajectory from bound laborers to *cimarrones* (runaways) to freedom fighters" (126) with African and Indigenous peoples in the Americas.

In the face of extreme socioeconomic inequality, new rulers relied on the use of force and repression to uphold stability "unleashing a vicious cycle of repression whose impact would be felt into the new millennium" (Cardenas 25). The complicated hemispheric history of the region with the United States is also partly responsible for the human rights abuses that have characterized it. As a result, Latin America often is perceived as a place of human rights violations and not necessarily as a region that has greatly contributed to the development of human rights. The region's relatively recent dictatorial past, as it became a central battlefield for the Cold War, especially after the Cuban revolution in 1959, erroneously gives the impression that Latin America is a newcomer to the terrain of international human rights. Not only is Las Casas' complex legacy still felt in the region; we need to know that the leading human rights organization in Chiapas, the home of the worldwide known Zapatista movement that has resisted globalization, is called "Fray Bartolomé de Las Casas Center for Human Rights" (8). Similarly, a growing number of scholars acknowledge the crucial role of Latin American intellectuals in drafting the *Universal Declaration of Human Rights* (10). Despite gross human rights violations against the citizens of many Latin American states, it is also true that new models of response to state violence that have been emulated worldwide materialized in the region.

During the military dictatorship in Brazil (1964–1985), for instance, joining forces with advocates from diverse nations in the American hemisphere, Brazilian human rights activists began to use moral and political vocabulary to upend dominant "notions of state sovereignty" (Kelly 3) and "nonintervention" (7) in the 1970s with the aim to deprive dictators of the legal protection that enabled them to carry out acts of internal state repression with impunity. In 1977, at the height of repression the Mothers of the Plaza de Mayo (*Las Madres de la Plaza de Mayo*), a human rights organization that emerged as women found the courage to publicly and nonviolently protest the "disappearances" of their children at the hands of organized state terrorism during the Argentine military dictatorship, between 1976 and 1983. Their fame enabled the Mothers, who made skillful use of traditional views of "the mother" that makes her pain public, to create transnational alliances that pressured the Argentine junta military and inspired activists worldwide even if in the process some mothers were also disappeared, tortured, and murdered.

After more than 40 years, the Grandmothers of the Plaza de Mayo (*Asociación Civil Abuelas de la Plaza de Mayo*) continue to look for children stolen and illegally adopted during the dictatorship. Similar to Argentina, making use of traditional notions of women's roles Chilean women chose to create "*arpilleras*, tapestries with a political content" (Agosín 20) to counteract the culture of death and silence imposed by the dictatorship. Despite the government prohibited the sale of the tapestries, the items were smuggled to the United States, Canada, and Europe and made the international community aware of the horrors of Pinochet's regime and the privations people endured.

During the transition to democracy, and unlike many other regions of the world, again Latin American women have been at the forefront demanding *accountability* for past state-sponsored terrorism and creating memory commissions that request public historical record of crimes against humanity. Seeking restorative justice, the region, along with Africa, has the highest number of "truth commissions" and demands for punishment; it is the place where "human rights trials" most frequently have been held (Cardenas 159). The groundbreaking trial of General Pinochet revealed to the world possibilities of legal prosecution of heads of state for human rights crimes committed while in office (173–177). More recently, mobilizing against torture many Latin American countries have organizations devoted to victims, such as, CINTRAS (*Centro de Salud Mental y Derechos Humanos* or Center of Mental Health and Human Rights) in Chile or the *Movimento Tortura Nunca Mais* (MTNM) (Movement Torture Never Again in Brazil) (Cleary 123–126). Partly because of "the Latin American multicultural turn" (Rahier 7), a growing number of scholars problematize *mestizaje* processes of invisibilization of Black populations in official versions of Latin American history and their erasure from the region's consciousness. National governments accounting for the past have created commissions that have accepted the fact of structural discrimination against Black and Indigenous peoples and massive rights violations.

In the case of Afro-descendants in Latin American societies, for instance, intellectuals forcefully call attention to the tenacious social classification that ranks them below Indigenous peoples and how the insidious hierarchy perpetuates the negation of their "contribution, culture, and humanity" as well as "their invisibility in contemporary policy and law" (Walsh 18). Latin American Afro-descendants are increasingly claiming the concept of diaspora in the awareness that borrowing Mark Sawyer's terms from another context, "the experience of African people cannot be confined within the boundaries of the nation-state" (273). Even if contemporary Afro-Latinidades are still marginal in "most mappings of the African diaspora" (Lao-Montes 172) and Latina/o Americanist discourses, there is a growing awareness of Afro-transnational collaborations in the Americas that can be traced back to earlier historical moments. We need to recall that oblivious of recognized political boundaries in the quest for hemispheric emancipation, "Haiti assisted movements to overthrow Spanish rule in Venezuela (1806) and Mexico (1816) and, most notably, Simón Bolívar's expedition in Venezuela (1816)" (West and Martin 80), thereby directly contributing to weaken Spain's colonial grip in the Americas. Finally, with the expectation that the "21st century will be the century of global reparatory justice," the Barbadian historian Hilary Beckles has proposed that "indigenous, African, and Asian experiences of genocide and slavery" be grasped "as 'three acts of a single play'" in the context of colonial exploitation of the Americas (Beckles qtd. in López 130). People of Asian descent are increasingly exploring "race and culture through literature, poetry, art, and politics" (López 128) as is the case with the movement called "Coolitude" (129) that addresses issues of identity, belonging, language, and culture as well as the history of indentured laborers and their descendants in the region.

In fact, global changes in technology have reinforced human rights advocacy in Latin America as activists (Indigenous advocates, relatives of human rights victims, Black social movements, women's groups, LGBTQIA+ groups, disability rights groups, street children's movements, etc.) are able to create invigorating transnational alliances and empower the prominence of human rights struggles in the world. However, the unfortunate side effect of these advancements is that "today's activists constitute one of the primary targets of abuse" (Cardenas 112). Although the struggles of Indigenous peoples for human rights are far from over, Indigenous movements have moved to center stage politics thanks to technology. Case in point is the Zapatista uprising in Chiapas against the North American Trade Agreement (NAFTA) in 1994, in one of the poorest regions of Mexico with a large Mayan population, displayed to the world how "human rights, globalization, and network activism intersect" (117) and in some cases can improve human rights conditions. The movement that challenged the inevitability of globalized capitalism located itself in the historical continuum of 500 years of struggle against colonization and oppression and enabled the emergence of a broader Indigenous ethnic identity that emphasizes the elements that diverse Indigenous communities share with one another "in revindication of economic, social, and political exploitation" (Collier qtd. in Castells 81). Indigenous women have also profited as their leadership has been reinforced because of the achievements of the Zapatista movement (Belausteguigoitia 31). These observations, however, do not diminish the persistent gendered violence Indigenous women and their movement encounter due to what human rights groups call "a low-intensity war" Indigenous peoples have been enduring "in the context of militarization and paramilitarization" of the region (Hernández Castillo 150).

The end of the Cold War has seen the proliferation of human rights violation in Latin America as new conflicts have replaced anti-Communist activities that justified state terrorism against its citizens. As a response to the global war on terror, some governments, e.g., Peru and Colombia have enacted antiterrorism laws that open spaces for human rights abuses. In the Americas, post-9/11 anxieties and the War on Terror have often resulted in strong expressions of hostilities and even acts of violence, against Arabs, Muslims, and Middle Easterners are becoming more common. Though it is true that these communities have been increasingly acknowledged in Latin America, it is also true that they are often perceived with ambivalence (Shohat and Alsultany 3–41). In her book propitiously called, *Human Rights in Latin America: A Politics of Terror and Hope,* Sonia Cardenas rightfully identifies "poverty, impunity, and militarization" (203) as the main sources for the ongoing violation of human rights in a region that remains deeply divided by class, race, ethnicity, and gender. The region has also experienced the resurgence of religious fundamentalism with its notions about traditional gender roles and heteronormativity, which linked to the unfolding of neoliberalism and the intensification of all forms of violence and deprivation has effected "extreme forms of violence against women" that remain neglected by the "masculine state" (Sagot 213).

Indeed, scholars theorize "systemic sexual feminicide" as a gender-based crime "that sends punitive and hierarchical messages" (213). Since to date most *femicidios* (the murder of women with impunity) remain uninvestigated, families and human rights groups seek justice through different grassroots movements. The most visible one is *Ni Una Más* (Not One More) launched by family members, human rights activists, and representatives of the border community to protest the Juárez murders. In 2007, failing to find support from the Mexican government, mothers of three of the victims filed human rights complaints in "first the Inter-American Commission on Human Rights and later in the Inter-American Court of Human Rights Organization" (Heiskanen 2). The Inter-American Court of Human Rights found the Mexican government responsible for the murders in 2009 (2) and thus established "the first basis for interpreting the right of women to live free from violence and responsibilities of States to guarantee these rights" (3). The case was also relevant because the reports made explicit use of "the concept of femicide" (3); by now, the causes and ramifications of misogynist violence are increasingly viewed as "inherently transnational in nature" that require "conjoined transnational effort" (3). In Canada, the Sisters in Spirit initiative similarly calls attention to the unresolved murders of Indigenous women and girls in a multicultural country that continues to struggle with its legacy of colonialism. Canadian activists are beginning to apply the term femicide (García-Del Moral) used in Latin American contexts to protest the crimes (*CFOJA*).

Correspondingly, Indigenous women in the United States protest the sexual violence that permeates their life. In *The Beginning and End of Rape: Confronting Sexual Violence in Native America* (2015), the best study of rape in the Native American context to date, Sarah Deer questions the tendency to refer to the high rates of rape of Native American women as a recent "epidemic" (ix). Deer instead proposes that the rape of Native American women has to be grasped as a product of a colonist rape culture that cannot be analytically separated from the history of the colonization, as it were, rape of Native peoples as a whole which have contributed to render Native women "rape-able" (9). Deer also questions liberal feminists who focus on patriarchy to account for sexual abuse but fail to theorize the trauma of "abusive colonial power" (24) on gender relations. Most recently, similar to Deer, the film *An Indigenous Response to #Me Too* (2018) by *Rematriation Magazine* on Vimeo problematizes the movement's one-sided emphasis on patriarchy. In the film, activists such as Michelle Schenandoah and Jonel Beauvois emphasize the need to ponder colonialism as integral to the culture of rape that sanctions the sexual abuse of Indigenous women and sustains gendered violence. Meanwhile, Latin American movements denouncing femicide have joined the more recent U.S. American *#Me Too Movement,* October 2017, in what has become the international struggle against widespread forms of sexual harassment and assault of women at all levels while emphasizing the global dimension of violence against women that concern all of us.

Finally, we need to be aware of critical posthumanism, a non-dystopic or utopic approach that calls for a different conceptualization of the Eurocentric Human that traditionally has been treated in the singular and placed the (free-willed, rational, sovereign, white) Man as the paradigmatic universal Human. This approach critically examines previously taken for granted categories of the human/nonhuman that have premised human rights debates for its "exclusivism" (Nayar 9). Humanism, as this introduction has shown, has too often resulted in the containment and natural exclusion of certain groups (objectionable "others") such as, for instance, women, children, slaves, homosexuals, transgender people, Jews, Muslims, Indigenous populations, differently formed bodies, immigrants, and so forth from the category of the human and encouraged the denial of their rights and their subjugation to murderous violence. It has similarly naturalized a hierarchical divide between the human and the nonhuman that has structured the utilitarian relationship of humans to animals, the environment, and the earth as a whole as well as disavowed the ecological dimension of the subject and its complex interaction with the nonhuman world. The critical posthuman turn also includes the technological creations that increasingly play a role in our lives "by stressing the primacy of digital mediation and electronic circuits in our self-definition and interaction" (Braidotti and Hlavajova, 2). While seeking to redraw the boundaries of the human, thinkers of critical posthumanism seek to overcome pernicious binaries and ethical hierarchies to broaden ethical accountability by acknowledging humanity's "interdependence with multiple, human and non-human others" (Braidotti 342). In this sense, as we problematize past frameworks, coin new concepts, question our ethical inconsistencies, and propose alternative ways of being in the world, we need to maintain the decisive balance needed for the ongoing, pragmatic work of honoring and protecting the life of all humans ever watchful that pre-given ideas of "the Human" may influence our work. This observation becomes an imperative, as governments in the Americas respond or fail to respond to the COVID-19 pandemic that has laid bare the persistence of inequity, exclusion, and authoritarianism and may reinforce the violation of human rights of millions of people as administrations impose restrictions on some human rights in order to protect public health.

The essays in this volume

Josef Raab offers the lead chapter in our *Human Rights in the Americas* anthology and bears the title: "Human Rights in the Americas: A Stony Path." Raab anchors his discussion on a foundational definition written in 1948 in the tract, "Universal Declaration of Human Rights" by the United Nations. He argues that although attempts at instituting human rights in the Americas have been extant from the inception of the Europeans landing in the Caribbean Islands and the mainland of the American continent as early as 1511, these early incursions were barely successful. Addressing positions by Antonio de Montesinos, Bartolomé de Las Casas, Toni Morrison, Dutty Boukman, Thomas Paine, Miguel Ángel Asturias, Rigoberta Menchú, and others his essay reveals how the desire for profit and the new cash crops that began to be farmed in the colonized lands such as rice, sugar, coffee, and tobacco were too lucrative to ignore. The need for workers was immense; thus the introduction of slavery. Human rights violations continued unabated in the Americas. In the 20th century, especially after World War II, the declaration of human rights became more popular. Unfortunately, from 1930 to the present 21st century, human rights have been consistently ignored, especially by the rise of the numerous dictators who instituted murder, imprisonment, and torture on their own populations.

Philipp Reisner, in his contribution "The Parallel Reception Histories of Carlos de Sigüenza y Góngora and Cotton Mather," offers an astute reading of two key figures who represent in some fashion the 17th and 18th centuries with respect to human rights in two distinct parts of the Americas: New England and Mexico. As pre-independence representatives and literary figures in their own right—particularly of the Baroque style—they are excellent examples that can be used for undertaking a close reading of what is termed "reception histories." Reisner highlights how these two colonial period authors are misconstrued throughout history. In large part, Reisner lays out the rationale for tracing the evolution of human rights in late modernity through Sigüenza y Góngora and Mather.

Roland Walter begins "Maps of Violence, Maps of Resistance, or, Where Is Home in the Americas?" by stating that "...home is the place (residence, city, nation) where one lives and works as an individual within a collective unit (family, society) enjoying the rights and obligations of citizenship." With this preliminary statement, he sets the stage for exploring in his essay the concept of home and human rights. Since the dawn of life on our planet, people have migrated to all parts of the earth's geographic spaces in search of food and shelter. The competition between groups of *Homo sapiens* and a search for a "home" in terms of geographic lands has led to enormous clashes of violence either to displace original inhabitants or to kill them off. Walter explores the search for "home" in the Americas through literary representations such as Gioconda Belli's *La mujer habitada*; Laura Esquivel's *Malinche*; Helena María Viramontes' novel *Their Dogs Came with Them* (2007); and T. C. Boyle's *When the Killing Is Done* (2007) to advocate for a return to respect for the earth, for animals, and human beings.

Xaver Daniel Hergenröther, in "The Human Rights Situation in Central America through the Lens of Literary Representations of Violence," offers a provocative analytical reflection on the issue of human rights in Central America in general and in Guatemala specifically. The author centers his analysis on the novel, *Insensatez*, by Salvadoran writer, Horacio Castellanos Moya who was part of the generation of disenchantment and thus is able to portray the brutal civil war in Guatemala that took place between 1960 and 1969. Castellanos Moya's objective is twofold: to demonstrate the workings of institutionalized violence (i.e., genocide) and to promote the idea of creating a memory about such situations. To accomplish his goal, the author resorts to a concept coined by Alexandra Ortiz Wallner who first proposed "*friccionalidad*," that is, a literary product composed of history, *testimonio*—a common form of capturing narrative substance in Central America since the 1950s—memory, and fiction. Essentially, the term encapsulates a fusion of "fiction" and "reality."

In "Rebellion, Repression, Reform: U.S. Marines in the Dominican Republic," *Breanne Robertson* offers an extensive case study on the Dominican Republic during a U.S. Marines presence. This serves well to document how American interests became intertwined with the country's internal affairs that subsequently led to using it as a political pawn for American intervention. This is related to the well-chronicled Marine invasion of 1916 that, although initially driven by a humanitarian campaign, ended up being a "misguided counterinsurgency campaign" with overt imperialist intentions. The Dominican Republic proved to be weak and unstable with its own internal problems and conflicting interests: how to find ways to modernize the country versus allowing the Americans to help them achieve that goal. However, the Marines became entrenched, viewing their presence as an attempt to protect the constitutional government, while most Dominicans saw it as an outright invasion. The relationship between Dominicans and the Americans began to deteriorate into a clear form of long-standing colonialism.

Isabel Caldeira's chapter "Black Women Writers in the Americas: The Struggle for Human Rights in the Context of Coloniality" examines Black women writers in the Americas by incorporating theories related to "coloniality of power," "coloniality of knowledge," (Aníbal Quijano); coloniality of gender (María Lugones), and intersectionality (Kimberly Crenshaw); as well as feminist theories and human rights. In her perceptive article, Caldeira warns of the dangers regarding an uncritical acceptance of human rights since these theories and movements have been crafted by Western colonialists civilizations. For Caldeira, a more productive understanding of the structure of domination and exploitation that has subjugated Black women in particular can be gleaned in the works of Lugones and Nigerian Oyéroké Oyewùmí. She also highlights the concept of intersectionality proposed by Black feminist thinkers to address issues of violence against Black women by Black men by examining literary works such as Edwidge Danticat's *Breath, Eyes, Memory* (1994), Nourbese Philip's *A Genealogy of Resistance* (1977), Ntozake Shange's *For Colored Girls Who Have Considered Suicide/When the Rainbow is Enuf* (1975) plus *Sassafras, Cypress and Indigo* (1982). Caldeira rightly points out that for a "true" liberation, both men and women need to come together in an all-encompassing quest for human rights.

In "Autobiography, Fiction, and Racial Hatred: Representation in Jamaica Kincaid's novel, *See Now Then*," *Gonçalo Cholant* explores the concepts of fiction and truth-telling in autobiographical and fiction writing. Through these explorations of two literary genres, he demonstrates how literature and the literary imagination are key areas of cultural production that delve deeply into relations of racial conflicts. Cholant analyzes Jamaica Kinkaid's novel and the traumatized central characters populating that literary universe: Mrs. Sweet, an African woman from the Caribbean traumatized by racial hatred, and her husband, Mr. Sweet, a Jewish man traumatized by the Holocaust. She has been impacted negatively by the African diaspora but Mr. Sweet encapsulated in his own pain inflicted by the more recent horrors of the Holocaust does not perceive or acknowledge the suffering of the African experience due to slavery and the crossing of the Atlantic.

Rita Santos explores in her contribution "The Rebirth of the Myth of the American hero and Feminism" the cyclical nature of time and world events. Although women's human rights are more widely recognized, the study discloses a powerful instance that unveils the U.S. inner resistance to women's full equality stemming from the September 11, 2001 attacks. The essay demonstrates how persistent domestic inequalities continue to muddle women's status in the Unites States, despite the country's professed superiority to other countries in terms of human rights as it problematizes the marginalization of the female fire fighters.

Ruth Hellier-Tinoco's groundbreaking "Dancing Resistance, Controlling Singing and Right to Name Heritage: Mexican Indigenous Autonomy,

P'urepecha, Practices, and United Nations" explores issues of appropriation, reappropriation, nationalists constructions of "mexicanidad" (Mexicaness), and "authenticity" through the history of the P'urhépecha dance of "La Danza de Los Viejitos." Included also in this outstanding analysis is a dance and music contest sponsored by the local government of this Indigenous community located in Zacán, Michoacán, Mexico. Hellier-Tinoco centers her study on the, "Danza de Los Viejitos," considering that this cultural artifact arose in the village of Zacan as an attempt by the local elders to encourage the younger generation in the 1920s to retain their Indigenous traditions. Nevertheless, the author points out that as the traditional dance and contest gained popularity, the Mexican government agencies began to appropriate the dance and contest to further expand nationalist objectives of nation-building and national identity formation. Attempts by the local community of Zacán to reappropriate their Indigenous traditional dance became a form of resistance. However, the designation given by UNESCO to the local tradition of Zacán left Indigenous people feeling exploited once again, since they were not consulted or asked for their approval.

María José Canelo develops in "Carey McWilliams's Activism and the Democratic Human Rights Tradition" a detailed historical profile of a central human rights figure from the 1940s and 1950s in the United States. The author proposes to present this leader from "an alternative tradition of democratic activism" according to James Tully's philosophical precepts. Both believed that human rights should not be something proposed from above to attempt to establish them as law by the state without first doing the necessary legwork to propose, discuss, and contest "diverse constituencies." McWilliams played a key role in spearheading a campaign to define and implement human rights, not as a privilege but a fundamental right. Specifically, he was instrumental in impacting labor law among migrant farm workers, something which later was resurrected by César Chávez in the early 1960s, consequently influencing the creation of the Chicano Movement in 1965. McWilliams proposed that cultural citizenship and cultural rights are legitimate issues to address in order to counter what some have called the internal colonial model within the United States.

Alexander Ullman's theoretical literary analysis titled "The Ontogenesis of Fear in Héctor Tovar's *The Barbarian Nurseries*" dissects this narrative in order to extract from it a series of concepts carried out by a deep narratological reading of the text. The author unpacks such key topics as fear, illegality, and deportability seeking to understand the actions and experiences of a humble, undocumented domestic worker in Los Angeles who oversees the household of an upper class couple with their two children. She is forced to flee with the two children and to be their "mother" when the couple acts out a violent confrontation between them with flashbacks of being in the United States illegally. The article proposes various readings of Tovar's book, revolving around fear as a thematic trait and a formal structuring device. As metafiction, the work exposes the media for perpetuating fear as well as a right-wing antagonism. The human rights of this humble woman are compromised through outside machinations outside of her will.

Wellington Marinho de Lira offers, in his chapter "Brazilian *Quilombos*: Castaínho and Its Struggles for Human Rights," an analysis and portrayal of the social phenomenon known as quilombos within Brazil to raise awareness of the contemporary quilombola community Castaínho. The *quilombo*, a community formed by mostly escaped African slaves, is used to examine how such communities have resisted since the late 1500s in a nation that historically has promoted biological and cultural "whitening" to the extent that upward mobility or racial equality for Blacks has remained elusive despite the myth of racial democracy in Brazilian race relations. The case study attempts a comparison, through accumulation, by first focusing on the community *Quilombo dos Palmares* that serves as the model for the remnant community of Castaínho in their ongoing struggle for the right to ensure the right of property over their land as well as the preservation of their ethnicity (culture, religion, social practices).

Luz Angélica Kirschner's study, "*Capá Prieto* and the Decolonial Afro-Latin(a/o) American Imagination," focuses on a collection of stories titled *Capá Prieto* (2009) by Afro-Puerto Rican Yvonne Denis Rosario that well illustrates an African diasporic and Caribbean consciousness with human rights as both front and end. Through the stories "El silenciamiento" (Silencing), "Periódicos de ayer" (Newspapers of Yesteryears), "Desaucio en el palmar" (Eviction), and "Ama de leche" (Wet Nurse), Afro-Latinidades are examined to understand a decolonizing text about identity and, particularly, Blackness. Writing at the intersection of U.S. Latina/o, Latin American, and Anglo-American narratives of culture, memory, and race, Kirschner addresses some of the complexities relative to national and ethnic identities that make up U.S. and Puerto Rican consciousness about culture, ethnicity, gender, and race, and how these have influenced the implementation, or lack thereof, of human rights in the country.

Matti Steinitz in his article, "We Got Latin Soul!" offers an excellent and detailed account on how African Americans and Afro-Latinos, namely, Puerto Ricans, sought commonalities through music to create new hybrid musical styles that forged alliances between the two groups for the sake of human rights during the Age of Black Power, 1966–1972. Rhythm and dance brought them together by creating popular music that they both related to, thus borrowing from each other. African Americans brought to the table Jazz, Rhythm and Blues, and Funk, and Puerto Ricans contributed Mambo, Cha-cha-cha, and later Salsa, which together later helped to produce Reggae and Hip Hop. As Blacks recalled the aftereffects of slavery from the South and Puerto Ricans problematized their status as colonial subjects, the combination of styles in Harlem and the Bronx promoted greater interactions on the issue of Blackness. What emerged, Steinitz reveals, was what some called a "Rainbow radicalism" which offered anti-essentialist strategies, a kind of mutual breeding ground, from both ethnic perspectives as they discovered a workable solidarity.

In "From Racism to Speciesism: The Question of the Freedom of the Other in the Works of J. M. Coetzee and J. M. Detela," *Marjetka Golež Kaučiĉ* deconstructs the artificial and anthropocentric separation humans have erected between animals and themselves to underline the incipient status of animals and their rights in many nations and societies of the world and the Americas where animal rights are in a nascent stage. Golež Kaučiĉ convincingly argues for animal rights and how literary works are essential in this advocacy project. To this end, the scholar compares how in an analogous manner to the rationale offered to justify racism, human-constructed speciesism arises out of artificial barriers that intend to separate humans and nonhumans. Golež Kaučiĉ analysis of speciesism and humans' inability to recognize the mistreatment of animals in the multiple forms these mistreatments arise, especially in the form of eating animals and using animals for sport and food. Golež Kaučiĉ provides an insight into human/animal discriminatory practices as her contribution calls the conceptualization of animals as part and parcel of the human life spectrum and should be treated as such: with dignity and respect.

Nicole Sparling Barco's chapter titled, "To Be Or Not To Be Human: The Plasticity of Posthuman Rights," delves into theorizing regarding a posthuman world. Postulating the right to *be* human as essential to any discussion of human rights, Sparling Barco analyzes Karen Tei Yamashita's experimental transnational novel, *Through the Arc of the Rain Forest*, through the lens of critical posthumanism. Relying on Rosi Braidotti's concept of the posthuman as a mode of "becoming-animal, becoming-earth, becoming-machine," she concentrates principally on the notion of "becoming-earth" in Yamashita's novel, as articulated in the figure of the spirited plastic narrator, Kazumasa's ball. Much of Barco's essay comes to terms with Yamashita's esthetic choice to personify plastic, and to imagine a world in which Kazumasa and his ball share a vitalist materialist posthuman identity. What this helps us to consider, Sparling Barco argues, is the danger not only in the disappearance of the human subject to which rights attach, but also of the power of a critical posthumanist reading to reveal the exclusionary process by which the human is constructed in a binary relation to its others, namely, dehumanization. Reimagining the posthuman in terms of becoming, she concludes, allows us to humanize the transnatural world and strengthen our ethical responsibility to it.

The essays included in our anthology, *Human Rights in the Americas*, explore the topic of human rights from different angles and in different time periods. The last essays bring to the fore issues of who is a human and who is not. The question is not as easily answered as the Enlightenment philosophers of the 17th and 18th century thought it was self-evident. However, their definition was restricted to the white male. People of color, women, and animals were all excluded from this very narrow definition. The 21st century, on the other hand, is greatly expanding the definition to include even inanimate objects. The essays are all thought provoking and provide new venues through which we can explore the subject of human rights.

Works cited

Agosín, Marjorie. *Surviving Beyond Fear: Women, Children and Human Rights in Latin America*. White Pine Press, 1993.

Anderson, Carol. "A 'Hollow Mockery': African Americans, White Supremacy, and the Development of Human Rights in the United States." *Bringing Human Rights Home: A History of Human Rights in the United States*. Abridged edition, edited by Cynthia Soohoo et al. University of Pennsylvania Press, 2009, pp. 68–99.

Anghie, Antony. "Francisco de Vitoria and the Colonial Origins of International Law." *Postcolonialism and the Law: Critical Concepts in Law*. Vol 1, edited by Denise Ferreira da Silva and Mark Harris. Routledge, 2018, pp. 152–167.

Anzaldúa, Gloria. *Borderlands/La Frontera: The New Mestiza*. Aunt Lute Books, 1987.

Arias, Arturo. "Indigenous Herencias: Creoles, Mestizaje, and Nations before Nationalism." *The Cambridge History of Latina/o American Literature*, edited by John Morán and Laura Lomas. Cambridge University Press, 2018, pp. 33–50.

Barreto, José-Manuel, editor. "Introduction: Decolonial Strategies and Dialogue in the Human Rights Field." *Human Rights from a Third World Perspective: Critique, History and International Law*. Cambridge Scholars Publishing, 2013, pp. 1–42.

Barreto, José-Manuel, editor. "Imperialism and Decolonization as Scenarios of Human Rights History." *Human Rights from a Third World Perspective: Critique, History and International Law*. Cambridge Scholars Publishing, 2013, pp. 140–171.

Bashi Treitler, Vilna. *The Ethnic Project: Transforming Racial Fiction into Ethnic Factions*. Stanford University Press, 2013.

Belausteguigoitia, Marisa. "From Indigenismo to Zapatismo: Scenarios of Construction of the Indigenous Subject." *Critical Terms in Caribbean and Latin American Thought: Historical and Institutional Trajectories*, edited by Yolanda Martínez-San Miguel et al. Palgrave, 2016, pp. 23–36.

Braidotti, Rosi and Maria Hlavajova, editors. "Introduction." *Posthuman Glossary*. Bloomsbury Academic, 2018, pp. 1–14.

Braidotti, Rosi, editor. "Posthuman Critical Theory." *Posthuman Glossary*, edited by Rosi Braidotti and Maria Hlavajova. Bloomsbury Academic, 2018, pp. 339–342.

Broeck, Sabine. "The Legacy of Slavery: White Humanities and Its Subject. A Manifesto." *Human Rights from the Third World Perspective: Critique, History and International Law*, edited by José-Manuel Barreto. Cambridge Scholars Publishing, 2013, pp. 102–116.

Caminero-Santangelo, Marta. *Documenting the Undocumented: Latino/a Narratives and Social Justice in the Era of Operation Gatekeeper.* University Press of Florida, 2016.

Cardenas, Sonia. *Human Rights in Latin America" A Politics of Terror and Hope.* University of Pennsylvania Press, 2010.

Castells, Manuel. *The Power of Identity.* 2nd edition. Wiley-Blackwell, 2010.

Castles, Stephen, Hein de Haas, and Mark J. Miler. *The Age of Migration: International Population Movements in the Modern World.* 5th edition. Palgrave, 2014.

Ceja, Granados, Luis, José and Jamal, Urooba. "Canada's Broken Pledge to Human Rights Defenders," *NACLA, 30 July* 2019, nacla.org/news/2019/08/01/canada%E2%80%99s-broken-pledge-human-rights-defenders.

CFOJA (Canadian Femicide Observatory for Justice and Accountability). "Murdered and Missing Indigenous Women and Girls." 8 Aug. 2018: www.femicideincanada.ca/about/history/indigenous.

Cleary, Edward. *Mobilizing Human Rights in Latin America.* Kumarian Press, 2007.

Deer, Sarah. *The Beginning and End of Rape: Confronting Sexual Violence in Native America.* University of Minnesota Press, 2015.

Dussel, Enrique. "Las Casas, Vitoria and Suárez, 1514-1617." *Human Rights from the Third World Perspective: Critique, History and International Law*, edited by José-Manuel Barreto, translated by James Terry. Cambridge Scholars Publishing, 2013, pp. 172–207.

Fischer, Sybille. *Modernity Disavowed: Haiti and the Cultures of Slavery in the Age of Revolution.* Duke University Press, 2004.

Fischer, Sybille. "Having Hitherto Interpreted the World, the Point is to Change It: Unthinkable History? The Haitian revolution, Historiography, and Modernity on the Periphery." *A Companion to African-American Studies*, edited by Lewis E. Gordon and Jane Anna Gordon. Blackwell, 2006, pp. 360–376.

García-Del Moral, Paulina. "The Murders of Indigenous Women in Canada as Femicides: Toward a Decolonial Intersectional Reconceptualization of Femicide." *Signs: Journal for Women in Culture and Society*, vol. 43, no. 4, 2018, pp. 929–954.

Goldberg, David Theo. *The Threat of Race: Reflections on Racial Neoliberalism.* Blackwell, 2009.

Grosfoguel, Ramón et al., editors. "Introduction: Latin@s and the 'Euro-American Menace': The Decolonization of the U.S. Empire in the Twentieth-First Century." Latin@s in the World-System: Decolonization Struggles in the Twentieth-First Century U.S. Empire. Paradigm Publishers, 2005, pp. 3–27.

Heiskanen, Benita. "Ni Una Más, Not One More: Activist-Artistic Response to the Juárez Femicides." *JOMEC Journal: Journalism, Media and Cultural Studies*, no. 3, 2013, pp. 1–21.

Hernández Castillo, R. Aída. "Fraticidal War or Athnocidadl Strategy? Women's Experience with Political Violence in Chiapas." *Engaged Observers: Anthropology, Advocacy, and Activism*, edited by Victoria Sanford and Asale Angel-Ajani. Rutgers University Press, 2006, pp. 149–169.

Kandiyoti, Dalia. *Migrant Sites: America, Place, and Diaspora Literatures.* Dartmouth College Press, 2009.

Kelly, Patrick William. *Sovereign Emergencies: Latin America and the making of Global Human Rights Politics.* Cambridge University Press, 2018.

Kirschner, Luz Angélica, editor. "Expanding Latinidad: An Introduction." *Expanding Latinidad: An Inter-American Perspective*. Bilingual Review Press, Arizona State University, 2012, pp. 1–56.

Lacroix, Jean-Michel. "Canadian and US Approaches towards the Americas: Similarities and Differences." *International Journal*, vol. 67, no. 3, Summer 2012, pp. 703–721.

Lamberston, Ross. "Domination and Dissent: Equality Rights before World War II." *A History of Human Rights in Canada: Essential Issues*, edited by Janet Miron. Canadian Scholars' Press, 2009, pp. 11–26.

Lamberston, Ross. "Introduction." *A History of Human Rights in Canada: Essential Issues*. Canadian Scholars' Press, 2009, pp. 1–8. Nayar, Pramod K. Posthumanism. Polity, 2014.

Langlois, Anthony J. "Normative and Theoretical Foundations of Human Rights." *Human Rights: Politics and Practice*, edited by Michael Goodhart. Oxford University Press, 2009, pp. 11–25.

Laó-Montes, Agustin. "Decolonial Moves: Trans-locating African Diaspora Spaces." *Globalization and the Decolonial Option*, edited by Walter Mignolo and Arturo Escobar. Routledge. 2010, pp. 163–192.

López, Kathleen. "The Asian Presence in *Mestizo* Nations: A Response." *Critical Terms in Caribbean and Latin American Thought: Historical and Institutional Trajectories*, edited by Yolanda Martínez-San Miguel et al. Palgrave, 2016. 125–131.

Lugones, María. "Heterosexualism and the Colonial/Modern Gender System." *Hypatia*, vol. 22, no. 1, 2007, pp. 186–209.

Mace, Gordon and Jean-Philippe Thérien. "Canada and the Americas: Making a Difference?" *International Journal*, vol. 67, no. 3, Summer 2012, pp. 569–582.

Mann, Charles C. "Columbian Exchange." *The Routledge Handbook to the History and Societies of the Americas*, edited Olaf Kaltmeier et al. Routledge, 2019, pp. 67–74.

McClennen, Sophia A. and Alexandra Schultheis Moore, editors. "Introduction: Aporia and Affirmative Critique." *The Routledge Companion to Literature and Human Rights*, Routledge, 2016, pp. 1–19.

McClennen, Sophia A. and Joseph R. Slaughter. "Introducing Human Rights and Literary Forms; or, The Vehicle and Vocabularies of Human Rights." *Comparative Literature Studies*, vol. 46, no. 1, 2009, pp. 1–19.

Mignolo, Walter. "Who Speaks for the 'Human' in Human Rights?" *Human Rights from the Third World Perspective: Critique, History and International Law*, edited by Barreto. Cambridge Scholars Publishing, 2013, pp. 44–64.

Miller, J.R. "Human Rights for Some: First Nations Rights in Twentieth-Century Canada." *Taking Liberties: A History of Human Rights in Canada*, edited by David Goutor and Stephen Heathorn. Oxford University Press, 2013, pp. 233–260.

Miron, Janet, editor. "Preface." *A History of Human Rights in Canada: Essential Issues*. Canadian Scholars' Press, 2009, pp. vii–viii.

Oboler, Suzanne, and Anani Dzidzienyo, editors. "Flows and Counterflows: Latinas/os, Blackness, and Racialization in Hemispheric Perspective." *Neither Enemies Nor Friends: Latinos, Blacks, Afro-Latinos*. Palgrave, 2005, pp. 3–35.

Oboler, Suzanne, and Deena J. Gonzáles, editors. *The Oxford Enciclopedia of Latinos and Latinas in Contemporary Politics, law, and Social Movements*. Two volumes. Oxford University Press, 2015.

Parikh, Crystal. "Bringing Human Rights to Bear in American Literature." *The Routledge Companion to Literature and Human Rights*, edited by Sophia A. McClennen and Alexandra Schultheis Moore. Routledge, 2016, pp. 380–388.

Patten, Wendy. "The Impact of September 11 and the Struggle Against Terrorism on the U.S. Domestic Human Rights Movement." *Bringing Human Rights Home: A History of Human Rights in the United States*. Abridged edition. Edited by Cynthia Soohoo et al. University of Pennsylvania Press, 2009, pp. 287–325.

Quijano, Aníbal. "Coloniality of Power, Eurocentrism, and Latin America." *Coloniality at Large: Latin America and the Postcolonial Debate*, edited by Mabel Moraña et al. Duke University Press, 2008, pp. 181–224.

Raab, Josef. "Dissent—Lifeblood of the Americas." Unpublished paper presented at the conference "Reinventing the Social: Movements and Narratives of Resistance, Dissension, and Reconciliation in the Americas" in Coimbra, Portugal, in March 2018.

Rahier, Jean Muteba, editor. "Introduction: Black Social Movements in Latin America: From Monocultural Mestizaje and 'Invisibility' to Multiculturalism and State Corporatism/Co-optation." *Black Social Movements in Latin America: From Monocultural Mestizaje to Multiculturalism*. Palgrave, 2012, pp. 1–12.

Sagot R., Montserrat. "Gender Travels South: A Response to Lawrence La Fountain-Stokes." *Critical Terms in Caribbean and Latin American Thought: Historical and Institutional Trajectories*, edited by Yolanda Martínez-San Miguel et al. Palgrave, 2016, pp. 209–215.

Sawyer, Mark. "Racial Politics in Multiethnic America: Black and Latin@ Identities and Coalitions." *Neither Enemies nor Friends: Latinos, Blacks, Afro-Latinos*, edited by Suzanne Oboler and Anani Dzidzienyo. Palgrave, 2005, pp. 265–279.

Schenandoah, Michelle and Jonel Beauvais. *An Indigenous Response to #Me Too by Rematriation Magazine*, 2018: https://vimeo.com/261177660.

Shohat, Ella and Evelyn Alsultany, editors. "The Cultural Politics of 'the Middle East' in the Americas: An Introduction." *Between the Middle East and the Americas: The Cultural Politics of Diaspora*. The University of Michigan Press, 2013, pp. 3–41.

Smith, Miriam. "Social Movements and Judicial Empowerment: Courts, Public Policy, and Lesbian and Gay Organizing in Canada." *A History of Human Rights in Canada: Essential Issues*, edited by Janet Miron. Canadian Scholars' Press, 2009, pp. 220–243.

Soohoo, Cynthia, et al., editors. "Preface." *Bringing Human Rights Home: A History of Human Rights in the United States*. Abridged edition. University of Pennsylvania Press, 2009, pp. vii–xi.

Soohoo, Cynthia. "Human Rights and the Transformation of the 'Civil Rights' and 'Civil Liberties' Lawyer." *Bringing Human Rights Home: A History of Human Rights in the United States*. Abridged edition, edited by Soohoo et al. University of Pennsylvania Press, 2009, pp. 198–234.

Stanton, Domna C. "Top-Down, Bottom-Up, Horizontally: Resignifying the Universal in Human Rights Discourse." *Theoretical Perspectives on Human Rights and Literature*, edited by Elizabeth Swanson Goldberg and Alexandra Schultheis Moore. Routledge, 2012, pp. 65–86.

Takaki, Ronald T. *Iron Cages: Race and Culture in the Nineteenth-Century America*. The Athlone Press, 1980.

Trouillot, Michel-Rolph. *Silencing the Past: Power and the Production of History.* Beacon Press, 1995.

Walker, Barrington. "Finding Jim Crow in Canada, 1789-1967." *A History of Human Rights in Canada: Essential Issues*, edited by Janet Miron. Canadian Scholars' Press, 2009, pp. 81–98.

Walsh, Catherine. "Afro In/Exclusion, Resistance, and the 'Progressive State: (De)Colonial Struggles, Questions, and Reflections." *Black Social Movements in Latin America: From Monocultural Mestizaje to Multiculturalism*, edited by Jean Muteba Rahier. Palgrave, 2012, pp. 15–34.

West, Michael O. and William G. Martin, editors. "Haiti, I'm Sorry: The Haitian Revolution and the Forging of the Black International." *From Toussaint to Tupac: The Black International since the Age of Revolution.* The University of North Carolina Press, 2009, pp. 72–104.

Part I
Early origins of human rights

1 Human rights in the Americas
A stony path

Josef Raab

Walls are detrimental to human rights. Those who build walls—whether physical or metaphorical ones—highlight difference. Difference, in turn, fosters inequality, and those regimes and individuals that are not held back by ethical concerns will use inequality as an excuse or as an encouragement to strengthen their own privileged position by violating the human rights of others. Human rights violations come in many forms, from dispossession to genocide, from slavery to sexual exploitation, from dispossession to torture, from arbitrary detention to a denial of freedom of speech, from capitalist exploitation to barring access to water and resources, from forced migration to abduction, and from pollution and hunger to a denial of political representation or of equal treatment before the law. The abuses occur in the public (often committed by representatives of the state) and private spheres (often committed by men against women). Countermeasures against human rights violations also come in myriad forms, from mass protests to civil disobedience, from social movements to impromptu coalitions, from artistic expression to political action, from media productions or testimonials to armed resistance, and from local to national, inter-American, and global initiatives. Both the threat to human rights and the struggles to defend them are omnipresent and very diverse—in the Americas and beyond.

But what *are* human rights? This question has been a bone of contention for centuries. The standard document on human rights remains the 1948 "Universal Declaration of Human Rights" by the United Nations. Article 1 states that "All human beings are born free and equal in dignity and rights. They are endowed with reason and conscience and should act towards one another in a spirit of brotherhood" (183). Article 2 specifies that when it comes to human rights, "no distinction shall be made" with regard to their applicability; these are universal rights. And Article 3 adds that "Everyone has the right to life, liberty and security of person" (183). Slavery, torture, unequal legal treatment, and infringements of individual liberties are castigated in the Declaration, while freedom of expression, the right to privacy, freedom from fear and want, the right to asylum, freedom of religion, and the right to own property are upheld. Other stipulations include "the right to rest and leisure" (Article 24), "the right to a standard of living adequate for the health and well-being of [a person] and of his [or her] family, including food, clothing, housing and medical care and necessary social services" (Article 25.1), the right to "special care and assistance" in "motherhood and childhood" (Article 25.2), the "right to education" (Article 26), and "the right freely to participate in the cultural life of the community" (Article 27). In view of how encompassing this array of rights and freedoms is, it seems not surprising that there are frequent quarrels over where the rights of the one group or individual start to infringe upon the rights of another group or individual. There is also a considerable danger that some may try to justify violent interventions, claiming that they are undertaken in pursuit of the "social progress and better standards of life" envisioned by the United Nations (182). While in the past some held that groups such as Indigenous peoples, persons of African descent, or even all women were in some manner lacking and therefore could not claim full human rights or citizenship rights, today there seems to be a danger of instrumentalizing human rights and human rights discourses as a pretext for extending one's own power. This extension of power can be through intervention in a foreign country or by claiming privileges for particular groups. Andrew Clapham goes so far as to assert that "human rights are under attack today, not because of doubts about their existence, but rather due to their omnipresence" (14). It seems that the deeper we dive into the matter, the more complex the issues become and the more room there is for contention and conflict. For centuries the Americas have been plagued by such human rights–related contention and conflict.

The history of the Americas is also a history of human rights struggles. The defense of human rights has been a stony path indeed. Since before the Conquest human rights have been advocated, challenged, and violated in conflicts over territory, resources, freedom, equality, the death penalty, labor, citizenship, the fate of so-called *desaparecidos* (disappeared), and organ trafficking. The sanctity of the human body, the preservation of a livelihood, and the right to freedom of expression remain under siege throughout the Americas. In this context—apart from political intervention and active resistance—scholarship, public discourse, literature, and the media constitute important venues for keeping human rights on the agenda. As well, they are important venues for pursuing the ideal proclaimed in the UN "Universal Declaration of Human Rights," namely the "recognition of the inherent dignity and of the equal and inalienable rights of all members of the human family [as] the foundation of freedom, justice and peace in the world" (182). Narrating and castigating human rights abuses is important because it involves moving from objectification and victimhood to a subject position that makes the individual or group a rights claimant demanding adherence to international principles of respect for human dignity (see also Coundouriotis 78). As I hope to demonstrate, human rights are a key issue in and for the Americas and as such, they deserve our full attention.

Although there is much that we do not know or understand about Indigenous American civilizations before the Conquest, these civilizations are known for their accomplishments in astronomy, agriculture, and architecture as well as for living in sustainable harmony with the natural environment. However, practices like slavery and human sacrifices were also common. While it makes little sense to apply the UN Declaration of Human Rights retroactively, practices of inequality and violence seem to be deeply ingrained in human history. In the Americas, inequalities and human rights violations were further inscribed by the Conquest and colonialism.

Colonialism—in the Americas and elsewhere in the world—was based on the idea of European, Christian, and white self-appointed superiority and on an assumed right to exploitation and subjugation, as well as (in the case of Spain and other colonial powers) a duty to missionize. The Papal Bull of 1452 granted to Christian European nations the right to conquer and subdue any lands held by non-Christians. This Papal Bull of 1452 was the basis of Pope Alexander VI's bull *Inter Caetera* of May 3, 1493, that granted to Spain the right to conquer the lands Columbus had already claimed for the Spanish crown as well as any lands that Spain might "discover" in the future. This so-called Doctrine of Discovery and the subsequent colonialist practices of inequality involved genocide and a wide disregard for the human rights of the Indigenous population on the basis of questioning whether the Indigenous have reason and a soul, whether they are full-fledged children of God, and whether therefore human rights even apply to them. Against the prevailing sentiment, the Dominican friar Antonio de Montesinos asked in his "Advent Sermon" of 1511, given on Hispaniola: "Are they not men? Do they not have rational souls?" (Little 19). Ambrose Mary Little explains de Montesinos' stance as follows:

> In the midst of a culture where slavery was permitted, few questioned the rights of Spaniards systematically to enslave and murder the native populations of the New World. However, among those few were the Dominicans of Hispaniola who denounced the actions of slave owners from the pulpit. On what grounds did they do this? Surely it was not based on any written law, for the law of Spain allowed the enslavement of peoples. Nor was it founded on some international law, for this controversy was partially responsible for the development of a recognized international law. Rather, the argument of Montesinos and his Dominican brothers depended on a higher law. This was not church law, however, since the ambiguities in ecclesiastical law allowed theologians, like Juan Ginés de Sepúlveda, to give credibility to the institution of slavery. Instead, Montesinos made his appeal to God's law by referring to human nature: "Are they not men? Do they not have rational souls?" (19)

According to Little, de Montesinos and his more famous disciple Bartolomé de Las Casas based their approach on St. Thomas Aquinas. They castigated the Spanish colonists for their mistreatment of the Indigenous population and refused absolution to anyone who "possessed" *indios*. While Las Casas did not focus on individuals and he was slow to recognize the equality of Africans, he did proclaim *group* rights (see also Cardenas 6–8). He believed, as he wrote in his *Apologetic History*, that "the entire human race is one" (qtd. in Cardenas 7). On this basis, every group among the human race should have the same rights. Accordingly, Las Casas broadcast his conviction that the native population of the Americas could not be massacred, enslaved, maimed, starved, or raped with impunity.

But the more common approach of Spanish colonialists was that of subjugation and decimation. The execution of the last Inca emperor, Atahualpa, by Francisco Pizarro in 1533 is just one of the innumerable human rights violations that characterized colonial rule in the Americas. Many Indigenous people were forced to work for Spaniards under the *repartimiento* or *encomienda* system. They were considered a commodity that the Spanish crown could use to remunerate Spanish colonialists. Abhorring the atrocities that this system brought with it, the Franciscan Order sent a formal protest note against the practice of *repartimiento* in the Spanish colonies to the *Consejo de Indias* in 1594. In a rational argument consisting of 20 articles, the authors castigated the practice of unfree Indigenous labor, which, they wrote, disregarded the human dignity of the *indios* and profited only a few Spaniards. Rather than having the common good as its goal, wrote the Franciscans, it was a practice of exploitation, humiliation, and decimation, a cruel and un-Christian practice of profiteers (Franziskaner 209ff).

The importation of enslaved Africans to the Americas was not far behind. European seafaring nations, especially Portugal, had been importing kidnapped Africans to Europe and to the Atlantic islands since the 15th century. By the late 16th century, the slave routes had shifted to the New World, initially especially to the Caribbean and Brazil.

David Brion Davis remarks in his book *Inhuman Bondage: The Rise and Fall of Slavery in the New World* that despite the differences among New World colonies, there was a persistent pattern. These pattern regarding slavery and its inhumanity was observed "from Hispaniola and Brazil in the sixteenth century to Virginia and Carolina in the seventeenth." The greed led to pillaging and forced Indian labor, a process followed by turning to cash crops like sugar cane, tobacco, and cotton, the profitable cultivation of which depended on African slave labor (99). The supply of enslaved Africans seemed limitless; it more than made up for the frequent deaths during the Atlantic crossing and for the low life expectancy of slaves, especially in the hot and humid climate of the Caribbean sugar cane fields. As Davis writes, "[m]uch of the New World ... came to resemble the Death Furnace of the ancient god Moloch—consuming African slaves so increasing numbers of Europeans (and later, white Americans) could consume sugar, coffee, rice, and tobacco" (99). The profits that sugar production promised were the main reason for the human rights violations inflicted upon enslaved

Africans. As Davis points out, "In the long era from 1500 to 1870, according to a recent estimate, it was sugar-producing Brazil that absorbed over 41 percent of all African slaves and the sugar-producing British, French, Dutch and Spanish Caribbean that imported over 48 percent more. The Spanish mainland in South America took only 4.4 percent of the Africans brought into the Americas, and the British mainland in North America only 5 to 6 percent" (104). African descent meant difference, and difference meant exploitation and atrocious violations of human rights; it meant bondage, starvation, maiming, habitual rape, the tearing apart of families, and unsanctioned killing.

Toni Morrison's novel *A Mercy* (2008) offers a captivating reimagining of the cruelties to which especially women of African descent were subjected. The narrative's fragmentation recreates the ways in which slavery rips apart individuals and families, tears apart their lives and stories. In this neo-slave narrative set in the 1680s, an enslaved mother tries to get a kind-looking Englishman to purchase her 7-year-old daughter before that daughter falls prey to the lusts of her Portuguese slave master: "Senhor is not paying the whole amount he owes to Sir. [who] will take instead the woman and the girl, not the baby boy and the debt is gone. ... Take the girl, she says, my daughter, she says. Me. Me. Sir agrees and changes the balance due" (7). The daughter is traumatized and will never see her mother again. She feels abandoned by her mother, who cannot explain to her daughter the common practice of rape and sexual abuse in slavery from which she tried to protect her by having her purchased by a slave master who might have more respect for her human dignity and her right to her own body.

The struggle to end slavery in the New World and the movement toward respecting the human rights of the population of African descent occurred in many different locations at different times. Dutty Boukman, also known as Boukman Dutty, is a central figure in this struggle. Probably born in Jamaica as a slave, he taught himself to read and started teaching reading to other slaves, upon which his British slave master sold him to a French plantation owner. Boukman was taken to the French colony of Saint-Domingue, where he worked as an overseer. He is said to have been a Muslim as well as a voodoo priest. In August 1791, he took part in a voodoo ceremony held at Bois Caïman in Northern Haiti, a meeting at which the Haitian Revolution is believed to have germinated. That uprising eventually led to the overthrow of the French colonialists and to the proclamation of the free republic of Haiti in 1804. At the Bois Caïman voodoo ceremony, Boukman allegedly spoke the following prayer:

> The God who created the earth ... You see all that the white has made us suffer. The white man's god asks him to commit crimes. But the god within us wants to do good. Our god, who is so good, so just, He orders us to revenge our wrongs. It's He who will direct our arms and bring us the victory. It's He who will assist us. We all should throw away the image of the white men's god who is so pitiless. Listen to the voice for liberty that sings in all our hearts. (n.p.)

Several of the issues that Boukman identifies here—suffering, crimes, wrongs, pitilessness, and especially the lack of "liberty"—will also be addressed in the UN Declaration of Human Rights over a century and a half later. But in the Haitian slave rebellion and subsequent revolution, the human rights violations committed under colonialism and slavery were answered with human rights violations in the spirit of what Boukman calls "revenge." Within 2 months, the number of slaves who joined the rebellion reached some 100,000; they had killed some 4000 whites and destroyed hundreds of sugar, coffee, and indigo plantations.

The Haitian Revolution, like the French Revolution and the American Revolution before it, likewise was fought to stop human rights violations, exploitation, and inequality. But while the "Declaration of Independence" of 13 British colonies along the Atlantic coast of North America in 1776 spoke of equality and "certain inalienable rights," including "life, liberty, and the pursuit of happiness," its provisions applied only to persons who were white, male, Protestant, and landowning. If we look at conflicts throughout the world today, Thomas Paine was too optimistic when he argued in his book *The Rights of Man* (1791) that it is an instinct of man to act toward the common good. Paine believed that

> by the simple operation of constructing government on the principles of society and the rights of man, every difficulty retires, and all the parts are brought into cordial unison. There the poor are not oppressed, the rich are not privileged. Industry is not mortified by the splendid extravagance of a court rioting at its expense. Their taxes are few, because their government is just: and as there is nothing to render them wretched, there is nothing to engender riots and tumults. (163)

Although he does mention concepts that will also be found in the UN's 1948 "Universal Declaration of Human Rights"—like "the rights of man," a just government, and freedom from oppression, exploitation, and privilege—Paine focuses on Protestant, landowning, white men and overlooks the human rights of women, Native Americans, African Americans, and many recent immigrants.

The constitutions of the Spanish American republics established in the early 19th century likewise tended to solidify privilege and inequality rather than aiming to protect the human rights of all in their diverse populations. As Daniel K. Richter and Troy L. Thompson argue, the end to colonialism in the Americas did not signify a social contract based on equality and on respect for human rights. With regard to the situation of the Indigenous populations, they write:

> Policy and ideology varied greatly across the many new nations that emerged from the ruins of the Spanish empire. In the wake of the Andean Insurrections, Peruvians and Bolivians paid little heed to indigenous rights. Elsewhere, juridical equality and *mestizaje* were proclaimed as

ideals, but nonetheless the practical result for indigenous people was a relentless assault on communal rights won under the Spanish regime. After Mexico won its independence in 1821, for example, legislators expanded the definition of *terrenos baldíos* (vacant lands that could be auctioned off to new owners) to include communal property that either lay fallow or was held for ceremonial purposes. By 1830, Mexico discontinued the practice of diplomatic gift-giving that had prevailed since the 1780s, joining the United States in depriving indigenous communities of political power as well as land. Similarly, in the 1820s, the Argentine regime of Juan Manuel Rosas had resettled what it called *indios amigos* in frontier locations and paid them annuities in the form of foodstuffs, clothing, livestock, and alcohol. In subsequent decades, Uruguayans, Chileans, and Paraguayans conquered autonomous peoples, resettled or enslaved the survivors, and expanded cattle production into their lands. Nearly everywhere autonomous Indian nations increasingly came to be described as irredeemable 'savages.' (513–14)

In the context of U.S. history, we are painfully reminded of the "Trail of Tears," the forced relocations of native tribes and Indian nations following the Indian Removal Act of 1830. In later decades, resistance to the many assaults on the rights of Native Americans came, for example, in the Ghost Dance Movement of the 1890s or in the American Indian Movement, founded in 1968.

While I have concentrated on human rights in colonial and early national contexts so far, there remains the important transnational component. In 1941, in their so-called Atlantic Charter signed on a navy ship off the coast of Newfoundland, British Prime Minister Winston Churchill and U.S. President Franklin Delano Roosevelt envisaged that the defeat of Nazi Germany would be followed by a peace "which will afford assurance that all the men in all the lands may live out their lives in freedom from fear and want" (qtd. in Borgwardt 4). As Elizabeth Borgwardt observes, "[c]ontemporaries quickly began to cite the charter as the foundational stone for an internationalized set of 'fundamental freedoms,' using a particularly emblematic term for these universalist principles popularized during the war, 'human rights'" (5). Nonetheless, the 20th and 21st centuries are far from having become an age of transnational human rights observation.

In the "Atlantic Charter," the United States saw itself as the defender of those (outside the United States) whose human rights had been trampled upon. But in the preceding and subsequent decades, many in Latin America would have characterized the United States as the biggest danger to the preservation of human rights. Foreign interventions by the United States in numerous regions of Latin America typically involved violations of human rights. President Theodore Roosevelt had laid the basis for such interventions when he proclaimed in his 1904 "Corollary to the Monroe Doctrine" that they may become necessary to ensure what he called "reasonable efficiency and decency in social and political matters" and to prevent, as he said, "chronic wrongdoing, or an impotence which results in a general loosening of the ties of civilized society" (Roosevelt, n.p.). Other U.S. interventions have been conducted to pave the way for U.S. companies to operate in those countries or allegedly to prevent the spread of communism, to wage the war on drugs, or to secure democracy (see also McPherson). Isabel Allende's multigenerational novel *La casa de los espíritus* (1982), translated as *The House of Spirits*, illustrates how national and transnational contexts foster human rights violations over generations and how the pursuit of U.S. interests in Chile aggravates the bloodshed there. Canada, by contrast, is presented in the novel as a safe haven.

U.S. American business interests are linked to many dictatorships in Latin America and to their disregard for human rights. The Rockefellers, Hearsts, and Guggenheims, for example, supported and profited from the dictatorship of Porfirio Díaz in Mexico between 1876 and 1911. And the United Fruit Company enjoyed close and profitable ties to Guatemalan dictator Manuel Estrada Cabrera, who ruled the country from 1898 to 1920. Guatemalan novelist, poet, journalist, and diplomat Miguel Ángel Asturias, who was later awarded the Nobel Prize in Literature, wrote his novel *El Señor Presidente* about Estrada Cabrera's authoritarian rule and human rights violations in 1933, but the work was not published until 1946. It is now regarded as a founding text in the literature on dictatorship and fear. A 21-century text in this genre is Edwidge Danticat's story cycle *The Dew Breaker* (2004), which takes readers into the torture chambers of a Haitian prison during the Duvalier regime, exploring the traumata of survivors and torturers as well as those of their children's generation.

In the 20th century, from Augusto Pinochet in Chile to Jorge Rafael Videla and other dictators in Argentina to the Duvaliers in Haiti and the civic-military dictatorship in Uruguay, Latin American strongmen counted on either a blind eye or active support by the United States. As Lars Schoultz wrote in his book *Human Rights and United States Policy toward Latin America* in 1981, "[i]t would not be difficult for a study of United States policy toward human rights [in Latin America] to become a diatribe" (xi). He adds that "[i]n the years between the beginning of the Cold War and the development of widespread opposition to the Vietnamese War, human rights all but disappeared as a component of United States foreign policy" (3) until President Jimmy Carter put them back on the agenda in 1977. With social and economic changes in many Latin American nations, struggles for political control intensified. According to Schoultz,

> Just as privileged groups fight back when their political existence is threatened by a popular government, so the supporters of popular governments can be expected to resist first the destruction of their ability to participate in politics and then the economic shock treatment administered by bureaucratic-authoritarian governments. Given this potential opposition, government repression must focus upon the complex task of

deterring political activity. Measures must be taken to forestall strikes, slowdown, and demonstrations. Labor unions must be destroyed, political parties disbanded, media silenced, conversations monitored. It is at this point that the violations of human rights became notorious in many of the major nations of Latin America during the 1960s and 1970s...

During the 1960s and 1970s, the human rights violations by bureaucratic-authoritarian governments in Argentina, Brazil, Chile, and Uruguay were supplemented by more traditional forms of repression in other Latin American nations. The governments of Bolivia, El Salvador, Guatemala, Haiti, Nicaragua, and Paraguay were frequently attacked by human rights activists in Washington and later by United States policy makers. But during most of these two decades, U.S. government officials tended to interpret repression as endemic in Latin America's most rudimentary political systems and to believe that elites were unable to respond positively to U.S. efforts on behalf of human rights. (11, 13–14)

Documents that have been released in close to four decades since the publication of Schoultz's book reveal, however, that his assessment of the role of the United States in human rights violations elsewhere in the Americas seems altogether too positive. In multiple cases, the U.S. role turns out to have been less that of a passive commentator and more of an active instigator. As factual fiction, Miguel Ángel Asturias' *Banana Trilogy* (published from 1950 to 1960) exposes the foreign control of the Central American banana industry and the concomitant exploitation of the Indigenous laborers.

For dictatorial regimes and those working for them—whether out of conviction or out of fear—no human rights violation seems too atrocious in their attempts to gain or retain power. Those who actively resist abusive regimes, speak out against them, or just happen to be in the wrong place at the wrong time suffer torture and terror. The process of a growing politicization of Indigenous communities in Guatemala in response to economic exploitation and political repression is documented in Nobel Peace Prize winner Rigoberta Menchú's testimonial *I, Rigoberta Menchú* (1983). Menchú was an activist for Indigenous and women's rights during the Guatemalan Civil War that lasted from 1960 to 1996, and she continues her political work, having run for the Guatemalan presidency in 2007 and 2011. In her classic testimonial, she recounts the oppression of the poor, especially the Indigenous poor, and she indicts the brutality of the military. Menchú believes that the arrival of Columbus brought hunger and suffering to the Indigenous population; it instituted white privilege, which is still dishonoring Indians. She tells of a brother as well as a friend of hers dying of pesticide poisoning while working on plantations, and she details atrocities and torture by Guatemalan soldiers. Among the most violent descriptions is a scene where the army forces a village community to watch the execution of tortured political prisoners, one of whom is the narrator's 16-year-old brother:

> My mother recognized her son, my little brother, among them. They put them in a line. Some of them were, very nearly, half-dead, or they were nearly in their last agony.... My brother was very badly tortured, he could hardly stand up. All the tortured had no nails and they had cut off part of the soles of their feet. They were barefoot. They forced them to walk and put them in a line. They fell down at once. They picked them up again. There was a squadron of soldiers there ready to do exactly what the officer ordered. ... No-one could leave the meeting. Everyone was weeping. ... Somewhere around half-way through the speech, it would be about an hour and a half, two hours on, the captain made the squad of soldiers take the clothes off the tortured people, saying that it was so that everyone could see for themselves what their punishment had been and realize that if we got mixed up in communism, in terrorism, we'd be punished the same way. (176–177)

That Menchú was not actually present at the scene described here, but relying on the testimony given to her by others does not diminish her account's truth or validity. It remains a powerful indictment of human rights abuses of the worst kind and it reminds us that all too often incidents of this sort occur without the outside world hearing about them.

While some totalitarian regimes have been overcome, others continue their repression and extortion. Gang- and drug-related crime, agro-business and extractivism, gendered violence, poverty, and a lack of employment opportunities create a climate in which human rights seem like a luxury or a chimera. Sonia Cardenas summarizes the situation in the early 21st century as follows:

> Human rights violations and impunity are an ongoing reality in Latin America. A recent [2005] annual report by Amnesty International observed that "Respect for human rights remained an illusion for many as governments across the Americas failed to comply with their commitments to uphold fundamental human rights." Amnesty International documents that at the outset of the twenty-first century, torture, disappearances, extrajudicial executions, and ill treatment persist throughout the region, alongside systematic violence against women; attacks on human rights defenders; and an endemic poverty that disproportionately harms society's most vulnerable members, including children and indigenous groups. Even if the "geography" of political violence has shifted over time or the overall magnitude of abuse has declined in recent decades, [...] oppression still is a way of life for many of the region's people. Despite the progress associated with truth commissions and legal trials, the vast majority of human rights violators continue to walk the streets of Latin America, often in close proximity to their victims. (3)

Not only in Central and South America, but also in the Caribbean and North America, politics, greed, fear, prejudice, capitalism, and systemic racism seem to be the major factors behind human rights violations. This also holds true for more current instances like the 2014 Iguala kidnapping and killing of 43 students, the continuing operation of Guantanamo Bay prison, or the unprovoked killing of African Americans stopped by U.S. police officers. In capitalist economies, the concern for profit usually outweighs the concern for human rights. If we look at the depletion of the jungle in Brazil, the showering of migrant farmworkers with pesticides in Guatemala, the drug war in Colombia or Mexico, the flow of purchased or stolen human organs from South to North, the exploitation, abuse, and sometimes the killing of maquiladora workers south of the U.S.–Mexican border, the destruction of First Nations' hunting and fishing habitats in Canada to make space for tar sands extraction, we can see that it is profit and not a desire for better, more equal ways of living or the respect for human dignity that determines economic processes. But even regimes in explicitly noncapitalist societies—like the one in Venezuela in early 2019—do not shy away from violating human rights and starving large parts of the population in the interest of their own political gain.

However, despite this century-long stony path of human rights in the Americas, there have always also been courageous women and men who demanded respect for these rights. Activists from Antonio de Montesinos, Bartolomé de Las Casas and Dutty Boukman to Martin Luther King, Jr., and the Madres de la Plaza de Mayo have reminded us that resistance can succeed. In this vein, Patricio Guzmán's three-part documentary *La Batalla de Chile*, released from 1975 to 1979, chronicles events in Chile during that time and ends on a hopeful note that despite repression, state brutality, and killings, popular resistance to the injustices inflicted by a military regime is possible and stands a chance. While human rights are constantly under attack by those who seek power and profit, human decency and solidarity are also a force to be reckoned with. Currently, one such popular force is the "Black Lives Matter" movement in the United States. Another one is the current media revolution. David Palumbo-Liu argues that social media can help create affective communities that can rally behind human rights causes. Social media, he writes, engage in "the posting, reposting, decontextualization, and recontextualization of posts as they circulate both linearly and nonlinearly across the Web" (234). Their users sift through fragments that often do not add up to a "properly recognized and purposeful 'story'" but that may engage those users in causes "which would have been invisible otherwise" (235). With new means of documentation like cell phone cameras (despite the danger of falsifications to create fake news for political gain) and new channels of publication like YouTube, it is becoming harder to hide human rights abuses and to limit the reactions to them to their immediate geographic vicinity or national context. The local abuse of human rights increasingly triggers an international response since it is part of human nature (for most people) to want to protect the rights, freedoms, bodies, and subsistence of other human beings against totalitarian regimes or violent exploitation.

In the efforts to internationalize human rights, Central and South Americans played key roles in the drafting of the United Nations' 1948 "Universal Declaration of Human Rights" (Cardenas 9–12). Twenty-one years later, in 1969, the Organization of American States convened a meeting in San José, Costa Rica to draft the "American Convention on Human Rights." The document has meanwhile been ratified by 25 American states (the United States and Canada are not among them), two of whom (Trinidad and Tobago and Venezuela) have since renounced their adoption of the document. It reiterates the UN Declaration's position that "the ideal of free men enjoying freedom from fear and want can be achieved only if conditions are created whereby everyone may enjoy his economic, social, and cultural rights, as well as his civil and political rights" (Cardenas 209). Governments in the Americas have, lamentably, been rather selective when it comes to deciding who should benefits from the conditions they create. The "everyone" (referred to in the Preamble) of the Convention remains a far-off vision. The demand of the Convention, stated in Article I, that "all persons subject to their jurisdiction [i.e., the jurisdiction of the ratifying American states]" should be able to enjoy "the free and full exercise of those rights and freedoms, without any discrimination for reasons of race, color, sex, language, religion, political or other opinion, national or social origin, economic status, birth, or any other social condition" remains a theoretical proposition that is often disregarded in actuality when it comes to the treatment of women, minorities, migrants, dissidents, or the poor (Cardenas 210).

The position of the United States is double-edged in this regard. While the country has a model democratic constitution and while it is the home of most nongovernmental organizations devoted to human rights, the treatment of migrants without proper documentation in 2018 (separating children from their parents and detaining them) or the refusal to ratify international agreements tied to human rights blemish the record. There is an "unwillingness to impose on itself general international rules that the U.S. government accepts in principle as just" (Moravcsik 148). This is why Andrew Moravcsik speaks of "the exceptional ambivalence and unilateralism of the U.S. human rights policy," which he ties to U.S. American exceptionalism (150). He concludes that "no other country pursues as ambivalent and unilateralist a human rights policy as does the United States" (197). Leaders in the United States and elsewhere have an easier time staying in power and corporations have bigger profit margins when they disregard the human rights of certain individuals and groups. Egotism and capitalism defeat ethical concerns.

Hannah Arendt wrote in "The Decline of the Nation-State and the End of the Rights of Man" (1951) that the issue of human rights asks what it is that makes us human and that it demands of us not to reduce the individual to just one feature. Arendt observes,

> all that which is mysteriously given us by birth and which includes the shape of our bodies and the talents of our minds, can be adequately dealt with only by the unpredictable hazards of friendship and sympathy, or by the great and incalculable grace of love, which says with Augustine, "*Volo ut sis* (I want you to be)," without being able to give any particular reason for such supreme and unsurpassable affirmation. (53)

But this element that makes us human, Arendt continues, is also what makes us different from one another. There is a great danger, she cautions, that individuals perceived as different are reduced to this difference in an act that can then be used as a justification for infringing upon their rights. Paradoxically, it is what makes a person a human individual that tends to be used as a basis for denying that person full human rights. Arendt gives the following example: "If a Negro in a white community is considered a Negro and nothing else, he loses along with his right to equality that freedom of action which is specifically human; all his deeds are now explained as "necessary" consequences of some "Negro" qualities; he has become some specimen of an animal species, called man" (54). Reducing an individual or a community to one attribute that we do not share fosters the construction of mental or physical walls between us and that individual or community. Such an exclusionist mentality might in turn motivate us to want to sanction that individual or community for the attribute we ascribe to them, and we may forget the other's human rights and humanity in the process. Social movements, public intellectuals, literature, the media, scholarship, and the International Association of Inter-American Studies can help keep the spotlight on human dignity and human rights. While the struggle for human rights in the Americas has been a stony path with many setbacks, abandoning it would mean abandoning our humanity.

Works cited

Arendt, Hannah. "The Decline of the Nation-State and the End of the Rights of Man." *Human Rights: An Anthropological Reader*, edited by Mark Goodale. Wiley Blackwell, 2009, pp. 31–57.

Borgwardt, Elizabeth. *A New Deal for the World: America's Vision for Human Rights*. The Belknap Press of Harvard University Press, 2007.

Cardenas, Sonia. *Human Rights in Latin America: A Politics of Terror and Hope*. University of Pennsylvania Press, 2010.

Coundouriotis, Eleni. "In Flight: The Refugee Experience and Human Rights Narrative." *The Routledge Companion to Literature and Human Rights*, edited by Sophia A. McClennen and Alexandra Schultheis Moore, Routledge, 2016, pp. 78–85.

Davis, David Brion. *Inhuman Bondage: The Rise and Fall of Slavery in the New World*. Oxford University Press, 2006.

Dutty, Boukman. "The Prayer That Started the Haitian Revolution." *Assata Shakur Forums RSS* http://www.assatashakur.org/forum/spirituality-connect-your-center/41228-boukman-dutty-prayer-sparked-haitan-revolution.html.

Little, Ambrose Mary. "The Foundation of Human Rights in Natural Universals." *Montesinos' Legacy: Defining and Defending Human Rights for Five Hundred Years*, edited by Edward C. Lorenz et al. Lexington Books, 2014, pp. 19–26.

McPherson, Alan. *A Short History of U.S. Interventions in Latin America and the Caribbean*. Wiley Blackwell, 2016.

Menchú, Rigoberta. *I, Rigoberta Menchú: An Indian Woman in Guatemala*. First edition, edited by Elisabeth Burgos-Debray, translated by Ann Wright. Verso, 1984.

Moravcsik, Andrew. "The Paradox of U.S. Human Rights Policy." *American Exceptionalism and Human Rights*, edited by Michael Ignatieff. Princeton University Press, 2005, pp. 147–197.

Morrison, Toni. *A Mercy*. Alfred A. Knopf, 2008.

Neu-Spanien, Franziskaner von. "Gutachten über die Ausbeutung der Indios durch die *Repartimientos*." *"Auch wir sind Menschen so wie ihr": Franziskanische Dokumente des 16. Jahrhunderts zur Eroberung Mexikos*, edited by P. Horst von der Bey OFM. Ferdinand Schöningh, 1995, pp. 209–213.

Paine, Thomas. *The Rights of Man*. 1791. www.ucc.ie/archive/hdsp/Paine_Rights_of_Man.pdf.

Palumbo-Liu, David. "Fragmented Forms and Shifting Contexts: How Can Social Media Work for Human Rights?" *The Routledge Companion to Literature and Human Rights*, edited by Sophia A. McClennen and Alexandra Schultheis Moore. Routledge, 2016, pp. 233–242.

Richter, Daniel K. and Troy L. Thompson. "Severed Connections: American Indigenous Peoples and the Atlantic World in an Era of Imperial Transformation." *The Atlantic World c. 1450 – c. 1850*, edited by Nicholas Canny and Philip Morgan. Oxford University Press, 2011, pp. 499–515.

Roosevelt, Theodore. "Corollary to the Monroe Doctrine." 1904. Transcript. www.ourdocuments.gov/doc.php?flash=true&doc=56&page=transcript.

Schoultz, Lars. *Human Rights and United States Policy toward Latin America*. Princeton University Press, 1981.

United Nations General Assembly. "The Universal Declaration of Human Rights." 1948. *Human Rights: A Very Short Introduction*, edited by Andrew Clapham, Oxford University Press, 2007, pp. 182–189.

2 Constructing rights and empires in the early Americas

The parallel reception histories of Carlos de Sigüenza y Góngora and Cotton Mather

Philipp Reisner

Recent scholarship on Cotton Mather has focused on recasting him as an early Evangelical (DiCuirci; Kennedy; Stievermann). This shift in perception is prompted by the current first edition of his voluminous Bible Commentary *Biblia Americana* (Smolinski and Stievermann). So far, the only more systematic attempt to assess his work from the perspective of inter-American studies has been made by Alina Mayer in her comparison of Cotton Mather (1663–1728) and Carlos de Sigüenza y Góngora (1645–1700). While this new assessment of Mather focuses on his theology, Sigüenza y Góngora is seen as the most significant intellectual of early modern Mexico (and possibly Latin America; Medina 1), and since the lives of both have been similarly marked by important shifts in the understanding of the rights of different social groups, an argument can be made for a comparison of their work with regard to societal change and ideas of (human) rights. This will be an important step toward a clearer view of theological developments in the Americas at the turn of the 18th century. Hemispheric studies is a relatively new field that has gained popularity among scholars but is still in its early stages (Barr and Countryman; Kirk and Rivett).

Mayer has pointed out that the lives of Sigüenza y Góngora and Mather exhibit interesting parallels. Both were "almoners" or polymaths that struggled for international recognition for the intellectual achievements of their respective colonies; both wrote about the heyday of piracy and published captivity narratives, almanacs, poems, historical writings, hagiographies, and scientific treatises; both had difficulty publishing parts of their vast oeuvre despite international academic recognition; both studied Native American languages and engaged in significant political events in 1692—respectively, in the Mexico City riot and the witchcraft persecution in Salem, Massachusetts; both opposed judicial astrology and superstition, in addition to being proponents of research based on empirical experience while critically engaging with their theological heritage; and both defended the right to education and the emancipation of marginalized groups, namely, women (Mather) and *criollos* (Sigüenza y Góngora).

These biographical parallels are also reflected in curious similarities in their reception histories: both were seen as literary figures and in hindsight accused of a "Baroque" style (Clark; Manierre; More; Prado 219; Ross; van Cromphout). This view persists more specifically in relation to Sigüenza y Góngora who is still qualified as a "baroque humanist" (Medina 1) and seen to partake in "baroque discourse" (Sabat de Rivers, 287). Politically, they were depicted as pre-Independence representatives of a religiously determined New Spain and New England exceptionalism in decline (Boyd; Breed 170–171; Canup 223; Gunn 186; Leonard, *Baroque Times in Old Mexico* 125; Lowance 160; Miller 1–15; More; Schweninger; Zivin 354). This has led to curious misreadings of their allegedly similar roles in the veneration of the Virgin of Guadalupe and of Boston, Massachusetts, as a New Jerusalem (Mayer 169).

The reception histories of these two figures were subject to similar distortions, in connection with the history of human rights leading up to early modernity in which both men played an important role. Comparing their reception histories offers a snapshot of present developments in the historiography of the late 17th and early 18th centuries, shedding light on historiographical tendencies in relation to Protestant and Catholic sensibilities. Their oeuvres may be examined for *theological* and *literary* convergences and discrepancies, allowing us to develop more nuanced and differentiated views of both Americas. The present study may serve as a first attempt at a comparative, inter-American (religious, literary, intellectual, and social) biography in early modernity, which may lead to more large-scale comparative histories within and between the Americas. Comparative biographies have been on the rise since the 1980s, though mostly within a modern context, and generally focusing on political history (Brinkley; Summy). That there is a need for more profound, *longue durée* studies in the form of comparative biographies with a greater focus on early modern history is well known, but it has not led to a sufficient change within the historiographical research landscape (Ambrosius). The two comparative studies on Mather are of great scholarly merit and point in the right direction, but they focus exclusively on New England. Plus, they need to be revised precisely because they predate more recent work which puts into question the regionalist and nationalist paradigms that shaped their research layout and methodologies (Breitwieser; Middlekauff).

In general, to understand the development of concepts of human rights during the 18th century, it would be worthwhile extending this approach more systematically into early modernity. Such research would entail a more thorough probing of the print and manuscript archives of both authors and examining more closely the context of their work. It would also consider the numerous texts that may have been lost (correspondences, manuscripts, and print editions in the case of Mather, unpublished writings in the case of Sigüenza y Góngora) (Sigüenza y Góngora, *Inventory*). It has been pointed out that, in the case of Sigüenza y Góngora, numerous scholars during his lifetime in New Spain have received little or no attention (Beezley passim), which is all the more striking given that the Society of Jesus has been increasingly interested in its own history in the Americas, both from a Jesuit and non-Jesuit perspective (Abé; Classen; Maryks; Stiles; Vélez). Given the significance of the complex relationship between Catholics and Protestants during the 17th and 18th centuries, such research would aid current efforts of hemispheric studies by deepening their theological perspective.

After all, the increasing importance of human rights in the 18h century should be seen within the context of religious history and theological developments characterized by religious revivals, waves of confessionalization, the rise of Methodism, the surge of anti-Protestant legislation and polemic within the Catholic Church, the dissolution of the Society of Jesus, rampant anti-clericalism, the gradual Catholicization of Protestant denominations, and the Sacralization of political institutions, including codifications of human rights (Juviler and Gustafson; Villa-Vicencio; Stackhouse). Both Mather's and Sigüenza y Góngora's life and work need to be seen in an early Enlightenment context that prepared the ground for these later developments. Their involvement in the (re-)formation of a sense of local identity as New Englander and Mexican can be constructively related to later developments only by carefully analyzing their understanding of themselves. Otherwise, attempts at projecting *late* modern understandings of national identity and human rights onto *early* modernity will hinder rather than further our understanding of modernity (Janssen).

This case study points to a larger problem within European approaches to American studies, a problem that mirrors the history of human rights: in European American studies in particular, there has been a persistent historical bias—which arose following the Second World War—toward focusing on the 19th and 20th centuries, that is, on a U.S. national history with all its post- and transnational redefinitions and reappraisals. This leads, however, to an ahistorical bias and a distorted understanding of modernity and the history of human rights. It has been repeatedly shown that new definitions and appraisals of history that go beyond national borders, while they may modify nationalist paradigms, do not ultimately succeed in displacing or overcoming them (Bieger, Saldívar, and Voelz; Siewert; Vormann). Early American Studies in Europe is a relatively small field much less developed than in North America. It nonetheless offers an important perspective, inspired by its different theological and denominational landscapes, which might eventually be essential to critically rethink the post-national strands of the discipline. Since questions of human rights are inevitably tied to the

48 *Philipp Reisner*

project of understanding modernity, research on human rights needs to be conscious of the historical context beyond merely the more recent modern past, and this in turn entails more thorough research in early modern American Studies. The hemispheric and biographical approach proposed here may serve as a useful avenue toward deepening our understanding of the historical development of human rights.

Mather's and Sigüenza y Góngora's impact on the publication landscapes of their times also had important effects on societal developments that are relevant to the question of human rights. The transformation of the public sphere (Gestrich), the rise of the bourgeoisie, and the emergence of a critical public during the 18h century laid the ground for the codification of human rights in national legislations, a view that has recently come under more critical scrutiny (Hofmann). Mather's and Sigüenza y Góngora's work is important for present-day understandings and interpretations of human rights because of the crisis that contemporary secular thinking is facing with regard to universal principles. The rise of public theology in recent decades has demonstrated that it is doubtful whether claims to a universal moral ground can be effectively articulated from a secular perspective (Juviler and Gustafson).

Sigüenza y Góngora and Mather both stand historically at the beginning of the development of national literatures that looked to the past for inspiration, and they inaugurated the spread of periodicals that emerged from almanacs. While the rise of periodicals is still too frequently associated with the 18th century (Steele), for it has been shown that they really arose at around the beginning of the 17th century (Bauer; Böning; Hillgärtner), both Mather and Sigüenza y Góngora lived in a time that saw the geographical spread and multiplication of periodical publications (Krefting, Nøding, and Ringvej). They both actively partook in this process. Mather's alleged involvement in Benjamin Harris's (c. 1673–1716) first New England newspaper *Publick Occurrences Both Forreign and Domestick* (1690) (Harris; Knights), which was suppressed by the colonial censors after its first issue, correlates with the suppression of significant parts of Sigüenza y Góngora's writings by the Inquisition (Carrasco 222). Both Mather's and Sigüenza y Góngora's roles in the early modern publishing world were similarly restrictive and innovative. Mather, too, called for expulsion, suppression, and censure, for example, in the Quaker controversy of the 1690s (Hebel 132). Besides contributing to periodical publications, both writers represented early mass publication on a scale that has rarely been matched: with over 400 published works and numerous unpublished texts, Mather may be considered the most prolific author of the 17th and 18th centuries in New England. Sigüenza y Góngora's printing output may be less copious, but his manuscript output certainly is not. More archival research and scholarly editions are needed to unearth not only new findings to help reevaluate his neglected work, but also to help answer questions on writing habits and the functions of note-taking, diary-writing, and correspondence in early modernity. Such findings will have repercussions for determining who was reading their writings and evaluating their engagement in the context of human rights.

Many of their works are also in need of being revised and updated: Sigüenza y Góngora's work does not exist in current scholarly editions, while some of the editions of Mather's work (including his diary, letters, church history of New England, and medical handbook *The Angel of Bethesda* [Mather 1957]) need to be re-assessed because of recent findings and flaws in the first scholarly editions. Mather's Protestant missionary attempts at reaching out to the Catholic populations of the Americas—he taught himself Spanish and even published some texts in Spanish—is a further point of contact in need of more comparative research (Mather and Johnston). It is not clear, for example, to what extent the opposite case— that is, Spanish Catholic missionary publications in English—existed as a genre in North America. Especially in light of the renewed attention to self-writing and life-writing in all its forms (Leader; Smyth), it will be necessary to investigate this dimension more fully as well. The work of both authors raises interesting questions concerning print and distribution history, also with regard to their audiences (Hall 7; 93–95). Given their ambivalent and changing theological outlook and roles, examining their writings in greater detail from the perspective of print history will allow us to reassess the religious history of the time in which they lived, and with it, the early modern discussion of rights as it prepared the way for modern understandings of human rights. The present article attempts a first assessment of the potential and necessary paths of investigation of such a larger, comparative research project.

In their current receptions, the evaluation of Sigüenza y Góngora as a forming figure of a New Spanish collective conscience precedes the recasting of Mather as an early American Evangelical which, given the religious historiography of New England Awakenings, makes him—to state the paradigm shift somewhat pointedly—an early Founding Father rather than the Last Puritan. Sigüenza y Góngora's reception, by contrast, does not exhibit such a pointed shift. A comparative reception history of both thinkers has the task of revealing much about confessional differences in the interpretations of early modern figures and history from a present-day perspective. Are the many shifts in Mather's reception history to be explained as a "Protestant" element in historiography, inspired by his own Protestantism? Since Evangelicalism encompasses both Catholic and Protestant theological positions, a comparative historical perspective may also shed light on developments within the spectrum of Catholic and Protestant Christianity: the current reception of Mather may then be seen as the culmination of centuries of "Catholicization" of diverse—not only American—forms of Protestantism into a mainstream Evangelical culture that increasingly blurs the boundaries and distinctions established during the Reformation. Recent research into the "Protestant mainline," the development of periodical mass publication in the religious sphere, and individual conversion histories and religious mobility corroborate this view (Coffman; Meyer and Moors; Millner; Ihrke-Buchroth). Speaking of a "Catholicization" of Protestant New England Christianity is no vaguer than contemporary references to "American Evangelicalism." On the contrary, it recognizes that there has been an Anglicanization of New England theology, taking into account the gradual establishment of Catholicism in British North America, and it inquires into its impact on Protestant theology.

Sigüenza y Góngora and Mather remind us that in North and South America and beyond, the question concerning the relation between the Reformation and the Enlightenment is still central to our understanding of modernity. To better comprehend early modernity, we must engage more critically with the reception histories and historiographical constructions that modernity retrospectively imposes upon it. In a time when hagiography still has a place in the humanities (Sparn 9), such interconfessional comparisons of hagiographers may help us to unravel and better understand our current desires to find saints in early modernity. We should acknowledge that biographies still have a didactic function. But instead of comparing figures from a similar or related cultural background, as Robert Lawrence Middlekauff famously did in *The Mathers: Three Generations of Puritan Intellectuals, 1596–1728* and Mitchell Robert Breitwieser in his *Cotton Mather and Benjamin Franklin: The Price of Representative Personality* (Breitwieser; Middlekauff), it may be more productive, also from an inter-American point of view, to compare contemporary figures in different, yet related cultures (and languages). Such biographical writing supplements the results of diachronic studies with more profound synchronic and transcultural knowledge of particular historical moments. Like a transcultural memoir, it may ultimately be more useful in forming a critical, metahistorical perspective on the past, rejecting the kind of religious affiliations characteristic of contemporary hagiography, which is arguably still en vogue in intellectual history.

In contrast to Mather's involvement in the Glorious Revolution and his opposition to the earlier Massachusetts regime of Governor Edmund Andros (1637–1714), Sigüenza y Góngora was generally on better terms with both the Viceroys of New Spain and the archbishop of Mexico. Both Mather's and Sigüenza y Góngora's early posthumous receptions seem to have been largely positive, in part due to the work they did for their local communities. While Sigüenza y Góngora was involved primarily in the work of the archbishop's almoner and in administrating the finances of the Hospital del Amor de Dios (Leonard, *Don Carlos de Sigüenza y Góngora*), Mather concentrated on pastoral activities. While he distributed and collected money for charitable purposes, he was most intent on distributing books, lessons, and spiritual support, encouraging the piety of his followers and those around him.

In a quite similar fashion, Mather and Sigüenza y Góngora engaged in a double mission as historians. They wrote hagiographies of the Royal Convent of Jesus Mary of Mexico City (Sigüenza y Góngora) and early New England "Puritan Saints" (Mather), but they also attempted to explain the place of the Americas in a biblical world history. In this context, the issue of conquest and questions related to Indigenous peoples posed significant challenges for thinking about human rights *avant la lettre*, challenges that both authors took up from their respective theological positions. South and Central America were crucial to this endeavor of explaining the place of the Americas in a biblical world history: Sigüenza y Góngora believed that the Mexicans and other nations of Anáhuac were descendants of Naphtuhim, the son of Mezrain and nephew of Chaim (Brading 365). The Mexican pyramids were considered very ancient. They were built shortly after the flood, which explains the similarity with the Egyptian pyramids, and the Aztec god Quetzalcóatl was the Apostle St. Thomas. Similarly, Mather was interested in theories of the Jewish descent of South American Indians, though he was more doubtful of this connection (Mather, *Magnalia*, III 193). Both Sigüenza y Góngora and Mather were looking for signs of the end of the times, a theological quest that—through potential identification with Israelite or Hebrew peoples—enhanced the status of Indigenous peoples in their eyes.

Comparing these two early modern intellectuals allows us to flesh out central concerns of their times and also reveal important differences. Some of these differences are surely due to the fact that Sigüenza y Góngora was a mathematician whereas Mather was a theologian. One may also see a Protestant element in Mather's reservation toward theories of the lost Jewish tribe which became the American Indians, whereas Sigüenza y Góngora's embrace of much grander theories like the Apostle Thomas's presence in Mesoamerica bespeaks a more Catholic theological thrust. While Irving Albert Leonard published a full-fledged hagiography of Sigüenza y Góngora in 1929 (Leonard, *Don Carlos de Sigüenza y Góngora*), casting him as "a Mexican Savant of the Seventeenth Century" and comparing him to the early Renaissance humanists— to which Mather too has been compared (van Cromphout 327)— Mather's early positive reception waned quickly, gradually turning him into a "Puritan gargoyle" throughout the 19th century and later into a "national gargoyle" (Silverman 425). The discovery of his role in the inoculation controversy and his medical achievements turned the tides somewhat at the end of the 19th century (Shryock 2). However, the shift in the reception of Puritanism during the early 20th century made him into a witch hunter—which he never was. This view colored his reception until another turn around the 1970s (van Arragon, passim). Neither Mather's nor Sigüenza y Góngora's writings have been edited or published in their entirety; their archives will demand further editorial work even once the current *Biblia Americana* project is finished.

Sigüenza y Góngora's reception, like Mather's, has periodically focused on particular famous works, and it will demand further editorial efforts to create a different, more balanced and nuanced account of both authors based on a broader selection of texts from modern scientific editions. Sigüenza y Góngora's reception may equally be linked to Catholic Church history of the past three centuries. That he is still seen as one of the greatest figures of American baroque may be due to the more consistently literary reception of his work in the Catholic culture in which it was conceived. Since he was perceived as an intellectual outside the more narrow bounds of the Church and theology, post-Tridentine reception did not differ substantially from earlier 20th-century hagiographies, including the one Irving Albert Leonard mentions. Mather's reception as a writer of American baroque was based on his church history of New England, *Magnalia Christi Americana* (Mather, *Magnalia*), and was generally a derogatory and anachronistic critique of early modern rhetoric. This betrays the persistent attempt to reclaim him for a Protestant tradition—which would be critical of any baroque effusion—and is one of the trends that future Mather studies will have to investigate more critically.

But perhaps the central point of convergence between the reception histories of Sigüenza y Góngora and Mather concerns the way they were both misread as proponents, on the one hand, of the veneration of the Virgin of Guadalupe in Mexico City and, on the other, of Boston, Massachusetts as a New Jerusalem. Marian devotion around the *Virgen de Guadalupe* was actually part of the flourishing of Marian devotion among priests wishing to ameliorate remaining tensions with Amerindians; this aspect has been neglected by modern politicized readings. It was partly brought to South and Central America as a translation of the Castilian Mariology that came by way of the Jesuit missionaries (Alves 170–171). Sigüenza y Góngora's *Indian Spring* (*Primavera indiana, poema sacrohistórico, idea de María Santíssima de Guadalupe*, 1662) has been seen as a key text for *guadalupanismo*, but the relation between the veneration and later forms of nationalism has been drawn more closely because the former has been viewed less theologically, but rather a historically from the perspective of later, modern national developments. This is problematic since Sigüenza y Góngora's life and work unfolded entirely within the 17th century, which is a major difference between him and Mather, whose mature work begins in the 1690s and witnesses major transformations in the early 18th century.

This further complicates any comparison of the two authors and their work because it faces the danger of conflating denominational and epochal differences. Besides, since Sigüenza y Góngora wrote this work at the age of sixteen, it would have to be considered more closely in light of him becoming a member of the Society of Jesus and how its frequent reprints and different editions are a product of its reception history. In this sense, with regard to its form, style, and function, this work is more similar to Mather's first published writing, his early funeral poem on Harvard president Urian Oakes (1631–1681), which Mather wrote at the age of 19. Rather than viewing Sigüenza y Góngora's work in a proto-national context of national politics, one should read it in the context of 17th-century eschatology, a fact that can already be gathered from the title referring to *primavera del mundo* (the spring of the world), the expected parousia, reinforced by Marian imagery (Sabat de Rivers, 283–285). The different strands of Creole identity, Marian devotion, and Christian (Catholic) eschatology within Sigüenza y Góngora's work need to be differentiated more clearly in order to better assess the relation between Creole and Mexican national identities. Mather's frequent references to the New Jerusalem have been similarly misunderstood and essentialized as a premodern prefiguration of the elect nation, whereas the idea of nation is doubly anachronistic since he was thinking and working in the two contexts of New England (which he never left) and "World Christianity" as he understood it, including his forceful engagement in the nascent Pietist Protestant missionary movement. In addition, the still persistent assumption that the people of New England viewed their land as a New Jerusalem has been rightly refuted because it is not only implausible, but theologically impossible: until the 1720s, all New England theologians believed the coming of the New Jerusalem required the conversion of the Jews and that the people of God, namely, the Jewish people, were in need of conversion before the end of times (Smolinski 1990, 1995).

Any claims that Mather saw Boston as a New Jerusalem and New England as the people of God thus misread early modern eschatology as modern political thought. Hence Sigüenza y Góngora as a *criollo*, belonging to a New Spanish colonial self-understanding, and Mather as a Pietist, belonging to a New English self-understanding, have been similarly misread from a modern perspective of nationhood, which sacralizes the nation and misses the theological facets of early modern eschatological thought by interpreting it in purely political, proto-national terms. In both cases, the main target, if read from the perspective of Sigüenza y Góngora's and Mather's thought and time, was to put New Spain and New England on a Christian world map, proving that they partake in a "world Christianity" (in case of Mather's New England) and Roman Catholic salvation history and Marian devotion (in the case of Sigüenza y Góngora's New Spain). This idea of a "world Christianity" in its late 17th-century and early 18th-century re-formulation was a major step in the universalizing that later led to the conception of human rights in modernity. Neither author intended to essentialize his respective geographical location, that is, to treat his own location as definitive for the future of Christianity, especially not within a providential or eschatological sense, which is theologically impossible from a Christian perspective. This mistaken view—which underlies the indelible yet false conceptions of a "Puritan errand" and which ascribes a sense of national mission to early New Spanish Mariology (Miller; Sabat de Rivers, 286)—flatly contradicts the now widely accepted idea that Sigüenza y Góngora and Mather, and the late 17th and early 18th centuries in general, ought to be situated in the context of the (early) Enlightenment, which had numerous centers and not one single world center (*"Weltzentrum"*) (Fischer, 106). Further theological research into early modern thought, possibly from the comparative perspective suggested here, may sharpen both our understanding of the origins of modern political culture and the sacralizing forms under which the religious impulse persists in modern thought. In conclusion, the work that both Mather and Sigüenza y Góngora did for marginalized social groups cannot be related to nascent ideas of human rights if their eschatological thought is misunderstood as proto-national politics. Theological research spanning both modernity and early modernity will help rectify these ahistorical assumptions.

A number of recent publications on human rights in the Americas have shown that human rights also serve an apologetic purpose. For example, Leonard Francis Taylor in his study *Catholic Cosmopolitanism and Human Rights* seeks to establish a connection between human rights and early modern Catholic internationalism. He attributes the 20th-century rise of human rights to the "Grotian tradition" and what he terms "cosmopolitan Catholicism." In the opening chapter, "Catholic Cosmopolitanism and the Birth of Human Rights," he makes a convincing case for reconsidering the origins of human rights in early modernity. Jo Renee Formicola argues that the Catholic Church was instrumental in the rise of human rights in the United States during the 20th century, and Margaret E. Crahan makes a similar argument for Latin America (Formicola; Crahan). Jon Witte has investigated the pre-Reformation origins of "rights talk" in the Protestant tradition, specifically in the Lutheran and Calvinist movements, whereas Rik Torfs has examined the Catholic Church's ambivalent relation to human rights (Witte; Torfs). These scholars demonstrate the central role that Christian denominations have played in the history of modern human rights and the significance of early modern studies in tackling these questions. A critical assessment of the secularization thesis may discover that the driving force behind modern human rights discourse is not secularization and humanist ideals but rather tensions between denominations, most notably between Catholicism and Protestantism. The works of Sigüenza y Góngora and Mather offer a broad range of material to reinvestigate and elaborate on these larger questions.

Upon closer scrutiny, many other differences emerge between these two early modern *hommes de lettres*, helping us to draw a more precise picture of the distinctions between Catholic and Protestant early modern milieus, while also permitting us to reflect upon and discover unacknowledged denominational biases in present-day historiography. In this sense, comparative early modern studies of the religious history of the Americas, when undertaken as the kind of biographical, personal history suggested here, may not only affirm the importance of biography as a historical genre but also shed light on early modern confessional history at large. Since some forms of New England Protestantism at the time of Mather and Sigüenza y Góngora were moving toward Catholicism, such comparisons may help to flesh out the complex developments that led to the gradual establishment of Catholicism in the United States over the course of the 18th century and the movement of *rapprochement* that this caused within the Protestant churches. In summary, these differences are obscured if they are regarded under the rubric of a Great Awakening, or even several Great Awakenings, as was characteristic in the 20th century (Bratt 57), or from the perspective of Evangelicalization, as is typical today (Cimino and Smith 30). Comparative inter-American early modern studies of important figures such as Cotton Mather and Carlos de Sigüenza y Góngora may yield insights that will ultimately reshape the field.

Works cited

Abé, Takao. *The Jesuit Mission to New France: A New Interpretation in the Light of the Earlier Jesuit Experience in Japan.* Brill, 2011.

Alves, Abel A. "The Sanctification of Nature in Marian Shrines in Catalonia: Contextualizing Human Desires in a Mediterranean Cult." *The Sacralization of Space and Behavior in the Early Modern World: Studies and Sources,* edited by Jennifer M. DeSilva. Ashgate, 2015, pp. 161–176.

Ambrosius, Lloyd E., editor. *Writing Biography: Historians & Their Craft.* U of Nebraska P, 2004.

Barr, Juliana, and Edward Countryman, editors. *Contested Spaces of Early America.* U of Philadelphia P, 2014.

Bauer, Oswald. *Zeitungen vor der Zeitung: Die Fuggerzeitungen (1568–1605) und das frühmoderne Nachrichtensystem.* De Gruyter, 2011.

Beezley, William H., editor. *A Companion to Mexican History and Culture.* Wiley, 2011.

Bieger, Laura, Ramón Saldívar, and Johannes Voelz, editors. *The Imaginary and Its Worlds: American Studies after the Transnational Turn.* Dartmouth College P, 2013.

Böning, Holger. *Deutsche Presseforschung: Geschichte und Forschungsprojekte des ältesten historischen Instituts der Universität Bremen: mit einleitenden Beiträgen zur Bedeutung der historischen Presseforschung.* Edition Lumiere, 2013.

Boyd, Richard. "Three Generations of Puritan Spiritual Autobiography: Problems of Self-Definition in a Time of Declension." Dissertation, 1985.

Brading, David A. "The First America: The Spanish Monarchy." *Creole Patriots, and the Liberal State 1492–1867.* Cambridge UP, 1991. Reprint transferred to digital press.

Bratt, James D. "The Reorientation of American Protestantism, 1835–1845." *Church History*, vol. 67, issue 1, 1998, pp. 52–82.
Breed, James L. "Sanctification in the Theology of Cotton Mather." Dissertation, 1980. Print.
Breitwieser, Mitchell Robert. *Cotton Mather and Benjamin Franklin: The Price of Representative Personality.* Cambridge UP, 1984.
Brinkley, Alan. "Comparative Biography as Political History: Huey Long and Father Coughlin." *The History Teacher*, vol. 18, issue 1, 1984, pp. 9–16.
Canup, John. *Out of the Wilderness: The Emergence of an American Identity in Colonial New England.* Wesleyan UP, 1990.
Carrasco, Rolando. "Buchkultur und Globalisierung von Almanachen im Peru des 18. Jahrhunderts." *Das Achtzehnte Jahrhundert: Zeitschrift der Deutschen Gesellschaft für die Erforschung des achtzehnten Jahrhunderts*, vol. 40, issue 2, 2016, pp. 219–228.
Cimino, Richard, and Christopher Smith. *Atheist Awakening: Secular Activism and Community in America.* Oxford UP, 2014.
Clark, Michael. "The Word of God and the Language of Man: Puritan Semiotics and the Theological and Scientific." *Semiotic Scene*, vol. 2, issue 2, 1978, pp. 61–90. Web. <http://www.pdcnet.org/scholarpdf/show?id=semioticscene_1978 _0002_0002_0061_0090&pdfname=semioticscene_1978_0002_0002_0061_0090. pdf&file_type=pdf>.
Classen, Albrecht. *Early History of the Southwest through the Eyes of German-Speaking Jesuit Missionaries: A Transcultural Experience in the Eighteenth Century.* Lexington Books, 2013.
Coffman, Elesha J. *The Christian Century and the Rise of the Protestant Mainline.* Oxford UP, 2013.
Crahan, Margaret E. "Catholicism and Human Rights in Latin America." *Papers on Latin America 10.* Institute of Latin American and Iberian Studies, School of International and Public Affairs, Columbia U, 1989.
DiCuirci, Lindsay. "Reviving Puritan History: Evangelicalism, Antiquarianism, and Mather's Magnalia in Antebellum America." *Early American Literature*, vol. 45, issue 3, 2010, pp. 565–592.
Fischer, Michael W. *Die Aufklärung und ihr Gegenteil: die Rolle der Geheimbünde in Wissenschaft und Politik.* Duncker & Humblot, 1982.
Formicola, Jo Renee. *The Catholic Church and Human Rights: Its Role in the Formulation of U.S. Policy, 1945–1980.* Garland, 1988.
Gestrich, Andreas. *Absolutismus und Öffentlichkeit: Politische Kommunikation in Deutschland zu Beginn des 18. Jahrhunderts.* Vandenhoeck & Ruprecht, 1994.
Gunn, Giles B. *Interpretation of Otherness: Literature, Religion, and the American Imagination.* Oxford UP, 1979.
Hall, David D. *Cultures of Print: Essays in the History of the Book.* U of Massachusetts P, 1997. Studies in Print Culture & the History of the Book 1996: 1.
Harris, Benjamin. Publick Occurrences Both Forreign and Domestick: 25 September 1690, Numb. 1, 1690. Web. 13 Mar. 2017. <nationalhumanitiescenter. org/pds/amerbegin/power/text5/PublickOccurrences.pdf>.
Hebel, Udo J. *"Those images of jealousie": Identitäten und Alteritäten im puritanischen Neuengland des 17. Jahrhunderts.* P. Lang, 1997.

Hillgärtner, Jan. *Die Entstehung der periodischen Presse: Organisationen und Gestalt der ersten Zeitungen in Deutschland und den Niederlanden (1605–1620).* Universität Erlangen-Nürnberg, 2013.

Hofmann, Michael. *Habermas's Public Sphere: A Critique.* Fairleigh Dickinson UP, 2017.

Ihrke-Buchroth, Uta. *Religious Mobility and Social Aspirations of Neopentecostals in Lima, Peru.* Lit Verlag, 2014.

Janssen, Geert H. "The Legacy of Exile and the Rise of Humanitarianism." Cambridge, UK: Murray Edwards College, Cambridge. 9 Sep. 2017. Lecture.

Juviler, Peter, and Carrie Gustafson, editors. *Religion and Human Rights: Competing Claims?.* Taylor & Francis, 2016.

Kennedy, Rick. *The First American Evangelical: A Short Life of Cotton Mather.* William B. Eerdmans Publishing Company, 2015.

Kirk, Stephanie, and Sarah Rivett, editors. *Religious Transformations in the Early Modern Americas. The Early Modern Americas.* U of Pennsylvania P, 2014.

Knights, Mark. Harris, Benjamin (c.1647–1720), 2004. Web. 13 Mar. 2017. <http://www.oxforddnb.com/view/article/48276>.

Krefting, Ellen, Aina Nøding, and Mona Ringvej, editors. *Eighteenth-Century Periodicals as Agents of Change: Perspectives on Northern Enlightenment.* Brill, 2015.

Leonard, Irving A. *Don Carlos De Sigüenza Y Góngora: A Mexican Savant of the Seventeenth Century.* U of California P, 1929.

Leonard, Irving A. *Baroque Times in Old Mexico: Seventeenth-Century Persons, Places, and Practices.* U of Michigan P, 1959.

Leonard, Irving A. *Don Carlos de Sigüenza y Góngora: A Mexican Savant of the Seventeenth Century.* Kraus Reprints, 1974.

Lowance, Mason I., Jr. *The Language of Canaan: Metaphor and Symbol in New England from the Puritans to the Transcendentalists.* Harvard UP, 1980.

Manierre, William R. "Verbal Patterns of Cotton Mather's Magnalia." *Quarterly Journal of Speech*, vol. 41, 1961, pp. 402–413.

Mather, Cotton. *Magnalia Christi Americana: Or the Ecclesiastical History of New England from Its First Planting.* Classic Textbooks, 1702.

Mather, Cotton. *Diary of Cotton Mather*, edited by Worthington C. Ford. New York: Two Volumes, 1957, pp. 1911–1912.

Mather, Cotton. *La Fe del Christiano*, Boston, MA, 1699; Thomas E. Johnston. "A Translation of Cotton Mather's Spanish Works: La Fe del Christiano and La Religion Pura." *Early American Literature Newsletter*, vol. 2, issue 2, 1967, pp. 9–15, 21.

Mather, Cotton. "The Angel of Bethesda (Manuscript, 1724)." *The Papers of Cotton Mather, 1676–1724*, edited by Matt B. Jones, Boston, MA: The Mather Papers 1, 1970. [Microfilm], Reel #14. Barre, MA, 1972.

Mayer, Alicia. *Dos americanos, Dos pensamientos: Carlos de Sigüenza y Góngora y Cotton Mather.* 1st edition. Universidad Nacional Autónoma de México, 1998.

Medina, Antonio Lorente. "Don Carlos de Sigüenza y Góngora en su context." Catedrático de Historia de la Literatura Hispanoamericana y de Novela Hispanoamericana Contemporánea de la Universidad Nacional a Distancia (UNED), 18.07.2012. Web. 7 Jan. 2018. <https://web.archive.org/web/20141106161153/http://www.larramendi.es/i18n/catalogo_imagenes/grupo.cmd?path=1000365>.

Meyer, Birgit and Annelies Moors, editors. *Religion, Media, and the Public Sphere.* Indiana UP, 2005.
Middlekauff, Robert. *The Mathers: Three Generations of Puritan Intellectuals, 1596–1728.* Oxford UP, 1971.
Miller, Perry. *Errand into the Wilderness.* Cambridge, MA, 1975.
Millner, Michael. *Fever Reading: Affect and Reading Badly in the Early American Public Sphere.* U of New Hampshire P, 2012.
More, Anna. *Baroque Sovereignty: Carlos de Siguenza y Gongora and the Creole Archive of Colonial Mexico.* U of Pennsylvania P, 2012.
Noll, Mark A. and David William Bebbington, editors. *The Rise of Evangelicalism: The Age of Edwards, Whitefield and the Wesleys.* InterVarsity Press, 2005.
Noll, Mark A., David William Bebbington, and George A. Rawlyk, editors. *Evangelicalism: Comparative Studies of Popular Protestantism in North America, the British Isles, and Beyond, 1700–1990.* Oxford UP, 1994.
Prado, Wendy L.M. "El triunfo parténico de Carlos de Sigüenza y Góngora: La participacíon festiva entropicá de la ideología del poder." *Teatro y poder en la época de Carlos II: Fiestas en torno a reyes y virreyes; [Congreso Teatro y Poder en la Época de Carlos II: Fiestas en Torno a Reyes y Virreyes celebrado en el] Tecnológico de Monterrey; Monterrey, 23–25 de agosto de 2006*, edited by Judith Farré Vidal. Iberoamericana, 2007, pp. 211–220.
Reisner, Philipp. "Cotton Mather als Aufklärer. Glaube und Gesellschaft im Neuengland der Frühen Neuzeit." *Reformed Historical Theology 21.* Vandenhoeck & Ruprecht, 2012.
Robert, Aleksander Maryks, editor. *A Companion to Jesuit Mysticism.* Brill, 2017.
Ross, Kathleen. "The Baroque Narrative of Carlos De Sigüenza Y Góngora: A New World Paradise." Dissertation. Cambridge UP, 1993.
Sabat de Rivers, Georgina. "Hacia una edición de *Primavera Indiana* de Carlos de Sigüenza y Góngora." *Calíope: Journal of the Society for Renaissance and Baroque Hispanic Poetry*, vol. 4, issue 1–2, 1998, pp. 283–295.
Schweninger, Lee F. ""Between fiction and reality": The Motif of the Jeremiad in American Literature." Dissertation. Chapel Hill, NC, 1984. Web.
Shryock, Richard H. *Die Entwicklung der modernen Medizin in ihrem Zusammenhang mit dem sozialen Aufbau und den Naturwissenschaften.* 2nd edition, translated by Hildegard Hönig. Enke, 1947.
Siewert, Stephanie. "'America at Large?' Inter-American Studies, Transnationalism, and the Hemispheric Turn." *Amerikastudien/American Studies*, vol. 60.4, 2016, pp. 533–547.
Sigüenza y Góngora, Carlos de. *Primavera indiana, poema sacrohistórico, idea de María Santísima de Guadalupe.* Mexico City, 1662.
Sigüenza y Góngora, Carlos de. *Carlos de Sigüenza y Góngora: An Inventory of His Collection at the Benson Latin American Collection.* The U of Texas at Austin, 2018. Benson Latin American Collection. Web. <https://legacy.lib.utexas.edu/taro/utlac/00057/lac-00057.html>.
Sigüenza y Góngora, Carlos de. Fundación Ignacio Larramendi > Sigüenza y Góngora, Carlos de, 1645–1700. Colección de Polígrafos Hispanoamericanos. Web. 7 Jan. 2018. <https://web.archive.org/web/20141106161153/http://www.larramendi.es/i18n/consult+a_aut/registro.cmd?id=3030>.

Silverman, Kenneth. *The Life and Times of Cotton Mather*. 1st edition. Harper & Row, 1984.

Smolinski, Reiner and Jan Stievermann, editors. *Biblia Americana: America's First Bible Commentary. A Synoptic Commentary on the Old and New Testaments*. 10 Vol. Mohr Siebeck, 2010.

Smolinski, Reiner. "Israel Redivivus: The Eschatological Limits of Puritan Typology in New England." *New England Quarterly*, vol. 63, 1990, pp. 357–395.

Smolinski, Reiner. "Die Neue Welt in der biblischen Typologie der Puritaner Neuenglands: eine revisionistische Betrachtung." In *Amerika: Entdeckung, Eroberung, Erfindung*, edited by Winfried Herget. Wissenschaftlicher Verlag Trier, 1995, pp. 67–94.

Smyth, Adam. "Almanacs, Annotators, and Life-Writing in Early Modern England." *ELR*, vol. 38, issue 2, 2008, pp. 200–244.

Sparn, Walter, editor. *Wer schreibt meine Lebensgeschichte? Biographie, Autobiographie, Hagiographie und ihre Enstehungszusammenhänge*. Gütersloher Verlagshaus Mohn, 1990.

Stackhouse, Max L. "Reflections on 'Universal Absolutes'." *Journal of Law and Religion*, vol. 14, issue 1, 1999, pp. 97–112.

Steele, Richard. *The Tatler: Volume 3*. Cambridge UP, 2015.

Stievermann, Jan. *Prophecy, Piety, and the Problem of Historicity: Interpreting the Hebrew Scriptures in Cotton Mather's Biblia Americana*. Mohr Siebeck, 2016.

Stiles, David. "The Imperial Horrification of Jesuit Frontier Sacred Space in South America, 1750–67." *The Sacralization of Space and Behavior in the Early Modern World: Studies and Sources*, edited by Jennifer M. DeSilva. Ashgate, 2015, pp. 237–275.

Summy, Ralph. "Comparative Political Biography: Jayaprakash Narayan and Thomas Jefferson." *Biography*, vol. 6, issue 3, 1983, pp. 220–237.

Taylor, Leonard Francis. *Catholic Cosmopolitanism and Human Rights*. Cambridge UP, 2020.

Torfs, Rik. "Human Rights in the History of the Catholic Church." *Human Rights and the Impact of Religion*, edited by Johannes A. van der Ven and Hans-Georg Ziebertz. Leiden: Brill, 2013, pp. 55–74.

van Arragon, William. "Cotton Mather in American Cultural Memory, 1728–1892." Dissertation. Indiana University, 2006.

van Cromphout, Gustaaf. "Cotton Mather: The Puritan Historian as Renaissance Humanist." *American Literature*, vol. 49, issue 3, 1977, pp. 327–337.

Vélez, Karin. "'By Means of Tigers': Jaguars as Agents of Conversion in Jesuit Mission Records of Paraguay and the Moxos, 1600–1768." *Church History*, vol. 84, issue 4, 2015, pp. 768–806.

Villa-Vicencio, Charles. "Christianity and Human Rights." *Journal of Law and Religion*, vol. 14, issue 2, 1999, pp. 579–600.

Vormann, Boris. "Who Needs American Studies? Globalization, Nationalism, and the Future of Area Studies." *Amerikastudien/American Studies*, vol. 59, issue 3, 2015, pp. 387–406.

Witte, John, Jr. "Rights, Resistance, and Revolution in the Western Tradition: Early Protestant Foundations." *Human Rights and the Impact of Religion*, edited by Johannes A. van der Ven and Hans-Georg Ziebertz. Brill, 2013, pp. 25–53.

Witte, John, Jr. "Between Sanctity and Depravity: Human Dignity and Human Rights in Classical Lutheran Perspective." *Human Rights and the Impact of Religion*, edited by Johannes A. van der Ven and Hans-Georg Ziebertz. Brill, 2013, pp. 9–24.

Zachary, Leader, editor. *On Life-Writing*. Oxford UP, 2015.

Zivin, Erin G. "Baroque Sovereignty: Carlos de Sigüenza y Góngora and the Creole Archive of Colonial Mexico by Anna More (Review)." *Hispanic Review*, vol. 84, issue 3, 2016, pp. 351–354. Web. <https://muse.jhu.edu/article/626904/summary>.

3 Maps of violence, maps of resistance, or, where is home in the Americas?

Roland Walter

In plain terms, home is the place (residence, city, nation) where one lives and works as an individual within a collective unit (family, society) enjoying the rights and obligations of citizenship.[1] According to the *Universal Declaration of Human Rights*, the basic rights we share as human beings in the world, regardless of age, sex, gender, location, nation, origin, language, religion, class, ethnicity, or any other status, are based on universal values, such as justice, freedom, independence, fairness, dignity, equality, respect, and peace. Once these basic rights and freedoms are guaranteed, human beings may feel at home in a place. However, literary works of writers from the Americas often cast a shadow of unbelonging over the resolution on universal belonging, a sentiment of postcolonial unease, a longing to belong, suggesting a schizophrenic, ambivalent dance on the glocal hyphen of coloniality linking and separating different times and places. In fact, many hemispheric Americans, pushed by economic hardship, violence, and natural disasters or pulled by professional opportunities and better living conditions, are on the move. This (trans)national migration, a dis/translocation between places, spaces, and cultural epistemes, has its roots in an inefficient and biased political, social, and legal system, the racial/ethnic divide, gender conflicts, drug trafficking, organ harvesting, widespread corruption, and the issue of land tenure.[2] These and other violations of human and nonhuman rights, according to the *Amnesty International Report 2017/18* (27), constitute ever-increasing levels of violence throughout the region.

The purpose of this essay is to reveal and problematize the issue of neocolonial violence and its effect on human beings and their environment in contemporary literature of the Americas. In the process, it examines how creative writing represents characters in search of home across a continent where according to Norma Alarcón, centuries of empire/nation-building and resultant migratory deracinations have imbued "home" with mobility: "a 'home' without juridically nationalized geopolitical territory" (49). To do so, let me begin with an overview of selected texts by inter-American writers from diverse sociocultural and multiethnic contexts. This textual juxtaposition allows me to present examples of a 500-year legacy of human and nonhuman rights violations. It will serve as the basis for a general discussion of violence and implicit violations of (non)human rights in the Americas. The last part of this essay focuses on a more particular aspect of this issue, namely, the connection between gender, race, and place at the interface of culture and nature in novels by Gisèle Pineau, Helena María Viramontes, and T.C. Boyle.

Both Gioconda Belli in *La mujer habitada* (1996), and Laura Esquivel in *Malinche* (2008) focus on the arrival of the Spanish colonizers, the resistance of the Nahua peoples, and the destruction of the Nahua way of being. The lootings, burnings, and killings by the colonizers, as Nahua warrior Itzá observes in Belli's novel, leave as legacy "una red de agujeros" (127; a network of holes). This nonlinear history, written by the colonizer and thus riven by lacunae, distortions, obfuscations, and silence from a Nahua perspective has, according to the musings of Malinalli in Esquivel's novel, another bloody underside, namely, the colonization and destruction of nature which connotes the homelessness of Nahua descendants and of modern man: "El maíz no ataca al maíz. El aire no ataca al aire. La tierra no ataca a la tierra. Es el hombre que no se reconoce en ellos quien los ataca, quien los destruye" (177; Maize does not attack maize. Air does not attack air. Land does not attack land. By not recognizing himself in these natural elements, man attacks and destroys them).

Pablo Neruda, in his 1950 epic *Canto General*, poeticized this physical and epistemic violence through a tree of life "nutrido por muertos desnudos,/muertos azotados y heridos" (478–71; nourished by naked corpses,/corpses scourged and wounded); a postcolonial tree with roots, branches, and leaves soaked in blood and tears—its (neo)colonial sap (479–72). In a similar vein, Guadeloupean writer Maryse Condé emphasizes the colonial past haunting the present when Xantippe, in *Crossing the Mangrove* (1995), reveals forgotten sites of past massacres and identifies with those who lost their lives in the plantation past, declaring that their spilled blood is also his own blood (204). This implicit resurrection of a forgotten memory—a counter-memory deconstructing institutionalized amnesia by introducing the festering wounds of the colonial past into hegemonic discourse—is an important means of identity reconstruction in that it enables consciousness to connect experiences and thus situate the "I" in the spatiotemporality of events. This mnemonic flourishing of the inside launches Xantippe into a worldly position and thereby reconceptualizes his otherization as the town's idiot. Furthermore, this type of resistance encoded in the text's memory construction decolonizes what Toni Morrison, in *A Mercy* (2008), has delineated as colonial orphanhood. One of the most insidious effects of the plantation system, enslavement of Africans and genocide of Native peoples was, according to Morrison, that all those involved as well as the following generations, became "orphans" characterized by a "withering inside that enslaves and opens the door for what is wild" (160). The silent roar of the question "who is responsible?" (3) echoes throughout the story line and, typical of Morrison's writing, rather than offering the reader clear-cut answers, opens a postcolonial crossroads constituent of a tangled, messy network of related issues and actors bearing responsibility.

In *The Round House* (2013), Native American writer Louise Erdrich problematizes the lack of sovereignty of First Nations people in North America and Canada. The novel denounces that by taking "from us the right to prosecute non-Indians who commit crimes on our land,"—in this specific case, a brutal rape committed by a white man—"the dispossession of our lands" continues (229). In light of the strong relation between sovereignty, land, and identity in Native American literature, one could add that as long as Indigenous peoples lack autonomy in judicial matters, the dispossession of their identities continues.[3] Moreover, as Mapuche poet David Aniñir Guilitraro in "Temporada Apológika" (2009) and Potiguara poet Graça Graúna in "Manifesto I" (2010) highlight, the plight of urban Mapuches in Chile and urban Potiguaras in Brazil is of a different order. For many urban Amerindians—in Canada, for example, almost half of the Aboriginal population lives in cities—the question is not so much to achieve sovereign self-government and determination, but to survive an ethnoracial and cultural in-betweenness.

Guilitraro poeticizes this liminal existence between the lost roots of the land and the yet unfound roots in the urban maze of Santiago as "Confusión tierra asfalto" (25; Confusion soil asphalt). Graça Graúna expresses anger and sadness about an ongoing deterritorialization of humans and nonhumans, a forced transculturation that does not end in cultural fusions but cultural fissures—cultural clashes—composed of dismembered biotic fragments without roots, unable to read each other, learn from each other. By declaring that she is afraid of not knowing anymore "o que ainda resta/do cheiro da mata/da água/do fogo/da terra e do ar" (what still remains/of the smell of the woods/of water/of fire/of the land and the air) that she has lost the wisdom of reading "a terra/sangrando por dentro" (the land/bleeding within), Graúna makes a strong statement about the necessity of decolonizing our technologized knowledge in the digital age.

For migrant workers and people of African descent, this cultural in-betweenness and inherent homelessness has yet another characteristic. In Tomás Rivera's *...Y no se lo tragó la tierra/...AND THE EARTH DID NOT PART* (1977), the narrative voice of a migrant worker expresses what it means to be constantly on the move. The migrant workers are not only pushed into an institutionalized system of migration in the *nepantla* borderlands linking and separating Mexico and the United States but also pulled by the American Dream of material well-being: "Arriving is the same as leaving because as soon as we arrive ... well, quite frankly, I'm tired of always arriving.

Maybe I should say when we don't arrive because that's the plain truth. We never really arrive anywhere" (115). Kept running, migrants, all over the Americas, have been on the move driven by a desire for home, or, as African American writer Ralph Ellison has once termed it, "seeking the homeness of home" (143).[4] In "América Negra" (2014), Afro-Brazilian poet Élio Ferreira denounces that in the "Américas,/o que passou, não passou" (31; Americas,/what happened is not over) but accumulates and explodes in poverty, misery, migration, and violence—a situation that transforms African Brazilians into homeless strangers. In view of past and present racial discrimination in Brazil, the poetic voice raises the issue of indemnification and asks: "quando você me pagará seus débitos?" (35; when will you pay me your debts?). For Dionne Brand, in *A Map to the Door of No Return* (2002), to live in the Black diaspora means to exist "in the sea in-between ... this inexplicable space" (20); a lived-imagined nonplace qua consciousness that haunts surviving generations because of its inherent ambivalence. This "inexplicable" nonplace, a spatiotemporal racist and sexist nightmare in Brand's creative works, is, as Émile Ollivier's novel *La Brûlerie* (2004) problematizes, also a xenophobic space of glocal worlding. Haitian immigrants, seeking shelter from a plethora of human rights abuses and natural disasters on their island, arrive in Canada facing a society "qui a peur de tout ce qui est différent" (142; that is afraid of everything that is different). As the narrator says, far from a nation praised for its tolerant, egalitarian multiculturalism (Adams 123), Canada is at best an anonymous and at worst an unlivable space because Canadians feel "incommodés par ces gens du voyage, ces hommes sans feu ni lieu" (153; bothered by travellers, those who have no home).

This patchwork of Pan-American writers and fragments of their texts shows the multilayered traces and tracks that diverse forms and practices of (neo)colonial violence have left over the centuries: a geographic, physical, mental, and epistemic violence that has a disastrous impact on humans and nonhumans in that it deprives them of their basic rights. Native peoples across the Americas argue that the balance of being-in-the-world is broken; Frantz Fanon (8) spoke of the collapse of the ego through "aberrations of affect" in the (neo)colonial "zone of nonbeing"; Belli, Neruda, Condé, Morrison, Erdrich, Ollivier, Brand, Ferreira, Guilitraro, Graúna, and Esquivel, among others, emphasize a double otherization: a self-othered through external and/or internal forces and images struggling to make sense of them. In the process, they inscribe subaltern subjectivities as a strategy of decolonization that establishes what Enrique Dussel has called the "reason of the Other" (69)—forms and practices of resistance that reveal, problematize, and deconstruct the Euro-American myth of modernity imbued with injustice and violence. In their difference, the textual excerpts emphasize that otherness, in all its shades and shapes, constitutes the interior and/or exterior alterity that marks the limits of personhood and/or nationhood. In other words, in the Americas nation-states mother some of their children and orphan others. The multidimensional tensions resulting from diverse forms and practices of otherization implode nation-states in the Americas, rendering them, according to Antonio Cornejo-Polar (147), heterogeneous, "dismembered" entities that enact, albeit in different forms, their traumatic past in the present. In the following, I will elaborate on this dismembered heterogeneity of American societies and nations.

Space, time, memory, and identity are linked; in that, identity is shaped by connections to the physical world within a temporal process. Words, through memory, recreate a world of references that (re)constitutes identity within a historical process: an identity rooted in a culturally specific ethos and worldview and expressed through language. If this equation of subject, language, ethos, and worldview is broken, then the ways of knowing are severed from their ontological premise and identity is dislocated. What links the previously quoted texts in their difference is the representation of cultural in-betweenness resulting from this broken equation.

One of the crucial reasons for existential deterritorialization resides in a broken spatial and temporal relation with the land. Land is a valuable commodity, and the expropriation of native-owned land by mining and lumber companies, drug cartels, or multi/transnational companies with the consent of local/national governments has led to transferred lives. Édouard Glissant has argued that inter-American literature is characterized by "a search for temporal duration" with writers "struggling in the confusion of time ... this exploded, suffered time ... linked to 'transferred' space" (144). Built on total aggression, a process that continues to write violent new chapters in the present, American places, spaces, and people(s) exist in a time-space continuum, in which a traumatic memory prevents "historical consciousness" from becoming collective memory (61–62). It is knowledge based on recall, the understanding of oneself in relationship to others (human and nonhuman) in a spatial and temporal framework, which enables consciousness to determine human creativity. When this ability to refer to past experiences to make sense of present events is interrupted through a process of interior or exterior colonization—forces and practices inherent in what Aníbal Quijano has analyzed as "colonialidad del poder" (coloniality of power)—it leads to cultural paralysis, alienation, and fragmentation of the self and may even result in genocide. This erasure of "collective memory" argues Glissant, renders "lived history as a steadily advancing neurosis" (65). Mapped on the body, soul, and mind of human beings and the environment they inhabit, the diverse forms and practices of (neo)colonial violence, I argue, constitute the sociocultural foundation of societies throughout the Americas. Of all the "misplaced" things and ideas across the Americas (Schwarz), it is this broken equation of subject, language, ethos, and worldview within a specific geographical setting that causes identitarian and cultural in-betweenness:

transferred lives within transferred spaces. A spatiotemporal displacement characterized by the outcries of subaltern discourses that echo across transcultural contact zones where ethnic, racial, gendered, and classist conflicts constitute the sign, and especially the access to the sign, as battle zones over social and semantic control.

Mythopoetic articulation is a means of revealing, denouncing, and perhaps transforming this situation of human rights violations through a *revision* of history in Adrienne Rich's sense, and thereby relocating identity within the categories of a re(-)membered, self-determined cultural episteme, that is, the validity issues providing cultures with an ethical, theoretical, and philosophical framework of knowledge, truth, and behavior. In Jeannette Armstrong's novel *Slash*, an old Native Canadian explains this link between culture, place, identity, and language by affirming that only if traditional ways, customs, and language are practiced and preserved, then "place can be protected because then it has a purpose to be protected" (211). In this sense, then, and in reference to Glissant's terms which I mentioned before, transferred space can be transformed into a re(-)membered place, a collectively shared site within a temporal flow whose rhythm is not characterized by confusion, explosion, and sufferance but governed by justice and mutual responsibility.

Multiethnic inter-American artists play, write, sing, paint, sculpture, and perform sites of memory through the process of remembrance in order to come to terms with a traumatic past. The importance of this *working through* the events of the past in the present resides precisely in the mnemonic sedimentation of a traumatically lived/imagined experience. In the process, a dislocated identity may be relocated not necessarily in one specific place but between places, that is, in a diasporic space characterized by overlapping and/or juxtaposed cultural epistemes: a translocation characterized by a transculturation whose imposed spatial and identitarian in-betweenness may be deconstructed through creative activities. In this sense, creative writing is part of a revision and an implicit prevision of a new, self-determined cultural ethos and worldview. As such, it contributes to the decolonization of (neo)colonial knowledge: a cleansing of the (neo)colonial insults to human and non-human rights and dignity; that is, following René Depestre, a mental/cultural "dézombification" (64).

Thus, one of the principal themes in inter-American literature is the conquest, exploitation, and destruction of place and space and their resurrection as *locus amoenus*, an Eden or El Dorado qua utopia or a material-spiritual place-world qua *Dasein*. On the basis of this double writing, I hypothetically contend that in inter-American texts what Edward Soja has termed *affective geography*, namely, "the concretization of social relations embedded in spatiality" (7), symbolizes a temporal, spatial, and cultural in-betweenness. This is characterized by the brutalization of space and people rooted in the past and disseminated in the present in rhizomic ways, as well as a traverse of this liminal experience, an effort of "transwriting" cultural displacement into an existentially understandable and emancipatory episteme where roots and routes often dance to syncopated rhythms.[5] In the process, the representation of this lived/imagined spatiality externalizes the spectral nature of inherent, repressed forms, and practices of violence that return in response to disavowal and suffuse the characters' lived experience, thoughts, imagination, emotion, acts, and discourse—forms and practices of violence which together constitute the political, cultural, and ecological unconscious of the inter-American experience.

One of the principal characteristics of this affective geography qua enforced liminality, I argue, is land tenure. Land ownership inequality throughout the Americas constitutes the common situation that links diverse nations and peoples in their difference: a dichotomy between basically two meanings attributed to land by the military industrial complex, governments, consumer society, and big landowners on the one hand, and, on the other, by Indigenous communities and subsistence farmers. Whereas for the former the land is a means of making a profit, for the latter it is the place where their ancestors and sacred beings live, a place giving identity to the community and used for subsistence farming. Herein resides one of the most important unresolved conflicts and traumatic sources of this double brutalization forming the unjust geography that characterizes the dismembered heterogeneity of Pan-American nation-states.[6]

If it is through memory that we make sense of our self and our position and experience in the world, a trauma cannot be remembered because the traumatic events are repressed from consciousness, that is, not codified in the narration, oral or written, of memory. According to Cathy Caruth, traumatic experiences provoke "a rupture in the experience of time, self and the world" (4). Thus, I believe, it is necessary to ask how and with what objectives writers translate traumatic events and experiences into written form. In order to examine how the colonial past haunts and nourishes neocolonial violence in the present, that is, how writers transwrite the brutalizations of space and people and thereby denounce human rights violations, I will now focus on Gisèle Pineau's novels *L'espérance-macadam* (1996) and *Morne Câpresse* (2008).

Antonio Benítez-Rojo, in his analysis of Derek Walcott's *Drums and Colours*, argues that according to Walcott the Caribbean region's most permanent problem is "sheer violence, historic violence ... discovery, conquest, slavery or colonialism" (300).[7] Pineau's novels estheticize violence to thematize contemporary issues of race, gender, history, culture, and their roots in the past. According to Rosette in *L'espérance-macadam*, the colonial past casts a shadow over the lives of present-day Guadeloupeans. It is as if "la honte et les blessures" (241; the disgrace and the wounds) constitute the traumatic unconscious pulsations of a "postmemory" (Hirsch) that creates a time-space continuum between the first enslaved Africans who arrived at the island's shores, and those who go about their daily affairs in the 1990s: "Non, rien n'avait change depuis qu'on avait transbordé les premiers Nègres d'Afrique dans ce pays ... cette terre violente où tant de malediction pesait sur les hommes et femmes de toutes nations. Rien n'avait change... Le sabre, la corde, les chaînes" (241–242; No, nothing had changed since the first Blacks from Africa were unloaded in this land ... that violent land where so many curses weighed on the men and women of all nations. Nothing had changed... The saber, the cord, the chains).

Situated in the post-plantation reality of the late 1990s, the novel's characters enact their "existential deviation" (Fanon 14) through the internalization of a hegemonic, hierarchical value system based on domination and exploitation; an internalized colonialism characterized by self-hatred and acts of violence which can be resumed in three words: "Fendre, hacher, couper" (99; Split, chop, cut). This existential alienation and the cycle of violence it entails are most tellingly symbolized by Hortense's brutal assassination at the hands of her partner. Accusing her of an extramarital affair, Regis kills her and cuts her into pieces, laying out her head, breasts, and vagina on banana leaves across the kitchen floor (88). The repetition of this image qua *Stilleben* throughout the plot reinforces the killed woman's silent accusation of male violence; an accusation echoing Pineau's criticism of a patriarchal society that objectifies women to the satisfaction of male whims. In this so-called postcolonial society, where the coloniality of the past writes endless neocolonial chapters, nothing changes because mental slavery, one of the effects of physical slavery and/or serfdom, causes violent acts with sequential traumatic replays. Regis, unable to work through the anxiety of castration he bequeathed from "the plantation machines" (Benítez-Rojo 9), to disassociate his libido from a negated autonomous sexual subjectivity, enacts it through a deviation of violence against Hortense—a violence that is of a psychological and physical nature. Rosette, on the other hand, is able to transform her disavowed colonial unconscious into a sedimented individual postmemory through an arduous process of consciousness-raising that frees her from the self-colonizing victimization of her fellow Guadeloupeans.[8]

In *Morne Câpresse* (2008), Pineau delineates a patriarchal society with women suffering from drugs, prostitution, infanticide, incest, and rape. This downgrading of women's rights, as the novel emphasizes, is just one particular aspect of a reified consumer society where the unredeemed horrors of the past permeate new forms and practices of human exploitation in the contemporary sugar, coffee, and cacao business. In the process, Pineau highlights ecological degradation as one important effect of the retrogression of human rights: earthscapes and seascapes polluted by "toutes les immondices de la société de consommation" (59; all the refuse of consumer society). This environmental degradation through consumer waste is the neocolonial highpoint of the island's ecosystem destruction that began at the moment of conquest. As the narrator muses, the effects of this interbiotic colonization of man, plants, trees, rivers, and animals live on as "fantômes de l'antan" (260; yesterday's phantoms). Her memorable question—"La terre se souvenait-elle encore de ce passé? Les chaînes, la douleur, le fouet, la colère devant l'ignominie et le silence des Nations..." (59; Does the land still remember the past? The chains, the pain, the whip, the rage before the ignominy and silence of the Nations...)—while emphasizing the fact that the traumatic past of the plantation system is present in the XXI century, connotes an interbiotic stance that challenges a mere anthropocentric perspective.

Pineau's fiction recreates diverse aspects of this issue, revealing a society where humans and nonhumans constitute a biota of "plantes aux racines coupées. Des arbrisseaux malingres qui avaient grandi à l'ombre de la haine" (259; plants with severed roots. Malicious small trees having grown under the shelter of hatred). Furthermore, generations of Guadeloupeans, whose collective consciousness disavows the past, are haunted by the pain, frustration, debasement, and abject nature of a past that devours them and seek solace in the use of drugs (122). Hence, the text's interbiotic memory instantiation links the human and plant worlds within a doomed space; a space where many vanished and/or disavowed memory traces haunt the violence-filled tracks of the island's present-day experience; a milieu in which the disintegration of the human capacity to synthesize impressions consciously leads to a fragmentation in the perception of the self, reality, emotions, and memories.

In her writings, then, Gisèle Pineau delineates a rootless people—characters traumatically and violently anchored in the deep waters of the Black Atlantic that link and separate the Americas and the African continent. By exploring the relation between "culture" and "nature" through an intersectional system of oppression in which race, gender, age, and class mutually construct one another, Pineau's fiction creates a rhetorical sense of place, space, culture, and history, and additionally, constructs an interbiotic belonging through an *engagement* with memory: the negotiation between the traces of a traumatic past that haunt the violent tracks of the present through denial. Thus, the recognition of the past does not disappear; it rather haunts identity and the land. It is in this sense that Pineau's esthetic translation of violence diagnoses questions of cultural identity within a historical, interbiotic process.

In Pineau's holistic vision of man and nature, *la terre* qua earth/land(scape) does remember the past. Chicano writer Rudolfo Anaya, with reference to people from the Southwest, points out that they are "affected by the land," that is, "[t]he landscape changes man, and the man becomes his landscape" (46). Other Pan-American writers, such as Margaret Atwood, Orlando Romero, Linda Hogan, Leslie Marmon Silko, Miguel Asturias,

Patrick Chamoiseau, Édouard Glissant, Maryse Condé, Derek Walcott, José María Arguedas, João Guimarães Rosa, Graciliano Ramos, and Manoel de Barros, to name just a few, have highlighted this existential interbiotic link between man and nature, outer and inner landscape, in some of their creative and critical texts. There is, then, in the words of Caribbean writer Wilson Harris, "a dialogue ... between one's internal being, one's psyche, and the nature of the place, the landscape" (Gilkes 33). In what follows, I will briefly examine this issue in two contemporary novels by Helena María Viramontes and T.C. Boyle.

In *Their Dogs Came With Them* (2007) by Chicana writer Helena María Viramontes, set in Los Angeles in the 1970s, the freeways with their noise and pollution winding through the plot, "amputated the streets into stumped dead ends and the lives of the neighbors itched like phantom limbs" in the memory of the characters (33). The construction of the freeway system crossing LA uprooted people, literally buried communitarian knowledge and memory under concrete. The result was an ethnocultural fragmentation and alienation that increased poverty and marginalization as well as gang criminality. Once the collective life of the place with its affective relations vanished, the meaning of the barrio disappeared for its inhabitants. The barrio became a war zone where human beings and dogs fought for survival. In Viramontes' novel, memory qua cultural code system, so crucial to decolonization, is lost not only because of the freeways per se, but because of the multidimensional violence that this invasion of private capital based upon "environmental racism"[9] provokes: an inferno where "tears," "blood," and "bullet wounds" (325) attest to a systematic and continuous human rights violation. Tranquilina's exclamation, "*We'rrrre not doggggs!*" (324), denounces the subalternization, animalization, and deterritorialization of the Mexican American community in Los Angeles driven by the continuous transformation and appropriation of space for corporate and real-estate gains as well as the inherent strategies of social marginalization, racial discrimination, cultural denigration, and the deprivation of human and civil rights that Mexican Americans have suffered since the arrival of the Anglo intruders.

Whereas in Viramontes' novel we witness another chapter of what Naomi Klein has called *disaster capitalism* (2007), destroying human beings and their environment, in *When the Killing's Done* (2007) by T.C. Boyle, ecologically sensitive human beings wage a "total war" (206) in the name of nature. Two clashing opinions about the protection of nature constitute the basis of a series of violent events and situations that reveal and problematize the domination human beings exert over nature and related issues, such as the explosion of population growth, pollution as a direct result of short-term economic growth policies, exploitative practices of agribusiness, a wasteful consumer society, etc. (1) that the endangered native creatures of California's Channel Islands should be saved

Maps of violence and resistance 71

from invasive species such as rats and feral pigs by killing the latter, as defended by Alma Boyd Takesue, a National Park Service biologist; and (2) that these native creatures should defend themselves as argues Dave La Joy, a local businessman, and all those who are against the killing of animals. The question problematized throughout the plot is whether to leave nature alone, seal it off to let it heal itself so to speak, or meddle with it once more to undo the effects of human interference. This issue is linked to biotic difference, otherness, as the narrative voice connotes in the phrase "... here was chaos, here was the other ..." (249). Chaos, according to the events of the plot, because human beings are incapable of understanding nature's languages and/or unwilling to communicate with nature in its diverse languages; that is, contrary to Nez Perce Hin-mah-too-yah-lat-kekht's statement in 1865, "the earth and myself are of one mind" (McLuhan 54), in Boyle's novel plants, animals, and human beings are of divergent minds. Western rational perception of reality as hierarchically arranged separate units rather than a network of interrelated phenomena, is, I believe, the root cause of the violence perpetrated by the two ecologically minded groups. Unable to accept difference, the many others, as an integral part of the self and give it a vote, to live in harmony with the biota, those who want to save the planet endanger it even more. Both Viramontes and Boyle, then, highlight the importance of geography (place, space, landscape, nature) for identity studies in post/neocolonial contexts. While Viramontes foregrounds the destruction of a milieu of human experience as social practice in the name of ruthless corporate interests, Boyle problematizes the destruction of a *milieu* of nonhuman experience through human interference.[10]

Thus, where and what is home in the Americas? Considering the stirrings of unhomeliness in the texts examined in this essay, does home mean a stable, fixed place, and/or a constant longing to belong, straddling places, and epistemes within a fragmented *transfrontera contact zone* (Saldívar 13–14), that is, a shifting in-between space where the roots, rhizomes, and routes of family, group, neighborhood, region, and nation constitute tangled crossroads? Does it reside in the conscientization of why, where, how, and for whose benefit mistakes were made?[11] One of the crucial objectives in this process of understanding and transcending the ambivalence inherent in the violent forms and practices of contemporary coloniality—the glocal logic of injustice and exploitation—is, according to Toni Morrison to tackle the issue of race: to "convert a racist house into a race-specific yet nonracist home" (Home 5), "to decipher the deracing of the world" (Home 11). In *Paradise*, Morrison's double writing, a transwriting of double-consciousness into double vision, emphasizes her view of a world qua "real earthly home"; a decolonized world where land is not sold, robbed, or unlawfully possessed but made up of homeplaces where mutual respect governs a balanced relationship between the species—a place that existed, according to the narrator, in the past, before "the whole of Western history, ... the beginning of organized knowledge, ... pyramids and poison bows, ... when rain was new, before plants forgot they could sing and birds thought they were fish" (213). In this sense, Morrison's *deracing of the world* is a "concrete utopia" (Bloch) of an existence without race, gender, class, property, and biological species functioning as principles of a hierarchical social organization and promoting differential patterns of the rights and duties of citizenship.

Across the Americas, different forms and practices of physical, epistemic, and ecological violence, then, constitute a system of connections generated by and based upon an ongoing *colonialidad del poder*. In the process, epistemic violence naturalizes material violence imposed upon all biotic species. Bodies, minds, lands, seas, and natural resources become neocolonial contact zones where ideological disguise and the opacity surrounding the intricate relationship between national institutions and supranational financial operations permit the establishment of diffuse networks of power who control and profit from the flows of corporate capital. It is needless to say that in many parts of the Americas (and the world) this market-driven relationship between the local and the global is based on the systematic negation of human rights and responsible land tenure as stipulated in various international agreements[12] and exacerbates existing inequalities between and within regions and nations. While some pretend to free us into technological paradise, contemporary relations of power orchestrate the marginalization, animalization, and demonization of diverse others to the syncopated rhythms of violent (trans)national deterritorializations and reterritorializations resulting in more precarious job opportunities, less education, health service, and humane living conditions. In this global panorama of "geopolitical chaos" (Ramonet), which according to Samir Amin is characterized by a subordination of "every aspect of social life to the imperatives of economic rationality" (136),[13] the Americas continue to be "invaded, occupied, whitewashed, gagged, suppressed, sanitized and at best, ignored" as Francisco Alarcón (34) has observed. Thus, throughout these violated Americas, the issue of home—its diverse locations, types, and desires[14]—is a matter of survival and decolonization.

Memory, as inter-American writers show in the writings previously examined, is central to survival and decolonization. In reference to Pineau's memory of *la terre*, they denounce that some parts of the Americas are not allowed to remember the past due to imperial neocolonial strategies masked in the guise of a racialized and genderized market-driven globalism. Furthermore, by dismantling colonially imbued ideologies through mnemonic strategies of conscientization these writers and their texts, together with local and translocal resistance movements, such as the Zapatista movement in Chiapas and the social philosophy of *sumak kawsay* (*vivir bien*/well-living) of the Andes—the vitality of Amerindian peoples—for example, contribute to the decolonization of what Eduardo Galeano has alternately termed "la mémoire brisée" (Passé 92; broken memory) and "la memoria secuestrada de toda América" (*Memoria* 12; the kidnapped memory of the Americas) and the inherent systematic violation of human, vegetal, and animal rights. In this regard, to go home signifies a mnemonic homecoming that counteracts hegemonically institutionalized amnesia. Furthermore, home in the Americas can be situated in the innumerous daily struggles, the fight against illegitimate land holding/grabbing, injustice, and exploitation as well as in the conception and materialization of an alternative sense of life. It can be found in the many attitudes, individual and collective, which attempt to decolonize our entanglement in the tightly woven networks of (neo)colonial power relations.

This human desire for a home, a circle of harmoniously interconnected people(s) based on equal rights and obligations, is illustrated in a ceramic mural called *World Peace Begins With Human Dignity* at the California Metro Center in Santa Cruz, California.[15] Here, human life on earth is celebrated: the freedom, joy, and dignity of some people should not be based on the unfreedom/invisibility of others. In this constellation, *la terre* qua earth/land(scape) in Pineau's sense, is conceived as lived and imagined social and cultural space; an anthropocentric space, however, which excludes other species of our planet. In this ceramic mural, human dignity is celebrated in the absence of nonhuman dignity. Hence, the mural's anthropocentric alignment tinges its implied message that alienation, fragmentation, separation, and exploitation—the driving forces of the diverse phases of our rational, progress-oriented and predatory consumerist way of life—lead to violence, destruction, dislocation, the inclusion of some based on the exclusion of others. In the novels examined in this essay, *la terre* qua earth/land(scape), this fictional site of memory, evokes the message that culture as a human product should not be seen in opposition to or the absence of nature because human culture resides in and is determined by nature. In other words, our human existence and history is inextricably intertwined with those of other species and the places/spaces we inhabit. Because of the injustice, the constant rape suffered—the brutalization of the human, vegetal, and animal worlds—*la terre* qua earth/land(scape) connotes, as it demands, a transformation of our sense of what it means to inhabit the earth: a sense of place as sense of space characterized by interbiotic harmony and justice. Thus, if according to the mural world peace begins with human dignity, it continues with nonhuman dignity: there is no peace without an all-encompassing interbiotic dignity based on mutual respect relating all species in their lived and imagined experiences. Without an ecological logos based on respect—*respicere*: to gaze at; to care for; to consider—that is, recognizing and admitting the vegetal and animal others, it is impossible to balance an unbalanced world; to recreate "the comfort of belonging with the land, and the peace of being with these hills" (117), as Old Betonie argues in Leslie Marmon Silko's *Ceremony*.[16]

Home in many parts of the Americas, then, is rather a desire for home, a temporal, spatial, social, and cultural interface where violence and violation meet diverse forms and practices of resistance; a tension-laden contact zone where peace and violence, injustice and justice, freedom and slavery/serfdom, joy and frustration dance cheek to cheek; or, in the words of Afro-Potiguara poet Graça Graúna (Resistência 120): "dançamos a dor/tecemos o encanto/de índios e negros/da nossa gente" ("We dance the pain/we weave the delight/of Amerindians and Blacks/of our people"). The pain of (non)human rights violations and the delight qua ethical satisfaction in fighting for these rights constitute one of the important common situations that unites inter-American peoples and nation-states in their difference.

Notes

1. If not otherwise indicated, the translations in this essay are mine.
2. Many writers have pointed to the issue of land as one of the crucial root causes of violence in the Americas. Let me just mention two examples. In 1928, José Carlos Mariátegui, in his memorable *7 ensayos de interpretación de la realidade peruana*, argues that the "cuestión indígena" ("indigenous issue") has its roots in "el régimen de propiedad de la tierra" ("the regime of land ownership", 153). In general, neoliberal policies combined with debt crises throughout much of Latin America have strengthened large landholding systems and furthered expropriation of land for export culture. In 2005, Dionne Brand, in the opening pages of her novel *What We All Long For*, emphasizes the general amnesia of multiethnic Torontonians in relation to the issue of Aboriginal land: "All of them sit on Ojibway land, but hardly any of them know it or care because that genealogy is willfully untraceable except in the name of the city itself" (4). For an ideal definition of land tenure, see the *FAO Voluntary Guidelines on the Responsible Governance of Tenure of Land, Fisheries and Forests in the Context of National Food Security*.
3. Whereas, according to the *United Nations Declaration on the Rights of Indigenous Peoples*, a resolution adopted by the General Assembly in 2007, Indigenous peoples "have the right to self-determination" (Article 3) and "self-government" (Article 4) and nation-states together with Indigenous peoples shall ensure the protection of Indigenous women and children against all forms and practices of violence, in the Americas, Aboriginal Peoples are subject to federal jurisdiction, that is, they have only partial or no autonomy in judicial matters. For many First Nations People throughout the Americas, an independent justice system is as urgent a matter as the rights to their lands traditionally owned, guaranteed by the Inter-American Court and the OAS Inter-American Commission on Human Rights, but, following the *Amnesty International Report 2017/18* (32), not (or insufficiently) enacted by inter-American nation-states.
4. According to the *Amnesty International Report 2017/18* (27), the number of hemispheric Americans on the move has increased in comparison to previous years with the refugee crisis in Central America leading the continent's migrant fluxes (31). In light of the *Declaration of OAS Human Rights* from

June 2016, adopted at the 46th OAS General Assembly, which urges inter-American nation-states to ask the International Organization of Migration, among others, for assistance to protect migrants from human rights abuses (23–24), the Amnesty findings emphasize the nation-states' lack of willingness and/or financial means to fulfill the objectives of the OAS *Declaration*, upholding human rights.
5. For a definition of "transwriting," see Walter (*Narrative* 31).
6. William Faulkner has once memorably delineated this brutalization as the "curse of the land," "that whole edifice intricate and complex and founded upon injustice and erected by ruthless rapacity" (291) transforming "wilderness" into "tamed land" (252).
7. Not only does the *Amnesty International Report 2017/18* emphasize the continent's retrogression in human rights, but it states that "Latin America and the Caribbean *remained* the most violent region in the world for women. The region had the world's highest rate of non-intimate partner violence against women, and the second highest rate of intimate partner violence" (27; my emphasis).
8. Pineau's novels are imbued with the most pernicious aspect of colonization, that is, the internalization of the imago of Black people imposed upon them by the white supremacist value system.
9. For Deane Curtin, "environmental racism" is "the connection, in theory and practice, of race and environment so that the oppression of one is connected to, and supported by, the oppression of the other" (145).
10. Both authors deal with what Soja, Lefebvre, and Raffestin, among others, have thematized as cultural, human geography; that is, the meaning of territoriality transmitted through the consciousness of spatiality, its social practices and relations of power. Unlike Soja, Lefebvre, and Raffestin, Viramontes and Boyle, in their difference, highlight the interbiotic link between social, cultural and ecological issues.
11. When Ralph Ellison's narrator in *Invisible Man* declares his acquaintance with "ambivalence" and confesses his confusion because a "mistake was made somewhere" (8–9), he stresses the important link between geography and experience and that ambivalence, a legacy of the colonial past coated in neo-colonial forms and practices of violence, refers to geographical, ethno-racial, social, cultural, and psychological in-betweenness in which basic concepts of human morality are dismantled.
12. Inter alia, the *Universal Declaration of Human Rights*, the *United Nations Declaration on the Rights of Indigenous Peoples*; the *OAS American Declaration on the Rights of Indigenous Peoples*; the Inter-American Commission on Human Rights; the Inter-American Court of Human Rights; the Inter-American Commission of Women.
13. In *The Guardians*, by Chicana author Ana Castillo, Miguel asks the following question regarding the transborder violence driven by predatory economic interests: "With so much money involved, how can anyone ever expect this savagery to stop?" (184).
14. For a discussion of home qua "homing desire," see Brah (178–210).
15. The tile mural *World Peace Begins With Human Dignity* was created by the artist Lark Lucas and was commissioned by *Good Times* a local Weekly newspaper. https://localwiki.org/santacruz/World_Peace_Begins_With_Human_Dignity.
16. Many inter-American authors use literary strategies of inter/transbiotic recall as counter-memory to evoke a post-rational order characterized by an egalitarian relationship between human beings and the rest of the biota. See Walter (2016).

Works cited

Adams, Michael. *Fire and Ice: The United States, Canada and the Myth of Converging Values*. Penguin, 2003.
Alarcón, Francisco. "Reclaiming Ourselves, Reclaiming America." *Without Discovery: A Native Response to Columbus*, edited by Ray González. Broken Moon Press, 1992, pp. 29–38.
Alarcón, Norma. "Anzaldúa's *Frontera*: Inscribing Gynetics." *Displacement, Diaspora, and Geographies of Identity*, edited by Smadar Larie and Ted Swedenburg. Duke UP, 1996, pp. 41–54.
Amin, Samir. *Capitalism in the Age of Globalism*. Zed Books, 2000.
Amnesty International. *Amnesty International Report 2017/18*, www.amnesty.org/en/documents/pol10/6700/2018/en/. Accessed 04 Feb., 2018.
Anaya, Rudolfo A. "A Writer Discusses His Craft." *The CEA Critic*, vol. XI, issue 1, 1977, pp. 40–47.
Armstrong, Jeannette. *Slash*. Theytus Books, 1988.
Belli, Gioconda. *La mujer habitada*. Emecé, 1996.
Benítez-Rojo, Antonio. *The Repeating Island: The Caribbean and the Postmodern Perspective*. Duke UP, 1996.
Bloch, Ernst. *Das Prinzip Hoffnung*. Suhrkamp, 1985.
Boyle, T.C. *When the Killing's Done*. Penguin, 2011.
Brah, Avtar. *Cartographies of Diaspora: Contesting Identities*. Routledge, 1996.
Brand, Dionne. *A Map to the Door of No Return. Notes to Belonging*. Vintage, 2002.
Brand, Dionne. *What We All Long For*. Vintage, 2005.
Caruth, Cathy. *Unclaimed Experience: Trauma, Narrative, and History*. Johns Hopkins UP, 1996.
Castillo, Ana. *The Guardians*. Random House, 2008.
Condé, Maryse. *Crossing the Mangrove*. Trans. Richard Philcox. Anchor, 1995.
Cornejo-Polar, Antonio. *O condor voa: literatura e cultura latino-americanas*, edited by Mario J. Valdés, translated by Ilka Valle de Carvalho. Ed.UFMG, 2000.
Curtin, Deane W. *Environmental Ethics for a Postcolonial World*. Rowman & Littlefield, 2005.
Depestre, René. *Encore une mer à traverser*. La Table Ronde, 2005.
Dussel, Enrique. "Eurocentrism and Modernity." *The Postmodernism Debate in Latin America*, edited by John Beverley, et al. Duke UP, 1995, pp. 65–76.
Ellison, Ralph. *Invisible Man*. Random House, 1952.
Erdrich, Louise. *The Round House*. Harper Perennial, 2012.
Fanon, Frantz. *Black Skin, White Masks*. Trans. Charles L. Markmann. Grove Press, 1967.
Faulkner, William. "The Bear." *The Portable Faulkner*, edited by Malcom Cowley. Penguin, 1977, pp. 197–320.
Ferreira, Elio. "América Negra." *América Negra & outros poemas afro-brasileiras*. Quilombhoje, 2014, pp. 25–36.
Galeano, Eduardo. "Memoria del fuego 1." *Los nacimientos*. Siglo XXI, 1982.
Galeano, Eduardo. "Ce passé qui vit en nous." *Manière de voir*, vol. 82, 2005, pp. 91–93.

Gilkes, Michael. "The Landscape of Dreams: Extract from a Conversation between Wilson Harris and Michael Gilkes." *Wilson Harris: The Uncompromising Imagination*, edited by Hena Maes-Jelinek. Dangaroo Press, 1991, pp. 31–38.
Glissant, Édouard. *Caribbean Discourse*. UP of Virginia, 1992.
Graúna, Graça. "Resistência." *Cadernos Negros 29*. Quilombhoje, 2006, p. 120.
Graúna, Graça. "Manifesto I." Overmundo.com.br/banco/manifesto-i, 20 Feb. 2010. Web. 07 Nov. 2017.
Guilitraro, David A. *Mapurpe: venganza a la raiz*. Pehuén, 2009.
Hirsch, Marianne. "Projected Memory: Holocaust Photographs in Personal and Public Fantasy." *Acts of Memory. Cultural Recall in the Present*, edited by Mieke Bal, et al. New England UP, 1999, pp. 3–23.
Klein, Naomi. *The Shock Doctrine: The Rise of Disaster Capitalism*. Metropolitan Books, 2007.
Lefebvre, Henri. *La production de l'espace*. Anthropos, 1974.
Mariátegui, José Carlos. *7 ensayos de interpretación de la realidad peruana*. Capital Intelectual, 2009.
McLuhan, T.C. *Touch the Earth: A Self-Portrait of Indian Existence*. Touchstone, 1971.
McLuhan, T.C. "Home." *The House That Race Built*, edited by Wahneema Lubiano. Vintage, 1998, pp. 3–12.
Morrison, Toni. *Paradise*. Alfred A. Knopf, 1998.
Morrison, Toni. *A Mercy*. Alfred A. Knopf, 2008.
Neruda, Pablo. *Canto General*. Trans. Jack Schmitt. U of California P, 2000.
Neruda, Pablo. *Obras Completas. V. I–V*. Editorial Galaxia Gutenberg, 2001.
Ollivier, Émile. *La Brûlerie*. Boréal, 2004.
Organisation of American States (OAS). *Declaration of OAS Human Rights. 46th Session of the General Assembly*, www.oas.org/en/topics/human_rights.asp. Accessed 28 Apr., 2018.
Organisation of American States (OAS). *OAS American Declaration on the Rights of Indigenous Peoples*, indianlaw.org/adrip/home. Accessed 04 May, 2018.
Pineau, Gisèle. *L'espérance-macadam*. Stock, 1996.
Pineau, Gisèle. *Morne Câpresse*. Mercure de France, 2008.
Quijano, Anibal. "Colonialidad del poder, cultura y conocimiento en América Latina." *Anuario Mariateguiano*, vol. 9, issue 9, 1997, pp. 113–120.
Raffestin, Claude. *Pour une géografie du pouvoir*. Librairies Techniques, 1980.
Ramonet, Ignacio. *Géopolitique du chaos*. Gallimard, 2002.
Rich, Adrienne. "When We Dead Awaken: Writing as Re-Vision." *On Lies, Secrets, and Silence: Selected Prose 1966–1978*. W.W. Norton and Company, 1979, pp. 33–49.
Rivera, Tomás. *…Y no se lo tragó la tierra/…AND THE EARTH DID NOT PART*. Editorial Justa, 1977.
Saldívar, José D. *Border Matters: Remapping American Cultural Studies*. University of California Press, 1997.
Schwarz, Roberto. *Misplaced Ideas: Essays on Brazilian Culture*. Trans. John Gledson. Verso, 1992.
Silko, Leslie M. *Ceremony*. Penguin, 1977.
Soja, Edward. *Postmodern Geographies: The Reassertion of Space in Critical Social Theory*. Verso, 1989.

United Nations. *United Nations Declaration on the Rights of Indigenous Peoples*, www.un.org/development/desa/indigenouspeoples/declaration-on-the-rights-of-indigenous-peoples.html. Accessed 24 Apr. 2018.

United Nations. *Universal Declaration of Human Rights*, www.un.org/en/universal-declaration-human-rights/. Accessed 14 May 2018.

Viramontes, Helena M. *Their Dogs Came with Them*. Washington Square Press, 2007.

Walter, Roland. *Narrative Identities: (Inter)Cultural In-Betweenness in the Americas*. Peter Lang, 2003.

Walter, Roland. "Inter/Transbiotic Memory Traces: Transculturation and Decolonization in Inter-American Literature." *Fiar*, vol. 9, issue 2, 2016, pp. 34–54.

Part II
Human rights in Central America and the Caribbean

4 Human rights situation in Central America through the lens of literary representations of violence

Xaver Daniel Hergenröther

Introduction

In the novel *Insensatez* (*Senselessness,* 2008),[1] published in 2004, as well as in others, Horacio Castellanos Moya portrays the civil war in Guatemala, particularly in contemporary Guatemalan society, while reaffirming the focus on its memory of violence. His way of intervening is to strongly criticize the way of life in Central America through sarcasm, cynicism, and vulgar exaggerations. The central question of this study is if and in what way this approach is a fruitful contribution to the process of reworking the violent past. The analyzed literature investigates the topic of genocide during the civil war in Guatemala and asks, for example, whether the genocide against the Indigenous people was adequately reworked and whether this memory is integrated and embedded deeply into the collective memory of Central American society. Castellanos Moya's writings and analysis of his novels is a valuable method of redefining the ways toward a new (national, institutionalized, collective, individual) memory in Central America.

In order to provide an example of the ongoing discussion on human rights and genocide in Central America, it is worth quoting from the preelection interview "Cara a Cara #Jimmy Morales con José Eduardo Valdizán"[2] with the then new president Jimmy Morales, who won the Guatemalan presidential elections in October 2015. He states his opinion on the question of whether Guatemala suffered genocide during the civil war or not:

> Según lo que yo interpreto del concepto y de la definición de la palabra genocidio, no hubo tal intento de exterminio. Pero quiero hacer una aclaración. Creo que en el conflicto armado hubo crímenes de la humanidad, detestables. Crímenes que no debieron darse, crímenes que son lamentables y que son parte de nuestra historia.[3]
>
> (According to the way I interpret the concept and the definition of the word genocide, there was no such intent to exterminate. But allow me to clarify. I believe that in the armed conflict there were crimes against humanity, detestable ones. Crimes that should have not happened, crimes that are regrettable and that are part of our history.)

To contextualize, Morales had won the elections as a candidate of The National Convergence Front, a political party that was established in 2008. It was initiated by a group of retired army officers, including veterans of the Guatemalan Civil War, affiliated with the Military Veterans Association of Guatemala.

Framework

The literary text was chosen for interpretation in this study deals, generally speaking, with the topic of the Guatemalan civil war (which lasted from 1960 until 1996; estimated casualties and losses between 150,000 and 200,000 dead and missing) and the after-war period in Guatemala and its daily violence. In *Senselessness*, the protagonist and narrator, a nameless middle-aged journalist, reports his points of view on the violent past and present. His form of narration resembles a sheer endless internal and external monologue, a *suada* (from the Latin verb suadere–to convince), which we categorize here as a *fictional* narration according to the theory developed by Alexandra Ortiz Wallner in *El arte de ficcionar* (2012). Within her perspective on contemporary Central American literature, she defines the discussed literature as belonging to the genre *novela centroamericana de posguerra* (Central American novel of the Post-War). By inventing the term *friccionalidad*, she categorizes this literature as "narrativa entre los polos de la H/historia, el testimonio, la memoria y la ficción" (90; a narrative between the poles of H/history, testimony, memory, and fiction). Therefore, for Ortiz Wallner, Castellano Moya's texts are narrations found in interplay somewhere between the areas and foci mentioned. The line of differentiation between fiction and reality cannot be drawn clearly. Regarding her research approach, the subversive character of literature in the Central American discourse becomes obvious. This function of literature is termed imperative in the immediate moment and at any time in states and nations in Central America and in the world at large. Different points of view regarding the past and the versions of history have to exist for the purpose of a fruitful reworking process of the past, including marginalized groups of society. In the Central American case, it is, for example, important to give voice to the Indigenous people in order to view their versions of history and take their memory into consideration. The discussion of how a collective identity can be produced through the memory process and how this process leads to a peaceful present is applicable to the Central American and especially the Guatemalan case. Next to monuments, museums, and politics, texts produce an abundance of memory, and the novel *Senselessness* produces a wealth of memory on violence.

Senselessness and its historical pretexts

To fully understand the circumstances and methods of the institutional and individual reworking process after the official end of the Guatemalan civil war in 1996, there are two important reports for historical clarification that need to be mentioned: the "D. R. Oficina de Derechos Humanos del Arzobispado de Guatemala" (The D. R. Office of Human Rights by the Archbishop of Guatemala) published in 1998 and part of the report *Guatemala: nunca más, informe del proyecto interdiocesano; recuperación de la memoria histórica* (Guatemala: Never Again, Report of the Interdiocesan Project; Recovery of Historical Memory—REMHI). The latter report by the Catholic Church was then followed by the United Nations publication titled *Guatemala: Memory of Silence (Guatemala: memoria del silencio) – Report of the Commission for Historical Clarification*. The commission was established by the U.N. because of the 1994 "[a]greement on the establishment of the Commission to clarify past human rights violations and acts of violence that have caused the Guatemalan population to suffer" (68). This UN report is the only official report on the violent Guatemalan past and the only one recognized by the two opposing parties of the civil war. The commission presented its final results in Spanish in front of representatives of the Guatemalan government, the Guatemalan National Revolutionary Unity (URNG), and the UN Secretary General in February 1999.

Herein we discuss how these institutional texts or any text are able to reproduce the truth about the armed conflict and what strategies the fictional text *Senselessness* by Castellanos Moya uses to capture that violent past. Hayden White's theory of the poetics of history as revealed in "The Historical Text as Literary Artifact" is very valuable with his four categories of narration (romance, tragedy, comedy, and satire). He is essentially asking how the discourse of the historian and the author of fictional literature is overlapping, similar, or equal. History and literary writings offer, in his opinion, norms of coherence and correspondence. *Senselessness*, for example, produces its own truth of the violent Guatemalan past and reproduces the REHMI report *Guatemala nunca más* as its fictional short summary. The meaning of the title can be translated in multiple ways, including as a lack of judgment and/or a lack of being reasonable. The interpretation of the title leaves room for speculation on the kind of absence or deficiency the author is describing in his novel. Stupidity is carried out by a person lacking intelligence and with unreasonable behavior that could occur in a wanton way, that is, senselessly. The question, then, is who lacks common sense with its subsequent consequence. All interpretations lead to the fact that there is a lack of human rights in Guatemala and that the novel is targeting the nuances of such a condition and how society could address it. Consequently, the title of the novel suggests the guilt embedded in Guatemalan society, thereby offering a sense of truth about the guilt, the perpetrators, and the victims produced through actions during the armed conflict.

In this regard, it is indispensable to first think about what Western society in general declares as a reasonable behavior in situations of armed conflicts.

At this point, the example of Francisco de Vitoria from the University of Salamanca helps illustrate how the philosopher and theologian addressed such questions in his lectures "De indis." After the Spanish Conquest began in 1492 of the newly encountered territories in the Western hemisphere, the Spanish Crown of Rey Carlos I considered how governing elites should legally deal with troublesome opponents on the Indian continent with regard to the case of armed conflicts. Based on the idea that the transgression of the *jus gentium*—the principle of reciprocity—would be an illicit transgression (van der Kroef 152), De Vitoria, for instance, concluded that if the Indians broke the laws of hospitality to foreigners and prohibited peaceful and unrestricted trade with the Spaniards, these "would be allowed to defend themselves, provided they have all acted in good faith and have not malevolently sought to subjugate the Indians" (154). In the 16th century, De Vitoria authorized what became a "justified" war (155) and fashioned the appropriate measures that were warranted in such conflicts based on "a concept of the fundamental rights of each nation under international law" (158). Laws that sought to establish evenhanded transnational relations were written over 500 years ago for the expressed benefit of the Spanish crown which established its wealth through the gold and silver found in the continent of the "easily frightened and by nature dumb" Indians (154). Moreover, scholars in the field of public international laws of nations have revived and revisited these colonial legal texts throughout the centuries. The same texts partly continue to be deployed in the same way today to justify humanitarian interventions in the name of progress that in reality hide "crass exploitation" (162) as Justus M. van der Kroef reveals in his ever relevant article "Francisco de Vitoria and the Nature of Colonial Policy." Our contention is that, on the one hand, as early as the 15th century, sound approaches toward creating a democratic society with high ethical and moral values may have been legislated. On the other hand, however, these laws have to be questioned on their applicability and relevance to today's societies. Reminiscent of De Vitoria's legislation, it is necessary to remember that authors of texts and law continue to be written in highly subjective ways, oftentimes influenced by authorities who instruct and pay intellectuals and lawyers to write such texts. It is not an exaggeration to propose that legal texts are constructions in a similar way that fictional texts are and that parallels can easily be drawn between 16th-century policy-making and contemporary practices in Guatemala, for instance, regarding the way in which truth is found and negotiated through written texts. This study, therefore, examines the border between subjectivity and objectivity of Castellanos Moya's novel and the questions surrounding it on the assumed versions of truth in history. One of the central questions entails the truth about the existence of genocide during the armed conflict in Guatemala in the second half of the 20th century.

The retelling of archetypal tales in Guatemalan examples

The novel *Senselessness* presents the understood truth of the violent Guatemalan past in the form of a fictional text. Furthermore, in the original Spanish edition, the author uses art to affirm his argument. The picture on the cover of the novel demonstrates in a vivid manner Castellanos Moya's perspective on the events of the Guatemalan civil war and exemplifies the situation of human rights in Central America. Two hundred thousand people were killed during the 36-year-long conflict and the fratricidal nature of this civil war is symbolically represented through the biblical figure of Cain in flames, running away from the murder scene.[4] Castellanos Moya takes part of this painting from William Blake, the English pre-Romantic poet, and frames it for the cover, choosing the part that only focuses on the figure of Cain (see the link).[5] The London Tate Gallery provides the following explanation of the painting:

> This work shows Adam and Eve discovering their dead son. His brother Cain, the murderer, flees the scene. Despite his evil deed, Cain appears as an ideal male figure. Here, Blake's approach is in line with that of Lavater, who argued that someone's appearance is often 'better than his actions'. However, Lavater also suggested that in performing an evil act the person could become disfigured, perhaps explaining Cain's contorted body. Rather than follow Lavater here, Blake's use of the body to invoke self-loathing, fear and, in the case of Eve, despair may be closer to pathognomy–a way of reading emotions about which Lavater remained skeptical.[6]

The physical idealization of the criminal acting on emotion, on the one hand, self-hatred, fear, and despair of the involved parties are, on the other hand, described as the main themes of the painting. This art-historical interpretation of William Blake's painting leads the discussion to questioning the function of the figure of Cain for Castellanos Moya's novel. According to the Book of Genesis, he is the first son of Adam and Eve. William Blake in *Songs of Innocence and Experience* (1789–1794, 2 volumes) describes two different states of the soul. As Bruce Woodcock writes, "He sees in the child a sign of ingenuous potential in which evil does not yet exist. Evil is only produced through experiencing the world and the consequent oppression of the human mind. Blake criticizes the conditions in society, in particular, established, institutional Christianity, while viewing his duty as a prophetic author in expressing a clear critique" (56).

The examination of the manifold contexture of the evil and the human potential for violence expressed by Blake is notably applied by Castellanos Moya to the Guatemalan situation. The question is why the cover picture only shows the murdering son Cain and not the murdered son Abel. Cain is escaping the murder scene, while burning up in flames, and the author analyzes the violent past of Guatemala by focusing on the person actively involved in murdering his own brother. The murderer is the guilty one, the perpetrator, but in Blake's painting, he himself is threatened by his act, lifting his hands to his head, wanting to rip out his hair or even part of his head into two. Castellanos Moya in this image suggests that the victims and their voices are not adequately represented, that is, their story and their version of the past is not heard by the Guatemalan and global public.

Castellanos Moya is trying to evoke empathy from the reader, and the selection of the cover image is a first hint and a first invitation to think about the identities of the perpetrators in the Guatemalan armed conflict. Next to evoking empathy implicitly, the author is also telling the reader explicitly his opinion about the genre of his own novel *Senselessness* in the editorial page: he essentially states that his novel is a work of fiction, in which names, characters, places, and incidents are a product of the author's imagination or utilized in a fictitious manner (n.p.).[7] His disclaimer emphasizes that any resemblance to real, living, or dead persons is a coincidence. Connecting this strategy with the theory of Hayden White on fictionality and the factuality of texts, it becomes obvious that Castellanos Moya is trying to create with his novel one of many truths about history, and this truth is as fictional as are all the available versions of the past.

The pre-assumed fictional text offers direct and indirect intertextual connections to the 1998 report by the Catholic Church and to the 1999 UN report, therefore described as a fictional short summary of the report of the Catholic Church. The novelist points out the fictionality of his novel and his imagination and rules out assumed similarities with existing personalities. The author in the year 2004 is aware of the shattering effect of his novel and of how difficult it is to speak about the armed Guatemalan conflict even 8 years after the official end of the civil war. He, on the one hand, wants to prevent problematic interpretations of his novel and, on the other, he provokes the perpetrators of the conflict directly and deliberately.

The dedication of the novel is directed to a person named S.D. and reveals that S.D. made the author promise him/her that he would never dedicate his novel to him/her. This dedication prepares the reader for the circumstances of the publication of the novel and makes them aware of the situation of human rights in Guatemala. S.D. fears reading his name in a dedication of a novel by Castellanos Moya and, therefore, the dedication demonstrates the author's strategy of making danger visible, while at the same time standing up to it and still preserving the whole name and hidden identity. So the reader cannot help but to ask if writing the full name of S.D. would make him/her fear for their life. The epigraph to the novel *Senselessness* (n.p.)[8] demonstrates how the author furthermore guides the reader toward the topic. Here, Castellanos Moya translated a direct quote of Ismene from Sophocles' Antigone into Spanish, in which she speaks directly to Sophocles saying that rationality never lasts among those who are unfortunate beings.

The quote of Ismene's speech from Sophocles' drama *Antigone* indicates that the wisdom will never last with the unlucky and miserable ones, nor the wisdom which is born through them, but it will withdraw, wither and fade away. The epigraph directly reflects the cover image. *Antigone* was written in 441 B.C. by the Greek philosopher and poet Sophocles. It deals with the consequences of the prohibited burial of a renegade criminal. The protagonist Antigone, the daughter and sister of Oedipus, buries her brother Polyneikes without permission; Ismene is Antigone's sister. Derrida, Lacan, and Butler have all written about Antigone in the context of psychoanalysis. The relationship between the dichotomy of wise and unwise human behavior in interhuman situations and in conflicts is thereby exposed. The connection between the prototype human and inhuman behavior, by extension including the (in-)human behavior of the Guatemalan society, is established through this epigraph. The topic of Antigone is a typical topic for the ancient Greek tragedy, as the audience is ethically and morally cleansed by watching the play. The cleansing or the catharsis in the Aristotelean poetic's definition is a catharsis of diverse effects. By living through lamentation and emotion, as well as fear and shudder (Greek *éleos* and *phóbos*), the audience of the tragedy receives a cleansing of the soul on the condition of agitation (Fuhrmann, *Poetik*, Kap. 6).

Castellano Moya's *Senselessness* is in this sense a Greek tragedy that leads the reader to a cathartic cleansing process through emotion and fear. It discusses, furthermore, the original and deeply human topos of the murdering of his own brother. The complete novel is, therefore, an allegory as the author is clouding his concrete intentions with his language and his style of writing.

Friccionalidad as a stylistic game

Castellanos Moya and other Central American authors are often referred to as the generation of disenchantment. In his novel *Senselessness*, he uses real persons, institutions, etc., which can be interpreted as a practice of the stylistic game of *friccionalidad* as theorized by Ortiz Wallner. In his midday break, the protagonist, for example, meets a friend in the bar *El Portalito*, which is in fact a real place and also 13 years after the publication of the novel the most famous bar in Guatemala City. While having lunch with his *compadre*, he makes him aware of people sitting at the table next to them and states that they are informants and torturers of the badly named Main Presidential State: men who generally drink alone, hardly lifting their eyes from the table but who can be easily recognized because of the gruesome aura that surrounds them (*Senselessness* 12). By naming the institution Presidential High Command, *Senselessness* shows the direct connection between the novel and reality. In the report of the *Commission for Historical Clarification of the Guatemalan Civil War* of the year 1999, the EMP and the Inteligencia Militar are accused of illegal kidnappings, interrogations, tortures, forced disappearances, and executions during the 35-year armed conflict (Tomuschat 249–251). Moreover, in a report of Amnesty International of the year 2003, the EMP is accused of participating in crimes against humanity. For instance, the murders of Myrna Mack Chang (anthropologist), Monseñor Juan José Gerardi (archbishop of Guatemala City), and Epaminondas González Dubón (President of the Court on Constitutionality), who were all important figures who fought for a peaceful solution of the Guatemalan conflict in opposition to the government and the military.

Naming the EMP and associating them with a bad smell quite obviously portrays what Ortiz Wallner calls *friccionalidad*: fictional players in the story (co)exist *in reality*. Consequently, Castellano Moya's novel is not only at the edge of fiction but also includes autobiographical literature. He left El Salvador after writing newspaper articles in that country and later moved to Montreal, Canada. In the 1980s he was connected to the original Frente Farabundo Martí de Liberación Nacional (FMLN or a coalition of the Salvadoran guerrilla)—ideologically and in terms of his function as a journalist. After the long difficult period of the civil war in El Salvador in 1991, he founded the magazine *Tendencias* in San Salvador. Thus, Castellanos Moya projected to become part of the creation of a new society and a new memory before and after the tragic civil war. The circumstances did not allow him a direct and unmediated contribution, as he, for example, had to once again leave the country after publishing another novel *El Asco* after facing death threats. This well illustrates how his approach and objective of changing the situation and the politics in El Salvador, and in Central America in general, to create a new memory is the way of language and literature.

Literary representation of violence

There appear a number of examples in the novel in which violence is represented and portrayed within the text:

> *I am not complete in the mind*, I repeated to myself, stunned by the extent of the mental perturbation experienced by this Cakchiquel man who has witnessed his family's murder.... (*Senselessness* 1; emphasis in original)[9]

The narrating protagonist moreover states that this man, while fully conscious of the breakdown of his psychic condition, injured and impotent, had to witness his country's soldiers of the military slaughter each one of his four small sons to pieces and then assault his wife. The protagonist comes to the conclusion after witnessing such inconceivable violence in which the man's small children are turned into throbbing pieces of human flesh that no one can be complete in the mind (*Senselessness* 2). The use of the real existing ethnic group *Cakchiquel* is another excellent example of the concept of *friccionalidad*. Besides, the very explicit narration of the violence used by the soldiers of their country, which is without a doubt Guatemala, makes the process of reading a painful experience. The sympathy of the reader for the victims (the Guatemalan Indigenous people) and the antipathy for the perpetrators (the Guatemalan military) is clearly evoked, as the horrendous practices of the soldiers are described in detail. Reflecting the process of reading on a deeper level, and connecting it among others with the Greek tragedy *Antigone* and other human original topoi, the ruthless choice of words and the author's method make sense as he wants to bring the reader to a certain catharsis.

In the following, the author's opinion is expressed through the protagonist's voice, reflecting the state of mind of the people of Guatemala in a provocative way. The phrase "*I am not complete in the mind*" (*Senselessness* 1; emphasis in original) is used in manifold ways and, according to the narrator, encapsulates in the most compressed manner the description of the mental state in which dozens of thousands of people found themselves after having suffered similar experiences as the one experienced by the Cakchiquel Indians. The narrator states that this phrase also summarizes the mental state of thousands of soldiers and paramilitaries that had slaughtered their so-called compatriots with the greatest pleasure. Yet, the narrator acknowledges a significant difference between victims and perpetrators: it is not the same to be out of your mind for having witnessed the brutal killing of your own sons versus massacring someone else's sons (2–3). The storyteller then comes to the overwhelming conclusion, "the entire population of [Guatemala] was not complete in the mind" (2–3). The result of the senselessness of the violence committed during the conflict and the failure of the post-war process to deal with its traumatic aftermath, and consequently the country's memory process, are described by narrating about the perturbed state of mind of the population. By referring to the violence committed during the war evokes sheer anger and hate against the perpetrators in the protagonist's voice. Within the novel, the military is repeatedly accused of cold-blooded viciousness and countless pointless massacres, all of which is expressed in vulgar tones. The repetition of the accusations demonstrates the author's understanding of the need to remember the violent past. If everyone engages more often in the idea that the inhabitants of Guatemala cannot be right in their minds, only then can the society be cathartically freed of the violent consequences of the memory of the civil war and possibly look forward to a peaceful future. In contrast to the official accusations through legal means, thanks in part to the United Nation's *Truth Commission on the Historical Clarification of the Armed*

Conflict in Guatemala, the novel as a work of fiction is the author's way to resort to language in order to accuse and represent such a memory of violence.

The author's cynical style is a way to describe, portray, and eventually define the problems of contemporary Central American society. With such a method, the reader is encouraged to rethink the situation of human rights and ideally change their behavior. As Wolfgang Iser elucidates, the process of auto-reflection evokes emotions within the reader, and this process is evoked by fiction, as this genre organizes reality and makes it communicable: "Fiction is for that reason a good tool of reflection, which serves the society to communicate and negotiate its practices and which can, in this way, recuperate a practical function of second degree" (Iser 68). And after a *willing suspension of disbelief*, as defined by Samuel Taylor Coleridge, only fictionality has the possibility, potential, and opportunity to interrupt the reader's doubt voluntarily. Coleridge's literary concept argues that the reader is consciously entering into a contract with the author, agreeing to suspend his/her disbelief throughout the reading process.

The Central American novel in question makes the reader willingly suspend their disbelief in the violent past of their Central American country. Consequently, a process of auto-reflection is evoked through fictional/frictional literature, and this is an important way to negotiate and reconsider the violent past all over again. In this way, the author addresses his claims to external and also global players and institutions, thereby explaining what is happening and has happened in Central America from his point of view. His fictional work is at least an important step toward bringing—borrowing Werner Mackenbach's and Karl Kohut's terms from the title of their book—the "dolorosa cintura de América" (painful waistline of America) into the spotlight. It is a cry for help demanding that the international community and the United States of America, in particular, do not forget what is occurring in the "American backyard." It is an appeal to these authorities to rethink how the situation of the Guatemalan state and all the affected Central American countries and why the situation has become what it is today. The effect and logic of this approach, when thinking about the (re)construction of a Central American state after the civil war, is nevertheless criticized. What else is it than a valve for the author's anger expressed through this type of language? Is he reproducing violence for his own purposes of reworking his past in order to survive in the present by selling his books? And of course he has the right to portray the situation from his point of view, but the next step is guiding a wider community of readers to reconstruct society in a responsible way, thanks to an intellectual's perspective of a society's moment of crisis. It is unfortunate Castellanos Moya is not consistent in evoking this effect through his language. The tone of disenchantment and cynicism is notably present but the supportive character of language needs for the process of reconstructing the past and society is somewhat diffused. On the other hand, it is useful to portray and provoke with fictional language in order to incite the powers that be by suggesting a deep process about solving problems after a process of self-reflection. Castellanos Moya offers in his way the creation of a new identity while delineating a reconstructive path via the memory of history and culture. His literature is aiming indirectly at such an important step of reconstruction after the long-standing civil war in Guatemala—and by extension, most of Central America—whose effects seem to be endless.

Conclusion

The analysis of the literary methods of fiction, "friction," and narration of the novel *Senselessness* illustrates that the author is writing about extra-textual events of the violent Guatemalan and Central American past. Castellanos Moya wants to create a new memory and a new identity of his region with the strategy of reworking the violent past of his country, but regrettably, his direct impact on Central American society is questionable. It is impossible to draw a line of differentiation between reality and fiction in his writings because the author (who is in this case, and according to Hayden White's theory, also a historic figure) provides a direct and an indirect insight into a language of social reality, but there is not only a single reality of the Guatemalan past nor of any past. Only if diverse images of what went on during the civil wars are adequately articulated can the media and global community become attentive and, therefore, focus explicitly on the situation in Central America. Without this attention, the current situation of day-to-day violence in Central America will not change any time soon. It is important to study the literary versions of the past to understand the violent situation in the present.

Finally, it is relevant to conclude with a discussion regarding Castellano Moya's focus on violence in his literature or more precisely on the violent and vulgar language he is using. Here we can reference an important yet analogous public reworking process of the 20th century: the televising of the Eichmann Trial in the 1960s on German television. During the broadcasting, it became clear that the horrific speeches of testimonies (for example, the statement of a Jewish woman who fell into a mass grave without being shot as more dead bodies kept falling on top of her) produced a certain emotional public response to the Holocaust. However, is it necessary to dramatically present violence graphically in order to provoke a more public reception? Furthermore, does this wide reception lead to a diverse and fruitful construction of memory?

In addition, we have to keep in mind that the UNO Charta on human rights of 1948 was defined out of the painful experience of the Holocaust (and colonialism), and this ghastly trauma led to the understanding of the indispensability of the existence of human rights. So, the foundational element of what might be termed the positive human rights is the traumatically experienced pain, and as a next step, the result is a "never-again" mentality.

In the case of the work by Castellanos Moya, it seems that the reproduction of violence in literature at least makes the author sell his books in the center of the Western hemisphere (given that he is the most known contemporary Central American author in Europe and the United States). But, can this reproduction of violence be accepted only because Castellanos Moya has good intentions (to develop a fruitful memory process which leads to a peaceful present) or does the danger exist that he consolidates, reaffirms, and forever stamps the image and perception that the Western world has of Latin America? In a way, his literature is—in the framework of Maria Todorova's self-balkanization concept—a form of a *self-Latinoamericanization* and *uneducated* readers of the Western world might think that Latin America is solely an exotic place of violence, sex, drugs, etc. And, finally, groups like the still active gang Mara Salva Trucha are proud of being violent and, consequently, the vicious circle is completed. Where does this pride of violence come from? Is it only influenced by human sadism or also by the media (the literature) that people consume? And coming back to the new Guatemalan president's opinion on genocide and his affiliation to the Military Veterans Association of Guatemala, it is worth quoting the statement of the internationally recognized *Commission for Historical Clarification (CEH) of the Guatemalan Civil War*:

> In consequence, the CEH concludes that agents of the State of Guatemala, within the framework of counterinsurgency operations carried out between 1981 and 1983, committed acts of genocide against groups of Mayan people which lived in the four regions analyzed. This conclusion is based on the evidence...of Article II, II. first paragraph, II.a, II.b, II.c. [....] The CEH has information that similar acts occurred and were repeated in other regions inhabited by Mayan people. (41)

This serves to confirm why it is indispensable to write and interpret literary works like the novel *Senselessness*. In addition, it helps to highlight the importance of continuing to produce a new (literary) memory on the violent Central American past and why the analysis of Horacio Castellanos Moya's novels, therefore, represents a valuable tool for redefining another viable method toward articulating new human rights strategies in Central America.

Notes

1. In this contribution, I work, to different extents, with the original *Insensatez* and the translation of the text *Senselessness* by Katherine Silver. However, I exclusively quote from *Senselessnes*, 2008.
2. "Cara a Cara #Jimmy Morales con José Eduardo Valdizán," (minute 34:5): https://www.youtube.com/watch?v=mm4I0i2S-II.
3. If not otherwise indicated, all translations in this essay are mine.
4. *Insensatez* (Spanish Edition), https://www.amazon.com/Insensatez-Volumen-independiente-n%C2%BA-Spanish-ebook/dp/B00LEWBVTM/ref=sr_1_1?crid=32TRT73A08E4F&dchild=1&keywords=insensatez&qid=1595971409 & s=books&sprefix=insensates%2Cstripbooks%2C184&sr=1-1
5. Tate Gallery London. William Blake, The Body of Abel Found by Adam and Eve, http://www.tate.org.uk/art/artworks/blake-the-body-of-abel-found-by-adam-and-eve-n05888 (consulted on 23.11.2019).
6. Tate Gallery London. William Blake, The Body of Abel Found by Adam and Eve, http://www.tate.org.uk/art/artworks/blake-the-body-of-abel-found-by-adam-and-eve-n05888 (consulted on 23.11.2019).
7. In the original *Insensatez,* the editorial page is on page 6.
8. In *Insensatez*, the dedication is on page 11.
9. *Senselessness* translations by Katherine Silver.

Works cited

"Cara a Cara #Jimmy Morales con José Eduardo Valdizán." TV Azteca Guatemala, https://www.youtube.com/watch?v=mm4I0i2S-II. Accessed from Youtube on Channel "Guatepolítica" 16 May 2015.

Castellanos Moya, Horacio. *Insensatez*. Tusquets Editores, Colección Andanzas, 2004.

Castellanos Moya, Horacio. *Senselessness*. Translated by Katherine Silver. A New Directions Paperbook Original, 2008.

Comisión para el Esclarecimiento Histórico (CEH). *Guatemala, memoria del silencio*. Guatemala City: United Nations, 1999.

D. R. Oficina de Derechos Humanos del Arzobispado de Guatemala. *Guatemala nunca más: informe del proyecto interdiocesano; recuperación de la memoria histórica*. Guatemala City: D. R. Oficina de Derechos Humanos del Arzobispado de Guatemala, 1998.

Fuhrmann, Manfred. *Aristoteles Poetik, Griechisch/Deutsch*. Philipp Reclam, 1997.

Iser, Wolfgang. *Prospecting: From Reader Response to Literary Anthropology*. JHU Press, 1993.

Mackenbach, Werner, and Karl Kohut. *Literaturas centroamericanas hoy; desde la dolorosa cintura de América*. Vervuert Verlag, 2005.

Ortiz Wallner, Alexandra. *El arte de ficcionar*. Iberoamericana Vervuert, 2012.

Sophokles. *Antigone*. Griechisch/Deutsch. Übersetzung, Anmerkungen und Nachwort von Norbert Zink, griechischer Text nach der Ausgabe von A. C. Pearson. Philipp Reclam, 1981.

Tate Gallery London. William Blake – The Body of Abel Found by Adam and Eva, http://www.tate.org.uk/art/artworks/blake-the-body-of-abel-found-by-adam-and-eve-n05888. Accessed 23 Nov. 2016.

Todorova, Maria. *Imagining the Balkans*. Oxford University Press, 1997.

Tomuschat, Christian. "Clarification Commission in Guatemala." *Human Rights Quarterly*, vol. 23, issue 2, May 2001, pp. 233–258. https://www.jstor.org/stable/4489334

Van der Kroef, Justus M. "Francisco de Vitoria and the Nature of Colonial Policy." *The Catholic Historical Review*, vol. 35, issue 2, July 1949, pp. 129–162. https://www.jstor.org/stable/25015004

White, Hayden. "The Historical Text as Literary Artifact." *Tropics of Discourse: Essays in Cultural Criticism*. The John Hopkins University Press, 1978, pp. 81–100.

Woodcock, Bruce, editor. "Kommentar zu den Songs." *The Selected Poems of William Blake*. Wordsworth Editions, 2000.

5 Rebellion, repression, reform
U.S. Marines in the Dominican Republic

Breanne Robertson

In the contest for American votes, a candidate's bluster on the campaign trail can have unintended, yet far-reaching consequences.[1] Franklin D. Roosevelt learned this lesson the hard way during the 1920 presidential campaign, when his remarks about the U.S. interventions in Central America and the Caribbean raised public furor over Marine Corps misconduct in Santo Domingo (now Dominican Republic) and Haiti. Touting his experience as assistant secretary of the navy, the Democratic vice-presidential nominee boasted before a group of Montana voters: "You know I have had something to do with the running of a couple of little republics. The facts are that I wrote Haiti's Constitution myself, and, if I do say it, I think it's a pretty good Constitution." Roosevelt further fanned the flames of opposition when he insinuated that President Woodrow Wilson's administration could compel several Latin American republics to support U.S. initiatives in the newly formed League of Nations. "We are in the very true sense the big brother of these little republics," he explained. "Does anyone suppose that the vote of Cuba, Haiti, San Domingo [sic], Nicaragua and of the other Central American states would be cast differently from the vote of the United States?" (qtd. in Cross 104).[2]

Popular outcry was both swift and strong. Roosevelt's comments elicited caustic responses from both liberal advocates for national self-determination and conservative opponents of Wilsonian internationalism. Senator Warren G. Harding, the Republican nominee for president, capitalized on the growing furor by staking his own foreign policy in Dominican soil. Speaking before an Indiana delegation of voters in late August 1920, Harding condemned current U.S. military actions in the Caribbean as "unwarranted interference" that had not only "made enemies of those who should be our friends, but have rightfully discredited our country as a trusted neighbor." If elected president, he promised "not [to] empower an assistant secretary of the navy to draft a constitution for helpless neighbors in the West Indies and jam it down their throats at the point of bayonets borne by the United States marines" (Harding 91). In denouncing the Wilson administration's Caribbean policy and the activities of Roosevelt, in particular, Harding effectively pledged to bring an end to the military occupation in the Dominican Republic.[3] It would take nearly 4 years to fulfill this promise.

Harding's victory in the general election signaled the final phase of the American intervention, which involved intense public scrutiny, difficult treaty negotiations, and sweeping internal reforms. To be sure, the 1920 presidential election reflected a pronounced shift in American public opinion since the first Marines landed in the Dominican Republic four years earlier. An examination of Marine Corps activities illuminates how the occupation evolved, for U.S. citizens, from a celebrated humanitarian campaign to a misguided counterinsurgency operation and military regime embodying imperialist overreach in U.S. foreign affairs. Tracking the diplomatic motivation, military invasion, and counterinsurgency efforts of Marines in the Dominican Republic elucidates the changing circumstances that not only shaped public perception throughout the occupation but also compelled reform measures to facilitate a peaceful and effective withdrawal.

Protecting "America's lake"

In the years leading up to World War I, Caribbean financial insolvency and political disorder appeared dangerous to U.S. national security. The completion of the Panama Canal in 1914 endowed the U.S. Navy with a strategic advantage over other naval fleets; the desire to protect the isthmian canal, as well as the sea lanes around it, renewed U.S. interest in the Monroe Doctrine and occasioned frequent military interventions in the name of national defense. On December 6, 1904, President Theodore Roosevelt formalized U.S. foreign policy in hemispheric affairs with an initiative that has since become known as the "Roosevelt Corollary to the Monroe Doctrine." Arguing that European efforts to enforce Latin American debt repayment necessarily violated the Monroe Doctrine, he announced that the United States needed to ensure the political and financial stability of its sister republics (Roosevelt 100–102).

With trans-Atlantic tensions hanging in balance, the Dominican Republic served as a testing ground for the first practical application of the Roosevelt Corollary. In 1905, the State Department worked out a series of agreements that placed the Dominican customs service under American management. Although the U.S. Senate would delay ratifying the treaty until 1907, Roosevelt implemented the customs receivership immediately by executive fiat. The initial results were encouraging. Financial experts arranged for new loans with American lenders for debt consolidation and a lower interest rate, and U.S. officials took charge of customs revenues, collecting duties at Dominican ports and dividing the proceeds between foreign bondholders and the incumbent regime. Furthermore, the popularity and stability of the new Dominican president, Ramón Cáceres, permitted the administration to direct attention toward modernization and economic development in the country, which State Department officials attributed to the beneficial influence of U.S. oversight. The Dominican customs receivership served as the cornerstone of President William H. Taft's foreign relations policy. Known popularly as "dollar diplomacy," Taft emphasized economic influence as a paramount consideration in diplomatic affairs and pledged to use bankers rather than battleships to influence international stability. Nevertheless, when such efforts failed to secure desired results, both Taft and his successor, President Woodrow Wilson, resorted to threats of military force, or as historian Max Boot has described it, "the brass knuckles hidden beneath the velvet glove" (129).

The assassination of President Cáceres in November 1911 shattered the relative peace and economic prosperity of the Dominican Republic and ushered in a new era of transitory regimes and revolutionary violence. Between 1911 and 1916, U.S. officials intervened in Dominican affairs with increasing frequency to compel reform measures that would ostensibly establish a stable, freely elected, and pro-American government. Employing both diplomatic pressure and military might, the United States regularly sent warships to observe or make shows of force against the Dominican government, to threaten revolutionaries, or to protect the lives and property of American citizens. Despite such heavy-handed tactics on the part of the United States, domestic political turmoil persisted in the Dominican Republic, resulting in eight separate administrations in Santo Domingo in less than 5 years.

The near-constant disorder reflected a long-standing political feud between *horacistas*, followers of General Horacio Vásquez, and *jimenistas*, partisans of Juan Isidro Jiménez, as well as the growing strength of regional leaders such as General Desiderio Arias of Santiago. Rebellion flourished especially in the interior valleys, north coast, and rugged frontiers where local dictators or *caudillos* held sway. The warring political factions quickly exhausted the national treasury, and the country assumed additional debt trying to suppress rebellion, circumstances the United States considered in direct violation of its 1907 treaty with the republic. Moreover, this relapse into political volatility and financial insolvency enflamed U.S. fears of European intervention. German designs on the Americas, in particular, seemed to pose a very real threat.[4]

The State Department began to consider seriously the possibility of full-scale military intervention and the imposition of U.S. demands—a solution it had already implemented in Haiti starting in the summer of 1915. In November, William W. Russell, the newly appointed American minister, arrived in Santo Domingo with an ultimatum compelling the Dominican Republic to accept the appointment of U.S. financial advisers and the formation of U.S.-controlled constabularies. The current president, Juan Isidro Jiménez, refused as the proposed treaty would have severely curtailed Dominican sovereignty. Even so, his political enemies pointed to American overtures to damage his prestige and bolster support for their revolutionary efforts.

In April 1916, Jiménez ordered the arrest of several insubordinate officers, chief among them his minister of war, General Desiderio Arias. Tall, thin, and of mixed race heritage, Arias was a powerful, charismatic *caudillo* with a large following in the northwestern province of Monte Cristi. He represented the most infertile and impoverished region in the country but, unlike other *caudillos*, banned his troops from stealing food from the poor. Rising from humble origins himself, Arias attracted a devoted following among darker skinned peasants, soldiers, and the urban poor. By early May, the popular and politically influential leader persuaded the Dominican congress to begin impeachment proceedings against Jiménez. He then seized control of the capital and declared open revolt. With this action, the United States sent Marines to Santo Domingo to protect the American legation and to assist the Jiménez regime.

On May 2, 1916, two warships carrying a small force of Marines arrived in the Dominican Republic. In the eyes of Washington politicians, Arias had raised a rebellion against a properly elected president. In addition, U.S. policymakers viewed Arias as being pro-German and a conduit of arms to Haitian *cacos* then resisting American military rule on the other side of the island (Boot 168). Humanitarian paternalism and racism further informed the State Department's decision to intervene militarily. Ill-informed on political and social conditions in the republic, American officials incorrectly attributed the endemic violence and debt to corrupt local leadership and aimed to stabilize the Dominican Republic by preserving the incumbent administration against attempts to usurp power by force.

The United States concluded that Jiménez could not dislodge Arias from the capital without American assistance. The rebel leader had marshalled hundreds of civilian irregulars armed with rifles from government arsenals and around 250 Dominican soldiers who had defected to his side. Captain Frederic Wise described the situation this way, "every male in town even boys were armed easily making over a thousand rifles, with five (5) Gatlings, unlimited ammunition … plenty of [artillery]" and "gunners who knew how to use it" (Wise 141). Jiménez's small army, by contrast, numbered around 800 soldiers and had very little ammunition, fewer than 20 rounds per person. Minister Russell pressured Jiménez to request a landing of U.S. Marines. Exiled from the capital, the president first accepted but later rejected American assistance, explaining that his authority would diminish if "regained with foreign bullets" (Ureña 87–88). As an alternative to U.S.-armed intervention, Jiménez asked Russell and Wise to meet with Arias and negotiate a peaceful surrender. The Americans agreed on the condition that, if Arias refused, Jiménez would consent to a combined assault of Dominican and U.S. forces to regain the capital.

Arias and his followers rejected the deposed president's détente. Wise returned to camp and prepared to disarm the rebels by force, but Jiménez balked at the attack. "I can never consent to attacking my own people," he declared (qtd. in Wise 143). Wise, incensed by this response, told the Dominican president that American prestige was on the line and that if he did not want U.S. military aid, he should resign. After some vacillation,

Jiménez agreed. A secretary drew up the paperwork, and the president resigned on the spot.

Now in the position of trying to uphold an administration that ceased to exist, the United States nevertheless determined to quash the revolution and reinstate a constitutional government. On May 13, Rear Admiral William Caperton, commander of the U.S. Navy's Cruiser Squadron, Atlantic Fleet, issued an ultimatum demanding that Arias disband the rebel army by 0600 on May 15 or else face a full-scale American attack. As the U.S. officer awaited an answer, Arias defiantly hoisted Dominican flags rather than white flags as anticipated for surrender. Captain Wise and Major Newt Hall, commander of the 4th and 5th Companies recently arrived from Haiti and a detachment of the 24th Company from Guantánamo Bay, made plans for the forcible disarmament of the revolutionaries, while U.S. warships proceeded to San Pedro de Macorís, Sánchez, Puerto Plata, and other important Dominican ports. On the appointed date, the Marines marched on the rebel-held city. Anticipating armed resistance on every block, they instead discovered that Arias had evaded military confrontation by evacuating his troops under the cover of night. The Marine Corps took control of Santo Domingo and made the city its base of operations ashore.

Outside the capital, authority remained in the hands of local governors and military chieftains who operated independently of the central government. In addition, Arias claimed to hold the legitimate power of congress. Having reestablished headquarters at Santiago, he refuted the partisan revolutionary title assigned to him by Jiménez and the United States. His flag belonged to the Dominican people, he proclaimed (Calder 8). Russell refused to recognize Arias as the rightful executive chief and instead elevated Jiménez's remaining four cabinet members to the status of an interim "Council of Ministers" to carry on the business of state. Worried that Arias or one of his followers would be elected to the presidency if the Dominican congress were allowed a vote, Russell worked closely with Caperton to block congressional action while seeking a suitable alternative (Healy 196–197). While this strategy had worked in Haiti, Dominican politicians refused to give advance assurances of U.S. cooperation. "I have never seen such hatred displayed by one people for another as I notice and feel here," Caperton confessed. "We positively have not a friend in the land" (Caperton 9). Encountering near-universal hostility to U.S. governance, the commander feared a national uprising and called for reinforcements to secure the country's main coastal towns and disperse Arias' army in the Cibao Valley.

The march on Santiago

Arias retreated 85 miles inland to Santiago de los Caballeros, located in the northern agricultural valley of Cibao, where the distance to the sea precluded bombardment by a man-of-war or amphibious landing force. Caperton ordered Colonel Joseph Pendleton, the commanding officer of the

4th Regiment, to proceed against Arias' stronghold in the northern interior. Pendleton devised a plan, in which two columns of Marines would converge on Santiago from ports on the northern coast, since the country contained no roads that could accommodate large attack forces moving from the south. One column, commanded by Major Hiram Bearss, would follow a railroad inland from Puerto Plata, while the other, led by Pendleton, would march by road from Monte Cristi. The two forces would convene in Navarette, a village located 18 mi south of Santiago, for a full-scale drive on the objective.

Before the operation began, Pendleton defined the Marines' mission in the Dominican Republic and established guidelines for appropriate troop conduct. "[O]ur work in this country is not one of invasion," he announced to his men. Clarifying that their aim was to restore order, protect life and property, and support the constitutional government, he exhorted his fellow officers and enlisted men to "realize that we are not in an enemy's country, though many of the inhabitants may be inimical to us." Pendleton instructed his audience to treat the Dominican people with courtesy and dignity so as "to inspire confidence among the people in the honesty of our intentions" and to avoid generating antagonism and perceptions of an armed invasion (Pendleton).

In the early morning hours of June 26, Pendleton's column embarked on its 75-mile journey inland. The Monte Cristi force, consisting of the 4th Regiment and some artillery, had a greater distance to travel and would

Figure 5.1 13th Company, 4th Marines traveling with Colonel Joseph Pendleton's column on the road from Monte Cristi to Santiago, 26 June to 6 July, 1916. Official Marine Corps photograph #521541, Marine Corps History Division, Quantico, VA.

operate as a "flying column" without communications or supplies once it passed the midpoint of its assigned route. A two-mile long supply train of trucks, automobiles, mule carts, pack mules, and a caterpillar tractor followed in the wake of the main column. The Marines proceeded slowly along the main road. The Dominican insurgents had sabotaged bridges and railroad tracks on their retreat to impede the Americans' progress toward Santiago. At one ravine, the Dominicans had destroyed a 300-ft bridge, so the Marines crossed the ravine using an improvised trestle. The resourceful troops nevertheless confronted an array of obstacles as they trudged across the rough terrain. Forcing the Marines to walk secured tactical advantages for the insurgents by delaying the troops' advance and leaving them vulnerable to Dominican attack.

The northern resistance began at Las Trencheras, a defensive outcropping where insurgents had built a defensive network of trenches. The site had long been held by revolutionary armies, because government troops had never successfully captured the ridge, Dominicans considered it impenetrable (McPherson 41). As Pendleton's column approached, Marine officers watched the armed insurgents' movements through their field glasses and judged artillery to be the best means to counterattack. The next morning, Captain Chandler Campbell's 13th and 29th Companies hauled the battery into position on a ridge overlooking the road. The artillery fired 40 rounds while Captain Arthur Marix's 1st Battalion, supported by Major Melville Shaw's 2nd Battalion, advanced slowly through the jungle foliage. The insurgents, impervious to the artillery barrage, concentrated heavy fire on the closing ranks. Sergeant Major Thomas Carney reported that "the whole hillside was enshrouded in a pall of smoke through which the flashes of rifles constantly stabbed like light[n]ing through a cloud" (Carney 2). Suddenly, he perceived through the smoke a long line of bayonets gleaming in the morning sun. Pendleton's chief of staff, Major Robert Dunlap, sounded his whistle, and with a wild cheer, the Marine infantry units charged up the slope. The supporting artillery and machine gun platoon continued to suppress enemy fire, allowing the Marines to perform quick rushes and rout the insurgents from the trenches. Within 45 minutes, they seized the dominating ridge and drove the rebels into retreat.

On July 3, Pendleton's column again encountered resistance at Guayacanas. Eighty Dominicans, having dug defensive trenches and constructed a roadblock of felled trees, awaited the Marines from a camouflaged position. Although the insurgents remained well concealed, Marine patrols had earlier captured a prisoner who provided accurate information about terrain and size of the Dominican force. Without any tactical alternative, the machine gun platoon carried their Benet-Mercier light machine guns within a few 100 yards of the trenches and opened fire. The Dominicans countered the automatic weapons with single-shot rifle fire, yet their assault was so intense that several Marines were killed within minutes (Carney 3). Pendleton, disregarding the advice of his chief of staff to remain with the artillery, advanced to the firing line. He surveyed the enemy's position and issued instructions for an enveloping movement. Although a direct frontal attack would almost certainly fail, he correctly predicted that small parties could approach through the jungle on the right and left sides and thereby secure a protected position from which to enfilade the enemy. Amidst the din of automatic weapons, the infantry charged from their flanked positions.

In the center Marine advance, where action was thickest, First Sergeant Roswell Winans was working a jam-prone Colt-Browning Model 1895 machine gun from an exposed position. "They seemed to be just missing me," he recalled. "I don't know how the other men felt, but I expected to be shot any minute and just wanted to do as much damage as possible to the enemy before cashing in" (qtd. in "Two Marines"). When the last round jammed in his weapon, Winans calmly inspected the gun, returned it to working order, and resumed firing for the remainder of the engagement. Meanwhile, Corporal Joseph Glowin set up his Benet-Mercier behind a fallen log and began firing on the enemy. Twice wounded, he continued his assault until other Marines forcibly dragged him from the front line to safety. For these exploits Winans and Glowin received Medals of Honor.

Having forced the entrenched snipers to retreat, the Marines loaded their wounded into the wagon train and resumed the drive toward Navarette, where the column joined the smaller Puerto Plata contingent, consisting of the 4th and 9th Companies as well as Marine detachments from the battleships *Rhode Island* and *New Jersey*. Under Pendleton's orders, the force had proceeded from Puerto Plata, a town about 80 mi east of Monte Cristi on the north coast. Although traversing a shorter distance than Pendleton's crew, the column followed a destroyed railroad course that was inaccessible to a supply train. Tasked with reconnecting Santiago with the port city and establishing a line of supply for the combined attack force, the Marines traveled as far as they could in four boxcars pulled by a dilapidated locomotive, which, in turn, pushed a flatcar carrying a 3-in. artillery piece. On June 29, Bearss' contingent encountered a Dominican force at La Cumbre, a critical position near Alta Mira where the railroad track passed through a 300-yard tunnel. The 4th Company scaled a nearby mountain trail and signaled the enemy presence approximately 3000 yards away. Captain Eugene Fortson unloaded his 3-in. gun and began shelling a shack overlooking the rebel lines. On the ground, a combination of frontal and flank attacks forced the insurgents to retreat. When the Dominicans quit their position and ran for the tunnel, Bearss gave chase with a detachment of 60 men. The major, furiously pumping a handcar, rushed into the dark tunnel entrance. Despite the possibility of ambush or worse, Bearss emerged safely from the railroad corridor to watch the rebels hasten toward Santiago (Dominican Republic).

The reunion of Marine columns at Navarette set up the final stage of the campaign: the capture of Santiago. Before the troops even made camp at the rendezvous point, a delegation approached and requested an audience with Pendleton. With the insurgents decimated and demoralized following three decisive but lopsided battles, the Dominicans negotiated terms for surrender, including a pardon for their leader, Arias. The agreement took effect on July 5, 1916, and the 4th Regiment peacefully entered the city of Santiago the following day.

This military success did not resolve the State Department's desire for a pro-American successor regime, however. Russell used financial leverage and threatened further military action to dissuade the Dominican congress from electing anyone unwilling to support U.S. demands. On July 25, the Dominicans thwarted Russell's coercive maneuvers and elected Dr. Francisco Henríquez y Carbajal as provisional president. When Henríquez arrived in the capital, the American Minister refused to recognize the election as valid until he submitted to U.S. conditions. Henríquez defended the Dominican right to manage its own affairs, so Russell impounded all government funds. The ensuing political stalemate lasted until November, when the State Department declared the establishment of a military government. Over the next 8 years, the Marine Corps acted as an army of occupation supporting a variable and sometimes oppressive American regime.

The army of occupation, 1917–1920

In the United States, press coverage of events in Hispaniola touted American military operations for restoring peace on the troubled island. Despite the challenges of unmapped terrain, sabotaged roads and railroads, the Marines had exhibited tactical skill and professional discipline. Furthermore, the success at Santiago helped to validate the Marine Corps as an elite fighting force ready for deployment on behalf of American foreign affairs. Walker Vick, the former Receiver General for Dominican customs, told the *New York Times* that he regretted only that the United States had not intervened sooner. This high regard represented a welcome change for the Marine Corps, whose very existence had come under attack in Congress less than a decade before.

In the Dominican Republic, by contrast, public opinion of the Marine Corps deteriorated rapidly. The Marines' mission, clearly defined during the initial campaign, grew murky after the capture of Santiago and declaration of military government. Whereas U.S. Marines and sailors initially performed brief land excursions to quell the revolution, their operations evolved to encompass long-term occupation and the management of internal political affairs. Consequently, the rules of engagement changed as well. Tasked with maintaining order, the troops engaged in counterinsurgency operations for which they were neither prepared nor trained to handle. Moreover, the long duration and lack of measurable progress in pacifying an increasingly hostile population resulted, for many Marines, in a breakdown in the distinctions separating civilians from enemy insurgents.

Many Dominicans opposed the American occupation from the start. On the same day that Knapp declared the U.S. military government, First Lieutenant Ernest Williams led an assault on the *fortaleza* at San Francisco de Macorís where Juan Pérez, a local governor and supporter of Arias, and his followers had taken a stand and refused to surrender their weapons. As district commander, Williams initially dispatched a message to the governor demanding that he abandon the fort, but the Dominican allegedly scrawled "Come and get me!" across the ultimatum in reply (Considine 16). In plotting a course of action, Williams conferred with other Marines who argued that the fort would require at least an infantry battalion and artillery battery to take. The district commander, however, determined an alternate course of action. Early the following evening, he led a detachment of 12 Marines from the 31st and 47th Companies in a surprise attack. Williams and his crew rushed the gate, and a brief but intense battle ensued. Within minutes, the detachment of Marines, eight of them wounded, gained control of the fort as well as 100 prisoners confined therein.[5] Williams received a Medal of Honor for his actions.

Williams's successful operation proved the exception rather than the rule in the Dominican campaign. Initially Marine officers focused on establishing garrisons in major cities, disarming the civilian population, and defeating known insurgent leaders, whose capture American commanders believed would curtail rebellion; however, the confiscation of weapons and ammunition failed to stem insurgency in a society that placed a high social value on gun ownership. Neither officers nor enlisted Marines understood Dominican culture. Few could speak Spanish, and most held then-prevailing racist views that upheld whiteness as the epitome of cultural and

Figure 5.2 U.S. Marines searching Dominican homes for arms. Official Marine corps photograph #5012, Marine Corps History Division, Quantico, VA.

intellectual achievement. With a patronizing sense of superiority, many Marines approached their service in the Dominican Republic, a country whose populations Military Governor Harry Knapp characterized as being "almost all touched with the tarbrush," as an extended colonialist endeavor to "civilize" the natives (qtd. in Evans 123).

Early in the campaign, Marine operational reports indicate that captains or lieutenants led combat patrols of 40 or 50 men in response to collected intelligence. After the first year, operations transitioned to smaller patrols spread thinly across the countryside. In many areas, the rainforest underbrush was so thick that Marine patrols limited their searches to established trails. Commanded by noncommissioned officers, these detachments consisted of 10–15 Marines marching single file along narrow footpaths. To avoid ambush, Marines sometimes conducted reconnaissance by fire. When approaching terrain ideal for an attack, the patrol point guard would shoot into the jungle, tricking insurgents into returning fire and exposing their position before the Marines had fully entered the trap (Bickle 121). This practice was not without its dangers, however. In August 1918, insurgents ambushed a patrol of four Marines as they were rounding a trail bend and crossing a stream. Only Private Thomas Rushforth survived the attack. Bleeding from more than six wounds, including a severed right hand by a machete blow, Rushforth managed to mount a horse and escape amid enemy gunfire. Despite being gravely wounded, the Marine returned to camp, reported the skirmish, and asked to lead a rescue party back to the scene of the attack (Dominican Republic 1). As the occupation dragged on, the military forces grew increasingly edgy and frustrated.

The military government established a local constabulary to assist with the counterinsurgency campaign, but the Guardia Nacional Dominicana struggled due to the lack of funds and a shortage of competent officers and recruits. As with cabinet positions in the military government, no members of the Dominican elite would submit to a commissioned post in the Guardia Nacional. Consequently, many recruits came from the lower classes. The brigade commander looked to Marines to organize the Guardia until such time as Dominicans could be trained and found competent to fulfill leadership positions, but only 1 of the first 13 American officers was a commissioned Marine officer. Unlike in Haiti, American officers in the Guardia did not draw double pay, making it difficult to attract even noncommissioned officers to the organization. Neglected by the military government and despised by Dominican residents, who considered Guardia members traitors to the nationalist cause, the constabulary force was neither large enough nor well enough trained to effectively assist the Marines in policing the country (Tillman).

Further, the expansion of the Marine Corps in Europe during World War I siphoned many of the best officers from the Caribbean, and those remaining or newly deployed to the Dominican Republic were inadequately trained and ill-prepared for counterinsurgency operations. Many Marines resented what they perceived as a slight in their service record and a hindrance to their potential for career advancement (Evans 109). The enemy remained elusive, and Marines began to regard all Dominicans with suspicion. Throughout the occupation, Marine leaders asserted that their primary goal was to protect a law-abiding majority against a minority of insurgents. They deliberately labeled opponents "bandits" to emphasize this distinction and to uphold the righteous aims of American efforts, but when women and children began accompanying guerrilla bands in 1918, the American troops found it extremely challenging to distinguish insurgents from refugees and ordinary inhabitants in rural precincts (Evans, 124, 137). Many turned against the population they were assigned to protect, meting out gratuitous punishment regardless of an individual's guerrilla involvement.

Complaints against Marine conduct surged as it became common for patrols to burn rural homesteads and personal possessions. If the inhabitants fled, Marines often fired after them. The rationale for this practice, as Captain William Harlee explained, was the incorrect assumption that "People who are not bandits do not flee the approach of Marines" (qtd. in Evans 125). Not surprisingly, such brutal treatment created more insurgents and guerrilla supporters among previously uninvolved Dominicans. As one prominent Dominican explained, "When someone… was killed, his brothers joined the *gavilleros* (professional highwaymen) to get revenge on the Marines …. Some joined the ranks inspired by patriotism, but most of them joined the ranks inspired by hate, fear or revenge" (qtd. in Evans 126).

Popular protest in the United States

For all intents and purposes, World War I pushed Marine actions in the Caribbean into the background. The declaration of armistice in 1918, however, meant that German interest in Hispaniola no longer represented an imminent threat to U.S. national security. Accusations of Marine atrocities, which peaked during this period, further discredited the American occupation. Dominican peasants charged the occupying forces with committing rape, torture, imprisonment, and even murder. Among the most egregious culprits of Marine misconduct was Captain Charles Merkel, who in 1918 faced a military tribunal for allegedly beating and disfiguring one Dominican prisoner and ordering four others shot during patrol operations near Hato Mayor. Reported to the authorities by his own men, Merkel committed suicide while awaiting trial in Marine custody (Folse). Organized opposition to the American occupation grew rapidly in response. Government representatives from Brazil, Uruguay, Colombia, and Spain condemned the intervention and advised the United States to end the occupation, while Latin American newspapers launched a determined campaign against U.S. policy in the Dominican Republic. In the United States, articles on the occupation appeared regularly in *The Nation*, *Journal of International Relations*, and *Reforma Social*, a New York-based publication distributed throughout Latin

America. This groundswell of anti-imperialist agitation erupted in popular backlash against American policy during the 1920 presidential campaign.

By highlighting the Marine Corps' role in enforcing U.S. occupation in Hispaniola, Senator Warren G. Harding followed the lead of outspoken editorials in *The Nation*. As early as 1917, the leftist weekly magazine had pronounced the United States guilty of "[i]mperialism of the rankest kind" for imposing foreign rule by force of arms. The periodical devoted increasing attention to the topic after World War I, when critical essays by Oswald Garrison Villard, founder of the Anti-Imperialist League and editor of *The Nation*; James Weldon Johnson, president of the National Association of American Colored People; and foreign affairs journalists Lewis S. Gannett and Kincheloe Robbins censured the military government in Santo Domingo for its oppressive treatment of local residents. Harding therefore evoked a spate of evidence when, quoting nearly verbatim from *The Nation*, he called his opponent's utterances "the first official admission of the rape of Haiti and Santo Domingo by the present Administration" (qtd. in "Constitution or League").

Opponents of the American military government considered the provost court system and censorship of the press especially egregious. Throughout the occupation, all insurgent-related crimes funneled through the military courts, where the Marine Corps exercised wide powers of arrest as provost marshals. Many captains and lieutenants serving in this capacity did not speak Spanish and received no special training, yet wielded the authority to detain and sentence suspected enemies. Prisoners were occasionally shot without trial or killed while trying to escape, prompting military authorities in Santo Domingo to admonish Marines in the field to secure captives more carefully so as not to raise suspicion of judicial misconduct (Evans 125). Even with efforts to ensure due process, military records indicate that court officials did little to hide their derision for Dominican defendants and complainants, favoring instead the word of their American compatriots as a matter of course (Calder 128–129).

In 1920, the case of Captain Charles Buckalew spurred intense criticism of the military courts in the Dominican press, inciting outrage and leading some social clubs to close in response to rising U.S.-Dominican tensions. Dominican lawyer Pelegrín Castillo accused constabulary Captain Buckalew with murdering four Dominican prisoners and committing other atrocities, such as crushing the testicles of a suspected guerilla with a stone. When the prosecution's witnesses suddenly "voluntarily recanted and acknowledged that they falsely testified," the provost court dismissed the charges due to unreliable evidence (McPherson 96). In addition, Castillo faced a military tribunal for allegedly making false accusations. The provost court eventually exonerated him, and mounting evidence against Buckalew compelled the military court to bring the Marine officer to trial. Despite strong indications of guilt—including a partial confession—American officials again acquitted the Marine captain on technical grounds. As historian Bruce Calder has observed, the defendant's statement largely corroborated

Castillo's charges, suggesting that the original witnesses may have recanted their testimonies under duress (126).

Press censorship emerged as another flashpoint of controversy in the summer of 1920, when the trial of Dominican poet Fabio Fiallo elicited indignation and criticism throughout Latin America and the United States. Under American occupation, Dominican newspapers could not legally publish commentary on military government actions nor could they print evocative concepts such as "national," "freedom of thought," or "General" as a title for Dominican leaders (Munro 321). Infractions landed offenders in the American provost courts. In July 1920, Dominican newspapers published several stridently hostile articles and speeches that leaders delivered during "patriotic week," a fundraising event for the oppositional movement. Several individuals, including Fiallo, landed in jail and were convicted by a military commission. Their sentences initially remained a secret, and rumors swirled that they had been condemned to death. The story spread throughout Latin America, and news of the injustice reached Washington by way of Mexico City and Uruguay. Although the verdict had been exaggerated, Fiallo's sentence remained extreme. The poet was levied a $5000 fine and began serving a 3-year term of imprisonment at hard labor. The State Department endeavored to arrange Fiallo's release, but he remained imprisoned for several weeks and was subsequently freed under the condition of military surveillance.

The following month, Harding's vehement campaign rhetoric thrust Dominican allegations of Marine brutality and oppressive military governance into the political limelight. He intended the charges to reflect poorly on the Wilson administration, especially Franklin D. Roosevelt and his superior, Secretary of the Navy Josephus Daniels. The strategy worked. Almost immediately, newspapers and publications that previously supported the occupation or failed to report on it assumed a more critical stance. Then, in the closing weeks of the national election, a private letter written by Brigadier General George Barnett, Commandant of the Marine Corps, leaked to the press. The missive, directed to the commander of Marine forces in Haiti, seemed to corroborate the worst charges of troop misconduct. Referring to the proceedings of a recent court martial, Barnett expressed shock and dismay over what he believed to be the "indiscriminate killing of natives" in Hispaniola (qtd. in *The Nation*). Journalists clamored for an official investigation and immediate withdrawal of U.S. troops. Daniels responded to the negative publicity by ordering an internal investigation, but the findings failed to quell public protest. Even *The New York Times*, which a few months earlier had printed a front-page editorial against Harding's nomination, issued regular updates on the Republican candidate's charges, Roosevelt's campaign rebuttals, and the Wilson administration's formal inquiry into the matter.

Harding won the presidential election in a landslide victory. Receiving nearly twice the popular vote as the Democratic ticket, he appealed to war-weary Americans who craved peace and domestic prosperity in the aftermath of the Great War. Exposing the failures and vulnerabilities of military occupation, the election marked a turning point in U.S. military action in Hispaniola. The persistence of armed rebellion 4 years after the initial intervention and reports of oppressive American governance spurred opposition to the occupation, while charges of atrocities further hardened popular opinion and damaged the reputation of the U.S. Marine Corps. The impact was far greater in the Dominican Republic than in Haiti, where U.S. troops would remain until 1932. Efforts toward U.S. withdrawal from the Dominican Republic began immediately; the outgoing Wilson administration submitted a proposal for U.S. departure before the end of the year. Although the initial plan was unsuccessful, Harding's administration resumed negotiations with Dominican leaders the following spring and enacted a complete transfer of power by September 1924.

Withdrawal

Harding's secretary of state, Charles Evans Hughes, entered protracted negotiations with Dominican representatives over the terms of U.S. withdrawal. The State Department encountered resistance from both the Dominicans and from the military government until Brigadier General Harry Lee, a veteran with 24 years of service in the Marine Corps, replaced the much-maligned Rear Admiral Thomas Snowden and his successor Rear Admiral Samuel Robison as military governor. Acting as brigade commander as well as military governor, Lee formulated a plan that would lay the groundwork for a peaceful transition of power. He reduced the 2nd Brigade garrisons of the northern and southern districts to the capital and other principal cities, and he dedicated significant resources toward improving the Guardia Nacional Dominicana as the primary peacekeeper in anticipation of U.S. withdrawal.

The centerpiece of Lee's plan was the reorganization of *policía* training to reform the Guardia Nacional. He aimed to train an enlisted force of 1200, replace the remaining 44 American officers, and assign Dominican forces to all Marine outposts by the end of the following year. To this end, he planned to bring in 24 Dominican officers and all enlisted men for formal training at Haina, a new officer candidate school established in 1921. Marine officers oversaw the accelerated training program, but Buenaventura Cabral, a regional governor, assumed command of the constabulary. Under the new system, all officers and enlisted men would complete 6 months of training at Haina and an additional 6 months of supervised field work before advancing from probationary status. With instruction in counterinsurgency tactics, the Dominican constabulary organized elite anti-guerrilla outfits and began conducting successful patrols. In time, these paramilitary auxiliaries, renamed the Policía Nacional Dominicana, would take over Marine outposts, thereby allowing the American troops to garrison in principal cities.

Figure 5.3 Acting Military Governor, Brigadier General Harry Lee, USMC (first row, far right) and Executive and Military Staffs. Official Marine Corps photograph #530542, Marine Corps History Division, Quantico, VA.

Lee also announced a more benevolent policy toward the Dominican civilian population. He curbed the excesses of the provost courts, investigated charges of Marine misconduct, and ordered culprits to trial. He made the guards subject to civilian law. He also began an intensive indoctrination program for the troops. His primary purpose was to convince the Marines that Dominicans were not the enemy and that their mission was to make the U.S. withdrawal a success:

> The Forces of the United States did not enter this Republic to make war on the Dominican people. Far from it! ... It has been throughout the occupation to this time of returning the government to the Dominican people an unselfish object, looking only toward the betterment of the Dominican people and at great expense to the United States.
>
> ... Now ask yourself if your conduct in your attitude toward the Dominican people is as worthy as that of your country, and bear in mind that your conduct represents the United States in the eyes of the Dominican people (qtd. in Lane 6–7).[6]

Lee ensured that subordinate commanders followed his rigorous training plan. Weekly reports from these years include program summaries and preliminary self-assessments for the indoctrination of enlisted Marines. Film screenings and sports, especially baseball, eased troop boredom and contributed to more harmonious Marine-civilian cooperation. Such measures not only worked to contain the civilian population's disaffection but also helped to soothe the many grievances Dominicans had harbored against the occupying forces since their arrival in 1916.

The guerrilla conflict ended in the spring of 1922, after the United States and Dominican Republic signed an agreement terminating the military occupation. This definite plan for withdrawal hastened the drawdown. Equally important was the internal evaluation of the operational effectiveness and subsequent recalibration of Marine policy and tactical procedure. For instance, Lieutenant Colonel Charles Miller, chief of staff of the 2nd Brigade during the final years of occupation, identified five separate groups within the Dominican resistance: professional highwaymen or *gavilleros*; discontented politicians who used crime to advance their personal ambitions; unemployed laborers driven by poverty; peasants recruited under duress; and ordinary criminals. Such analytical writing not only generated invaluable insights into the personal motivations of guerrilla fighters but also inspired novel responses and solutions from the military government. Most of the insurgents Miller identified surrendered to American forces in exchange for nearly total amnesty.

Conclusion

In the immediate aftermath of World War I, U.S. society shifted its moral orientation to a more negative opinion of imperialism, patently rejecting military invention as a justifiable course of diplomatic action. As the most visible imprint of U.S. presence in the island republics, the Marine Corps came under intense scrutiny for its apparent lack of discipline. In the United States, formal investigations—one by a naval court of inquiry and one by a special committee of the United States Senate—gave vivid detail to a litany of stories involving Marine misconduct. In the process of developing counterinsurgency tactics in the Dominican Republic, the Marine Corps committed—and learned from—its mistakes. Nevertheless, the stalemate of guerrilla warfare, oppressive policies of press censorship, and sensational reports surrounding Marine abuses overshadowed its efficiency in the early phase of the intervention and produced conditions by 1920, in which military occupation was no longer tenable.

Notes

1. The views expressed in this article are those of the author and do not necessarily reflect the official policy of any U.S. Government organization.
2. Although Roosevelt's reputation in U.S.-Latin American affairs today rests largely with the Good Neighbor Policy, a foreign policy initiative which pledged nonintervention and equitable trade agreements in the 1930s and 1940s, the future-president did not espouse such progressive thinking with regard to Wilsonian internationalism.

3. Contemporary audiences understood that the assistant secretary of the navy referred to in Harding's speech was Franklin D. Roosevelt, the Democratic vice-presidential nominee.
4. For more on Germany's "secret war" in the Americas, see Friedrich E. Schuler, *Secret Wars and Secret Policies in the Americas, 1842–1929* (University of New Mexico Press, 2010).
5. Pérez retreated, stealing a train for his getaway. Rapidly converging detachments of the 4th Regiment intercepted and captured him, and Pérez was sentenced by a U.S. military court.
6. *Santo Domingo* (n.p., 1922).

Works cited

"Constitution or League – Harding," *New York Times*, 18 September 1920, p. 11.
"Two Marines Win Medal of Honor," *New York Times*, 18 March 1917, p. 10.
Bickle, Keith B. *Mars Learning: The Marine Corps' Development of Small Wars Doctrine, 1915–1940*. Westview Press, 2002.
Boot, Max. *The Savage Wars of Peace: Small Wars and the Rise of American Power*. Basic Books, 2003.
Calder, Bruce J. *The Impact of Intervention: The Dominican Republic during the U.S. Occupation of 1916–1924*. University of Texas Press, 1984.
Caperton, William B. Letter to William S. Benson. William B. Caperton Papers, Library of Congress, Washington, D.C. 15 June 1916
Carney, Thomas P. "Adventures of 'San Diego's Own' Fighting through Santo Domingo," unpublished manuscript, 1-5. Gordon L. Pruner Papers, Historical Resources Branch, Marine Corps History Division, Quantico, VA.
Considine, Bob. "The Marines Have Landed," *American Weekly Washington Post & Times Herald*, 5 October 1958, pp. 7–9.
Cross, Graham. *The Diplomatic Education of Franklin D. Roosevelt, 1882–1933*. Palgrave Macmillan, 2012.
Dominican Republic Subject Files, *Historical Resources Branch, Marine Corps History Division*, Quantico, VA.
Evans, Stephen S., ed. U.S. Marines and Irregular Warfare, *1898–2007: Anthology and Selected Bibliography*. Marine Corps University Press, 2008.
Folse, Mark. "The Tiger of Seibo: Charles F. Merkel, George C. Thorpe, and the Dark Side of Marine Corps History," *Marine Corps History*, vol. 1, issue 2, 2016, pp. 4–18.
Harding, Sauthor G. Speeches of Senator Warren G. Harding of Ohio, *Republican Candidate for President: From His Acceptance of the Nomination to October 1, 1920*. Republican National Committee, 1920.
Healy, David. *Drive to Hegemony: The United States in the Caribbean, 1898–1917*. University of Wisconsin Press, 1988.
Henríquez Ureña, Max. *Los yanquis en Santo Domingo: la verdad de los hechos comprobada por datos y documentos oficiales*. M. Aguilar, 1931.
Lane, Rufus H. *Santo Domingo*, 1922. Santo Domingo: n.p., 1922.
McPherson, Allan. *The Invaded: How Latin Americans and Their Allies Fought and Ended U.S. Occupation*. Oxford University Press, 2014.
Munro, Dana G. *Intervention and Dollar Diplomacy in the Caribbean, 1900–1921*. Princeton University Press, 1964.

Pendleton, Joseph H. "Memorandum (Dominican Republic)," Joseph H. Pendleton Papers, Historical Resources Branch, Marine Corps History Division, Quantico, VA. 24 June 1916.

Roosevelt, Theodore. "The Roosevelt Corollary to the Monroe Doctrine." *Latin America and the United States: A Documentary History*, edited by Robert H. Holden and Eric Zolovs, Oxford University Press, 2000.

Schoenrich, Otto. "The Present American Intervention in Santo Domingo and Haiti." *The Journal of International Relations*, vol. 11, issue 1, July 1920, pp. 45–62.

Schuler, Friedrich E. *Secret Wars and Secret Policies in the Americas, 1842–1929*. University of New Mexico Press, 2010.

Tillman, Ellen D. *Dollar Diplomacy by Force*. University of North Carolina Press, 2015.

Wise, Frederic M. *A Marine Tells It To You*. J.H. Sears & Company, Inc., 1929.

Part III
Human rights and gender

6 Black women writers in the Americas

The struggle for human rights in the context of coloniality

Isabel Caldeira

Introduction

To address the topic—"Black Women Writers in the Americas: the Struggle for Human Rights in the Context of Coloniality"—three theoretical premises have been selected: [1](1) Aníbal Quijano's "coloniality of power" and "coloniality of knowledge" ("Coloniality of Power");[2] (2) María Lugones' "coloniality of gender" in the "modern/colonial gender system" ("The Coloniality of Gender"), which implicates "intersectionality" (Kimberlé Crenshaw); and (3) Feminism and its approach to human rights.

From its inception, Feminism has been known for its struggle to obtain a more humane and equitable society. The rights of women and of non-conforming sexual identities are all human rights, and any sort of discrimination contravenes the essence of the very concept of human rights. We owe to Black U.S. American women the gesture of critical disruption that questioned Western hegemonic feminism and paved the way to the inclusion of other women in feminist struggles—Black, working-class, "Third World," and so forth. By emphasizing the need to problematize hegemonic ways of knowing in struggles for equity, Patricia Hill Collins indeed reminds us that the suppression of "the knowledge produced by any oppressed group makes it easier for dominant groups to rule because the seeming absence of an independent consciousness in the oppressed can be taken to mean that subordinate groups willingly collaborate in their own victimization" (5). To Black feminists, we also owe the intersectional lens that helps to disentangle the divisiveness of identities—race, gender, class, sexuality, age, and so forth—and to disclose how the interplay of these socially constructed variables perpetuate relations of power, domination, and normalization that serve the divisive interests of coloniality and the violation of human rights.

Resistance and not victimization is also a very important concept in feminist movements and feminist theory. In the Americas, women of color have been on the forefront of resistance against repression and inequality. As the Chicana feminist theorist Chela Sandoval observes, in those struggles often "women of color become survivors in a dynamic which places them as the final 'other' in a complex of power moves" (64). Yet, while the system of interlocked power not only forces them into the margins through the destructiveness of sexism, racism, and classism, it also "provides them visions, intuitions and values which work to charge the definitions of 'liberation' and of 'feminism' with new and different meanings" (64). As Mary DeShazer meanwhile argues, their resistance is an achievement of citizenship: "their goals in challenging the system extend beyond self-interest toward a shared commitment to an alternative world view that nurtures new citizen-subjects" (10). In addition, Jacqueline Jones Royster writes,

> Among the most persistent desires that human beings over the course of human history have exhibited are desires for: freedom, justice, and the capacity to function with agency and authority within an accommodating environment. These, in the United States of America, are deemed our civil rights, and we have slowly come to understand that in global context, they are our human rights. (15)

Berta E. Hernández-Truyol and Mariana Ribeiro further reflect on human rights to question the "Universal Declaration on Human Rights" that separates civil and political rights from social, economic, and cultural rights.[3] The scholars certainly argue for a restructured model that embraces the indivisibility and interdependence of human rights and instead propose the incorporation of

> [t]he feminist critique that the human rights agenda as crafted fails to consider the condition and needs of women, the Asian critique that challenges the framework as Western, the third world critique that underscores the system as Northern and industrialized, and the anti-colonialist critique that notes the structure was crafted during colonial days and has not accommodated changes. (Hernández-Truyol and Ribeiro 32) This implies to question any manifestation of hegemony, to detach critical thinking "from the perspective of coloniality" (Mignolo, "DELINKING" 451) and no longer accept the totalizing ideas coming from the European center, since the "crooked rhetoric that naturalizes 'modernity' as a universal global process and point of arrival hides its darker side, the constant reproduction of 'coloniality'" (450).

Hernández-Truyol and Ribeiro similarly problematize the international model of human rights, approved by the so-called developed nations, for the imprint of the positioning of its writers at the center, thus presenting the subject of universal human rights as a "white, Anglo, Western, European, Judeo-Christian, educated, propertied, heterosexual, able-bodied male norm" (32). It is true that regional agreements such as the American Convention on Human Rights, the European Convention for the Protection of Human Rights and Fundamental Freedoms, and the African Charter on Human and Peoples' Rights are widely acknowledged for promoting important human rights agendas. However, it is also true that human rights international agreements focused on specific groups such as The Convention on the Elimination of All Forms of Discrimination Against Women or the Convention on the Elimination of All Forms of Race Discrimination enjoy limited support while nations that define themselves as global defenders of universal human rights, for instance, the United States has not ratified the agreements. Hernández-Truyol and Ribeiro also point out that though apparently progressive, the agreements approach the socially constructed categories of sex and race as independent from one another: CEDAW is silent on race and CERD is silent on sex (38). An intersectional lens necessary to analyze how different forms of social discrimination interact to create detrimental hierarchies and social inequality that may impede peoples of color, specifically, women of color to attain human rights is missing in these documents. It is not the same to be discriminated against because one is recognized as a "woman," or as a "Black lesbian," or as an undocumented female worker of color.

Intersectional sensitization and gender production

It is worth pointing out that coloniality—the logic of oppression and exploitation as the invisible and constitutive side of cultured European modernity continues to produce racial and sexual difference through the racialization and sexualization of labor, as well as the invention of forms of labor and sexual control. Though coloniality is related to colonialism, they are indeed distinct. Historical colonialism as such (e.g., territorial occupation) may largely have had its end, while coloniality (in the form of surviving colonial structures of domination) goes on and permeates all the aspects of social existence and perpetuates detrimental social, geo- and ethno-cultural identities. Quijano calls this persistent logic "coloniality of power" that is also and inevitably a "coloniality of knowledge" since the Eurocentric model of thinking continues to be promoted as the only valid, objective, and universal narrative while dismissing other forms of non-Western knowledge as subjective and inadequate.

In discussing Quijano's concept of coloniality of power, María Lugones argues that the intersection of race and gender that he proposes is based on global, Eurocentered, capitalist notions of gender, and therefore too narrow to understand the oppressive modern/colonial constructions of gender. The philosopher indeed proposes that colonialism "created very different arrangements for colonized males and females than for white bourgeois colonizers" ("Heterosexualism" 186). In other words, Quijanos' coloniality of power precludes an understanding of the ways in which, for instance, non-white colonized women have been subjugated and disempowered historically: understanding these features of the organization of gender in the modern/colonial gender system—the biological dimorphism, the patriarchal and heterosexual organizations of relations—is crucial to an understanding of the differential gender arrangements along "racial" lines. Biological dimorphism, heterosexual patriarchy are all characteristics of what I call the "light" side of the colonial/modern organization of gender. Hegemonically, these are written large over the meaning of gender. Quijano seems not to be aware of his accepting this hegemonic meaning of gender (Lugones, "The Coloniality" 2).

In order to develop a more inclusive concept of coloniality that incorporates a more complex and diverse understanding of gender, Lugones borrows the concept of intersectionality from the tradition of Black feminist thought to reveal, she writes, "what is not seen when categories such as gender and race are conceptualized as separate from each other" ("Heterosexualism" 192). Intersectionality brings to light aspects that remain invisible when research is unidimensional by making visible those who are victimized in terms of both categories (Crenshaw). While focusing on the conceptualization of how the control of gender, race, class, and sexuality was created within the matrix of colonial power during the European capitalist conquest and colonization of the world, Lugones proposes that the dehumanization of colonized non-white women and men correlates with the creation of "white bourgeois womanhood" ("Heterosexualism" 202) and the introduction of gender differences, dualisms, and binaries into cultures/traditions/communities were there were none" ("The Coloniality" 377). The capitalist colonial order produced a violent social order of hierarchical subjugation and degradation that turned some people, among them colonized Indigenous, Black, and other non-white colonized peoples into beasts of burden (202), while, even if given close to no political, economic, and social rights, white women were constructed as feminine, childlike, pure, small, and helpless (202–203). As for compulsory heterosexuality, its dominance in the colonial system, and its role in the construction of a power system, in her essay "Heterosexualism and the Colonial/Modern Gender System," Lugones poses two important questions:

> How do we understand heterosexuality not merely as normative but as consistently perverse when violently exercised across the colonial modern gender system so as to construct a worldwide system of power? How do we come to understand the very meaning of heterosexualism as tied to a persistently violent domination that marks the flesh multiply by accessing the bodies of the unfree in differential patterns devised to constitute them as the tortured materiality of power? (187–188)

Returning to the work of two feminists, the Nigerian Oyéronké Oyewùmí, and the Native American Paula Allen Gunn, Lugones mentions the absence of a hierarchical social organization based on gender, as the one Europeans spread throughout, respectively, in Yoruba society and Amerindian nations.[4] Genderization of labor was after all one of the constituent factors of capitalism. Yet, Lugones' important revision of Quijano's "coloniality of power" by means of intersectionality does more than just reveal the precarious position that non-white peoples occupy in the Euro-centered capitalist model of power. While the philosopher aims "to make visible the instrumentality of the colonial/modern gender system in subjecting ... both women and men of color – in all domains of existence" ("The Coloniality" 1), in reality her main concern is another. Lugones seeks to grasp the indifference, and more importantly, the construction of the indifference that men "who have been racialized as inferior, exhibit to the systematic violences inflicted upon women of color" (1). She elucidates,

> The indifference is found both at the level of everyday living and at the level of theorizing of both oppression and liberation. The indifference seems to me not just one of not seeing the violence because of the categorical separation of race, gender, class, and sexuality. That is, it does not seem to be only a question of epistemological blinding through categorical separation. (1)

For Lugones, it is not enough to try to "arouse in those men who have themselves been targets of violent domination and exploitation, any recognition of their complicity or collaboration with the violent domination of women of color" (1). The theorist actually denounces these men of collaboration with the violent system that perpetuates global domination of women of color. Based on Lugones' problematization of this complicity, one can more explicitly ask: what about the violence that these men themselves perpetrate against non-white women, more specifically, against Black women? This question will be examined further to join the decolonial turn, which as Nelson Maldonado-Torres states,

> refers to efforts at rehumanizing the world, to breaking hierarchies of difference that dehumanize subjects and communities and that destroy nature, and to the production of counter-discourses, counter-knowledges, counter-creative acts, and counter-practices that seek to dismantle coloniality and to open up multiple other forms of being in the world. (10)

In a 2008 publication, Madina Tlostanova reflects on the colonized female in the Soviet colonies in Central Asia and the Caucasus. Aligning herself with Lugones' theoretical arguments, and, like Lugones, also recurring to the contributions of O. Oyewúmi on the culture and language of the precolonial Yoruba and Gunn Allen on Indigenous women, she extends her analysis to the Russian empire. Here, Tlostanova identifies colonial policies and practices identical to the West, but she recognizes important specificities to emphasize the need to deconstruct the Western feminist perspective, since it does not apply or conform to other social and cultural contexts. By appropriating Gloria Anzaldúa's metaphor, Tlostanova refers to the forms of internal colonialism and imperial dependence as the colonial "herida" still "abierta" (still open colonial wound)[5] that affects the formation of subjectivities while forming interpersonal interaction in Latin America, Central Asia, and the Caucaus. We do not live in a postcolonial world. Resonating with Tlostanova, Lugones similarly states, coloniality is recognizable today by relating to gender relations and intersubjectivities, calling for the rejection of the modern gender system "to perform a transformation of communal relations" ("The Coloniality" 370). Oyéronké Oyewùmí, in *The Invention of Women*, furnishes Lugones with clear arguments on this matter, as she asserts, "gender was not an organizing principle in Yoruba society prior to colonization by the West" (Oyewùmí 31); "the fundamental category 'woman' – which is foundational in Western gender discourses – simply did not exist in Yorùbáland prior to its sustained contact with the West." (ix). "In pre-colonial Yorùbá society," Oyewùmí adds, "body-type was not the basis of social hierarchy: males and females were not ranked according to anatomic distinction" (xii). She concludes, "Gender was simply not inherent in human social organization." (xii). Looking at the present-day Yorùbá society, however, Oyewùmí finds it as a product of the colonial past, "because Yorùbá life, past and present, has been translated into English to fit the Western pattern of body-reasoning" (30). Oyewùmí adds, "The creation of 'women' as a category was one of the very first accomplishments of the colonial state" (124). Women were excluded from the colonial public sphere, defined by their anatomy and were from then on subordinated to men. The creation of the category had its detrimental impact on men too. "For females," as the author remarks, "colonization was a twofold process of racial inferiorization and gender subordination." (124) In "Toward a Decolonial Feminism," Lugones further underlines the process of dehumanization that the inferior gendered colonized had to undergo in the context of the Americas in relation to the superior, heterosexual, "white" European colonizers. Colonized men were simply categorized "as not-human-as-not-men," while colonized women became "females as not-human-as-not-women" (744). Colonized females were hypersexualized and turned into viragos, while males were humiliated in their sexuality, forced to be passive in the face of the females' rape. According to Lugones, colonial oppression caused the disaggregation of subjective–intersubjective relations among the colonized subjects. The logic of the "modern/colonial gender system" worked not only to subject both men and women of color, but also to disrupt the "bonds of practical solidarity" ("The Coloniality" 1). The dehumanization process also entailed the reproduction of patriarchal roles by colonized men and the construction of colonized women as actually "without gender," since they were sexually marked as female, but lacked the femininity that characterized white women (10). In other words, non-white colonized women were excluded from being gendered the way white women were.

In the modern/colonial world, masculinity was defined as power over women, but Black maleness, in parallel terms to Black femaleness (Lugones' "not-human-as-not-men" and "not-human-as-not-women"), was marked by ambiguity. Virility as defined in Western codes of masculinity was not fully accessible to Black males, as they were subjected to a process of "feminization" ("Toward" 744), among other things, by being forced to remain passive and disempowered whenever Black females were subjected to violence. Eventually, as history has shown, they were constructed as oversexualized Black men who represented a threat to white women's virginity.[6] Yet, the affirmation of masculinity too often involved the performance of violence over Black female bodies, unprotected by prevalent codes of white femininity and purity that may have warranted some form of protection. As Maldonado-Torres posits, for white masters the assertion of violence over colonized non-white female bodies "does not indicate any substantial amount of real power in a system where they do not even properly represent the idea of the feminine" (17). Devoid of the femininity conferred to white women, in fact, "there does not have to be an ultimate purpose for violence to be exercised over the black, native, and colonized women" (17).

Black female bodies as targets of violence

By using this theoretical framework, the logic of the "modern/colonial gender system" still influences present-day subjectivities and intersubjectivities, or permeates interrelations between the sexes, as reflected in symbolic representations in literary texts by Black women in the Americas. These texts present to us a persistent theme of violence against the female Black body perpetrated by Black males. In her widely read study of rape, Susan Brownmiller claims that the historical oppression of Black men has deprived them of many of the "legitimate" modes of expressing their male supremacist proclivities (26). The long-standing notion of the emasculated Black man was created by white scholarship in colonial contexts and adapted and reformulated at later stages. However, in the late 1960s, it was the Black woman who was accused of emasculating the Black man, precisely when more liberated women started to compete with men in the public space. Sociologist Calvin

C. Hernton devoted his book *The Sexual Mountain and Black Women Writers* (1987) to the defense of Black women writers who by that time were frequently attacked by Black male writers as "feminist bitches" for their negative depiction of male characters (47).[7] He rebukes Black men for their copious writing about the "castrating" Black females and recognizes that, "when black women write that black men are castrators and oppressors of black women, black men accuse the women of sowing seeds of 'division' in the black community" (47). *The Sexual Mountain* confronts Black men with their "feelings of envy, jealousy, resentment and paranoia" (47) because they feel threatened by successful women: "black men have a philosophy of manhood that relegates women to the back burner ... Therefore, it is perceived as an offense for black women to struggle on their own, let alone achieve something of their own. Such are the mortar and bricks out of which the mountain of sexism is constructed both before and on top of black women" (47).

Counterpointing the image of the emasculated Black man, we have the strong Black woman as—"too domineering, too strong, too aggressive, too outspoken, too castrating, too masculine" (Wallace 91), this would mean the myth of the superwoman as Michelle Wallace chooses to call it in *Black Macho and the Myth of the Super Woman*. Meanwhile, bell hooks also believes that the Moynihan report *The Negro Family: The Case for National Action* of 1965, which underlined the female dominance in African American families, and thus reproduced the stereotype of the Black matriarch, had a tremendous influence on Black men who felt Black women were their enemies. This divisive propaganda turned Black against Black. Indeed, in her trailblazing work *Ain't I a Woman*, bell hooks confronts the difficulty that Black women face in carrying out their struggle against Black men' sexism, because they are accused of disloyalty and of forgetting that their main enemy is racism. As she recalls, during the years of the Civil Rights Movement, "[f]ollowing the example of white male patriarchs, black men were obsessively concerned with asserting their masculinity while black women imitated the behavior of white women and were obsessive about femininity" (177). As Candice Linette Pipes argues in her work on abuse, resistance and recovery in Black women's literature,... the Black female body becomes the objectification of the Black male's castration, and it is for this reason that the harm of the Black female body seems to be central to the Black male's choice, in the context of modern rape, to rape Black women. The Black man's rape of the Black woman is symptomatic of larger racial and gender conflicts. The rape is at once an expression of racial self-hatred and an expression of gender self-worth, a denial of Blackness as valuable and an assertion that masculinity deserves power (98–99).

Coloniality of gender is clearly embedded in these intersubjectivities and feeds Black-on-Black violence. There is no need to dismiss the fact that Black men are also victims of the same modern colonial logic, thus persecuted equally by controlling stereotypes, such as the rapist, or the criminal. Importantly, the issue of sexual violence can be used to perpetuate racist perceptions of communities of color and justify discriminatory penalties. A historical consciousness of this risk often has silenced women of color on issues of domestic violence, as Kimberlé Crenshaw discusses in her study of intersectionality. Crenshaw writes, "while gang violence, homicide, and other forms of Black-on-Black crime have increasingly been discussed within African American politics, patriarchal ideas about gender and power preclude the recognition of domestic violence as yet another compelling incidence of Black-on-Black crime" (164). The barriers faced by these communities are built and strengthened through the work of the coloniality of gender, one vulnerability upon another creating several dimensions of disempowerment.

Literature as instrument of decoloniality

Heather Duerre Humann, in her book *Domestic Abuse in the Novels of African American Women* (2014), analyzes the issue of domestic abuse in contemporary African American female writers' fiction. She also refers to the silencing—once taboo—of intra-racial gender-based violence in the African American community, and the role of literature in shedding light on the subject and raising awareness about it. Humann's book comes in the wake of Hernton's *Sexual Mountain*. But, while Hernton identifies the roots of sexual violence in the hierarchies of race and gender built by the slave system, Humann examines the socially constructed system of abuse of women as a political issue, doing justice to the feminist assertion "the personal is political."

The purpose of analyzing fictional texts by Black women in the Americas is to examine the ways they address the intersectionality of questions of subjectivity/intersubjectivity, race, class, ethnicity, gender, and community within "the modern/colonial gender system," in order to unveil the reach and consequences of "coloniality." Marlene Nourbese Philip, Ntozake Shange, Gayl Jones, Jamaica Kincaid, or Edwidge Danticat are the writers chosen here. Their voices expose realities of repression, exploitation, and violence that find their logic within the same colonial frame. The critical stance and social solidarity they exhibit as writers-as-citizens (Caldeira 2017a; 2017b) contribute to contest a hegemonic production of knowledge about regions, groups, and individuals that have been historically dispossessed and deprived of full human rights. Writers-as-citizens cannot ethically afford to remain silent. They do not speak either for oppressed women, or in their name, but instead to rewrite history, empower women, and be accountable. Their writing calls forth solidarity and complicity from their readers to engage their active participation and intervention and enlarge the community of resistance.

In the history of the Americas, Black women have been besieged by negative stereotypes enmeshed in a colonial history: Mammy, Sapphire, Jezebel, bad woman, loose woman. Countering the negativity associated with their oversexualization, we have, on the one hand, the mother's cautionary advice in Jamaica Kincaid's text "Girl." Expressing cooperation with the mainstream morals and order, the mother declares, "this is how to behave in the presence of men who don't know you very well, and this way they won't recognize immediately the slut I have warned you against becoming" (4). Another example is the successive generations of mothers in Edwidge Danticat's *Breath, Eyes, Memory* (1994), who reproduce an old, Haitian, patriarchal ritual of control of their daughters' sexuality, when they turn 18. They test their virginity by inserting a finger in their vaginas to make sure the hymen is not broken.

As a counterpoint to these mothers' conservative attitudes, Nourbese Philip, the writer born in Tobago and based in Canada, entitles her book of essays intermingled with poetry *A Genealogy of Resistance* (1997). She boldly ascertains the long-standing traumatic mark of coloniality on Black women's lives, pinpointing the ways the patriarchal system in the colonial context targeted the Black female body. Unmasking language of all euphemistic, hypocritical, moralist veils, she boldly expresses the constant "uninvited forceful invasion of the space between the legs – rape" as a weapon of control (20). She is referring to the Black woman's body in the economy of the colonial plantation, and specifically to her sexual management and abuse. Philip relates the "inner space" with the "outer space"—the former serving the latter, i.e., the place of oppression. But this vision and management of the Black body is not the white man's prerogative alone (20). As Philip implies, "the 'black magic' of the white man's pleasure" is also "the 'bag o' sugar down dey' of the Black man's release" (77).

Ntozake Shange, the African American writer and artist, may be responsible for having led to a climax the topic of Black male violence against women. The staging of her dramatic poem (or "choreopoem," as she called it) of 1975, *for colored girls who have considered suicide/when the rainbow is enuf,* was a great success on Broadway. Notwithstanding, it elicited attacks from Black men who felt offended by her negative depictions of Black males. The intersectional poetic drama that identitifes friends and friends' friends as the main sources of sexual violence inflicted on Black women (17) establishes racism and sexim as the main sources of their distress. In general, the liberatory poem in which women reclaim their voices and bodies earned criticism from Black audiences that expressed their dismay for what they perceived as Shange's betrayal of her race.

In her novel *Sassafras, Cypress & Indigo* (1982), Shange narrates the story of Hilda Effania's three daughters, whose names echo memories of the plantations of the South: sassafrass, the second-largest export from the British colonies in North America after tobacco; the cypress, especially prized for its wood and indigo, a major crop through slave labor in Jamaica and South Carolina. Sassafrass is the first example chosen. She is a weaver, the one who has inherited the family looms and preserves the tradition of a generation of female ancestors who worked for white colonial families. Yet, Sassafrass raises the handicraft to the level of artistry, loving it for "the sense of womanhood that was rich and sensuous" (92). She understands herself as a proud carrier of a legacy of women in her family who, despite limitations, were busy living their lives beyond the gender roles imposed on them: "they could make something besides a baby" (91). This self-expression against social normalization is liberating, because when women are weaving "they have time to think …" (91). This passage not only suggests Sassafrass' potentiality for self-liberation, but also her desire to extend liberation to other women, in the sense of a transnational empathy (Russo) or a coalition (Spivak; Butler). But Sassafrass is trapped in her love for a man, Mitch, who once beat her after subjecting her to the role of a whore, with the collaboration of two friends who meet in her house to "celebrate her good pussy" (87). The three Black men perfectly reproduce the discourse of colonial dominance and exploitation of the Black female body. In the face of the humiliation, Sassafrass is at first speechless until she gathers strength to react and shout in their faces; "I am not bout to sit hea and listen to a bunch of no account niggahs talk about black women; … don't you ever sit in my house and ask me to celebrate my inherited right to be raped" (89). Alluding to the history of violence endured by Black women, the moment Mitch beats her, striking her in the face with his tube (97), Sassafrass remembers the occasion when as a young girl, she witnessed her own father beating her mother (98). This scene in *Sassafrass, Cypress & Indigo* offers us an eloquent enactment of the ongoing cycle of violence against Black women since slavery times. It is noteworthy that the violence is inscribed in the same patriarchal logic of the "modern/colonial gender system," although ironically it is perpetrated by someone who has also been racialized as inferior by the same system. As Calvin Hernton notes, "Similar to other people who have been colonized and oppressed at one time or another, the oppressive experiences of black men have not deterred them from being oppressors themselves" (7–8).

Gayl Jones is another example. In a quotation from her 1994 essay, "The Quest for Wholeness: Re-imagining the African American Novel," she clearly conveys a sense of intersectionality: "the female African American novel – of which I may be one – must be twice decolonized, not only from the context of racial dominance but also the context of sexual dominance" (512). Both her novels *Corregidora* (1975) and *Eva's Man* (1976) use characters and situations that are significant in this same context. In *Corregidora*, Ursa is the descendant of a generation of slave women who were raped by their white owner, Corregidora, whose name, besides his seed, they were forced to carry. They are determined not to let this traumatic memory fade, because it is the only way "to leave evidence:" "They burned all the documents, Ursa, [...] we got to keep what we need to bear witness. That scar that's left to bear witness" (72). On the one hand, Ursa is haunted by the responsibility to have children imposed by her forebears to keep memory alive. On the other hand, she is also the victim of violence at the hands of a man. In her case, however, it is Mutt, a Black man and her husband; and it is not rape, but a beating. She is newly pregnant and he pushes her down a flight of stairs, causing her to become sterile and preventing her from passing her memory on to the next generation.

Eva's Man, her next novel, is a most violent text. Jones presents a Black woman in her 40s, Eva Medina Canada, who has been incarcerated in a psychiatric prison in upstate New York for the brutal murder of her lover, Davis Carter. After killing him by poisoning his drink with arsenic, Eva bit off his penis and wrapped it in a silk handkerchief. The narrative, delivered in her own voice, finds this woman completely isolated since her arrest, throughout the 5 years she has spent in prison, both in her madness, her total silence, and everyone's incapacity to understand her insane acts. A life of sexual violence and abuse since she was a little child slowly and painfully starts to unfold through the chaotic fragments of a narrative of trauma. As Toni Morrison would say, we cannot access the "why," only the "how," the succession of traumatic events that may have had a bearing on the woman she became. Is this narrative that hurts to read, and is this character so hard to identify with the ultimate attempt to render the effects of all the violence that Black women have been subjected to? Are we faced with the monster just to realize how monstrous the coloniality of gender can be?

Throughout these texts, the Black woman's body is targeted for aggression; it is dehumanized as it is decomposed in its parts: face, hair, vagina, womb, "like a mannequin" (Shange, *Sassafrass*, 88). NourbeSe Philip inscribes that dehumanization and decomposition in the mechanism of the colonial plantation, seeing the body of the African woman as a whole fractured in pieces—"breasts thighs belly buttocks" (88), turned into a commodity that is a target of sexual abuse and historical silence. Philip uses "inner" and "outer space" as tropes, respectively, for the female body and societal rules; the control of the inner space being part and parcel of the regulation of women within society. Slavery, like colonialism, may seem to be a regulating system of the past. However, "coloniality" reveals a persisting trace of the colonial structuring of society, the enslavement of women, which we find represented in the literary text. This also remains in symbolic terms as a slavery's sequel marking interpersonal relations and specifically the oppression of Black women.[8]

However, all these women resist and liberate themselves. The most appropriate term is "liberated" instead of "emancipated" with reference to the counter-hegemonic proposals of intellectuals, activists, and social movements in Africa and Latin America (Fanon; Dussel; Mignolo). Liberation awakes a sense of the movement for self-determination taken by the subalterns in their own hands against colonization and coloniality. These writers and intellectuals move, as bell hooks states, "out of their place" (145) and seize the word to transgress and debunk master narratives, thus decolonizing the mind (Thiongo) that was subjected by the "coloniality of knowledge" (Quijano). That is why it is so important for them to reconnect with history in a critical way, committed as they are to a "cultural politics of resistance" (hooks 5).

Yet, this is just one, incomplete piece of the story. A true liberation and a true conquest of human rights need to bring men and women together in the same struggle. As in Toni Morrison's *Beloved*, where Paul D. wants to put his story next to Sethe's, it also needs coalitions beyond geographical and national borders toward a reconstructed pluralistic human rights framework (Hernández-Truyol and Ribeiro).

Notes

1. A presente publicação resulta do apoio da Fundação para a Ciência e a Tecnologia portuguesa, ao abrigo do Projeto Estratégico (UID/SOC/50012/2013).
2. A footnote cannot do justice to the category of the "coloniality of power." For the immediate purpose of this contribution, it is important to know that Quijano's coloniality of power is based on the racial social stratification of the world population (e.g., "whites" or "Creoles," "Mestizos," "Indians," "Negroes," "Blacks," "Reds," etc.) that was implemented during the European colonization of the Americas and later of the rest of the world. Coloniality of power proposes that the colonial racial structuration of humanity that took place over 500 years ago during the conquest and colonization of the western hemisphere remains in place and affects life conditions and options of non-white, non-European people who often continue to live under extreme forms of European or Euro-American exploitation and domination in the new millennium. Coloniality similarly affects intersubjective relationships and the problematic if not divisive way we often encounter difference in terms of race, gender, ethnicity, sexuality, culture, etc.
3. Latin American and African countries were the ones that opposed the separation of the rights included in the *Universal Declaration* and have created their own system that integrates civil and political rights and economic, social, and cultural rights (Hernández-Truyol and Ribeiro, 33).
4. Julieta Paredes (2012) criticizes Lugones for dismissing the centrality of gender in patriarchal Indigenous societies ("Las trampas del patriarcado." *Pensando los feminismos en Bolivia*. Serie Foros 2. La Paz, Bolivia: Conexión Fondo de Emancipación, 2012, pp. 89–112).
5. Gloria Anzaldúa uses the expression in *Borderlands/La Frontera: The New Mestiza*. Aunt Lute Books, 1987, 1999, p. 25 ("The U.S.-Mexican border *es una herida abierta* where the Third World grates against the first and bleeds.").
6. The myth of the Black rapist and the paranoia lived around it in the United States in the late 19th century and the first decades of the 20th century, which led to numerous lynchings in the South, is a clear symptom of that.
7. Calvin C. Hernton had already been provoking with his former book on *Sex and Racism in America* (1965), for daring to examine a taboo in American society, namely, the roots of modern race relations in the system of sexual dominance in slavery times.

8. The idea of representing the oppression of Black women using the codes of slavery grounds Hernton's reading of *The Color Purple* in one of the essays included in the above mentioned book—"Who's Afraid of Alice Walker? *The Color Purple* as Slave Narrative" (Calvin C. Hernton. *The Sexual Mountain and Black Women Writers: Adventures in Sex, Literature, and Real Life.* New York: Anchor, 1990, pp. 1–36).

Works cited

Anzaldúa, Gloria. *Borderlands/La Frontera: The New Mestiza.* Aunt Lute Books, 1987, 1999.

Brownmiller, Susan. *Against Our Will: Men, Women and Rape.* Fawcett Books, 1975.

Butler, Judith. *Gender Trouble.* Routledge, 1993.

Caldeira, Isabel. "'What moves at the margin': As vozes insurretas de Toni Morrison, bell hooks e Ntozake Shange". *"The Edge of One of Many Circles:" Volume de Homenagem a Irene Ramalho Santos.* Imprensa da Universidade de Coimbra, 2017b, pp. 140–162.

Caldeira, Isabel. "Toni Morrison and Edwidge Danticat: Writers-as-Citizens of the African Diaspora, or The Margin as a Space of Radical Openness." *Companion to Inter-American Studies*, edited by Wilfried Raussert. Routledge, 2017a, pp. 207–218.

Collins, Patricia Hill. *Black Feminist Thought: Knowledge, Consciousness, and the Politics of Empowerment.* Routledge, 1991.

Crenshaw, Kimberlé, editor. "Mapping the Margins: Intersectionality, Identity Politics, and Violence Against Women of Color." *Critical Race Theory.* The New Press, 1995, pp. 357–383.

Danticat, Edwidge. *Breath, Eyes, Memory.* Abacus, 1996.

DeShazer, Mary K. *A Poetics of Resistance: Women Writing* in *El Salvador, South Africa, and the United States.* University of Michigan Press, 1994.

Gunn Allen P., *The Sacred Hoop. Recovering the Feminine in American Indian Traditions.* Beacon Press, 1992.

Hawkesworth, Mary and Lisa Disch, editors. "Introduction. Feminist Theory: Transforming the Known World." *The Oxford Handbook of Feminist Theory.* OUP, 2016, pp. 1–15.

Hernández-Truyol, Berta E. & Mariana Ribeiro "María Lugones's Work as a Human Rights Idea (1)". *Berkeley La Raza Law Journal*, vol. 18, issue 29, 2015, pp. 29–45.

Hernton, Calvin C. *Sex and Racism in America.* Grove Press, 1965

Hernton, Calvin C, *The Sexual Mountain* and *Black Women Writers: Adventures in Sex, Literature, and Real Life.* Anchor, 1990.

hooks, bell. *Yearnings: Race, Gender and Cultural Politics.* South End Press, 1990.

Humann, Heather Duerre. *Domestic Abuse in the Novels of African American Women: A Critical Study.* McFarland, 2014.

Jones, Gayl. "The Quest for Wholeness: Re-imagining the African American Novel: An Essay. Third World Aesthetics". *Callaloo*, vol. 17, issue 2, Spring 1994, pp. 507–518.

Jones, Gayl. *Corregidora.* Beacon Press, [1975] 1986.

Kincaid, Jamaica. "Girl". *At the Bottom of the River.* Vintage, 1983, pp. 3–5.

Lugones, María, "The Coloniality of Gender". *Worlds & Knowledges Otherwise*, vol. 2, issue 2, Spring 2008, pp. 1–17.
Lugones, María. "Heterosexualism and the Colonial/Modern Gender System", *Hypatia*, vol. 22, issue 1, Winter 2007, pp. 186–209.
Lugones, María. "On *Borderlands/LaFrontera*: An Interpretive Essay". *Hypatia*, vol. 7, issue 4, Nov. 1992, pp. 31–37.
Lugones, María. "Toward a Decolonial Feminism". *Hypatia*, vol. 25, issue 4, Fall 2010, pp. 742–759.
Maldonado-Torres, Nelson. "Outline of Ten Theses on Coloniality and Decoloniality", 26 October, 2016. Web. 23 May 2017.
Mendoza, Breny. "Coloniality of Gender and Power: From Postcoloniality to Decoloniality". *The Oxford Handbook of Feminist Theory*, edited by Lisa Disch and Mary Hawkesworth. OUP, 2016, pp. 100–121.
Mignolo, Walter D. "DELINKING". *Cultural Studies*, vol. 21, issue 2, 2007, pp. 449–514. 13.02.2014. DOI: 10.1080/09502380601162647
Mignolo, Walter, ed. *Género y descolonialidad. Colección Pensamiento Crítico y Opción Descolonial*. Ediciones del signo, 2008.
Oyewùmí, Oyéronké. *The Invention of Women: Making an African Sense of Western Gender Discourses*. University of Minnesota Press, 1997.
Philip, M. Nourbese. *A Genealogy of Resistance and Other Essays*. The Mercury Press, 1997.
Pipes, Candice Linette. "It's Time to Tell: Abuse, Resistance and Recovery in Black Women's Literature." Diss. The Ohio State University, 2010.
Quijano, Aníbal. "Coloniality of Power, Eurocentrism, and Latin America." *Neplanta: Views from South*, vol. 1, issue 3, 2000, pp. 533–580.
Royster, Jacqueline Jones. "Literacy and Civic Engagement." Civil Rights Symposium: An Interdepartmental and Interdisciplinary Conversation on Civil Rights Reform 2007. Web. 12.09.2017.
Russo, Ann. "'We Cannot Live Without Our Lives': White Women, Antiracism, and Feminism." *Third World Women and the Politics of Feminism*, edited by Chandra Talpade Mohanty, et al., Indiana University Press, 1991, pp. 297–3013.
Sandoval, Chela. "Feminism and Racism: A Report on the 1981 National Women's Studies Association Conference." *Making Face, Making Soul/Haciendo Caras: Creative and Critical Perspectives by Feminists of Color*, edited by Gloria Anzaldúa, Aunt Lute Books, 1990, pp. 55–71.
Shange, Ntozake. *For Colored Girls Who Have Considered Suicide/When the Rainbow is Enuf*. Bantam, 1975.
Shange, Ntozake. *Sassafrass, Cypress & Indigo*. St. Martins' Press, 1982.
Spivak, Gayatri Chakravorty. "Can the Subaltern Speak?" *Marxism and the Interpretation of Culture*, edited by C. Nelson and L. Grossberg. Basingstoke, 1988, pp. 271–313.
Tlostanova, Madina. "'¿Por qué cortarse los pies para caber en los zapatos occidentales?:' Las ex colonias soviéticas no europeas y el sistema de género colonial moderno." *Género y descolonialidad*, edited by Walter Mignolo. Colección Pensamiento Crítico y Opción Descolonial. Ediciones del Signo, 2008, pp. 65–91.
Wallace, Michele. *Black Macho and the Myth of the Superwoman*. Verso, 2015.

7 Autobiography, fiction, and racial hatred representation in Jamaica Kincaid's *See Now Then*

Gonçalo Cholant

Equality is a central concept for the establishment, development, and maintenance of human rights as a universal reality. Discrimination is its polar opposite, as it creates realities in which not all have the possibility of developing their full potential, thus creating hierarchies that often are based on violence. Discrimination may function in several different ways, which are often co-formative and intrinsically interrelated. Race, sex, class, gender, sexual orientation, disability, national origin, religion, ethnic affiliation, among many other, are some of the factors that have determined the existence of many subjects in society, and legislation created toward the protection of these vulnerable groups has tried to create protections for them, and ultimately promote a safer and more equitable reality for all. Efforts toward the creation of a more equitable world are found in legislation that fosters an anti-discriminatory reality, in which citizens are able to fully enjoy their inalienable rights. The United Nations states,

> The international human rights legal framework contains international instruments to combat specific forms of discrimination, including discrimination against indigenous peoples, migrants, minorities, people with disabilities, discrimination against women, racial and religious discrimination, or discrimination based on sexual orientation and gender identity. (United Nations)

The denunciation of these inequalities may happen either by protest, with the engagement of social movements, by reports given by the media, by activism and politics, or even by culture and the arts. Literature, more specifically, may function as a platform for the denunciation of these realities, as a locus in which these subjects may voice their concerns, exposing the ways in which the violence against them takes shape and affects their existence. *See Now Then,* the novel that is the departure point of analysis in this work, is a text that reports on how domesticity crumbles to pieces and race becomes a weapon of personal injury. Jamaica Kincaid exposes the inner workings of the mind of the perpetrator of violence, whose frustration and unhappiness with his personal life takes a turn into racist reveries.

Autobiography and fiction are both present in Kincaid's work, in a form of hybrid life story that is scattered in different texts. Fiction takes center stage; yet, the autobiographical creates an enriched experience when dealing with her texts, as it is going to be further investigated later in this work.

The attempt of representation of violence trauma in literature makes the readership more aware of the experience of different subjects, possibly becoming an empathizing tool that may work toward the creation of a more equitable reality. Toni Morrison, in *The Origin of Others* (2017), asserts this point, stating,

> The resources available to us for benign access to each other, for vaulting the mere blue air that separates us, are few but powerful: language, image, and experience, which may involve both, one, or neither of the first two. Language (saying, listening, reading) can encourage, even mandate, surrender, the breach of distances among us, whether they are continental or on the same pillow, whether they are distances of cultures or the distinctions of gender, whether they are the consequences of social invention or biology. (35–36)

Literature may be considered a rich source of representations, where processes of identity construction are capable of informing the readership of the life experience of others, which contribute in the construction of a more plural knowledge about such experiences and the world. Backing such perspective and drawing from the writings of other African diasporic female authors, Isabel Caldeira writes in her essay, "Toni Morrison and Edwidge Danticat: Writers as Citizens of the African Diaspora, or 'The Margin as a Space of Radical Openness'": "I submit that literature is an important mode of re-appropriating history and offering a counter-hegemonic perspective to create social awareness and promote a critical competence to resist the entanglements of wealth and power" (207). Through its political, ethical, and aesthetic features, literature is capable of disturbing the ways in which hegemony functions, demonstrating the radical possibilities of other points of view, as well as humanizing subjects who have long been produced as inferior and unequal by the status quo. Caldeira expands: "[l]iterature has indeed the power to give us the emotional access to experience and either humanize our world or reveal its/our (in)humanity, displaying the universe in a new light, and sharpening our senses and intellectual perspicuousness" (208). Toni Morrison calls this ability the "moral imagination," connecting the life experience of authors, and especially the experience of trauma, to the capacity of refiguring language in meaningful ways:

> Certain kinds of trauma visited on peoples are so deep, so cruel, that unlike money, unlike vengeance, even unlike justice, or rights, or the goodwill of others, only writers can translate such trauma and turn sorrow into meaning, sharpening the moral imagination. A writer's life and

work are not a gift to mankind; they are its necessity. (*Burn This Book* 4) *See Now Then* is one of these instances where trauma is translated into meaning, and the (in)humanity of experience is brought into vision. In this novel Kincaid explores the dismantling of a marriage, between a Black Caribbean writer and an American composer of Jewish descent.

One can see an atomized kind of autobiography in Kincaid's production, where the author is present in some form, or some aspect of her life is explored in different texts, under different names, in different places, yet there is something that holds the thread. Kincaid's production can be classified in several different genres, from fiction to essays, (auto)biography and travel writing, though none is capable of encompassing it exclusively. Kincaid's life story can be traced to *At the Bottom of the River* (1983), *Annie John* (1986), *Lucy* (1990), *Autobiography of My Mother* (1996), *My Brother* (1998), *Mr. Potter* (2002), and *See Now Then* (2013). The nonfiction titles *A Small Place* (1988), *My Garden Book* (2001), *Talk* Stories (2001), a collection of her writings for *The New Yorker*, and *Among Flowers – A Walk in the Himalayas* (2005), they all, someway, also express this sense of continuity. In these titles, we are able to visit some different stages in the identity construction of the author, from her childhood in Antigua and her coming-of-age in the Caribbean, to her migration to the United States, as well as her travels to Nepal, and in the latest installment her adult life with her children and her ex-husband.

"Everything I say is true, and everything I say is not true. You couldn't admit it to a court of law. It would not be good evidence" (Bonetti, "Interview"). This is how Kincaid best exemplifies her relation to truth telling and fiction in a 2002 interview with Kay Bonetti for the *Missouri Review*. It is not specifically a question of trying to find truth among the fiction, neither of regarding her fiction as a disguised form of autobiography. The matter might better be understood when seen through the perspective of expanding boundaries of genres, or rather, the dismantling of them, as Kincaid exposes the fragility of the concept of truth telling in the autobiographical discourse. While describing the creative processes of the protagonist of *See Now Then,* Kincaid clarifies her own writing, stating that the protagonist would alter reality, or more precisely, would embellish it, adding details that would not actually be present in the actual reality it was referring. There is also the matter that though Kincaid is dealing with a genre that tends to be individualistic, the writing of one's self into text(s), in this serial autobiography effort she explores the lives of those people who surround her; first, her mother (who figures in all her texts), her absent father, her dying brother, and, in her latest installment, her ex-husband and her children. In *My Brother* (1998), her only work labeled as memoir, Kincaid writes about the life and death of Devon Drew, her youngest brother, who died of AIDS in 1996. In a memorable passage, Kincaid's notion of truth telling comes at play again, as her brother inquires about a character in a book published some time earlier. Ironically, Devon is referring to *The Autobiography of My Mother*, a 1996 work marketed as fiction. In this text, Kincaid describes a pivotal moment in which her brother, in his deathbed, asks her whether the child in a novel she had previously written was himself. We need to know that in this novel the mother had continuously tried to abort this child, unsuccessfully. To which the author replies, while laughing, that the specific character he is referring to is in a novel, and thus it is not reality. The author concludes, "... he did not tell me that he did not believe my reply and I did not tell him that he should not believe my reply" *(My Brother* 174). In another interview, Kincaid reveals to Moira Ferguson that the form of writing was not something that shaped what she produced, stating that,

> As far as I am concerned I am only happy to write. Often the voices that flow into each other because I am at a point where if I am writing supposedly different things, a fiction piece and a non-fiction piece, I often have just the same concerns. I am so happy to write that I don't care what you call it. (166)

What Kincaid ends up revealing in the interview and in these passages is that the reader should always be suspicious when dealing with her texts. Claudia Marquis also points to the hybridity of Kincaid's work in her article "'Not at Home in Her Own Skin': Jamaica Kincaid, History and Selfhood," referring to Kincaid's work as autobiographical fiction, and sometimes as narrative fiction, and claims that the relation between reality and fiction are only approximate in Kincaid's work. Moira Ferguson in, "Lucy as the Mark of the Colonizer" describes Kincaid's production as "a fictional/ semi-autobiographical saga" (238). Gilmore categorizes Kincaid's works in a genre called serial autobiography, a mode of inscribing autobiographical instances into complex networks of texts from which the readership is capable of identifying common features, even if the variants of name, context, or progression are in dissonance. Marquis commenting on the matter states,

> Kincaid, in fact, has repeatedly declared her lack of interest in any fiction that is not autobiographical – in this sense, at least, that in her stories she works through the problematic of her own experience. In that regard, Kincaid's narrative fiction has the relation of the asymptote to real history—a tangential relation where narrative and the line of actual events come very close to each other, but never exactly meet, where, necessarily, the narrative can never deliver its central character complete. ("Not at Home", par. 18)

Applying the modality of a term such as "autobiographical" to text comes with its own set of expectations and tensions, which must not limit the reader's interpretation of the text, but rather, enlarge its possibilities. Leigh

Gilmore in *The Limits of Autobiography–Trauma and Testimony* addresses the matter of the tension between fiction and autobiography. In a chapter dedicated to Kincaid's work, "There Will Always Be a Mother–Jamaica Kincaid's Serial Autobiography," Gilmore explores how Kincaid is able to build a sense of autobiography in her fiction through a network of recurring themes, exploring repeatedly how fracturing the mother-daughter (trauma) theme is present in many different works (96). The mother trauma is first explored in the difficult process of individuation brought by puberty, and later is transformed into a critique of colonialism centered in the mother's abidance to the imperial order, as also pointed by Laura Abruna in "Jamaica Kincaid's Writing and the Maternal-Colonial Matrix":

> Kincaid's greatest contribution to the full presentation of female life is her exploration of the mother-daughter bond, and specifically, the effects of the loss of the maternal matrix on the relationship between the mother and the daughter. In *Annie John*, as well as in *Lucy* and *The Autobiography of My Mother*, the alienation from the mother becomes a metaphor for the young woman's alienation from the island culture that has been completely dominated by the imperialist power of England. (54)

This refusal to contain life into a single text, or rather, to contain experience into a single character as a definite account, demonstrates that the modes of canonical autobiography are under scrutiny and new forms of experimentation in self-representation are possible. Gilmore expands, "Instead of respecting the sufficiency of each text unto itself (and why should she adopt that constraint without being able to rework it? And why should her readers?), Kincaid extends what appears to be the same character, with different names, into book after book" (101). Kincaid subverts the contracts of the traditional autobiographical pact, in Philippe Lejeune's terms, first by refusing the end of the text (and therefore of life) as a definite account through her texts' open-endedness. In addition, she escapes the convention regarding the coincidence of the trifold confluence of the author's name with the narrator's and the protagonist's as a proof of veracity and verifiability of the story. Interestingly, in *See Now Then*, a passage toward the end of the narrative plays with all these elements in a meta-reading of her own autobiographical production. In this passage, Mrs. Sweet is reading her son a book called, *See Now Then,* telling the story of how his parents had met, and why they married (she was about to be deported back to her small island). In addition, the character in the book is called Jamaica. Gilmore states,

> Kincaid avoids the ways autobiographical writing splits (or doubles) the "I" into "myself" and "herself" by coming up with different names for herself and her characters. In so doing, she exposes a crucial limit: that identity exceeds its representation and the violence of splitting

(or doubling, or extending) the "I" into autobiographer and character makes possible for both alienation and nostalgia for the fictional unity of an "I", even as serial autobiography offers a textual environment for refusing this split. (103)

This means that serial autobiography is capable of offering the writer different chances of responding to the questions "who am I?" or "how did I come to be this way?" instead of having to provide a definitive answer that is already destined to fail in its inflexibility. There is always the chance of coming back to this narrative exercise of the self, of returning to the autobiographical scene. This instability between fiction and autobiography subverts the contracts and pacts between reader and writer, creating an experience that is richer, as truth is constitutive of fiction in Kincaid's texts, and her personal life story is reconfigured in ways that expand both fictional and autobiographical discourses. Gilmore states, "[t]he autobiographical may [...] function critically as an expansive, extendible system of meaning, one that enables readers to do much more than search out sources, proof, or evidence of a corresponding reality" (*The Limits of Autobiography* 100). What Kincaid's work does, instead, through this autobiographical stance, is question the limits of truth telling, or rather, expose the limits of the construction of reality as text in autobiography, a feature that creates more room for the possibility of the representation of trauma.

Another feature found in many of these texts is a critique of colonialism and imperialism, writing from the position of a Black woman who is utterly and painfully aware of her situation as a postcolonial subject in contemporary-white-dominated-capitalist-patriarchal America, here understood in its hemispheric dimension. The rejection of Britain and its overbearing colonizing presence in her childhood, found in *Annie John,* continues in critiques of the complicit obliviousness of upper middle class Americans to the racial questions that shape everyday experience in *Lucy.* In *See Now Then*, there is also this consciousness, now turning into the microcosmos of domestic life in a peaceful New England town.

Mrs. Sweet, the protagonist in *See Now Then* and the fictional iteration of the author in this autobiographical installment, is the target of a series of attacks to her personhood, all based in her race and origin. However, the attacks happen mostly in the mind of Mr. Sweet, who is not capable of performing any of the vicious acts that he imagines toward his wife. The narrative unfolds in two different stages: the reality of a housewife being left by an unfaithful husband, and the interpretations of various moments of their past in comparison to their present. There is a progression in time, but it is complex and heavily punctuated by memories of the past. Time flows in a similar mode to Virginia Woolf's stream of consciousness. *See Now Then* brings memories of *To the Lighthouse* and *Mrs. Dalloway*, with its long sentences, scarcity of pauses, multiplicity of narrators, and shifts from one perspective to another without impediments, which allows the reader to experience both the minds of the perpetrator of the violence and the victim. From this perspective, one might infer that we can see another intermingling layer of fiction and autobiography, as the experience of the real is enlarged by the possibility of representing the inner workings of others. Most importantly, *See Now Then* is an investigation about the perception of time and about the shaping of memory, in which Kincaid explores aspects of life from different perspectives, as the title implies. The text is filled with the hypnotic repetition of the three title words, and in different order, making evident the malleability of memory, as one learns to see the past and the present, and possibly the future, from different perspectives. All this back and forth serves the purpose of showing how memory is pliable, and therefore subject to reinterpretations, it is imprecise and subject to multiple layers of (re)construction that depend on the circumstances they are remembered and (re)created. Hate as an extension of love, being its polar opposite, seeps into the life of this family. Kincaid explores how the spectrum of sentiments stretches out in this specific relationship. The author seems to describe the sentiment of hatred felt by Mr. Sweet as a reality that is natural, if not inevitable. Violence, in its symbolic stance, is very much present in this work, just like geography is a result of the constant and violent struggle of natural forces, the microaggressions of everyday life are what eventually shifts the reality of the Sweets. She states, "... Mr. Sweet hated his wife, Mrs. Sweet, and as she looked out on this natural formation of landscape: mountain, valley, lake, and river, the remains of the violence of the earth's natural evolution: she did not know it" (*See Now Then* 10).

As far as characterizations go, Mr. Sweet is not only described as a bitter small man, likened to a rodent, lurking in dark spaces and fearing the world around him, but also is remembered in a more positive light. He reflected the values of his upbringing, that is, a cultivated Manhattan man of Jewish descent, a sensitive composer, who could comprehend very complex musical pieces and composers, as well as culture at large (*See Now Then* 7). He was a person from whom bigotry would not be expected, as he was able to perceive the shifting of realities and mentalities (7). In comparison, Mrs. Sweet stands six-foot tall, with dark brown skin, taking care of her garden and her family, writing books and receiving checks by the mail, hinting a much more successful career than her husband's, who fails to gather an audience for his performances. They have two children who are highly mythologized, the young Heracles and the beautiful Persephone, and both seem to follow the ideas associated with the mythological characters they are named after, creating a creative and protective distance for the possible real counterparts. When describing the past of Mrs. Sweet, Kincaid plays with the autobiographical scene, in Gilmore's terms, and inserts some of her own life story as the background for this character, describing a past story that might be clearly associated with the author's. Mrs. Sweet is described also as an immigrant from the Caribbean. Differently from the author, the protagonist is said to have come to the United States on a banana boat, or some other obscure way, a parallel with cargo that imbues her story with the stigma of chattel slavery and colonialism (97–98). The protagonist's background is heavily related to her maternal figure, another association that is widely explored in Kincaid's production, as well as the absence of her father during her early years. Her identity is described as completely foreign to the experience of the husband, who would never visit the place from which his own wife came from (97–98). Her foreignness is stressed once again in questions such as, "Who knew what she was capable of? People who come on banana boats are not people you can really know and she did come on a banana boat" (14). Another frequent epithet used by Mr. Sweet to describe his wife is, "that bitch of woman born of beast" (10), once again making evident the nonhumanity of her character in his perspective. Her foreignness is not to be trusted. She is not part of his experience of whiteness. She is not one of them. Mr. Sweet goes even to the point of questioning if his wife was a passenger in a banana boat or even a banana herself, which should have been inspected upon entry in the country. The trope of the immigrant fresh off a banana boat is repeated 26 times in this novel, a metaphor that although repeated, does not feel like overplay, but simply as a testament of the persistence of the stereotypes and microaggressions that are embedded in the daily life of a Black body in the United States. Mrs. Sweet, an immigrant from Antigua (just like the author, another similarity between them), and the reference to the banana boat leads to an impression of foreignness and commodification. This depiction creates a display of inferiority clearly based on racial discrimination, as well as class discrimination. It signifies that she, just as the bananas (or the immigrants), is one of the cheap produces that come in batches from distant lands, to be consumed by the fine citizens of big cities in the developed world, to be seen as exotic and different, and therefore, inferior.

Conversely, when she first met Mr. Sweet, Mrs. Sweet's difference as a Caribbean writer in New York was seen as positive and compelling. This version fell apart as the years passed and in the narrative's present this *then* seems far and disconnected to their everyday experience of *now*. Mr. Sweet's frustration leads him to hate his *now*, and forget their *then*. These tensions in Mrs. Sweet's life are the way Kincaid chooses to demonstrate how the unfamiliar, even in the domestic environment, is perceived as inferior. Similarly, in *The Origin of Others,* Morrison presents a series of essays on the creation and maintenance of the Other and Otherness as foundational characteristics of Americanness, since the beginnings of the colonization of the continent, and continuing as a mark of inferiority until the present day. Morrison explores this difference in the construction of the binaries human/nonhuman later understood as a matter of race and color. She writes,

> The necessity of rendering the slave a foreign species appears to be a desperate attempt to confirm one's self as normal. The urgency of distinguishing between those who belonged to the human race and those

who are decidedly non-human is so powerful the spotlight turns away and shines not on the object of degradation but on its creator. Even assuming exaggeration by the slave, the sensibility of slave owners is gothic. It's as though they are shouting, "I am not a beast! I am not a beast! I torture the helpless to prove I am not weak." The danger of sympathizing with the stranger is becoming a stranger. To lose one's racialized rank is to lose one's own valued and enshrined difference (29–30).

Color became then one of the marks of Otherness for non-whites that kept the social hierarchy clear, and defined the humanity of subjects. Mr. Sweet's musings translate precisely the creation of otherness through the mark of color. The representation of these feelings of hatred touch matters of racism and sexism, echoing descriptions of Nativist theorists, linking the African diaspora to concepts of animality and oversexualization, concepts that still trickle down to contemporary sexist discourses of discrimination and prejudice.

Another matter Mr. Sweet brings to the fore is related to cultural ignorance, or at least historical awareness. At a given moment in the narrative, Mrs. Sweet is questioning what is the essence of love, that feeling from which all the others derive, including hate. For Mr. Sweet is Jewish, and his history, the history of his people, is permeated with questions of life and death, of extermination, and she was instructed by him on such history of collective trauma (*See Now Then* 12). However, when it comes to her personal history of collective trauma, he is completely oblivious. Despite having grown up in a Jewish household, and taught the horrors of the Holocaust and the diaspora, Mr. Sweet seems incapable of fathoming the Atlantic Slave Trade and the foundational trauma of his wife's experience as a Black person in the Americas (12).

While being deeply invested and solidary to the plight of Jewish people, the diaspora, and the Holocaust, Mr. Sweet seems incapable of recognizing the Atlantic Slave Trade as a generator of trauma and pain for an entire part of the world's population. His complete unawareness of her reality demonstrates how unfamiliar her Blackness is to him, showing how selective his understanding of humanity might be. By ignoring her history, and the history of all African diasporic subjects, he demonstrates the extent to which his suffering is more legitimate than hers. Mr. Sweet claims his superiority, and therefore his humanity, by evincing the ways in which his wife is incapable of sharing his values and perceptions, which is illustrated in the episode regarding a coat, the quality of which his wife would never appreciate. Even though he was able to perceive the quality of the garment, since it was a gift by his "beastly wife of his" (*See Now Then* 9) he came to hate it, as if she had diminished the coat's status with her own perceived inferiority.

As previously stated, repetition is key in Kincaid's work, and here the repetition of the adjective "benighted" (*See Now Then* 9) in several passages of the book reveals the clear inferiority of Mrs. Sweet in relation to her husband, in the character's perception. Another example comes from her children. On one occasion Mrs. Sweet is late to pick them up after school, and the resentment felt by them at this disappointment is taken upon her writing routines, which seem to separate the mother from her children (129). Her commitment to sharing her past and her origins seems to be perceived as a hindrance even to her children, which is illustrative of the unbearable discomfort that conversations regarding colonialism, racism, poverty, and discrimination create in a white supremacist society and even in the microcosmos of domestic life. Mrs. Sweet is the agent that reminds every one of the history of a people that the rest of the world would be glad to forget. Her obsession in emphasizing this reality encounters utter bitterness by the rest of her family.

Mr. Sweet often fantasizes about murdering his wife, and their son, though he never acts on these feelings. His frustration seems to stem from the life he was led to live, seemingly not by choice, but by circumstance. In a chilling passage in the first chapter, the reader is informed of these murdering desires, in images that mix domesticity, violence, and extreme frustration, as he pictures his wife's severed head on top of the kitchen counter, her body missing, and therefore the obstacle that has prevented him from achieving his full potential is eliminated (10). This episode is illustrative of the attitudes and feelings described by Morrison previously, since it seems that Mr. Sweet is prevented from becoming his real self because of the association with the foreignness of his wife. The violence inflicted upon her body would finally liberate him to express his full potential as a white heterosexual male. In the conclusion of this violent act of imagination, the reality of not having found his wife dead is brushed aside. However, her presence in the form of the decoration of their home serves as an expression of her foreignness as much as anything she touches (14–15). The ornamentation is perceived as a direct assault on his being; the bright colors selected to decorate the kitchen, which remind him of her Caribbean foreignness, stand in clear contrast with his sober white man sensibility. The fact that his mother had warned him about this possible development in their marriage (14–15) stresses Mr. Sweet's colonialist upbringing that reinforces the hierarchies derived from a colonialist perspective. As a woman perceived to lack proper upbringing, who is loud and chooses loud colors, Mrs. Sweet is the embodiment of everything Mr. Sweet was not meant to pursue, given his social status and family heritage. The figure of his mother is brought into the scene as a witness to all the devastation this Other would bring into Mr. Sweets life project.

The microaggressions seen through fiction here are very much real in the lives of people of color, immigrants, and social minorities. Writing gives us a chance to see the world through the eyes of the victim, as well as the perpetrator of violence. Fiction allows us to see violence from different perspectives, as it gives us room to attempt to understand how and why these feeling arise and develop. Though Kincaid does not seem to be trying to deconstruct any of these racial paradigms in an activist political kind of literature, her investment in the private and the particular suffices in exposing how the creation of the other takes place in everyday realities. The autobiographical stance of Kincaid's production helps construct the idea of verisimilitude, as her life experience, which might not have been precisely that of her characters, contributes to demonstrate that the reality of racism is highly active in our day. Ta-Nehisi Coates writes about his own experience with racism in *Between the World and Me*, positing that we must not let the language that we have developed about this reality obscure the immediateness and physicality of racism:

> It is hard to face this. But all our phrasing—race relations, racial chasm, racial justice, racial profiling, white privilege, even white supremacy—serves to obscure that racism is a visceral experience, that it dislodges brains, blocks airways, rips muscle, extracts organs, cracks bones, breaks teeth. You must never look away from this. (12)

Kincaid clearly explores the visceral perspective when dealing with the representation of racism, exposing the brutality of a prejudiced mind. Simultaneously, she reiterates her own humanity in each page. In his examination of contemporary United States, Coates declares bluntly that one of the traditions that has helped to create and maintain the idea of unity in this country is the abuse of the body of the other, a racialized reality that has pervasively contaminated many sectors of everyday life.

> Racist dehumanization is not merely symbolic – it delineates the borders of power. ... In America, part of the idea of race is that whiteness automatically confers a decreased chance of dying like Michael Brown, or Walter Scott, or Eric Garner. And death is the superlative example of what it means to live as an "Other", to exist beyond the border of a great "belonging". ("Foreword" XV)

Coates concludes with a maxim that completes the ideas of Toni Morrison that have been previously discussed: "In America, it is traditional to destroy the Black body—it is heritage" (*Between the World and Me*, 90). Kincaid does not explore the reality of physical violence in her text, but she portrays the ideology that fosters the racist dehumanization of human beings, clearly exposing us to questions of prejudice and discrimination, all of which must be continuously re-examined in order to achieve a better and more equitable society.

Works cited

Abruna, Laura Niesen de. "Jamaica Kincaid's Writing and the Maternal-Colonial Matrix." *Caribbean Women Writers: Fiction in English*, edited by Mary Condé and Thorunn Lonsdale. Macmillan Press, 1999, pp. 172–183.

Bonetti, Kay. "Interview with Jamaica Kincaid." *The Missouri Review,* Fall 2002, www.missourireview.com/article/interview-with-jamaica-kincaid/. Accessed 03 October, 2017.

Caldeira, Isabel. "Toni Morrison and Edwidge Danticat – Writers as Citizens of the African Diaspora or 'The Margins as a Space of Radical Openness'." *The Routledge Companion of Inter-American Studies*, edited by Wilfried Raussert. Routledge, 2017, pp. 207–218.

Caliban French Journal of English Studies, vol. 21, 2007, caliban.revues.org/1883#-text. Accessed 24 October, 2017.

Coates, Ta-Nehisi. *Between the World and Me*. Spiegel & Grau, 2015.

Coates, Ta-Nehisi. "Foreword." *The Origin of Others*. Harvard University Press, 2017, pp. VII–XVII.

Ferguson, Moira. "Lucy as the Mark of the Colonizer." *MFS Modern Fiction Studies*, vol. 39, issue 2. Johns Hopkins University Press, 1993, pp. 237–259.

Ferguson, Moira and Jamaica Kincaid. "A Lot of Memory: An Interview with Jamaica Kincaid" *The Kenyon Review*, New Series, vol.16, issue 1. Kenyon College, 1994.

Gilmore, Leigh. *The Limits of Autobiography – Trauma and Testimony*. Cornell University Press, 2011.

Kincaid, Jamaica. *My Brother*. Farrar Straus Giroux, 1998.

Marquis, Claudia. "'Not at Home in Her Own Skin': Jamaica Kincaid, History and Selfhood." *Caliban: French Journal of English Studies*, vol. 21, pp. 101–114.

Morrison, Toni. *Burn This Book: Writers Speak Out on the Power of the World*. Harper, 2009.

Morrison, Toni. *The Origin of Others*. Harvard University Press, 2017.

United Nations. "Equality and Non-discrimination." 2018. https://www.un.org/ruleoflaw/thematic-areas/human-rights/equality-and-non discrimination/. Accessed 18 June, 2018.

8 The rebirth of the myth of the American hero and feminism

Rita Santos

Introduction

The attacks of September 11, 2001 remain as one of the most traumatic events in American history. With Susan Faludi's *The Terror Dream: What 9/11 Revealed about America* as my main reference, in this Chapter I explores the ways in which 9/11 trauma may have awoken old myths present in the American imaginary, giving way to the rebirth of the American hero/John Wayne-esque myth. Part of the objective is to then explore the implications this new construction of the American hero had on feminism and which role was attributed to women afterward.

First, a general framework is provided on the notions of collective and cultural trauma in order to understand the recourse to the past. Then the focus becomes on how captivity narratives set a pattern for the hero/victim dichotomy and women's passive role in times of crisis. After exploring the ways in which feminism and feminists were attacked and partially blamed for the attacks, we move onto the consequences of such beliefs. Afterward, it is imperative to delve into all the ways 9/11 affected the heroification process in American society and culture and how that process ended up pushing women into the private sphere while men were driven to the public sphere. Finally, the analysis will lead to examining the ways in which the American hero myth is currently being portrayed and how those portrayals affect women's role in these mythical constructions.

Trauma: grasping the past to make sense of the present

When discussing trauma, some authors make the mistake of having in mind only individual events. One of the authors known for focusing on the difference between individual and collective trauma is Kai Erikson. He defines individual trauma as "a blow to the psyche that breaks through one's defenses so suddenly and with such brutal force that one cannot react to it effectively" (qtd. in Alexander 4). On the other hand, by collective trauma, he means "a blow to the basic tissues of social life that damages the bonds attaching people together and impairs the prevailing sense of communality" (qtd. in Alexander 4).

The exploration of collective trauma focuses mainly on the feelings of powerlessness and hopelessness that consume and affect the sense of collective self. In this sense, the main difference between individual and collective trauma is that the latter has more extended repercussions, affecting the main structures of a community, while the former is singular, putting at stake a single individual's relationships and personal identity.

The events of September 11, 2001 are part of a collective trauma. Although they represent crimes committed against individuals, they targeted the American community. Therefore, it is essential to briefly explore the notion of collective trauma in order to understand the impact that the events had on the American sense of self. Ganzevoort and Veerman discuss the effects that collective trauma has on the way the damaged community relates to other communities, "Common phenomena are withdrawal and isolation, identifying enemies and scapegoating, or surrendering to external forces" (5). The American people became more isolated after the events, with high levels of mistrust and wariness taking over their community. Furthermore, the identification of enemies was also easily achieved by holding grudges against Muslims.

When talking about collective trauma, it is impossible not to think about culture. Trauma and culture are connected, and collective trauma will reveal just that intricate connection. Whenever an event brings pain and trauma to individuals of a community, the pain and grief is collective because of their shared culture. Culture is the glue bringing trauma and community together. Both concepts are intrinsically associated not only to each other, but also to the notion of identity (both of the community and of the individuals who belong to it). When faced with the aftermath of cultural trauma, the sense of community identity may either be strengthened or disrupted (Baelo-Allué 64).[1] This reveals that culture will play a vital role in the overcoming of the collective trauma.

Given the traumatic nature of the 9/11 events, the entire phenomenon was difficult to understand or explain. Therefore, in an attempt to make sense of what was happening around them, it is normal that Americans looked at history and tried to hold onto historical and national myths to try to grasp some conclusions out of it and make sense of what had happened.

From captivity narratives to John Wayne

Nancy Gibbs' words in *Time* magazine in October, 2001 revealed very clearly this connection between culture, trauma, identity, and the past, by stating "we are seeing it in our nation and sensing it in ourselves, a new faith in our oldest values" (2001). Included in these values are also the national myths and narratives that played such a decisive role in Puritan America and its subsequent heritage to contemporary United States. One of the most important contributors to these myths are the captivity narratives of the

17th century, taking us back to the early core of Puritan society. According to Richard Slotkin,

> In [a captivity narrative] a single individual, usually a woman, stands passively under the strokes of evil, awaiting rescue by the grace of God. The sufferer represents the whole, chastened body of Puritan society; and the temporary bondage of the captive to the Indian [a] is dual paradigm - of the bondage of the soul to the flesh and the temptations arising from original sin, and of the self-exile of the English Israel from England. In the Indian's devilish clutches, the captive had to meet and reject the temptation of Indian marriage and/or the Indian's "cannibal" Eucharist. (94)

These narratives played a crucial role in the American imaginary because they set a pattern for the hero/victim dichotomy still present in the world of today. In the Indian captivity narratives in early puritan America, women were captured by Native Americans and held captive by them. These narratives not only had an important impact on the establishment of a European-American identity, but they also illustrated how women were "doubly victimized" in Puritan America: they were captured and held as prisoners by the Indians, but their stories were then used as propaganda to demonize the Indians (Derounian-Stodola 33). A similar phenomenon would happen again with the Afghans and Iraqis after 9/11 under the Bush administration, as I will focus on ahead in this chapter.

Furthermore, captivity narratives helped shape the role of women in the American puritan society, a role which was already oppressed and submissive, totally devoid of any powerful position in the state and in the church. As a result, women started being seen as victims in need of rescue. This was an idea that persisted in the American imaginary until today. Due to length constraints, I will not discuss the evolution of this notion, but it is important to have in mind that there was a resurgence of this myth mainly in the 1950s. This revival may have been caused by the significant turn in the feminist movement during WWII, when women were pushed to work outside of their homes to occupy the jobs left vacant by men who were fighting in the war. Although once the war was over they were encouraged to get back to their domestic life and dedicate their lives to their families, many women continued to work outside the home. Even the 1950s media promoted the idea that men would only regain their masculinity if women reclaimed their femininity (Faludi 282). Such notion was expanded to Hollywood, where the film *The Searchers*, with John Wayne, became the basis of all Hollywood films of the time, carrying and exacerbating the national myth of the happy ending where the good guys prevail over the bad guys and save the girl.

Due to the characters he portrayed, John Wayne became one of the true American heroes. Still today, his popularity in the United States is a remarkable phenomenon to be witnessed. When asking Americans who their "favorite star" is, John Wayne's name is the only one appearing on the annual Harris poll since it first began, in 1994. On the poll conducted in 2014, John Wayne remained the favorite star among men and conservatives. These are interesting results which allow us to understand even better how these core values are still present in the American imaginary (Shannon-Missal 2015). In my view, the Golden Age of comic books (from the 1930s to early 1950s) and the subsequent rising popularity of the superhero archetype were also important contributors that allowed for this John Wayne myth to gain momentum, as I will explore later on in this chapter.

After the events of 9/11, while facing terror, the United States clung to what it has always been thought to be its best formula of security—by living immersed in mythical fiction instead of reality. This generated a series of mechanisms diverting people from the real problem—the U.S. foreign policy. Instead of trying to understand why the attacks had happened and how the United States could be partially responsible for them, the nation saw itself as the ultimate victim, as the ever so often reckless comparisons to the Holocaust prove. As I will explain, in doing so, the United States chose to turn the 9/11 into a domestic issue, with the feminist influence being a major culprit of the current American vulnerability. This caused a major uproar of attacks to feminism and female voices who dared to call out attention to this issue.

Backlash against feminism

According to Faludi, days after the attacks, feminism and feminists became one of the main targets in media. For some reason, everything that had gone down at the World Trade Center and the Pentagon had proved how female independence should be disclaimed. Perhaps the most striking examples of such attacks are those of Rev. Jerry Falwell, who said,

> The abortionists have got to bear some burden for this because God will not be mocked. And when we destroy 40 million little innocent babies, we make God mad. I really believe that the pagans, and the abortionists, and the feminists, and the gays and the lesbians who are actively trying to make that an alternative lifestyle, the ACLU, People for the American Way, all of them who have tried to secularize America, I point the finger in their face and say, 'You helped this to happen.'
>
> *(Goldstein 2001)*

Although the following opinions are strictly directed at feminism, they are just as prejudiced as those of Falwell's. Cathy Young (2002) believes, "after years of male-bashing, it is good to see some appreciation for male heroism and even for the fact that traditional machismo always included not only dominance but protection and rescue." Charen (2001) states, "perhaps the new climate of danger – danger from evil men – will quiet the anti-male agitation we've endured for so long."

One can only understand these positions by referencing something Faludi does not acknowledge—that the misconception of the term feminism is the root of such dubious statements. If the term feminism were not in a continuous process of pejoration, its meaning would not have the degrading connotations that encouraged Falwell, Young, or Charen to believe they are stating universal truths. Feminism, as a movement, does neither promote male hatred or bashing nor does it associate men with evil forces.

Despite disregarding the misconception of the term feminism, Faludi argues that these positions come from the fact that, in the perspective of this particular group of people, feminism has "softened" men in the United States. It is interesting how this already challenging claim has another problematic notion associated to it: that "femininity" stands for weakness, fragility, and vulnerability while strength, power, and roughness are associated with "masculinity."

During times of indecision, changes on any spectrum are often feared. With feminism being one of the most prominent social changes, this fear held by the American society toward feminists would not only lead to attacks on them, but also to the silencing of female voices in general.

Silencing of female voices

According to an analysis of the newspaper *The Guardian*, there was a significant drop of female representation on television and newspapers right after 9/11 (Bunting), with white men dominating the public opinion. Faludi successfully presents examples that confirm this male favoritism, from which the most striking one is perhaps a study on the female representation on Sunday talk shows that revealed a drop of 40% in the number of appearances by American women (35). It is important to clarify that not all women were silenced, but even those who had the opportunity to have their voices heard became the target of abusive and sordid name-calling. Susan Sontag's provocative article for *The New Yorker* on September 24, 2001, where she suggested that the attacks were a response to the controversial and problematic U.S. foreign policies, instantly warranted her with a panoply of insults. Magazine editors and columnists called her "deranged" and "an ally of evil," accusing her of suffering from "moral idiocy" and of "hating America and the West and freedom and democratic goodness" (27). It is interesting to note how there were left-wing men who were just as provocative and critical as Sontag (such as Gore Vidal and Bill Maher) and yet they were not nearly as insulted as Sontag. Although Faludi extensively explores how women were ignored, I have identified two main problems in her analysis. While she is successful in providing with examples of female opinions on the events, she could have focused more on the women who actually died on that day and whose courageous acts were either ignored or forgotten while men were elevated to hero status. For example, in the following weeks after the attacks, Eileen Shulock, an unemployed woman at the time, decided

The rebirth of the myth 149

to use all of her internet knowledge and managed to recruit online 3000 volunteers for rescue agencies, such as the Red Cross and the United Way (Dollarhide 2001a). Rosemary George, an African American ironworker, was called to help clear the site of the collapsed World Trade Center and put her own life at risk by spending three days digging through the rubble and clearing debris with her own hands in search of survivors (Dollarhide 2001b). These are just some of the examples Faludi could have mentioned in her book. I will talk about other brave women of 9/11 later on in this paper when analyzing the way male firefighters and police officers were heroicized.

However, even when Faludi is not centering her attention on the women who perished that day, the examples she chose to talk about could be more inclusive and intersectional, which constitutes the second problem in her analysis. For instance, at a certain point, Faludi mentions how even feminists "across the border" were not safe from criticism, giving only an example of a Canadian columnist for the *Toronto Star* (32). Were there no opinions by female Latin Americans on the 9/11 that Faludi could have mentioned? Nonetheless, this does not mean that the author completely neglects women who, in the center/margin dichotomy, do not belong to the center. Faludi references Anastasia Soare (120), a Romanian woman who has become an icon in the American beauty industry, and Belen Aranda-Alvarado, a Latin American member of the Harvard Business School (132). Still, when it comes to account of the actual survivors or their relatives, the stories chosen by Faludi refer to white middle-class women. Given the wide array of information on how minorities were subjected to exponential levels of discrimination in the aftermath of 9/11, I wonder why Faludi did not address this double invisibility of women who belong to the margins and how their silencing greatly contributed for the general lack of female voices being heard.

For instance, in 2011, *Time* magazine published a photographic commemorative edition of the 10th anniversary of the attacks. Despite the 12 African American firefighters who perished on that day, there were no pictures of African Americans in *Time*'s remembrance issue. When faced with such situation, the mothers of these firefighters decided to struggle to keep their sons' memories alive (Prince). Also Luz María Mendoza, a Mexican widow whose husband, Juan Ortega, died during the attacks worked to keep his memory alive. Because Ortega was an undocumented migrant, his wife struggled for several years of overlooking to prove that he worked at the World Trade Center (Good). Or after losing her partner, Sheila Hein, in the terrorist attack on the Pentagon, Peggy Neff was denied compensation by Virginia's Criminal Injuries Compensation Fund, a decision that had solely to do with the fact that same-sex partners do not have the same rights as heterosexual couples (Lombardi).

The abovementioned examples given above did not receive the same amount of attention and exposure as several other stories of white middle-class families of the victims coping with their losses. Addressing such situations (or those with similar outlines) would have made Faludi's argument more diverse and intersectional. By also silencing the voices of minorities, Faludi ends up putting to practice what she accused the United States of doing.

Surprisingly enough, at the same time female voices were being silenced and ignored, the Bush administration tried to take advantage of women's rights to legitimate the U.S. welfare interventions as a response to the 9/11 attacks. Gender has always been an efficient tool to legitimize war and national security (Tickner 336), a point also highlighted by Susan Faludi. George W. Bush used women's liberation in a rather opportunist attempt to gather more supporters on the Afghanistan invasion, by presenting the inexistent education of Afghan women as one of the reasons why the United States should intervene in that country. It is also interesting to note the importance and influence of the First Lady during this campaign. In November 2001, Laura Bush used the president's weekly radio address to call out attention to the "brutality against women and children by the al-Qaida terrorist network and the regime it supports in Afghanistan, the Taliban" (2001). One may conclude that a female voice talking about other women's rights would have a greater emotional impact on other women. Nonetheless, this concern about women's rights proved to be disingenuous when Bush supported Afghan president Hamid Karzai, who would later be responsible for the passing of laws that allow husbands to deny wives food if they fail to follow their sexual demands (Boone). In addition to this, once the war started, there were suddenly no more allusions to the Afghan women's liberation movement, proving just how much Bush's real interests did not lie on women's rights.

One piece of information that may seem contradictory, and that Faludi does not mention, is how the Bush administration was one of the most gender diverse in history, until Obama's first term (Page). However, regardless of this diversity, what is truly important to retain is to look at the political decisions favoring women and other minorities, an aspect that does not favor the Bush administration in the slightest. From supporting anti-feminist organizations to shutting down women's offices in the government, we are able to conclude that Bush was likely trying to take advantage of such a demonstration of inclusiveness to gain popularity amongst women and other minorities. But regardless of his intentions, these people still had positions of power in the White House and such a fact should not have been disregarded by Faludi when discussing the ways in which women have become invisible in a post-9/11 United States. Such invisibility, however, would become especially noticeable when compared to the elevation of men as heroes.

9/11 and the rebirth of the myth of the American hero

Besides silencing women, the trauma of 9/11 also contributed to the reemergence of the notion of the American hero, in which Faludi describes as a promotion of "American chivalry." Unsurprisingly, the main character trait of the American hero was his manliness, in a revival of the problematic equation of manliness and masculinity with power and strength.

The rebirth of the myth 151

All over the country, "manly man" politicians and other powerful figures, such as George W. Bush, Donald Rumsfeld, Dick Cheney and Rudy Giuliani, had their bodies and faces edited in magazines to make them look like superheroes. 9/11 attained a mythic stamp from the very beginning in the way President George W. Bush handled the situation. Disregarding any possible connection between the events and U.S. foreign policy, Bush was quick to assert, "America was targeted for attack because we're the brightest beacon for freedom and opportunity in the world." (2001). From here on, Bush was known to acquire a dualistic and one-dimensional view of the events, where the United States stood for good and the terrorists stood for evil. According to Faludi, this "cartoonish" comic book storyline where Americans were the heroes and the terrorists the villains helped Bush in gaining more supporters (47). This is in direct dialog with what I mentioned earlier in this chapter: that the myths brought along with this "cartoonization" of the events and the role of comic books, together with the heritage of the captivity narratives, were the two main factors contributing to the resurgence of the John Wayne myth of the American hero.

An interesting trend right after the attacks was the way in which the event affected the comic book and cartoon industry. To help people cope, the responses from this industry took a variety of forms and appeared shortly after September 11 with DC Comics and Marvel releasing projects related to the events. This trend was highly visible in other forms of popular culture, expanding to television and cinema. Television shows like *Heroes*, *Lost*, and *24* offered these "manly man" representations of heroes. In cinema, there was a new wave of superhero movies in the 2000s, with the *X-Men* series, *Spider-Man*, *Daredevil*, *Batman*, and *Catwoman*, just to name a few. Meanwhile, in the series of the most iconic characters in the comic book universe, superheroes were portrayed as being powerless, in an attempt to make these characters more relatable to the American people through the transposition of their recent fragility to the classic ultimate heroes.

However, at the same time that the established fictional superheroes were portrayed as powerless, in real life, the "manly man" *John Wayne-esque* hero prevailed. Faludi describes this phenomenon as a "reversal in hero worship," where Superman and company were replaced by ordinary people in the true American hero podium (51). But who were these heroes "of its own" in the United States after 9/11? And what role did women play in this new redistribution of heroism?

Joseph Campbell, an authority in the superhero mythology, developed the concept of the Classical Monomyth:

> A hero ventures forth from the world of common day into a region of supernatural wonder: fabulous forces are there encountered and a decisive victory is won: the hero comes back from this mysterious adventure with the power to bestow boons on his fellow man. (qtd. in Jewett and Lawrence 6)

Borrowing from this definition, Robert Jewett and John Shelton Lawrence argued for an American variation of this concept, naming it "The American Monomyth":

> A community in a harmonious paradise is threatened by evil; normal institutions fail to contend with this threat; a selfless superhero emerges to renounce temptations and carry out the redemptive task; aided by fate, his decisive victory restores the community to its paradisiacal condition.
>
> *(Jewett and Lawrence 6)*

In this concept proposed by Jewett and Lawrence, it is also visible the presence of the John Wayne myth in this "selfless superhero" who saves the day and defeats evil. But how did 9/11 fit in this "American Monomyth" narrative?

Police officers, firefighters, and citizens who offered their efforts to help those struggling with the terror-taking place on Ground Zero and the Pentagon were instantly on the front page of newspapers and featured on TV. These were the John Waynes of our time – the noble, heroic, and regular strong "macho men" of the New York Police Department (NYPD), the Fire Department of New York (FDNY), and the citizens who selflessly put their lives at risk to save as many people as possible. Even if many perished and were not able to "restore the community to its paradisiacal condition," their efforts were still considered courageous and heroic. However, amidst this heroification process, one has to wonder where the "Jane" Waynes were.

After 9/11, while men were elevated to heroes, women were relegated to forgetfulness. Most of the stories being publicized the following weeks after the attacks featured men as the gallant rescuers, mainly of women. Just to provide an example, this was particularly visible in the story with high media coverage of how a group of firefighters inside the North tower of the World Trade Center refused to leave a woman behind even when the tower was collapsing, saving her life in the process (Dale). This association of action and bravery with masculinity while passivity and helplessness equate femininity is another important heritage of the myths originated from the captivity narratives I have explored in the beginning of this study. As a result, this ever-growing tendency to equate masculinity with action and heroism, while femininity was associated with passivity and helplessness, eclipsed the efforts of many women who, on that day, were just as brave and courageous as their male counterparts.

One year after the attacks, Lt. Brenda Berkman, a veteran New York City firefighter, pointed out that the passing over of women firefighters was so common that the sexism had spread to language, with the term "fireman" returning to vogue (Miller). Berkman was one of the many women firefighters who expressed her resentment on the way so many of the female fearless acts on that day went unnoticed: "Women were down there from the time that the first plane hit the first tower [...] Women were trapped in the rubble.

The rebirth of the myth 153

Three women rescue workers were killed that day," including paramedic Yamel Merino, Port Authority Capt. Kathy Mazza and police officer Moira Smith. According to witness accounts, the last two women displayed great bravery that day. Mazza is said to have oriented her officers on the World Trade Center, where they were killed while trying to carry a woman out of the building. After helping an injured man out of the World Trade Center, Moira Smith ran back into the South Tower, and was later killed in the collapse while trying to rescue other people (Drexler). Smith was even photographed moments before returning to the South Tower, but that still did not prevent her story to be considerably less covered or promoted than those of her male colleagues. As Berkman put it,

> I've been a firefighter for 20 years and I've never seen the contribution of women firefighters, police officers and paramedics so completely ignored. Suddenly, we've become invisible. It's as though we were wearing the American equivalent of the veil.
>
> *(qtd. in Faludi 82)*

Faludi calls our attention to the fact that, despite 75–80% of the 9/11 victims being men (CNN Library), the several images of men rescuing women could be deceptive. Despite this, it would be false to claim women were completely silenced or ignored. There were instances where women were the main focus of attention. I will explore next how even in those occasions of apparent protagonism, women kept being pushed to the private sphere.

Female survivors, male heroes

In the months after the attacks, the media focused most of their attention on the families of the victims, trying to understand how they were coping with their losses. This coverage, however, was not equally distributed and, unlike what was happening with the construction of the narratives of the 9/11 heroes, women became the center of all attention. The stories of pregnant widows whose babies were going to be born after the death of their fathers were the preferential option for headlines and newspaper covers. In 2002, *People* magazine even organized a photoshoot in New York, gathering 9/11 widows and their newborn babies for a group photo (Faludi 95). Nevertheless, the 9/11 widowers became invisible. Their stories were not as widely distributed as those of the widows and they certainly were not given the chance to take a group photo with other widowers and their children. Despite this, the narratives that now pushed women to the foreground (and men to the background) were focused solely on their role as mothers and wives. In this situation, the media attention was on women while men in a similar position were being dismissed. However, since the reasons that pushed women to public attention were led by their private sphere role of family caretakers, it can be argued that, despite now being in leading roles in the media, the essence of that protagonism still pushed women to the private sphere. A good example of this was Lisa Beamer, wife of Todd Beamer, one of the Flight 93 passengers who was proclaimed a hero. After learning she was pregnant by the time of the attacks, reporters hounded her. Regardless of her cooperation in being in the spotlight, all the questions directed at her were extremely personal and intrusive, as Faludi illustrates:

> This Christmas doesn't it make you sadder? [...] Now, how do the boys like having a little sister? [...] Does she sleep well at night? [...] What do you have, one boy in a bed and two in cribs now? [....] (qtd. in Faludi 100)

All these questions revolving around Lisa Beamer demonstrate this obsession of the American media in portraying the 9/11 widows as perfect suburban wives. Those who did not engage with the media were then warranted with public judgments on the way they were spending their money, "They seized on rumors about widows who supposedly had face-lifts, Botox injections, breast implants, and cosmetic surgery – one was even said to have gone under the knife 'on her wedding anniversary'" (Faludi 104). This attempt to push women into the private sphere fits the portrayal of men as heroes and women as victims, resulting in the idea of the woman in distress who needs to be protected by the fierce man.

With this new resurgence of the American hero and its misogynist consequences that jolted women into the private sphere, it is important to now explore how all the processes explored so far in this study have changed since 2001. I will try to show what shape the American hero myth is currently taking and what the implications for feminism are.

What about today?

Earlier on in this study, I have talked about the pejoration of the term "feminism." Unfortunately, there have been no significant changes in this process that encourages people worldwide to distance themselves from "the F word." To this very moment there are campaigns comparing feminists to terrorists, where the most bizarre example of that association is a petition circulating online whose goal is to officially consider feminism as a terrorist movement (Wilkinson). On social media, there have been movements, such as, "Why I don't need feminism" or "I need meninism because ..." where both men and women talk about everything but what feminism truly stands for. Overall, feminism is still acknowledged as a bad word that is understood as a synonym for misandry.

Just like feminists were to blame for the American male "softness" registered pre-9/11, today feminists are blamed for a whole new variety of events. Just to give some of the most controversial examples: earlier this year, a Catholic Cardinal stated, "radical feminism" was to blame for the pedophile acts by priests (Ferguson). He argued that feminists were responsible for the current established "fluffy" view of sexuality, making way to pedophile priests. According to Charlotte Allen, the lack of male aggression in the "feminized setting [that] is a setting in which helpless passivity is the norm" at Sandy Hook Elementary was an important factor that allowed the shooting to take place (Allen).

In 2007, when talking about the silencing of female voices on the media after 9/11, Rebecca Traister accused Faludi of focusing only on the side that better serves her interests. She claimed that during the years mentioned by Faludi, there were women occupying positions of power on the media, such as Jill Abramson, Ariel Levy, among others (Traister). However, just as Faludi should look at the big picture instead of generalizing, so should Rebecca Traister. According to the Women's Media Center, gender representation statistics from 2014 show that, in newspaper newsrooms, women occupied only 37.2% of the positions. This is actually 0.01% less compared to the numbers gathered in 2001. The report also demonstrates how gender inequality among journalists, whether online, on television or in print still persists. The results reveal that men dominate media by 62.1% against women's 37.3% (Women's Media Center). While I could not get access to reliable statistics on the US media gender gap in 2001, what is important to retain is that these numbers are still troublesome. Little has changed since 2012, when the first report by the Women's Media Center came out. It is a reality that women are still underrepresented on the U.S. media and, as a result, female voices are still being silenced, allowing for Faludi's argument to be taken in consideration.

Considering my earlier focus on the way 9/11 affected female firefighters and police officers, I think it is relevant to look at the current number of women present in the FDNY and the NYPD. In FDNY, as of May 2015, out of 10,500 firefighters, there were 46 women, constituting an historic high for the department and an improvement since 2001 (Marcus and Otis).

As for the NYPD, the latest data I was able to find is from 2009 and revealed an increase of female police officers to 40% since 2001, according to Police Commissioner Raymond W. Kelly (NYPD). These numbers reflect an increasing number of women being admitted both in the FDNY and the NYPD, but the gender gap is still astonishingly high.

Considering how the American Hero myth has such intrinsic origins that are deeply engrained in the American subconscious, one could assume that this myth is static, generating narratives that perpetuate the "American Monomyth" concept. To understand how this myth has been recently presented, I will focus on two popular movies that came out in 2014: *American Sniper* and *Interstellar*. Although both films deal with this notion of what (and who) is an American hero, I will be focusing more deeply on *American Sniper* due to its autobiographical character and representation of real life events.

In *American Sniper*, directed by Clint Eastwood, the presence of the "American Monomyth" is very noticeable: the selfless unexpected hero puts upon himself the responsibility of restoring the community order against all obstacles. The narrative that was built around Chris Kyle fits this pattern:

an unknown humble ranch worker in Texas who then becomes a Navy Seal and is deployed to the Iraq war, where he fights to protect his country and is considered the most lethal sniper in U.S. history. But was Chris Kyle an American hero?

In his memoir, he claimed, "shooting the machine gun was fun!" (96) and dwelled on how he "couldn't give a flying fuck about the Iraqis" (271) because he "hated the damn savages" he had been fighting (301). In fact, Chris Kyle seemed to adopt the same one-dimensional perspective on the Iraq war perpetuated by George W. Bush. Given the way Iraq had not invaded or attacked the United States, when deciding to attack that country, Americans became the aggressors. However, in the American rhetoric, the aggressors were the heroes while the Iraqis, who were protecting themselves against the invaders, were the villains and "the savages." This was a dangerous position that legitimized the dehumanization of Iraqis, an act that Chris Kyle himself engaged in "Every person I killed I strongly believe that they were bad [...] When I do go face God, there is going to be lots of things I will have to account for, but killing any of those people is not one of them." (Hegarty). This dehumanization of the Iraqi people is also very apparent in the film as they are portrayed as coldhearted vicious monsters (Eastwood). This portrayal ended up encouraging some Americans to tweet about their desire to take action against Iraqis. As Kolhatkar reports, "*American Sniper* makes me wanna go shoot some fuckin' Arabs," "Great f...king movie and now I really want to kill some f...king ragheads" (2015). Nonetheless, the movie has divided the country mainly in two. Some Americans say Chris Kyle was a hero while others believe he was far from being one. Representing one side, we have Kolhatkar demystifying the film narrative based on true facts of Chris Kyle's life.

> *American Sniper* exemplifies a sense of macho, white male braggadocio that is symbolic of all that is wrong with the right-wing, pro-war, pro-gun, bully culture of the United States. Should we really be surprised that both the American public and the Academy are rewarding a film about a man who, judging by his own words, appeared to be a psychotic mass murderer?
>
> *(Kolhatkar 2015)*

On the other side, there is Lauri B. Regan supporting the acts committed against the Iraqis and the American need of heroes such as Kyle to fight "the enemy."

While watching *American Sniper*, the viewer is observing events that occurred recently and that may well take place tomorrow. There is no escaping the fact that the "evil f—king savages" as Kyle so aptly calls them are alive and well—and coming for us (2015).

Judging by the way the film celebrates Kyle as a hero, Clint Eastwood is clearly on the latter side, sharing a warped view of the events.

We have seen before how women do not have a leading role in the "American Monomyth" narratives. *American Sniper* is not an exception. Taya Kyle, the sniper's wife, is portrayed solely as an attentive and concerned wife and mother, in which her only purpose is to be a support system to Chris. Again, while men are heroicized, women are pushed to the background.

In *Interstellar*, another movie that came out 2014, the "American Monomyth" narrative present in it breaks this tradition of women being pushed to the background. In this respect, the film does something innovative: Cooper, an "average Joe" farmer, becomes the unlikely hero of a space mission to save humanity and his heroification process begins when he succeeds. Nonetheless, unlike in other "American Monomyth" narratives, as Cooper is elevated to hero status, the women in his life are not pushed to the background. Instead, his daughter, Murph (one of the two female main characters) goes through the heroification process along with him and eventually becomes the real hero of the story (Nolan).

Both films demonstrate that Americans still have not moved "beyond mythical consciousness" (Jewett and Lawrence 6)—they are still trapped in the "endlessly repeated story of innocent communities besieged by evil outsiders" (Jewett and Lawrence 16) who are then saved by an average Joe.

Still with no release date as of this moment is the movie "Ashley's War," an adaptation of the homonymous book telling the story of a team of women soldiers fighting on the front line in Afghanistan (Brown). In what is expected to be a female heavy film, it will be interesting to see how the American hero myth is explored and what role(s) women will play in it.

Conclusion

Recently after Susan Faludi published her book, Rebecca Traister accused her of seeing a "vast national conspiracy to put women back in the kitchen and alpha males like John Wayne [...] back in their lost positions of power" (2007). I hope this study has demonstrated how I disagree with Traister's assessment. Naming this process, a conspiracy would mean that the agents perpetrating it are entirely aware of it. As I have shown, due to the trauma inflicted upon Americans with 9/11, resorting to history and national myths to make sense of what happened came as a coping process. These myths, particularly captivity narratives and the patriarchy engrained in Puritan America, helped give rise to the American hero myth, where men are the strong and manly heroes and women the powerless and weak victims in need of rescue. With the resurgence of this American hero myth, women were portrayed as the victims who did not have a primary role in the heroification process of regular civilians, firefighters, and police officers. As the manly heroes were being exposed to the public sphere, the female invisibility cloak pushed women to the private sphere. Even in the very particular occasions when women were the protagonists, what propelled them to the foreground concerned their dutiful roles as mothers and wives, in a process that only pushed them even more to the private sphere. These myths and all of their consequences to women are still present in the American imaginary. More than a conspiracy, Faludi was trying to alert us to the dangers of an internalized misogyny. Through the rebirth of the American hero myth perspective, I have tried to explain how this engrained prejudice against women also appears to intensify and gain momentum in times of crisis. We need to be aware of these mechanisms and processes so that, in the future, we can prevent women from being pushed to the background while men are distinguished as heroes. Human beings are capable of great deeds—why should not both men and women be celebrated for their bravery amidst chaos?

Note

1. Sonia Baelo-Allué rightly points out how coloniality continues to produce racial and sexual differences through a racialization and sexualization of labor. In her article, she further critiques Quijano's concept of "coloniality of power" as Eurocentric and male centric.

Works cited

Alexander, Jeffrey Charles; Eyerman, Ron; Giesen, Bernhard; Smelser, Neil; Sztompka, Piotr. *Cultural Trauma and Collective Identity.* University of California Press, 2004.

Allen, Charlotte. Newtown Answers. *National Review,* 19 Dec., 2012, http://www.nationalreview.com/article/335996/newtown-answers-nro-symposium. Accessed 14 Nov., 2017.

Baelo-Allué, Sonia. "9/11 and the Psychic Trauma Novel: Don DeLillo's Falling Man." *Atlantis: Journal of the Spanish Association of Anglo-American Studies,* no.34, 2012, http://www.atlantisjournal.org/old/ARCHIVE/34.1/SBAELO_2012.pdf. Accessed 14 Nov., 2017.

Boon, Jon. "Afghanistan passes 'barbaric' law diminishing women's rights." *The Guardian,* 14 August. Accessed 14 Nov., 2017, http://www.theguardian.com/world/2009/aug/14/afghanistan-womens-rights-rape. Accessed 15 Nov., 2017.

Brown, Kat. "Reese Witherspoon to star in 'female American Sniper'." *The Telegraph,* 12 March 2015, http://www.telegraph.co.uk/culture/film/film-news/11467280/Reese-Witherspoon-to-star-in-female-American-Sniper.html. Accessed 14 Nov., 2017.

Bunting, Madeleine. "Women and War." *The Guardian,* 20 September 2001, http://www.theguardian.com/education/2001/sep/20/socialsciences.highereducation. Accessed 14 Nov., 2017.

Bush, George Walker. "Address to the Nation on the Terrorist Attacks." *The American Presidency Project,* 11 September, 2001a, http://www.presidency.ucsb.edu/ws/index.php?pid=58057&st=&st1=. Accessed 14 Nov., 2017.

Bush, Laura. "Radio Address by Mrs. Bush." *The American Presidency Project,* 17 November, 2001b, http://www.presidency.ucsb.edu/ws/?pid=24992. Accessed 14 Nov., 2017.

Charen, Mona. "Hooray for Men." *Townhall.com,* 31 December 2001, http://townhall.com/columnists/monacharen/2001/12/31/hooray_for_men. Accessed 14 Nov., 2017.

CNN Library. "September 11th Fast Facts." 2015, http://edition.cnn.com/2013/07/27/us/september-11-anniversary-fast-facts/. Accessed 14 Nov., 2017.

Dale, Richard. *Inside the Twin Towers*, Dangerous Films, 2006.

Derounian-Stodola, Kathryn Zabelle. "The Indian Captivity Narratives of Mary Rowlandson and Olive Oatman: Case Studies in the Continuity, Evolution, and Exploitation of Literary Discourse." *Studies in the Literary Imagination*, vol. 27, issue 1, 1996, pp. 33–46.

Dollarhide, Maya. "Using E-mail List, Shulock Finds 3,000 Volunteers." *Womensenews.org,* 5 November 2001a. http://womensenews.org/story/our-history/011105/using-e-mail-list-shulock-finds-3000-volunteers?page=0,1. Accessed 14 Nov., 2017.

Dollarhide, Maya. "Ironworker George Cleared Debris With Her Hands", Womensenews.org, 22 October, 2001b, http://womensenews.org/story/our-history/011022/ironworker-george-cleared-debris-her-hands. Accessed 14 Nov., 2017.

Drexler, Peggy. "This Time, the Brother Is a Sister." *Womensenews.com,* 3 April, 2002, http://womensenews.org/story/commentary/020403/time-the-brother-sister. Accessed 14 Nov., 2017.

Eastwood, Clint. *American Sniper.* Warner Brothers, 2014.

Faludi, Susan. *The Terror Dream: What 9/11 Revealed about America.* Atlantic Books, 2007.

Ferguson, David. "Demoted Catholic Cardinal: 'Radical feminists' are to blame for pedophile priests." *Raw Story,* 7 January 2015, http://www.rawstory.com/2015/01/demoted-catholic-cardinal-radical-feminists-are-to-blame-for-pedophile-priests/. Accessed 14 Nov., 2017.

Ganzevoort, R. Ruart and Alexander L. Veerman. *Communities Coping with Collective Trauma.* Paper presented at the Conference of the International Association for the Psychology of Religion, Soesterberg, The Netherlands, September, 2001.

Gibbs, Nancy. "The Swords of Justice." *Time Magazine,* 1 October, 2001, http://content.time.com/time/world/article/0,8599,2047952,00.html. Accessed 14.11.2017.

Goldstein, Laurie. "Falwell: Blame Abortionists, Feminists and Gays." *The Guardian,* 19 September, 2001, http://www.theguardian.com/world/2001/sep/19/september11.usa9. Accessed 14 2017.

Good, Alastair. "September 11: Mexico's Forgotten 9/11 Victim." *The Telegraph,* 6 Sept., 2011, http://www.telegraph.co.uk/news/worldnews/september-11-ttacks/8745821/September-11-Mexicos-forgotten-911-victim.html. Accessed 14 Nov., 2017.

Hegarty, Stephanie. "What Goes on in the Mind of a Sniper?." *BBC News,* 25 January 2015, http://www.bbc.com/news/magazine-16544490. Accessed 14 Nov., 2017.

Infoplease. "Live Births and Birth Rates, by Year", 2007, http://www.infoplease.com/ipa/A0005067.html. Accessed 14 Nov., 2017.

Jewett, Robert and John Shelton Lawrence. *The Myth of the American Superhero.* William B. Eerdmans Publishing Company, 2002.

Kolhatkar, Sonali. "'*American Sniper*': American Hero or American Psycho?'." *Truthdig,* 22 Jan., 2015, http://www.truthdig.com/report/item/american_sniper_american_hero_or_american_psycho_20150122. Accessed 14 Nov., 2017.

Kyle, Chris; McEwen, Scott; DeFelice, Jim. *American Sniper: The Autobiography of the Most Lethal Sniper in U.S. Military History.* Harper Collins, 2013.

Lombardi, Chris. "'Partners of Sept. 11 Victims Denied Compensation'." *Womensenews. org,* 19 January 2002, http://womensenews.org/story/lesbian-transgender/020119/partners-sept-11-victims-denied-compensation. Accessed 14 Nov., 2017.

Marcus, Chelsea Rose and Ginger Adam Otis. "'FDNY Welcomes 305 Rookie Firefighters, Including 3 Women'." *Daily News,* 5 May 2015, http://www.nydailynews.com/newyork/fdny-welcomes-305-new-firefighters-including-3-women-article-1.2211289. Accessed 14.11.2017.

Miller, Kay. "The Invisible Women Firefighters of Ground Zero." *Star Tribune – Minneapolis,* 13 January 2002, http://www.rense.com/general19/zero.htm. Accessed 14 Nov., 2017.

New York Police Department. "NYPD Celebrates Women in Policing." 2009, http://www.nyc.gov/html/nypd/html/pr/pr_2009_ph07.shtml. Accessed 14.11.2017.

Nolan, Christopher. *Interstellar.* Paramount Pictures, 2014.

Page, Susan. "Bush is Opening Doors with a Diverse Cabinet." *USA Today* 12 September 2004, http://usatoday30.usatoday.com/news/washington/2004-12-09-diverse-usat_x.htm. Accessed 14 Nov., 2017.

Prince, Richard. "No Blacks Pictured in 9/11 Commemorative", *The Root 10 September* 2011, http://www.theroot.com/blogs/journalisms/2011/09/no_blacks_pictured_in_911_com memorative.html. Accessed 14 Nov., 2017.

Raimi, Sam. *Spider-Man.* Columbia Pictures Corporation, 2002.

Regan, Lauri B. "An American Hero… and Obama." *American Thinker,* 20 January 2015, http://www.americanthinker.com/articles/2015/01/an_american_hero_and_obama.html. Accessed 14 Nov., 2017.

Shannon-Missal, Larry. "The Equalizer Knows No Equal: Denzel Washington is America's Favorite Movie Star." 2015, http://www.harrisinteractive.com/NewsRoom/HarrisPolls/tabid/447/mid/1508/articleId/1544/ctl/ReadCustom%20Default/Default.aspx. Accessed 14 Nov., 2017.

Slotkin, Richard. *Regeneration through Violence.* Wesleyan University Press, 1996.

Sontag, Susan. "Tuesday, and After." *The New Yorker,* 24 September 2001, http://www.newyorker.com/magazine/2001/09/24/tuesday-and-after-talk-of-the-town. Accessed 14 Nov., 2017.

Tickner, J. Ann. "Feminist Perspectives on 9/11." *International Studies Perspectives,* no.3, 2002, pp. 333–350.

Traister, Rebecca. "The 9/11 Backlash Against Women." *Salon,* 3 October 2007, http://www.salon.com/2007/10/03/faludi/. Accessed 14 Nov., 2017.

Wilkinson, Janet. "It's Time To Class Feminism As a Terrorist Group." 2014, https://www.change.org/p/the-government-its-time-to-class-feminism-as-a-terrorist-group. Accessed 14 Nov., 2017.

Women's Media Center. "The Status of Women in the US Media 2015." 2015, http://wmc.3cdn.net/83bf6082a319460eb1_hsrm680x2.pdf. Accessed 14 Nov., 2017.

Young, Cathy. "Feminism's Slide since September 11." *Reason Magazine,* 17 September 2002, http://reason.com/archives/2002/09/17/feminisms-slide-since-september. Accessed 14 Nov., 2017.

Part IV
Human Rights: Mexican Indigenous groups and Mexican Americans groups

9 Dancing resistance, controlling singing and rights to name heritage

Mexican Indigenous autonomy, P'urhépecha practices, and United Nations

Ruth Hellier-Tinoco

Autonomy and the artistic contest of the P'urhépecha people as Nation[1]

It is October 18, 2016. A crowd waits expectantly inside a large auditorium in the highland village of Zacán, Michoacán, Mexico. In front of the stage, judges sit taking notes and conferring. To the back of the stage, above the faux red-tiled roof and stone doorways, a large banner states "Zacán, Michoacán. XLV Concurso artístico de la raza P'urhépecha"—The XLV Artistic Contest of the P'urhépecha People.[2] Long colored streamers made of *papel picado* and featuring the four colors of the P'urhépecha Autonomous Nation and the Supreme Indigenous Council of Michoacán converge above the heads of the audience. At the highest point in the center, the distinctive flag and insignia of the P'urhépecha Nation is suspended across the space.

A line of masked "old men" dancers stumbles onto the brightly lit stage, supporting themselves on wooden canes. Suddenly they break into frenetic footwork and execute precise choreography, before feigning exhaustion. This is the Dance of the Old Men—la Danza de los Viejitos—of the Island of Jarácuaro. After 5 minutes of set pieces, the dancers struggle off the stage amid enthusiastic whoops, cheers, and applause from the audience.

Following a brief pause, the announcer, speaking in the P'urhépecha language, introduces the next act, as three performers enter, carrying guitars, and position themselves in front of the microphone. They are *pireris*—singers of *pirekuas*, the P'urhépecha song form sung in the P'urhépecha language. To the accompaniment of exquisitely plucked and strummed arpeggios and chords, they sing a few *pirekuas*. Moving from a gentle three-time song, to a more upbeat six-time song, they always include the distinctive and complex rhythmic shifts. The auditorium resounds and resonates with these vibrant sounds. As with each ensemble, the audience claps and shouts in appreciation (Figures 9.1–9.3).

This seems to be a space and place where P'urhépecha dance and music are performed by P'urhépecha for P'urhépecha. Here, the Dance of the Old Men seems to be reappropriated from the long-standing role as heritage of the nation. Here, the *pirekua* seems to be sung in a local context. Here,

164 *Ruth Hellier-Tinoco*

Figure 9.1 The auditorium for the XLV Artistic Contest of the P'urhépecha People (XLV Concurso artístico de la raza P'urhépecha), October 18, 2016, Zacán, Michoacán, México. The long paper streamers, displaying the colors of rights movement for the P'urhépecha Autonomous Nation and the Supreme Indigenous Council of Michoacán, are strung around the auditorium. Photography by Ruth Hellier.

Figure 9.2 The insignia and flag of the P'urhépecha Autonomous Nation and the Supreme Indigenous Council of Michoacán is suspended high above the heads of the audience and performers at the Artistic Contest of the P'urhépecha People. Photography by Ruth Hellier.

Figure 9.3 An ensemble of the Dance of the Old Men (los Viejitos) at The XLV Artistic Contest of the P'urhépecha People (XLV Concurso artístico de la raza P'urhépecha), October 18, 2016, Zacán, Michoacán, México. This group is Tzipikua, Los Viejos Alegres, led by Procopio Cázares Patricio from the Island of Jarácuaro, Lake Pátzcuaro, winners of the 2016 Tata Gervasio López prize. Photography by Ruth Hellier.

the Zacán P'urhépecha Contest seems to exist as a site of the Indigenous P'urhépecha Autonomous National movement for self-determination and Indigenous rights. Yet, even here, the reach of heritage is global. In 2010, the *pirekua* was designated as Intangible Cultural Heritage of Humanity, through the program of the United Nations Educational, Scientific and Cultural Organization (UNESCO). The Dance of the Old Men and the Zacán P'urhépecha Concurso are both featured in the promotional video on the UNESCO *pirekua* site (see UNESCO, "*Pirekua*, traditional song of the P'urhépecha").[3]

Dance and music may not appear to be the most obvious focus for discussing issues of human rights. They are often considered to be somewhat inconsequential, despite or perhaps because of their ubiquity. They are "just entertainment" and available for all, especially when labeled as traditional, popular, or folkloric. Yet, all cultural practices—dance and music included—take place in specific sociopolitical-economic contexts within ideological-historical environments and trajectories. They are therefore clearly embedded in matters of power relations and inherently involve issues of human rights. In some cases, dance and music practices involve overt abuses of more obvious human rights, involving death, imprisonment, punishment, and censorship. But what of less obvious and more covert forms of human rights violations in contexts of dance and music? What of contexts involving dance and music categorized as "heritage"?—heritage to unite a nation?—heritage to unite all nations? Who controls these designations and labels? Who controls proprietorship? Who controls artistic production? How do cultural materials of embodied knowledge, including dance and music, become commoditized?

In discussions of value, culture tourism, and heritage, Regina F. Bendix has referred to the coloniality of heritage thinking, describing how cultural heritage does not exist but is made. As cultural heritage is transformed into a commodity, so social, ideological, political, and economic motivations intertwine.[4] When dance and music are labeled as cultural heritage and utilized within commoditized and commodified structures of nationalism and tourism, multifarious questions around dynamics of sociocultural practices, memories, and cultural property surface. Within matrices controlling dance and music as "heritage," matters of rights involve complex and contradictory issues concerning the interconnectedness of values, power structures, histories of colonization, dominion, control of the narrative, and controlling lives.

Constructing national unity through shared heritage is, of course, a well-known political and authoritarian technique. Selected forms of dance and music are appropriated and designated as heritage for processes of creating a united nation. Similar procedures of heritage-making are utilized for processes of touristification. Thus, dance and music as public heritage are mobilized for strategic uses. There are well-documented connections between uses of designated heritage for nationalism and tourism. Through this symbiotic relationship, dance and music practices are given exposure. Symbols of dance and music are used to unite a nation through the notion of shared national heritage, even as the inherent processes disempower and obscure or objectivize those people at the heart of these practices.

Expanding from uniting a nation to uniting all nations, dance and music as heritage are also utilized in the global sphere. According to Bendix, "the concept of 'a common heritage of mankind' emerged..." into a global scope post World War II. This concept of common heritage was formalized through UNESCO, and in 2002, the UNESCO program for and declarations of Intangible Cultural Heritage of Humanity was launched. In this context, dance and music practices have often been designated as global heritage without the practitioners themselves being consulted. Here, then, is the progression of the problematics of heritage and human rights.

The opening vignette portrays a contemporary Indigenous P'urhépecha context that encompasses many complexities around dance, music, and human rights as heritage. Uses of the dance practice—Dance of the Old Men—, song form—*pirekua*—, and event—the Zacán P'urhépecha Concurso—indicate some of the key questions around rights of control and self-determination.

When dance and music practices involve Indigenous peoples in Mexico, their lives are entrenched in hundreds of years of colonial, post-, and neo-colonial oppressions. These are histories of disempowerment and minimal justice, with long trajectories of domination and destruction from the Spanish invasion onward. Even in the 20th century, such practices were entangled in complex and contradictory contexts of postrevolutionary and neo-liberal state-driven nationalism and tourism. In the 1920s, the P'urhépecha dance form of the Dance of the Old Men of the Island of Jarácuaro was appropriated through state-driven nationalist processes as "our heritage" for uniting the nation. Simultaneously the Dance served as an icon for touristification. In the 21st century, the spheres of power have grown to a more overt global reach through the UNESCO program for Intangible Cultural Heritage. The P'urhépecha song form of the *pirekua* was mostly performed in local communities in the 20th century, yet in 2010, the designation of the *pirekua* as Intangible Cultural Heritage of Humanity has moved this into another global sphere: a sphere of United Nations.

As with multiple other Indigenous peoples, P'urhépecha are seeking status as an autonomous nation; seeking self-determination, autonomy, and self-governance; seeking rights through multiple strategies and processes. This includes controlling designations and contexts around cultural practices of dance and music. My aim, then, in this chapter is to raise questions concerning dance, music, heritage, and human rights that connect local, regional, national, and global spheres of power. The specific examples in this chapter offer insights into matters of human rights and social justice in relation to histories of appropriation, heritage, and strategic resistance.

Ethics, research positionality, allyship

In any discussions of human rights in the Americas, it is vital to question how research processes and writing are part of institutionalized power structures. This is particularly necessary when a context such as this seems to be contrary to the very heart of the problematic, in other words, global institutions appropriating local knowledges.

In this case, I am overtly discussing questions of P'urhépecha Indigenous control and self-determination, yet I am not myself a P'urhépecha. I am a British woman currently working in a U.S. public higher education institution. I therefore position myself through allyship, the practice of emphasizing social justice and human rights to advance interests of an oppressed or marginalized group.

My involvement with and correlations to processes of P'urhépecha dance and music practices is one of complex and perhaps seemingly contradictory issues. I am intimate with lifeways of P'urhépecha people, especially of the Lake Pátzcuaro area, through many years of living in the region. I have long and on-going relationships with many P'urhépecha individuals, particularly musicians, dancers, teachers, and their families of the Lake Pátzcuaro region My role is therefore enacted through practices which have involved researching and writing occluded and less discussed stories, and also on-the-ground activities as a musician. The discussions in this chapter are part of my long-term research examining contexts and processes of nationalism and tourism specifically in relation to the Dance of the Old Men of the Island of Jarácuaro and the celebration of Noche de Muertos of the Island of Janitzio. I use interviews, article and object analysis (tourist paraphernalia, films, brochures), and documental archival work (news media, audio recordings, and government documents). For many years, I also played violin with an ensemble of the Dance of the Old Men from the Island of Jarácuaro.

In my writing and dissemination, I have always sought to examine processes of appropriation, control, and exploitation, particularly in relation to consequences of governmental and institutional processes. As an ally, I am interested in understanding and communicating complexities and contradictions of implicit and explicit contexts of power relations, hierarchies, and inequities and strategies for resistance and reappropriation. I have specifically *not* engaged in detailed ethnographic writing of P'urhépecha lifeways, although there are key aspects of my research processes and relationships that incorporate various forms of reciprocity.[5]

Yet, I recognize the contradictions and my own complicity in perpetuating long-standing institutional processes. By writing this chapter, I raise the problem of potentially contributing to essentializing narratives of "P'urhépecha peoples." Even though I discuss these issues with many individuals who self-identify as P'urhépecha, their individual voices are not reflected in this chapter. I therefore open myself up here to this writing and questions of human rights.

In relation to research and activism in the area of UNESCO, the *pirekua*, and Intangible Cultural Heritage of Humanity, I particularly draw attention to the work of scholar Georgina Flores Mercado. In recent years, she has written extensively on these very problematical issues and has also been active with many P'urhépecha musicians in seeking explanations from UNESCO.[6] My discussion of dance, music, and human rights in this chapter is situated within many conversations in a range of scholarly areas in the humanities and social sciences, most obviously performance studies, dance and music studies, history, tourism studies, critical heritage studies, and critical memory studies.[7] This chapter moves chronologically through three key contexts: the postrevolutionary processes involving appropriating the Dance of the Old Men for national heritage, the Zacán P'urhépecha Concurso, and the designation of the *pirekua* as Intangible Cultural Heritage of UNESCO.

Movements, Revolutions and The Dance of the Old Men: "our heritage" to unite the nation

To situate this particular case of dance, music, and human rights, it is crucial to recognize the long histories of P'urhépecha struggles and movements. Prior to the Spanish-European invasion in the early 16th century, the P'urhépecha empire was one of the major civilizations in meso-America, with the grand capital city of Tzintzuntzan located on the edge of Lake Pátzcuaro. In the 1520s, the civilization was decimated. The P'urhépecha peoples survived and continued to speak their distinctive and intricate language. They perpetuated many forms of cultural practices, often as syncretic forms, and always in environments of severe economic deprivation.

In the last decades of the 20th century, the movement for the autonomy of the P'urhépecha nation was formed. Obviously, the nationwide Indigenous rights movement of the Zapatistas (Ejército Zapatista de Liberación Nacional—the Zapatista Army of National Liberation) is also crucial to the more regionalized processes for the recognition of P'urhépecha Indigenous rights. In Michoacán, the movement is particularly active through the Supreme Indigenous Council of Michoacán— el Consejo Supremo Indígena de Michoacán (CSIM).[8] As with all movements for Indigenous rights in Mexico, CSIM aims to reclaim agency that was forcibly and violently removed in the 1520s by Spanish conquistadores and missionaries and which has been perpetuated since that time. In one notable action, since 1984, the reintroduction of the ritual ceremony of the P'urhépecha New Year—the New Fire ceremony on February 1— has become a potent performance of autonomous self-identification. As a designation of tradition and heritage by P'urhépecha community members and activists for the P'urhépecha peoples, the yearly ceremony incorporates overt forms actions and symbols of the movement for P'urhépecha Autonomous Nation. As Bendix notes, "Traditions are always defined in the present, and the actors doing the defining are [] concerned [that] the manifestation will accomplish what they intend it to accomplish."[9] In the 21st century, the movement has grown in strength and numbers, with its four-color flag (green, turquoise, purple, and yellow) and insignia much in evidence.

In any discussion of Mexico and human rights, the Revolution (1910–1920) figures as an overt period of struggles for land and liberty for Indigenous and rural-dwelling peoples. These were ostensibly processes to wrestle power from the elite government of Porfirio Díaz. The revolution was therefore embedded in issues of social justice, redress for long-term oppressions, educational and linguistic rights, and territorial rights. However, the postrevolutionary decades were deeply conflicted in relation to rights of Indigenous peoples. Dance and music practices were embedded in postrevolutionary political and ideological processes, as some Indigenous cultural practices were deemed useful for creating a united nation.

Through government-driven processes of appropriation for both nationalism and intertwined tourism, practices were given the label of "our" heritage in national terms, effectively removing them from local control as they were given a national role. This produced contradictory states of valuing the practice (and people for their practice), yet simultaneously removed agency as they were incorporated into national collective memory.[10] Such processes relied on generating and disseminating icons of *mexicanidad* and *lo mexicano*—authentic Mexicanness. These implicated Indigenous people through double processes of incorporation and appropriation. Indigenousness (through *indigenismo*) became a central component of the rhetoric, policies, and ideologies, enacted through state-controlled delineations of otherness, and the reification of practices, peoples, and places.

P'urhépecha peoples served as an ideal model of Indigenousness, and in the 1920s, the Lake Pátzcuaro area, comprising P'urhépecha islands and villages, was the focus of state attention. Although these actions were undertaken in a context of purported improvement and progress for all Mexican citizens, in actuality, the consequences for P'urhépecha peoples were, and continue to be, those of continued marginalization and discrimination. It was in this context of uniting the nation that a P'urhépecha masked dance of old men (viejitos) from the Island of Jarácuaro was transformed into an icon of national heritage. A dance of old men was staged and theatricalized in Mexico City and converted into the Dance of the Old Men, a process that took place through the state-directed engagement of one man from the Island of Jarácuaro (Nicolás Bartolo Juárez).[11] By the 1930s, the Dance of the Old Men was firmly part of a national repertoire. There is a subsequent long trajectory of official uses for intertwining and often symbiotic processes of nationalism and tourism.

Significantly, two other P'urhépecha practices and a location were simultaneously incorporated into the symbolic network of heritage to unite the nation: the P'urhépecha celebration of Noche de Muertos on the Island of Janitzio, a form of fishing known as mariposa (using *redes de mariposa*—butterfly nets), and the Island of Janitzio as landform.[12] Specific for the focus of this chapter, it is notable that the P'urhépecha song form *pirekua* was *not* successfully appropriated and remained separate from nationalistic and touristic frameworks.[13] Pirekuas continued to be sung and composed prolifically and informally in local P'urhépecha contexts, in the same way that multifarious dances were performed in local contexts (including many different dances of old men).

Subsequent to the 1920s, over the ensuring decades, nationalistic and touristic processes intensified the role of the Dance of the Old Men of Jarácuaro as heritage of the nation. Yet, P'urhépecha rights of control have been limited. Musicians and dancers from the Island of Jarácuaro are fundamentally part of the Michoacán and Mexican state tourism projects, regarded as objects of cultural heritage. Displays of the Dance enable P'urhépecha performers to be valued, even though paid minimally, while also being essentialized within a delimiting system. From the 1950s onward, one man from Jarácuaro, Gervasio López, performed a role as the principal exponent of the Dance. He participated in countless official representations as an icon of Mexico, Michoacán, and Indigenous P'urhépecha peoples, in national and international contexts. López was utilized as a valuable artifact of cultural patrimony and treated as public property belonging to the nation. Although López attempted to make the most of opportunities that were presented to him, he was frequently caught in a context of constructed authenticity that required a utilitarian response. For all his official performances, he was often recompensed with little or no payment.[14]

Even in the 21st century, the act of deploying the Dance as a valuable narrative of the nation's past continues to perform a hierarchical exercise. It is a valuable commodity and resource that is part of a web that is both complex and firmly rooted, serving large institutions of state government and the tourism industry. The so-called success of this process is evident today, almost 100 years after the initial acts of appropriation, as the Dance of the Old Men continues to be reified as patrimony of the nation. To complicate notions of "our heritage" further, since the 1940s, the Dance of the Old Men of Jarácuaro has also been danced by hundreds of ballet folklórico groups in Mexico, the United States, and elsewhere in the world. In such contexts, notions of "our heritage" reveal multiple contradictory options.[15]

Resistance and reappropriation?

To draw attention to rights for controlling artistic production and heritage and to processes for reclaiming P'urhépecha rights and power, particularly in relation to the Dance of the Old Men, I return now to the opening context of the Zacán P'urhépecha Contest. The almost 50-year history of the Zacán P'urhépecha Contest itself provides insights into struggles and strategies for self-determination and management of dance and music. The Zacán P'urhépecha Contest was initiated in 1971 by a group of professional P'urhépecha men from Zacán, all of whom had left the region at a young age. Zacán is a small village in the P'urhépecha sierra.[16] In 1943, the nearby volcano Paricutín erupted, compelling people to move away from the area to look for land and work elsewhere.

The Zacán event was an initiative of local P'urhépecha people who returned to the region and who sought to rescue and recultivate certain customs through reinstating a traditional fiesta.[17] Modeling the event on usual practices for Saints' Days, the aim was to reestablish P'urhépecha identity amongst the young P'urhépecha people. It was an occasion solely for the people of Zacán and nearby communities in the P'urhépecha highlands. Music, dance, food, and fireworks were all important elements of the festivities, and, as with most traditional fiestas, a dance and music contest (*concurso*) took place, with participants competing for prestige and prize money. Local groups performed one after the other in front of a small community audience on the basketball court, and judges, with the power to adjudicate and control criteria, were an important feature.

By the mid-1980s, numbers attending the event had increased to such an extent that a stage and auditorium were erected for the contest. P'urhépecha communities from the widest region traveled to the Zacán event. The Dance of the Old Men was performed by islanders from Lake Pátzcuaro, including Gervasio López and his family from the Island of Jarácuaro. The situation had changed dramatically by the late 1990s, as non-P'urhépecha ballet folklórico ensembles were also participating. In this context, the Dance of the Old Men was performed numerous times by both P'urhépecha and non-P'urhépecha groups.

By the new millennium, another specially constructed auditorium capable of accommodating a crowd of thousands was built on the edge of the village. In 2005, there were 1000 contestants comprising P'urhépecha and non-P'urhépecha ensembles: dance groups, wind bands (bandas), mixed string and wind ensembles (*orquestas*), and *pireris* (singers of P'urhépecha songs in the P'urhépecha language). State and national representatives attended the live event, and the contest was promoted heavily through television and other media, and an overt tourist connection became prevalent. Thus, in just a few decades, the localized and autonomous right to designate P'urhépecha heritage in the context of the P'urhépecha nation had been usurped and expanded into Mexican cultural heritage.

Yet, the movement for the P'urhépecha autonomous nation has become present and highly visible. Centering the flag and insignia for the P'urhépecha movement for autonomy and rights above all the participants and audience members acts as an overarching framework. Articles published before and after the contest function to publicize the event and to define the competition as an important context for reviving and strengthening traditional P'urhépecha dance.[18] In recent years, performance elements have been introduced that indicate counter-processes of resistance and reappropriation. As the Zacán event is fundamentally a formal competition (rather than a festival), the organizers and judges are able to control contestants, criteria, narratives, and terminology. Each year, the parameters are set out in in a printed and well-distributed convocatoria (a call). The convocatoria is produced in P'urhépecha and also Spanish (side by side) locating the P'urhépecha language firmly at the core of the event. One key change over the past few years concerns who may participate. The criteria has altered from allowing anyone to enter (Convocatoria 2012), to permitting only P'urhépecha people to enter (Convocatoria 2013), to permitting only P'urhépecha people who can show a form of identification to establish themselves as authentically P'urhépecha (Convocatoria 2016). This demonstrates an obvious power shift back to P'urhépecha-only contestants. In a similar way, a set of judging criteria has changed to control of the notion of "P'urhépecha tradition." This has been made more overt, with references to identifying elements that are "not part of the P'urhépecha culture" (Convocatoria 2013).

In relation specifically to the Dance of the Old Men, processes also signal strategies to reappropriate this dance from the sphere of the nation to P'urhépecha self-control. A special prize was established in 2000 named "La Danza de Los Viejitos, de Jarácuaro." This was specifically created "In memory of the illustrious master Tata Gervasio López from the Community of Jarácuaro," who had died the previous year.[19] In the context of the Zacán P'urhépecha Concurso, generating the Dance prize in memory of López performs the functions not only of honoring López's memory and commemorating his life-long role in promoting the Dance and acting as representative of Indigenous peoples even though in a utilitarian position, but also of reclaiming his name and the Dance of the Old Men from national constructs through acknowledging López's role and providing a marker of P'urhépecha self-designated authenticity. Deploying the very icons and symbols that are used in national and international constructions of Mexicanness, as generated and shaped by hegemonic processes of state projects, is paradoxical. So, in some ways, although the Dance of the Old Men in the Zacán Concurso perpetuates notions of "our heritage" initiated in the 1920s by the authoritarian governmental institutions in the aftermath of the revolution, in other ways, it performs acts of reappropriation and of self-authentication. These are the politics of autonomy and self-determination, of recognition and rights, enacted through self-legitimation, all of which are efficacious for establishing rights, presence, and ideological territory through self-representation.

Significantly, the Zacán Concurso encompasses a multiplicity of dance and music practices, making evident the richness of the diverse expressions of the P'urhépecha people, and therefore countering the state-constructed stereotypical practices. In this context, pirekuas are sung multiple times— always in the P'urhépecha language, by P'urhépecha for P'urhépecha. The Zacán Concurso decenters and brings power to a periphery, even as self-assertion is performed through the control of tradition and contestants, through the organizational management, and through the displays of P'urhépecha politics in the form of the insignia and language. Notions of "our heritage" are those of P'urhépecha heritage.

Song as UNESCO world heritage: a violation of rights?

Even as the Dance of the Old Men and the *pirekua* as song form with the Zacán P'urhépecha Concurso appear to be reclaiming rights and control of heritage, other actions tell a different story: a story that incorporates these P'urhépecha dance and music practices into a global sphere of heritage to unite nations. In 2010, the *pirekua* was appropriated into a framework of "global heritage" when it was inscribed on the UNESCO Representative List of the Intangible Cultural Heritage of Humanity under the title "*Pirekua*, traditional song of the P'urhépecha people"—"La *pirekua*, canto tradicional de los p'urhépechas."[20] P'urhépecha practitioners (singers, musicians, and composers) have described this designation as "a violation of rights."[21] Degenerating the processes for P'urhépecha rights over artistic production and cultural heritage further, both the Dance of the Old Men and the Zacán P'urhépecha Concurso are already part of the same global framework through inclusion on the official UNESCO video for the *pirekua*.

UNESCO is fundamentally concerned with notions of human rights. Since its inception in London in 1945 at a specific moment of global history of outright war, UNESCO has formulated strategies for establishing global peace "on the

174 *Ruth Hellier-Tinoco*

basis of humanity's moral and intellectual solidarity," striving to build "intercultural understanding: through protection of heritage and support for cultural diversity" and establishing "a holistic cultural governance system based on human rights and shared values."[22] Despite the rhetoric of global peace and shared values, it is important to raise questions about the many inherent problematics of UNESCO, which implicate global spheres of power through configurations of centers and peripheries and gendered patriarchal structures.[23]

One specific remit of UNESCO is a procedure for the protection of human rights, by dealing with alleged violations of human rights. Thus, UNESCO's purpose is "to contribute to peace and security by promoting collaboration among the nations through education, science and culture in order to further universal respect for justice, for the rule of law and for the human rights and fundamental freedoms which are affirmed for the peoples of the world."[24] In terms of specific rights that fall within UNESCO's competence (which are included in the Universal Declaration of Human Rights and also appear in the United Nations Covenants of December 16, 1966), I am particularly interested in Article 27: the right to the protection of the moral and material interests resulting from any scientific, literary, or artistic production.[25]

Between 1972 and 2005, UNESCO generated four conventions and declarations with connections to the notion of artistic production, which encompass cultural heritage, diversity, and expressions.[26] Dance and music practices are incorporated into the last of these: the Convention for the Safeguarding of the Intangible Cultural Heritage. Making the global reach obvious, this convention and designation exists under the title and rubric of "Protecting Our Heritage and Fostering Creativity." Such terminology raises an obvious question: Who is the "our" of "our heritage"?[27] Since 2006, Mexico has been particularly active in the realm of generating heritage, as many cultural practices have received the designation of Intangible Cultural Heritage of Humanity.[28]

Turning specifically to the *pirekua*, as I noted, unlike the appropriation of the Dance of the Old Men, the *pirekua* had remained largely outside of, or at least less central to, state-organized nationalistic and tourist frameworks. Although pirekuas have been performed within certain tourist and public festivals (particularly for state-organized festivals around Noche de Muertos), these musical performances did not have the same traction as the Dance of the Old Men.[29] Yet, from the moment that the *pirekua* was designated as Intangible Cultural Heritage, touristic promotion has been strategic and widespread. Even the process for designation was the initiative of the Secretary of Tourism and was wholly concerned with promoting regional, national, and international tourism.

The situation regarding the *pirekua* is complex and multifaceted, and rights of consent are at the very heart of the matter. Scholar and activist Georgina Flores Mercado has undertaken in-depth research into the processes leading to and consequences of the designation, discussing many problematic aspects in her publications. The very title of one of her articles indicates the core issue of decision-making: "And with the *pirekua* they didn't even ask us"—"Y con la *pirekua* ni siquiera nos preguntaron."[30] The negative responses of the musicians, pireris, and composers to the declaration, and the identification of "the violation of their rights," is evidence of a new sphere of conflict between the Mexican state and the P'urhépecha peoples: which is classified as intangible cultural heritage.[31] Provocatively posing the question of plans for safeguarding as "instruments to maintain domination?," Flores Mercado discusses deep problems relating to who decides and how the decisions are made. She notes that, "it is important to mention that the concept of safeguarding and the process of generating a plan for safeguarding is not a neutral action and is not beyond ideology. They are created within governmental institutions and the plans and projects correspond with the dominant ideology of the government. As we know, in the case of Mexico the governments that have signed and ratified the 2003 Convention are conservative and neoliberal, whose primary interests in creating plans and measures of safeguarding ... are with the tourist market."[32] In efforts to challenge these authoritarian processes, Flores Mercado has taken an active collaborative role with many P'urhépecha artists in order to officially challenge the UNESCO designation.

Pirekua, traditional song of the P'urhépecha (Mexico)
Representative List - 2010
Film 'Pirekua, the P'urhépecha sings to life'
© 2009 by Montes/Secretaría de Turismo

Figure 9.4 A frame displaying the Dance of the Old Men of Jarácuaro, within the official video for the *pirekua* on the UNESCO website, Intangible Cultural Heritage of Humanity, United Nations Educational, Scientific and Cultural Organization (UNESCO). See www. unesco.org/culture/ich/en/RL/pirekua-traditional-song-of-the-purhepecha.

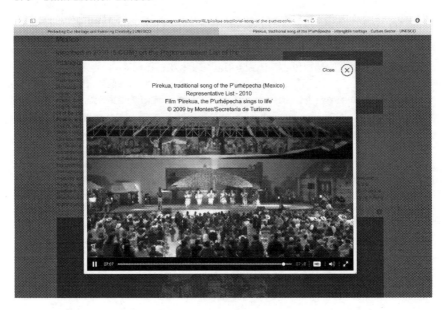

Figure 9.5 A frame displaying the Zacán Concurso, within the official video for the *pirekua* on the UNESCO website. See www.unesco.org/culture/ich/en/RL/pirekua-traditional-song-of-the-purhepecha.

What then of the Dance of the Old Men and human rights in relation to intangible heritage? And the Zacán P'urhépecha Contest? Both are already visually incorporated into the global agenda of UNESCO, tangibly visible inside the signifying frames, overtly featured in the official video created to showcase the *pirekua* on the official UNESCO website.[33] The photos are even labeled "Secretary of Tourism." The relationships to state-generated national and global touristic frameworks are overt. The Dance of the Old Men of Jarácuaro, along with mariposa fishing and the island of Janitzio—the very practices that were appropriated, reframed and structured for nationalistic objectives in the postrevolutionary era—are all featured and presented as traditionally P'urhépecha heritage as designated by a transnational organization. Now, within the UNESCO designation relating to the P'urhépecha *pirekua*, these same practices are further appropriated, reframed, and structured to construct "United Nations." The Zacán Concurso, as a P'urhépecha-controlled event, seems to have been drawn into the "United Nations" sphere of control.

These P'urhépecha practices and peoples are therefore incorporated into an ever-wider sphere of custody and international memory. The "our" is extended to a global context, contained by the notion of "shared values" and "holistic cultural governance." Where in this UNESCO framework are the rights of the P'urhépecha communities for self-determination and autonomy? When the very cultural practices labeled as "authentically

Mexican and P'urhépecha" are contained as "our" within the UNESCO configuration and by the highest level of Mexican governance, where are the opportunities for resistance? These dance and music practices may, in some ways, seem insignificant in the realm of human rights. Yet, they are deeply embedded in power relations, in the politics and rights of control over heritage, over history, over memories, and over lives.

Notes

1. I dedicate this chapter to, and I stand in solidarity and as an ally with, the movements for all rights of Indigenous P'urhépecha peoples and all Indigenous peoples of Mexico and the world. I acknowledge and thank all the dancers, musicians, composers, teachers, and community members of the broadest P'urhépecha region who I have been privileged to know.
2. All translations are mine, unless otherwise stated.
3. https://ich.unesco.org/en/RL/pirekua-traditional-song-of-the-purhepecha-00398. Accessed 7/11/2020.
4. See Bendix 2018.
5. See, for example, Hellier-Tinoco 2003, 2004, 2010a and b, 2011, 2019.
6. See Flores Mercado 2014 and 2017, and Flores Mercado and Fernando Nava, eds. 2016.
7. See, for example, International Journal of Intangible Heritage; Diana Taylor. 2003. The Archive and the Repertoire: Performing Cultural Memory in the Americas. Durham, NC: Duke University Press; Eric Zolov. 2001. "Discovering a Land 'Mysterious and Obvious': The Renarrativizing of Postrevolutionary Mexico." Fragments of a Golden Age: The Politics of Culture in Mexico Since 1940, edited by Gilbert Joseph, Anne Rubenstein, and Eric Zolov, Duke UP, 2001, pp. 234–72; Naomi Jackson and Toni Shapiro-Phim, eds. Dance, Human Rights and Social Justice: Dignity in Motion. Scarecrow Press. 2008; Barbara Kirshenblatt-Gimblet, 1998. Destination Culture: Tourism, Museums, and Heritage. U of California P, 1998.
8. See the Facebook page Consejo Supremo Indígena Michoacán.
9. Bendix 2019: 25.
10. These were complex and contradictory processes. In referring to postrevolutionary Mexican state formation processes and projects, cultural historian Derek Sayer has noted that "if this project does confine, it does so in very complicated ways," going on to emphasize the "polysemic, ambiguous, contradictory quality of these putative state forms: even as they oppress, they also empower," 1994:369–79.
11. As part of my ally work, I have been seeking to put the hidden story of the role of Nicolás Bartolo Juárez on the map. Although Bartolo Júarez is recognized for his *pirekuas* and other compositions, a few of which were transcribed by the state-sponsored scholar Rubén M. Campos, in his 1928 publication *El Folklore y la música mexicana*, his role in the foundational institutionalized history of the Dance of the Old Men remains mostly obscured. In collaboration with Gilberto Cázares and Leobardo Ramos, two of Bartolo Juárez's family, we are working on disseminating more on the life and works of Bartolo Juárez.
12. See Hellier-Tinoco 2010a,b, 2011, 2019 for further discussions.
13. It was sung by a few P'urhépecha musicians in national contexts, including by Nicolás Bartolo Juárez, and, as noted earlier, notations of *pirekuas* by Nicolás and his brother Alejandro were published in 1928 in *El folklore y la música Mexicana* by Campos.

14. Up until the end of life, Gervasio was still performing for a few hours on a Sunday in a restaurant in order to continue earning enough money to make ends meet. According to his sons, López died in poverty, with a sense having been taken advantage of, and even exploited financially, despite being given high status and utilized to the full by government agencies. Interview with Atilano and Pedro López (interview with Ruth Hellier, 1999).
15. For example, in the United States, performances of the Dance of the Old Men by ballet folklórico ensembles perpetuate stereotypes of Mexicanness, even as they embody insertion into the national narrative of marginalization (see Hellier-Tinoco 2011 for this discussion).
16. The full name is San Pedro Zacán, in the municipality of Los Reyes.
17. Aguilera Ortiz 1985.
18. See, for example "En aras de recuperar y fortalecer elementos tradicionales" in "Emiten convocatoria..." 2015.
19. "En memoria del ilustre maestro Tata Gervasio López, oriundo de la Comunidad de Jarácuaro" (Convocatoria 2000). Q.E.P.D.
20. https://ich.unesco.org/en/RL/pirekua-traditional-song-of-the-purhepecha-00398.
21. Flores Mercado, 2014, 34.
22. See www.unesco.com.
23. These include even the most basic divisions of the world according to UNESCO, which places Mexico into the category of "Latin America and the Caribbean," and designates North America as "Canada and USA." It also creates a binary of "Latin American and Caribbean States" and "Western European and North American States," and sets up notions of development through reference to "least developed countries."
24. See "UNESCO's Procedure for Dealing with Alleged Violations of Human Rights" https://en.unesco.org/about-us/procedure104.
25. See "UNESCO's Procedure for Dealing with Alleged Violations of Human Rights" https://en.unesco.org/about-us/procedure104.
26. These are, The Convention for the Protection of the World Cultural and Natural Heritage (1972); The Universal Declaration on Cultural Diversity (2001); The Convention for the Safeguarding of the Intangible Cultural Heritage (2003); The Convention on the Protection and Promotion of the Diversity of Cultural Expressions (2005).
27. I raise here the obvious linguistic issues of the Spanish term "patrimonio," which is inherently male and references male rights to inheritance.
28. Even in 2003, "the Indigenous Festivity Dedicated to the Dead"—"Las fiestas indígenas dedicadas a los muertos"—was designated as a UNESCO Masterpiece of the Oral and Intangible Heritage of Humanity.
29. Reasons for this include the use of the P'urhépecha language (unfamiliar to visitors and tourists) and a complex rhythmic musical form with frequent time changes. Both of these preclude non-local audiences from being able to "sing along."
30. 2014.
31. Complicating the institutional framework of critique, the article by Flores Mercado critiquing the processes for designation of the P'urhépecha *pirekua* as Intangible Cultural Heritage of Humanity was published by the National Institute of Anthropology and History (el Instituto Nacional de Antropología e Historia (INAH)). My aim here is not to examine Mexican institutions in detail; however, connections between INAH and European frameworks is discussed by one of Mexico's most renowned historians, Enrique Florescano, in his reflections on the founding of INAH (see "80 years of INAH, interview

with Enrique Florescano"). See also Florescano's influential volume *El patrimonio cultural de México*, 1997.
32. 2014: 36.
33. https://ich.unesco.org/en/RL/pirekua-traditional-song-of-the-purhepecha-00398. Accessed 7/11/2020.

Works cited

"Emiten convocatoria del XLIV concurso artístico de la raza p'urhépecha." *La Jornada Michoacán*. 28 Sep 2015.

Aguilera Ortiz, Porfirio. "Antecedentes." *Zacán: renacimiento de una tradición*, edited by Jesús Bugarini. Morelia, Michoacán: Instituto Michoacano de Cultura, Gobierno del Estado de Michoacán, 1985, pp. 13–19.

Bendix, Regina F. *Culture and Value: Tourism, Heritage and Property*. Indiana University Press, 2018.

Campos, Rubén M. *El Folklore y la música mexicana: Investigación acerca de la cultura musical en México (1525-1925)*. México: la Secretaría de Educación Pública, 1928.

Flores Mercado, Georgina and Fernando Nava, editors. *Identidades en venta: múiscas tradicionales y turismo en México*. UNAM, 2016.

Flores Mercado, Georgina. *La pirekua como Patrimonio Cultural Inmaterial de la Humanidad. Efectos del nuevo paradigma patrimonial*. México: Universidad Nacional Autónoma de México. UNAM IIS, 2017

Flores Mercado, Georgina. "Y con la *pirekua* ni siquiera nos preguntaron... La declaración de la *pirekua* como Patrimonio Cultural Inmaterial de la Humanidad: una perspectiva crítica." *Diario de Campo*, vol. 3, issue 2, 2014, pp. 32–38.

Florescano, Enrique, coord. *El patrimonio cultural de México*. Vols 1 and 2. México: Consejo Nacional para la Cultura y las Artes, 1997.

Florescano, Enrique. 2019. Interview. Instituto Nacional de Antropología e Historia (INAH), 1939–2019. INAH TV, 3 Feb, 2019, https://www.youtube.com/watch?v=8hSsNa2m8fs

Hellier-Tinoco, Ruth. "Experiencing People: Relationships, Responsibility and Reciprocity." *British Journal of Ethnomusicology*, vol. 12, issue 1, 2003, pp. 19–34.

Hellier-Tinoco, Ruth. "Power Needs Names: Hegemony, Folklorisation and the *Viejitos* Dance of Michoacán, Mexico." *Music, Power and Politics*, edited by Annie J. Randall, Routledge, 2004, pp. 47–64.

Hellier-Tinoco, Ruth. "Corpo/Reality, Voyeurs and the Responsibility of Seeing: Night of the Dead on the Island of Janitzio, Mexico." *Performance Research*, vol. 15, issue 1, 2010a, pp. 23–31.

Hellier-Tinoco, Ruth. "¡Saludos de México (el auténtico)!: postales, anuncios espectaculares, turismo y cuerpos actuantes." *Fractal*, vol. 46, 2010b, pp. 79–98.

Hellier-Tinoco, Ruth. "Embodying Mexico: Tourism, Nationalism and Performance." Oxford UP, 2011, and Companion Website: www.oup.com/us/embodyingmexico. 42 video resources recorded by R. Hellier-Tinoco.

Hellier-Tinoco, Ruth. "Embodying Touristic Mexico: Virtual and Erased Indigenous Bodies." *Meet Me at the Fair: A World's Fair Reader*, edited by Laura Hollengreen, Celia Pearce, Rebecca Rouse & Bobby Schweizer, ETC and Carnegie Mellon Press, 2014, pp. 71–80.

Hellier-Tinoco, Ruth. "Re-appropriating Choreographies of Authenticity in Mexico: Competitions and *the Dance of the Old Men*." *The Oxford Handbook of Dance and Competition*, edited by Sherril Dodds, Oxford University Press, 2019.

Sayer, Derek. "Everyday Forms of State Formation: Some Dissident Remarks on 'Hegemony'." *Everyday Forms of State Formation: Revolution and the Negotiation of Rule in Modern Mexico*, edited by Gilbert Joseph and Daniel Nugent, Duke University Press, 1994, pp. 367–377.

10 Carey McWilliams' activism and the democratic human rights tradition

María José Canelo

Introduction

It is a common assumption, especially for those of us born after the 1950s that human rights are natural and universal or are self-evident.[1] Nevertheless, if people were indeed entitled to them by birth, their simple invocation would immediately solve many of the world's worst problems. A closer look shows that the forms we perceive and develop in relation to human rights are largely historical and contextual. Attesting to this assertion, the *Universal Declaration of Human Rights* is less than one hundred years old and it has been amended on several occasions, demonstrating how rights are not only constructed but also require both official articulation and recognition. Culture as a right, for instance, was added to the United Nations list in 1966, in the *International Covenant on Economic, Social and Cultural Rights* that in turn came into effect only 10 years later.[2]

This study examines one instance of the development of a human rights discourse, taking as a case study the critique and activism of a California intellectual and lawyer one might also call a legal activist, Carey McWilliams. The objective is to read McWilliams' critique and activism in light of the alternative tradition of democratic activism for human rights identified by political philosopher James Tully in "Two Traditions of Human Rights" (see Note 1) who signals the struggle for rights that are proposed, discussed, and contested among diverse constituencies, and not just state-driven and imposed on people (139). While analyzing McWilliams' work I intend to highlight, on the one hand, the discursive construction of rights and, on the other, the democratic practices he developed in order to take that discourse to its final conclusion.

McWilliams' endeavors were framed by World War II, the Civil Rights Movement, and what he himself called the Second Reconstruction, the "racial revolution" (*Honorable* 114). Using his knowledge of the law and of legal mechanisms, he challenged the view that legislation was transparent, objective, and of universal access. In point of fact, he invested much of his life denouncing the disempowerment of particular ethnic groups in terms of access to justice and demonstrating how the law itself was key to explaining and sustaining their forms of oppression.

As a part of these struggles, McWilliams focused on the inclusion of culture in the discourse of rights, which will be the particular target of this reflection. Of central interest is his attempt to free culture from its role as a vehicle for prejudice and exclusion and turn it into a tool for affirmation and inclusion instead. Building on such theories of internal colonialism and having the Mexican American community as his target subject, he made a case for what came to be defined, decades later, as cultural citizenship and cultural rights.

Having specialized in labor law, McWilliams came to work closely with migrant farmworkers in California in the late 1930s after his nomination by Democratic Governor Culbert Olson, as Head of the California Division of Immigration and Housing. His ideas were largely practical in the sense that they derived from his own experience working with migrants and workers. Gathering personal testimonies was a technique he employed while visiting factories and talking to workers. This was similar to the way he brought big farmers and farmworkers together in state public hearings. He invited to California both the La Follette State Committee on Education and Labor and the Tolan Committee on National Defense Migration so that they could engage in public discussions on the poor working conditions and the lack of rights migrant workers had in the ever-prosperous agro-business of the region. Initiatives such as these created an uproar among the sector of big business in agriculture and won him the title of enemy no. 1 from the Associated Farmers, one of the most powerful constituencies in the state, which they relentlessly attempted to remove him from the position (*The Education* 77).

Developing a democratic tradition of human rights

Political philosopher James Tully distinguishes what he calls the two dominant traditions of human rights: the High Enlightenment tradition and the democratic tradition. In general, humanity has understood human rights in light of the former: as a set of declarative principles whose "institutionalization and processes of socialization all precede democratic participation" (Tully 149). As the author adds, this assumption entails that human rights develop somehow independent from the people who are subjected to them. Obviously, the latter comes as a flaw because it conceives of rights in a legalistic manner, as monolithic that must apply blindly to different constituencies and need approval only from the institutions that impose them. As an alternative to this tradition, Tully proposes democratic activism, which sheds light on an array of existing or envisioned plural practices, institutions, and relationships that bear a human rights dimension. One might say that Tully humanizes human rights in the sense that he calls attention to the actors or agents who deal with the realities of oppression, articulate claims, and, above all, assume the people's humanity beforehand, instead of waiting for the validating stamp of a formal institution. In Tully's words, "human rights are proposals made by and to [be] free and equal persons and people. They are proposed as tools for cooperating together and for contesting and changing unjust forms and means of cooperation" (149). This is a dynamic understanding of human rights. They are supposed to be interpreted, debated, contested, revised, and negotiated by both groups who claim them, i.e. human rights activists and institutions. Accordingly, the authority of human rights lies not in their being declared and imposed, but rather in their "being questioned, interpreted, expanded and fought over" (150).

Carey McWilliams' activism comes in line with many of the tenets expounded by Tully. Actually, the former always rejected political affiliation, although his activism was framed within Popular Front politics. This fitted his principles, for he believed that social justice was an ethical value that responded to the critic's individual responsibility alone. This capacity to be politically active without the limitations of political dogmas or the pressure of particular institutions can in fact explain the originality of many of his proposals (Critser 255). Above all, McWilliams was a contextualist who understood his own critical and social accounts of California as a way of challenging official histories and examining facts anew (*Factories* 9). Obviously, this examination entailed an intervention by the masses and involved cooperation with those systematically rendered invisible.

McWilliams described the California valleys as "large feudal empires," (*Factories* 6) once farming gave way to industrialized agriculture and the farm to the farm factory, a type of agriculture comparable to the "plantations and estates" typical of the U.S. South (*Factories* 24). Fieldworkers came from different ethnic groups who had migrated to California barely a century earlier. For instance, in the 1940s, California had been receiving Mexican immigrants for over 25 years and the vast majority of the current Spanish-speaking community had already been born, raised, and educated in the United States. He wrote on virtually every ethnicity present in the state at the time and was a pioneer in ethnic studies and race relations.[3] However, he took a particular interest in Mexican Americans, partly deriving from his direct involvement both in the defense of the criminalization of the groups involved in the Sleepy Lagoon case and the Zoot Suit Riots.

This experience, before McWilliams was invited to move to New York and lead the left-leaning magazine *The Nation*, during two decades (1955–1975), made him a loud spokesperson for civil liberties, organized labor, and race relations, first in California and later nationwide. He became an enthusiastic and influential contributor to what was then known as "the racial-cultural situation" (Denning 445–454). From his perspective, the war and its aftermath created the conditions for a Second Reconstruction, a period when the United States was called to face its internal crisis directly and acknowledge the resilient problem of race. In his view, legislation was ripe to tackle the remnants of prejudice while informing the legal system. California's history had much to teach on this subject because of the ethnic variety of migrants it had always hosted, the forms of segregations the state had developed to manage this population, and also the forms of cooperation that, against all odds, the migrants themselves might develop to claim their rights.

Still, according to the democratic tradition of human rights activism, James Tully traces the profile of the human rights promoter as someone who, "must always act as if the *other* is already a person or people with democratic dignity. The human rights activist brings a human rights *ethos* into being by interacting with others in this free and equal democratic manner.... The intersubjective practice of human rights **is** the socializing *ground* of human rights" (151; italics and bold in original). Carey McWilliams eventually combined his knowledge and practice of the law as a labor attorney with his learnings about culture from working closely with oppressed ethnic communities. He expected to develop what he called a legal imagination by attempting to envision, on the one hand, specific legal or cooperative mechanisms aimed at a better integration of ethnic communities and, on the other, request the direct intervention of the federal government on issues of racial discrimination. His ultimate ideal was that of "an ethnic democracy" ("What We Did" 98).

In the early 1940s, McWilliams' idea of culture was already dwelling on that of lived experience. He defended the contextualized and differentiated analysis of legal cases according to the minorities' experiences of discrimination, for instance. This implied listening to all parts involved, visiting factories, and having workers narrate their personal testimonies—or what critical race theorists Richard Delgado and Jean Stefancic came to call the "counterstories"–to identify the perspectives of the oppressed groups themselves and supplement the understanding of a situation (*Critical Race* 38). Practices such as these would allow the oppressed groups to achieve their own voices in the future and to learn to struggle for access both to legal tools to fight for social justice and to claim their rights.

McWilliams proposed the assessment of the main problem in California as one of cultural conflict, arguing against the culturalization of racism or any form of prejudice that replaced racism with the belief that intergroup conflict was inevitable. To combat those ideas, he did not, however, advocate a simple brand of cultural pluralism but tried to devise mechanisms by means in which culture could be an instrument for social integration.

Difference

Difference was a category McWilliams constantly struggled with and ultimately tried to articulate in the legal field. Besides the larger critical debate, he contributed to via his articles published in magazines and newspapers about what Louis Adamic called the racial–cultural situation (Denning 447), he also put his knowledge and practice as a lawyer to the service of the oppressed communities in 1940s California. For this reason, he is considered a legal activist,[4] since he defied the belief that legal actors were as objective and abstract as the law they practiced and openly stated his concerns with the interconnectedness of legislation and forms of oppression affecting particular social groups.

Ethnic migrants had come primarily to work in California's flourishing agriculture. But what they met was often different from what they expected, with the factories quickly replacing or displacing farmhands. As McWilliams also wrote in *Ill Fares the Land* (1942), rural migration not only underwent a revolution as it became itself the symptom and sign of a wider change in U.S. agriculture. This revolution was based on a "new triumvirate"—"agriculture, chemistry, and industry" (326) that relied on a politics of an indelible fascist bent. The factories were brought into the fields with the same violence as the imperial occupation of the previous century, a "second invasion of the borderlands" (*Brothers* 126), as economic penetration had neatly followed land expropriation. Since the beginning of the century, the face of U.S. agriculture had been subtly changing, keeping in the dark the social and labor problems it was generating. The seasonal character of many of the crops increased difficulties, forcing workers to move constantly. The labor camps that became their homes throughout the "feudal estates" appeared as shantytowns, if not "concentration camps, American style," as McWilliams called them (*The Education* 103). Working conditions were miserable, the pay was low, the varied ethnic composition of the groups made communication difficult, and permanent mobility allowed for no effective form of organization. Unionization took much longer to become effective among farmworkers than among industrial workers; in the decade when labor made its biggest gains through the Congress of Industrial Organizations, migrant workers and farm laborers were still by and large unorganized.

If that was the situation of migrants who worked in the fields, the situation of the largest immigrant communities in the state, second-generation Mexican Americans in the urban *colonias*, also faced many problems. McWilliams could not have ignored the question of racial difference because he also acted as Chairman of the Sleepy Lagoon Defense Committee (1943–44) and drafted the Appeal on behalf of the group of young Mexican Americans arrested on allegations of the crime. The incident had occurred at the Sleepy Lagoon, a place Mexican Americans attended because they were barred access to the Los Angeles public swimming pools. The trial was a typical case of production of abjection, soon becoming a "gang" trial when the Chief of the Foreign Relations Bureau of the Los Angeles sheriff's office, Edward Durant Ayres, openly made racist accusations. These were largely publicized by the sensationalist Hearst press in what came to be the largest mass trial for murder ever held in the country up to that point (*North* 229).[5] The arguments aimed at a complete dehumanization of the Mexican American youths by associating the groups' cultural habits to the tribal practices of sacrifice identified with ancient Native American cultures (i.e. the Aztecs) and what Ayres called a primitive thirst for blood. Dehumanization accounted for the fact that the accused were deprived of all their rights: besides the racist arguments, all common legal procedures were overrun, witnesses were ignored, and the defendants were refused clean clothes to appear in court. However, Ayres's discourse ultimately backfired as the construction of criminality and marginality as markers of the Mexican American community raised great resentment in the public opinion and ultimately led to several civil actions to gather support for the defendants, one of which was the creation of the Sleepy Lagoon Committee that Carey McWilliams was invited to chair.[6]

However, the dissemination of racist views by the Hearst press only unleashed more violence. Despite McWilliams' warnings to the authorities in another of his famous public testimonies, before the Los Angeles County Grand Jury in 1942, the situation only worsened with the coming of the war and the mounting racial hatred against the Mexican American community. Eventually, the Zoot Suit Riots exploded in Los Angeles in 1943, with the street fight between opposing young white marines and the so-called *Pachuco* zoot-suiters. Servicemen and civilians attacked several Mexican Americans dressed in the zoot-suit style (and also a few Filipinos and Blacks who shared the style). The zoot-suiters marked a specific cultural choice that entailed separating themselves from mainstream culture, adorning their bodies with tattoos and wearing long jackets with exaggerated shoulders, pegged pant legs, thick-soled shoes, long watch chains, and wide-brimmed pancake hats worn over ducktail haircuts. The white marines blamed their attacks on the *Pachucos*' cult of esthetics and play, which they deemed as insulting in a time of war, containment, and masculinity. Aggressions normally involved stripping the youths of their zoot-suits in an attempt to emasculate them while spanking them in a spectacle "normally" watched by the police, who patiently waited for the end of the show to take the victims to jail rather than the aggressors.

Hate against Mexican Americans at this time was not accidental. Riding on top of the emergencies of the Great Depression first and the war later, there were a number of atypical assaults on citizenship and human rights. From the deportation of Mexican Americans during the Depression, as of Filipinos alike (these being considered at the time wards of empire) to the Internment Program of Japanese Americans, not to mention the curtailment of individual liberties during the anti-Communist witch-hunt not much later. Attacks on citizens' rights by the state were imposed as legitimate and necessary. Neither were racial riots particular to California at the time[7] but the resentment that motivated the attacks on Mexican Americans in the 1940s had a particular tinge that McWilliams decided to analyze.

In California, this group clearly occupied the place of African Americans in the U.S. South due to historical issues of conquest and annexation. Institutional segregation in schools and other public places attested to the sanction by the law to practices of discrimination. Although the nature of inequality of these two groups was historically different, McWilliams argued that the root question was the same and colonial in nature: discrimination against Mexican Americans related to "the eternal question for cheap exploitable labor" (*Brothers* 341) and formed a case for domestic imperialism (*Brothers* 130). McWilliams actually set California in the front run for discrimination, asserting that the post-Reconstruction segregationist South had sought inspiration in California's nineteenth century anti-Chinese legislation, subscribing NAACP Herbert Hill's denunciation (*Honorable* 180). Moreover, the Zoot-Suit Riots had also been clearly influenced by the recent evacuation of the Japanese Americans to the camps, which had deprived the public opinion of the obvious scapegoat; hence the displacement of hate from the Japanese onto the Mexican Americans (*North* 227). The zoot-suit style, an overtly extravagant cultural marker, had been the pretext for the white marines to vent their hatred.

McWilliams noted that cultural discrimination was often used to disguise racial arguments. In several of his writings, he examined the ways the law sustained and added cultural substance to racism and thereby continually reproduced social inequality, anticipating arguments later defended by critical race theorists. Fighting against the ideological legacy of Plessy v. Fergusson, he defended that the courts did not have to wait until the mores changed, but rather legislation itself had an active role to play against systemic inequality (*Honorable* 179).

"Race" and law

McWilliams clearly perceived race as a strategy of power. He acknowledged that prejudice was culturally produced but did not neglect the economic and political dimensions of that manufacture. Race served a particular economic system that benefitted some groups by means of subjugating others and whose ramifications stretched into the world system. Therefore, segregation was for him an "instrument of social order," a "legal device" ("Race Discrimination" 11)—or "a policy of systematic exclusion" ("Does Social" 410)—that made it easier for a democracy to discriminate: "[i]n a democracy, social discrimination require[d] the exclusion of *groups*, since the comparative fluidity of the social structure ma[de] the exclusion of *individuals* both difficult and awkward" ("Does Social" 410; italics in original). The fact that his approach took into account not just the social but the political dimension of the issue allowed him to back political action regarding race that was not traditionally sanctioned by the law. Hence the responsibility he assigned to the federal government is what he termed its "positive obligation" to intervene in the enforcement of rights, assuming the need for institutions to respond to claims made by the people and not just produce and impose rights on the people in the traditional High Enlightenment rights fashion identified by James Tully (139).

McWilliams' project therefore relied on a committed—and *active*—involvement of the federal government on the issue of race relations through legislative reform called for by those on the ground: he proposed the development of a "Fair Racial Practices Act," following the footsteps of President F.D. Roosevelt's Fair Employment Practices legislation ("Race Discrimination" 22). F.D.R. had already subscribed to this position by signing Executive Order No. 8802, which prohibited discrimination in the workplace, although it was not really a binding law because it was mainly concerned with keeping order in the war industry during the war (*Prejudice* 290). Despite the legislative limitations so far, McWilliams maintained that the Fair Racial Practices Act was "a new federal civil rights status ... enforced by modern administrative methods as a matter of public policy rather than by individual action as a matter of personal privilege" ("Race Discrimination" 22). This understanding of race would eventually lead him away from that of individual rights to a communitarian argument: the law should acknowledge special, or differentiated, rights to particular groups. He also argued, "[t]endencies towards certain kinds of behavior are to be found, not in the bloodstream of a people, but in their cultural heritage. Cultural conflicts produce certain patterns of behavior, not only in individuals but in groups" ("Testimony" 152). He began working on this hypothesis in his Testimony to the Los Angeles County Grand Jury (1942), where he rejected the biopolitics employed to incriminate and demonize the Sleepy Lagoon youths and proposed instead a reformulation of race into ethnicity that stressed the centrality of *culture* to a group's social integration ("Testimony" 152). In essence, he transferred the focus of prejudice onto culture in an argument that also called for an understanding of the interdependence of civil, economic, social, and political rights.

The group involved in the turmoil, the zoot-suiters, was identified with the *Pachucos* (or *Cholos*)—the first Mexicans in the early 20th century who immigrated to California—and formed an economically and educationally oppressed group whose particular form of speech was itself taken as the mark of a poor education. McWilliams' Testimony to the Grand Jury also reconstructed the identity of the Mexican American youths on the basis of their particular experience of the law. His discourse related their integration failure as a reflection of their ambiguous citizenship status and corresponding inequality. In fact, after the Mexican–American War, Mexicans in the conquered territories had become citizens by default, under the Treaty of Guadalupe Hidalgo but the Treaty was omissive, namely regarding the racial identity of the newly created category "Mexican Americans," allowing for the assumption that they were white. Seizing the loophole, the law developed all sorts of obstacles to the enactment of the rights assigned by the Treaty in order to mitigate the Mexican Americans' degree of whiteness as well as the privileges inherent to it.

The argument that Mexicans were as white as Anglos and should therefore not claim the status of a minority ruled for many years. In fact, the categorization of "white" hid other disadvantages, such as the difficulty for Mexicans to claim discrimination since the law did not recognize discrimination against the "white race" (Delgado and Palacios 395). Richard Delgado and Jean Stefancic have described how Mexicans together with Asians in particular were historically a favorite target of racist legislation in California. In 1850, soon after the miners had begun to arrive after the Gold Rush, the Foreign Miners License Tax recently created aimed particularly at keeping Mexicans and Asians away, for it never applied to European miners. The tax imposed a monthly 20-dollar fee on noncitizens willing to mine gold and forced many Mexicans to abandon the activity. Although it was repealed 1 year later, it was brought into effect again against the Chinese a few years later. Mexicans, however, were perceived as posing an additional threat because they owned property. Discrimination against them always took specific forms. Some were exemplary violent, such as vigilantism and lynching, as Delgado and Stefancic explain ("California's" 1534) and in the mines, there was a double payroll that paid them less (even though they were fundamental in the development of the mining industry in the region, not just in terms of labor, but of technical knowledge as well). McWilliams used the Sleepy Lagoon case to highlight how, because official definitions of race did not sustain this group's discrimination, the distinction emerged in terms of markers of cultural identity instead.

One could actually base the whole question on the dispossession of oppressed groups on their right to equal access to the law. School segregation was perhaps one of the finest examples of that deprivation. McWilliams showed how education policies depended on the rights of ranchers, instead of those of the children, and were granted by the law. The case *Independent School District v. Salvatierra* in Texas in 1930 ruled against discrimination but for segregation on the basis of linguistic difficulties and migrant farming patterns, naturally in tune with Americanization programs. McWilliams was sent as an "envoy" of a civil rights organization to a similar case, *Mendez v. Westminster* from 1945 concerning a public school in El Modena, California, which was one of the first to rely on civil rights argumentation (Arriola 194), an episode he reported in the pages of *The Nation*. In this case, the court ruled for the existence of segregation, although in terms of language and culture/ancestry, not of race. Children were singled out because of their Spanish surnames alone, not for pedagogical reasons. However, in the El Modena case, the court did rule these practices as a violation of equal protection as defended by the Fourteenth Amendment (Arriola 167). So, it was not uncommon to have Spanish-speaking pupils in separate classes because of alleged "linguistic difficulties" and "migrant farming patterns," which justified both special syllabi for Mexican American pupils (Arriola 179)[8] and the adjustment of the school schedules to the children's work duties (Arriola 173). In effect, bilingualism (one of the characteristics most exclusively attributed to the Mexican American group) was often turned into language-based exclusion, being one of the nonofficial forms of discrimination upheld by the ruling stereotype of inferiority assigned to Mexican American children. Nevertheless, the reason why McWilliams emphasized the legal case of *Mendez v. Westminster* was the growing awareness among the Mexican American community of its power to protest against discrimination: as he stated, the case was, but one of many current indications that the Mexican minority throughout the Southwest has begun to attain social and political maturity. The suit was not "rigged," "inspired," or "promoted" by any cause committee. It was filed because rank-and-file citizens of Mexican descent in Southern California realized that they had long since "had enough." ("Is your Name" 304). Despite the shortcomings of the decision, the courageous struggle of Mexican Americans in the *Mendez v. Westminster* case certainly paved the way to the landmark case of *Brown v. Board of Education*, nearly a decade later, which overruled school segregation nationwide.

The experience led McWilliams to press for an analysis of the effects that a legal pattern might itself have had on the constitution or reinforcement of what had meanwhile become a commonsense notion and therefore disguised the ideological character of the law ("Race Discrimination" 2). He asserted that the law represented "an active manipulation of the *mores* to achieve purposes which find no sanction in the *mores* themselves" ("Race Discrimination" 6 [italics in original]). The mechanism of deliberation by precedent, for instance, after the ruling over segregation matters in the *Plessy v. Fergusson* case ("Race Discrimination" 11) was in place for over 50 years. It only contributed to the continuous disempowerment of oppressed communities, for it produced "legal myths" that crystalized social and political views in abstract and generalist principles, in complete disregard of historical contexts.

As Michael Omi and Howard Winant would establish later, race was a strategy of domination or a social formation (1994). Yet, McWilliams noted that, as such, race could provide only an illusory solution; for segregation in effect amounted to a social danger that threatened public interest, subtly promoting prejudiced and conflicting difference while continuously generating unequal competitive power ("Race Discrimination" 21–22). As oppressed communities gradually gained awareness of this reality, social turmoil ensued, as the Los Angeles riots had demonstrated. Hence the need to enforce measures such as the Fair Racial Practices Act as public policy for, as he explained, "[t]he individual may not feel injured by the discrimination; but society may well feel that its stability is being undermined by the practice" ("The Color" 639).

McWilliams' project had a material dimension as well, considering that he requested state responsibility and intervention in the issue. The Fair Racial Practices Act should be complemented by the elimination of the poll tax in federal elections and the enactment of an anti-lynching statute. As well, measures in the field of education and the guarantee of equal access to common facilities from publicly supported recreation to cultural facilities such as libraries and museums, and also civic conveniences from hotels and restaurants to buses and trains. This all implied that "race" be removed from the field of immigration and naturalization codes so that no trace of discrimination would remain: "no racial line ... [should] be drawn in determining eligibility to citizenship." This applied, in the particular war context to Asians as well: those who resided in the United States (following the Japanese American internment Order) should be immediately made eligible for naturalization and immigration quotas made equal to the various national groups as long as the government followed on an immigration program that was handled "purposefully and intelligently" ("The Color" 644).

Finally, McWilliams claimed that the creation of a federal agency expressly authorized to deal with the problem of race was urgent, which was undoubtedly a reference to what he also defined as the Institute for Ethnic Democracy. Moreover, the project was yet wider: in terms of Housing, a Fair Housing Practices Plan would enforce public policies and the end of restrictive covenants. Regarding equal access to health facilities, hospitals, and so forth, he defended the application of wider provisions. For equal access to work, McWilliams defended a state and federal Fair Employment Practices Committee and an amendment to the National Labor Relations Board. An important complement to this was what he conceived as yet another piece of legislation focused on civil rights, the New Federal Civil Rights Act.

Functional equality

Elaborating on a notion of culture that related closely to a community's lived contextual experience, McWilliams' stance relied on a relativist perspective on rights. He believed that a new concept of equality was needed: one who acknowledged and incorporated difference both as lived experience and as a distinguishing element in the identity of particular social or ethnic groups. He called it "functional equality," taking as a starting point that social justice could only be achieved if equality was conceived as differential (hence the modifier "functional"). Equality should thus be regarded as a practical, utilitarian value, maybe even a concrete method. This entailed that, instead of an abstract universal value, equality could be applied to specific cases. According to this rationale, equality was not a leveling of sameness (or the application of the same rule or benefit to everyone), but rather adapted to the conditions and needs of particular, contextually positioned, subjects. In McWilliams' project, functional equality included equal educational opportunities that required a series of measures, including, of course, the end of social segregation.

Functional equality took form in group rights even though the concept did not exist as such at the time. McWilliams conceived of it as "special rights" that should be assigned to ethnic groups once these had formally assumed their ethnic difference. That is, they should become aware of a common history of oppression marked by a particular experience of participation in society restrained by discrimination. This entailed specific understandings of citizenship that strayed from the universal, general, abstract definition of "equal to everyone" (*Prejudice* 294).

Once the oppressed groups had achieved this degree of perception of common grievances and cooperated with one another, they could claim group rights because discrimination was not an individual matter but the result of racial prejudice and the stereotypes attached to specific groups. The idea may sound farfetched or ahead of its time, but he found a solid justification in precedents to the practice in New Deal legislation, namely in the field of labor, as compensation for disadvantages regarding women and workers, e.g. the franchise or rest hours, in the case of women, and collective bargaining, in the case of workers (*Prejudice* 292). He, therefore, defended that citizenship rights be extended to minority groups not as an abstract generalist imposition from above, but in direct proportion to their specific needs and ambitions, their past and their future, their beliefs and expectations, their culture and education. Not long afterward and in spite of its shortcomings, the President's Committee Report of 1947, "To Secure These Rights," eventually recognized ethnic groups as minorities and for this reason McWilliams came to consider it "a turning point in the history of American racial minorities" (*Brothers* 345).

McWilliams' projects did not take immediate effect but their relevance is shown in their validity in current rights debates. For example, as shown in the critiques of political philosopher Will Kymlicka and his notion of "group rights" (1995), or legal sociologist Boaventura de Sousa Santos's notion of "equal differences" ("Para uma sociología" 252), or yet in political scientist Iris Marion Young's theory of "differentiated rights." While arguing that the oppressive past that marks a minority group's experience becomes part of its difference, that is, of its culture, Young denounced the law's alleged impartiality and universality as symptoms of cultural imperialism or markers of privilege (*Justice* 10, "Polity" 175) and therefore proposed a set of special rights attending to group differences ("Polity" 177). Where McWilliams wrote functional equality, Young writes contextual difference, a concept that acknowledges the interdependence of the different types of rights (economic, social, political, civil, and cultural) while allowing also for differentiated groups to recognize one another's specificity or difference without a necessary sense of conflict ("Polity" 157, 162–63).

Culture features precisely as one of the issues Young takes as a "differentiated" or a "special right," which includes "phenomena of language, speaking style or dialect, body comportment, gesture, social practices, values, group-specific socialization, and so on" ("Polity" 200) as well as very particular historical circumstances that in many cases have meant oppression. Instead of the historical definition of difference as otherness and exclusion, Young argues that it should be reassessed under a relational light, because both identity and difference revolve around interdependent, reciprocal relations, and "experienced meanings" ("Polity" 161). In both McWilliams' and

Young's critiques, the claim for context borders on the notion of cultural citizenship as the recognition that an individual can have multiple affinities and diverse loyalties, including to more than one country, and that his/her participation is not reduced to civic practices imposed from above or formalized through institutions. It implies that the individual's bonds to place can be assessed as forms of participation and therefore negotiated and acknowledged as contributions to the society s/he has settled in and developed associations. In other words, the individual appropriates participation in his/her own terms (according to his/her culture, for instance), as it were, rather than be appropriated by the institutionalized forms.

This understanding in turn calls to mind later elaborations such as cultural citizenship that link the development of an individual's cultural identity to active civic participation rather than roots, ranging from "trade unions, churches, [and] environmental groups, [to] charities [and] associations for women and ethnic groups" (Heater 120). However, given the history of the Southwest and its incorporation into the United States, the question for McWilliams would in fact be as simple as a rereading of history and the modes of social interaction that had developed on the ground. Social relations and routine practices and patterns of behavior showed that the people in these communities were integrated: they already exercised fundamental cultural rights they were denied from above:

Throughout the Southwest, the imprint of Spain and Mexico is indelible, not as Spanish or Mexican influence per se but as modified by contact with Indian and Anglo-American culture. The three influences are woven into nearly every aspect of the economy, the speech, the architecture, the institutions, and the customs of the people. The people of the Southwest share a mixed cultural heritage in which the mixtures, rather than the pure strains, have survived. In a Navajo rug, an adobe house, or an irrigated farm, one may find elements of the three cultures *inextricably interwoven and fused.* (*North* 301; my emphasis)

Conclusion: worldwide nationality and citizenship

The extent of McWilliams' project could not, however, be fully grasped without taking into account his cosmopolitan idea of a "worldwide nationality and citizenship code" ("The Color" 645). The topic would bring in complex questions beyond the scope of this essay, but I introduce it in a manner of conclusion because it evinces McWilliams' perception that, in what came to migrants and oppressed communities, rights granted within a national framework were important but not enough. Although he did not develop it in great detail, he conceived the worldwide nationality and citizenship code as a piece of legislation that would negotiate the conflicts between nationality and citizenship. Furthermore, it would grant migrants the basic rights related to hospitality, including preventing discriminated groups from falling prey to legal distinctions and arbitrary government decisions that trumped their human rights even before their citizenship rights. It was obvious that having witnessed the Sleepy Lagoon case or the internment of Japanese American citizens during the war that the struggle for rights was to endure both within and beyond national borders.

Notes

1. The publication of this text was supported by Fundacão para Ciência e a Tecnologia, under the Strategic Project (UID/SOC/50012/2015).
2. Tully, James. "Two Traditions of Human Rights" in *Human Rights, Human Dignity and Cosmopolitan Ideals,* Eds. Matthias Lutz-Bachmann and Amós Nascimento Farnham (Surrey: Ashgate Publishing Limited, 2014), pp. 139–158.
3. See his pioneering studies *North from Mexico* (1949) and *Brothers Under the Skin* (1943), for instance.
4. For a definition of legal activism, see Santos, Boaventura de Sousa. *Para uma revolução democrática da justiça* (Cortez Editora, 2008). See also Canelo, María José. "Carey McWilliams, the Public Intellectual: Reflections on Citizenship and Culture." *Intellectual Topographies and the Making of Citizenship,* Eds. Helena Gonçalves da Silva, Maria Laura Bettencourt Pires and Inês Espada Vieira (Catholic University, 2011), pp. 163–176.
5. Some of the youth were condemned of second-degree murder. The group was released of charges in 1944, for admitted lack of evidence.
6. The youngsters were only acquitted of charges in 1944 for lack of evidence.
7. Race riots also took place at Beaumont, Texas, Harlem, and Detroit.
8. See the *Independent School District v. Salvatierra,* taking place in 1930, in Texas, which ruled against discrimination but for segregation based on linguistic difficulties and migrant farming patterns, naturally in tune with Americanization programs.

Works cited

Arriola, Christopher. "Knocking on the Schoolhouse Door...." *La Raza Law Journal,* vol. 8, issue 2, 1995, pp. 166–207.

Critser, Greg. "The Making of a Cultural Rebel: Carey McWilliams, 1924–1930." *Pacific Historical Review,* vol. 55, issue 2, 1986, pp. 226–255.

Delgado, Richard and Vicky Palacios. "Mexican Americans as a Legally Cognizable Class Under Rule 23 and the Equal Protection Clause." *Notre Dame Law Review,* vol. 50, issue 3, 1975. http://scholarship.law.nd.edu/cgi/viewcontent.cgi?article=2759&context=ndlr. Accessed 9 October 2017.

Delgado, Richard and Jean Stefancic. "California's Racial History and Constitutional Rationales for Race-Conscious Decision Making in Higher Education." *UCLA Law Review,* vol. 47, issue 6, 2000, pp. 1521–1614.

Delgado, Richard and Jean Stefancic. *Critical Race Theory. An Introduction.* New York University Press, 2001.

Denning, Michael. *The Cultural Front. The Laboring of American Culture in the Twentieth Century* Verso, 1997.

Heater, Derek. *What Is Citizenship?* Blackwell Publishers, 1999.

Kymlicka, Will. *Multicultural Citizenship: A Liberal Theory of Minority Rights.* Oxford University Press, 1995.

McWilliams, Carey. "Does Social Discrimination Really Matter?" *Commentary*, no. 4, Nov. 1947, pp. 408–415. Carey McWilliams Papers (Collection 1319), Department of Special Collections, University Research Library, University of California, Los Angeles. Box 14, Folder "Copies of articles, speeches and pamphlets by Carey McWilliams, mostly from late 1930's, early 1940's."

McWilliams, Carey. "Is Your Name Gonzales?" *The Nation*, 16.3.1947, pp. 302–304.

McWilliams, Carey. "Race Discrimination and the Law." *Science and Society*, vol. 10, issue 1, 1945, pp. 1–22.

McWilliams, Carey. "Testimony to the Los Angeles County Grand Jury, October 4, 1942." *Viva La Raza!*, edited by Julián Nava. D. Von Nostrand, 1973, pp. 151–54.

McWilliams, Carey. "The Color of America." *The Antioch Review*, vol. 2, issue 2, 1942, pp. 35–650.

McWilliams, Carey. "What We Did About Racial Minorities," *While You Were Gone. A Report on Wartime Life in the United States*, edited by Jack Goodman. Simon and Schuster, 1946, pp. 89–111.

McWilliams, Carey. *Brothers under the Skin*. Little, Brown and Company, 1943.

McWilliams, Carey. *Prejudice: Japanese Americans: Symbol of Racial Intolerance*. Little, Brown and Company, 1944.

McWilliams, Carey. *Factories in the Field: The Story of Migratory Farm Labor in California*.Little, Brown and Company, 1939.

McWilliams, Carey. *Honorable in All Things*. Interview with Joel Gardner. Oral History Program. Los Angeles, CA: University of California, Los Angeles, 1982.

McWilliams, Carey. *Ill Fares the Land: Migrants and Migratory Labor in the United States*.Little, Brown and Company, 1942.

McWilliams, Carey. *North from Mexico: The Spanish-Speaking People of the United States*. Greenwood Press, 1949.

McWilliams, Carey. *The Education of Carey McWilliams*. Simon and Schuster, 1978.

Michael Omi, and Howard Winant. *Racial Formation in the United States. From the 1960's to the 1990's*. Routledge, 1994.

Santos, Boaventura de Sousa. "Para uma sociologia das ausências e uma sociologia das emergências," *Revista Crítica de Ciências Sociais*, vol. 63, 2002, pp. 237–280

Tully, James "Two Traditions of Human Rights." *Human Rights, Human Dignity and Cosmopolitan Ideals*, edited by edited by Matthias Lutz-Bachmann and Amós Nascimento Farnham. Ashgate Publishing Limited, 2014, pp. 139–158.

Young, Iris Marion. "Polity and Group Difference: A Critique of the Ideal of Universal Citizenship." *Theorizing Citizenship*, edited by Ronald S. Beiner. SUNY Press, 1995, pp. 175–207.

Young, Iris Marion. *Justice and the Politics of Difference*. Princeton University Press, 1990.

11 The ontogenesis of fear in Héctor Tobar's *The Barbarian Nurseries*

Alexander Ullman

"Let me assert my firm belief that the only thing we have to fear is fear itself—nameless, unreasoning, unjustified terror." Often tested as middle school trivia and adrenalized in fourth quarter football huddles, Roosevelt's famous phrase is part of the collective American memory. What is less remembered, though, is that Roosevelt uttered these words in response to the nation's unparalleled economic uncertainty.[1] Spoken at his 1933 inauguration and in the heights of the Great Depression, Roosevelt's speech goes on to condemn the "rulers of the exchange of mankind's goods" and calls for "engaging on a national scale in a redistribution" of industrial wealth (Roosevelt 11). While anchoring the source of the nation's fear in the greed of Wall Street, Roosevelt's hopeful tone of revelation and triumph belies a complex ontology of fear. "Fear itself" becomes a free-floating signifier, a disembodied affect that "we"—the implied citizenry of the United States—can withstand only by knowing it as such. How can fear be something a citizenry feels and at the same time be this disembodied, "nameless, unreasoning, unjustified" affect? In other words, how can it be the cause, the object, and the description of citizens' emotions, all at once? Roosevelt's complex philosophy suggests that fear shape-shifts and interpenetrates both the public sphere and the individual psyche.

The economic origins and protean ontology of Roosevelt's "fear itself" evade the collective memory of many Americans, but they are at the heart of Héctor Tobar's novel *The Barbarian Nurseries* (2011). In telling the story of Araceli, an undocumented domestic worker from Mexico City, and her employer the Torres-Thompsons, an upper middle-class nuclear family living in a gated community in Orange County, Tobar pulls back the veil of how neoliberal economic forces and modern media foster a culture of fear in 21st century America for citizens and noncitizens alike. Situated just after the financial crises of 2008, the novel begins when plummeting personal savings and increasing debt stir familial conflict for the Torres-Thompson family—conflict that culminates in an unforeseeable act of domestic violence. What ensues is a prolonged absence, where the parents Scott and Maureen abandon the house for several days without telling each other, leaving their bewildered domestic worker Araceli no choice but to lead the children, Brandon and Keenan, on a trip around Los Angeles to find their grandfather. What appears as a gesture of good will turns into a police search for the children and Araceli's fraught struggle with the media, public opinion, and the judicial system.

Fear is ever-present in this novel, yet Tobar does much more than simply document fear in 21st century America. The study will begin by exploring notions of what fear "is," especially in relation to philosopher Brian Massumi's 2005 essay on the "ontogenesis" of fear, and to Nicholas De Genova's analysis of how fear structures contemporary notions of migrant "illegality." The study will then continue by offering four readings of *The Barbarian Nurseries* in relation to these theories. With these readings, I will be arguing that both through telling Araceli's story, and specifically through the manner in which that story is told, Tobar offers the individual voice and the personal story of human mobility as productive counterforces to fear's destructive and totalizing gestures. By employing fear as both a thematic trait and a formal structuring device, Tobar at once fictionally dramatizes the media's promulgation of immigrant "illegality" while also deconstructing the fiction that is "illegality." *The Barbarian Nurseries*, through an immanent critique, offers a representation of and a riposte to the perpetuation of fear by neoliberal economic forces and mediatized spectatorship in 21st century America.

What is fear? Contemporary governmental representations of fear, from the Bush-era 9/11 terror alert system to the Obama administration's "ready.gov" ad campaign, at once function both to unsettle *and* to call to action.[2] They attempt to make something intangible—like "terror" or imminent aerial attack—tangible, visible, knowable, or even preventable. Brian Massumi, writing in direct response to the first Bush administration's color-coded terror alert system, posits that the anxiety these images evoke functions not simply as a protective shield against future threats, but that this anxiety is rather *itself* caught up in the process of fear's promulgation. Fear becomes the shadow cast by a looming threat: "futurity is made directly present in an effective [or fully realized, no longer virtual or potential] expression that brings it into the present without it ceasing to be a futurity" (Massumi 36). In this way, fear becomes its own "ontogenetic" force: an affect seemingly disembodied from any observable action, yet realized and perpetuated through the government's warning system *and* people's emotions. In the case of the domestic worker, like Araceli in the novel, the fear and anxieties of daily life are imminent and *immanent*—existing in the future, in the loss of one's job or the deportation of oneself, but always presently felt through the embodiment of affect. Of central importance here to Massumi's notion of the "ontogenesis," or the "birth of being" of fear, are two characteristics: first, the slippery temporality, or what he calls the "transtemporality" of fear, in that fear exists in the present and future and past, all at once (36); second, the spectral, affective ontology of fear—its ability to *appear* agentless while it is actually moved by larger forces and through individuals.

These two qualities provide a way of thinking about how fear functions in Tobar's novel, especially in relation to notions of "illegality." Nicholas De Genova, in "Europe/Crisis: New Keywords in the 'Crisis' in and of Europa" (2016), argues that fear functions not simply at the level of individual psyche, but also in concert with larger political, social, and economic forces as part of the modern public discourse. Because the U.S. economy demands low-wage labor, some migrants are deported so that the majority of migrants may remain in a state of "deportability" and thus are forced to work in low-wage jobs (De Genova 439).[3] The fear-inducing and right-less condition of deportability allows the American citizenry to spatialize migrant workers as "illegal," having crossed a militarized border, and to racialize them as "aliens" or "Mexicans" against a perceived "American"-ness. The militarization of the border thereby becomes a theater of war and control that plays out not only along the border, but also in the psyche of a scapegoating American citizenry and the ostracized migrant worker (436).

Such theoretical work offers a refined lens for close reading Tobar's novel: by emplotting the transtemporality of fear into the formal narrative structure of the novel in moments that thematically feature the affective characteristics of fear, *The Barbarian Nurseries* offers a representation and a critique of fear's ontogenesis—its seemingly agentless snowballing and perpetuation. The four vignettes from the novel below feature fear thematically—where the emotion of fear moves within the social milieu, the family unit, or the characters—and formally—in Tobar's use of paralepsis, analepsis, prolepsis, and metalepsis. In performing a Genettian reading of these four scenes, we attempt to show that Tobar uses narrative to represent how fear moves between the public and the private spheres, but also to thwart its affective potential. If the terms "illegal" and "deportable" are discursive functions—that is, part of the public discourse—which shape events, lives, and even political platforms, then *The Barbarian Nurseries* deconstructs the way this discourse functions by exposing its dependence on the media and giving voice to private stories. In "Incompleteness and the Possibility of Making: Toward Denationalized Citizenship" (2009), Saskia Sassen's optimism that "excluded actors and not fully formalized norms are factors that can make history" is not a theoretical fantasy in the fictional world of *The Barbarian Nurseries* (Sassen 232). Araceli's story, as well as the way it is told, suggests that traces of the future lie dormant in the present.

Fear of financial debt sets the plot of *The Barbarian Nurseries* in motion, but the novel quickly complicates both notions of fear and indebtedness. In the final chapter of the first of three sections, Scott and Maureen Torres-Thompson are fighting over the cost of a succulent garden Maureen put in the back of their idyllic home. Things quickly get out of hand, and Araceli at once hears Scott's "Be Quiet!," Maureen's scream in response, and then the shattering of the glass table that lies in the middle of their dining room. After this pivotal crisis that sets the rest of the novel into motion, Araceli rushes in to help—only to be startled that Maureen is screaming *her* name ("Araceli, help me. Please!"), not her husband's:

> The Mexican woman froze. *What have they done to each other, these people?* Araceli felt the need to restore order and understood that the violence in this room might spin into something unspeakable were it not for her presence. *Today I am the civilized one and they are the savages....* Stepping gingerly around the ruins of the table she had cleaned that morning, and too many other mornings to count, with blue ammonia spray, Araceli reached out and took the hand of her *jefa* and helped her to her feet. (114–115; emphasis in original)

The narrator later reveals that Scott's shove was prompted by Maureen's insulting of his dead mother. But there are four pages between the shattering of the table and the revelation of its exact cause, during which Araceli cleans up the mess that night in the living room and makes breakfast the next morning for the two boys in a conspicuously parentless kitchen. And it is in this narrative omission of four pages that fear looms both thematically and formally in the text as a means for Tobar to deconstruct its ontogenetic, that is, transtemporal and affective, power.

Massumi's theory of the ontogenesis of fear reminds us that fear can be felt in the absence of any observable action; through paralepsis, Tobar emplots this characteristic of fear into the level of form. Because the narrator focalizes through Araceli in the four pages between the shattering and the revelations of Scott's shove, the crises was only perceived through its result of the shattering of the glass table. Through this formal *hysteron proteron*—where the narrator reveals the effect before revealing the cause— the affect of fear emerges thematically. The shattered table symbolizes all of the work and affect that Araceli imbued into it, for it is the same table that "she had cleaned that morning, and too many other mornings to count, with blue ammonia spray" (Tobar 115). The phrase "too many other mornings to count" betrays Araceli's frustration at having to "clean up" after her quarreling employers. Such frustration arises from the fact that her labor is a contradiction: she must at once imbue that table with her affective labor, but at the same time erase it with an ammonia spray so it appears as if it has no origin. In this way, her affective labor resembles the ontogenesis of fear, which at once appears to be agentless but is actually driven by her feeling of economic precarity as an undocumented worker. Araceli's frustration is concomitant with a feeling of indebtedness, a need to "restore order" before the violence gets out of hand. Although she is not involved directly in this violence, she feels implicated in the prevention of its perpetuation. While her affective fear is emplotted into the narrative structure of the novel through omission, her voice emerges in the free indirect discourse of the italicized text, as both a representation of and a counter force to that uncertainty. When she tells herself, "Today, I am the civilized one and they are the savages," Araceli reappropriates the language of her employers, revealing how economic uncertainty and fear unsettle *both* Araceli and the nuclear family. It serves to comment on, even provoke empathy for, the economic struggles of both the family and the migrant laborer, not in a way that flattens their situations as equal but that calls attention to their common source: fear.

When she wakes up the next morning to a strangely silent house, Araceli fearfully opens the door to the living room and picks up the tiny shards that escaped her cleaning the previous night, "meditating not so much on the shards as on the unexpected violence that had produced them" (120). The reader, like Brandon and Keenan, only partially knows what happened inside that room but fully knows that Araceli is overwhelmed with the need to "restore order." The shards are metaphors for routines that are now broken, to be picked up and put back together by a domestic worker indebted to do much more than simply clean that table. The feelings of anxiety, fear, and indebtedness string the text together, foreshadowing not just the adventure to come but also deconstructing the manner in which it will be felt. Although her labor has been ammoniatized and erased, her voice is not erased in this section—providing one way in which Tobar offers the personal voice of the undocumented worker as a riposte to the ontogenesis of fear.

Again, the purpose in looking closely at the text here is to show how Tobar, by at once cueing up moments of the fear thematically as well as emplotting the transtemporal and affective nature of fear into the narrative structure, uses literary tactics to deconstruct fear. A second vignette in which Tobar enacts fear both at the thematic and formal level occurs after the Torres-Thompsons have abandoned Araceli at the house with the two boys. This is a parental absence that causes anxiety and stress for both the boys and their caretaker. Grappling with the responsibility thrust upon her now for three nights, Araceli thinks to herself, "*This is the third night I am spending alone with these boys. I should be the one crying out in my sleep. I should be the one screaming for my mother*" (150; emphasis in original). Such anxiety causes her and the boys to set out on an odyssey to find their grandfather in Los Angeles, which requires them to travel via public transport. After they hop on the bus, Araceli worries about the boys' safety, about the "bruises and bones an accident could bring" (157). The narrator shifts quickly to the exact moment when Araceli decided to leave Mexico City for America—when she came upon a bus accident in Coyoacán:

> Look. A young man is dying right here in front of us. This is something we don't normally see. It's all so more real than what's on television, isn't it? This isn't an actor. He is a poor man like us, just trying to make a few more pesos like the one he is still clutching in his hand. We can't help him; we can only look and thank the Virgin that it isn't us down there...(158; emphasis in original)

Fear and anxiety permeate Araceli's present and her past, but they are different types of fears. Her personal memory of Mexico City is striking in that fear is transformed into disgust and distaste. Araceli feels physically ill in response to the precariousness and disorderliness of Mexican life, prompting her desire to abandon any delay and set her plans leaving for the United States in motion. Some of the narrative of this memory is italicized, a technique often reserved for focalization through an individual voice, but the technique here also signifies the mediatized voices of Mexican bystanders to the accident, who observe this horror and immediately compare it to how it's been seen on television. This both singular and collective voice thinks, "*It's all the more real than television*," and yet, as if it *were* on television, no one does anything (158; emphasis in original). The dying boy is no "actor" but poor like everyone else; his blazing eyes mirror the emotionless stare of the mediatized spectators. There is a register of empathy here ("He is just like us"), but fear, because it is received through a mediatized violence, suppresses the bystanders action into inaction. In speaking of modern mediatized spectatorship, Michael Hardt writes that media, even as far back as Plato, is condemned for being superficial; what is less understood is how the media elicits a very specific type of subjectivity, one along an axis of activity and passivity.[4] Here, the spectators are induced into a death-like, comatose observation of this dying man, as if they were watching television, even though they are not.

The transtemporal character of fear is also working at the level of form: Araceli's anxiety provokes an analepsis—or flashback—to this moment in which she experienced horror in a similar setting. In a way, we can see this anxiety working in a Freudian way, where the flashback is a reminder for Araceli to protect the boys from any imminent danger.[5] But if the affect of fear, as Massumi suggests, functions imminently *and* immanently, both in the future and within the present, *The Barbarian Nurseries* also brings the past, present, and future into transtemporal, or what Massumi calls "infra-temporal" flux. When the narrative switches back to Araceli's narration of Mexico City, the reader is not just given her past experience of violence but also of her past hope. By glimpsing the hope for a better future in the past—what Paul Saint-Amour, in *Tense Future: Modernism, Total War, Encyclopedic Form* 2015), calls the future's past—Tobar's critique of neoliberal precarity emerges (Saint-Amour 22). Because of fear, Araceli remembers a past event in which she hopes for a better future in the United States, a future with better sensible traffic structures but also one with less "precariousness of life" (Tobar 158). Ironically, her time as a domestic worker has been no less precarious. The affect of horror in seeing the dying boy is not simply a reminder to protect Brandon and Keenan on the current bus, not just a resuscitation of the fear and horror that mediatized life suppressed in that past incident, but also an affirmation of how her current life is a variation on that same insecurity that she felt in Mexico City. Across the border, in two different countries, across time and space, fear has propagated itself and lingered on. Despite this, Araceli's movement provides a hopeful counterforce to fear's ontogenetic power—her present migration toward the city of Los Angeles mirrors her past migration to the United States. They are both hopeful gestures, both a leaving from and a going toward. This vignette emplots the transtemporality of fear onto the level of form, but in doing so, thwarts the destructive forces of fear with the counter force of hopeful mobility. Personal hope through migration—both to the United States and to Los Angeles—is a productive riposte to the ontogenesis of fear.

Tobar's technique of shifting the focalization from Araceli to that of other characters is one that repeatedly foregrounds the prevalence of fear. As Araceli and the two boys wander through Los Angeles' neighborhoods, there is a palpable feeling of fear and anxiety:

> "I think we're lost," the taller boy said.
> "*No seas ridículo, no estamos* lost," the Mexican woman answered, irritated. (175; emphasis in original)

Araceli is frustrated not just with the difficulty of locating the grandfather, but also with having been thrust into the role of maternal figure. This passage reveals her anxiety but it also betrays the emotion of Judge Robert Adalian, a traffic court jurist who happens to be driving by at the same time. The use of the dialog tags "taller boy" and "Mexican woman" here, instead of Brandon and Araceli, indicates that this dialog is focalized through his perspective, as he overhears and oversees their wandering from his car. As the shattering of the glass table disrupts the rhythms of the Torres-Thompson's family in an earlier scene, Araceli and the boys crossing the road breaks the rhythm of his normal commute. Just before the light turns green, Tobar uses italics to focalize through the inner monologue of Judge Adalian. "*It's not their skin tone that gives the boys away, it's their hair and the way they're walking and studying everything around them like tourists. Those boys don't belong here*" (175; emphasis in original). The word "here" is a deictic—one, the definition of which is dependent on context—and its use foregrounds how notions of belonging are dependent on such context as well. The Judge's spectatorship is imbued with racial categorization and gerrymandering, where the Caucasian boys don't belong, but Araceli *does*. Already, we see at the level of the sentence how Tobar deconstructs issues of "illegality," throwing the question of who "belongs" into a realm of spatial and racial context. The scene even stirs the judge's involuntary memory, recalling a time when Guatemalans and Salvadorans in the judge's own neighborhood were displaced by Armenian refugees from the Soviet Union. This imagery of displacement compounds with Adalian's more recent lament: he is the oldest person in the courtroom repeatedly that day, surpassed only by the accused defendant. Besides the feelings of irritation and displacement, fear underlies Judge Adalian's anxiety over aging, even becoming defunct in his own profession.

The ontogenesis of fear 203

Fear takes the reader back in time in *The Barbarian Nurseries* during the scene on the bus, but it also propels the reader forward in this scene with Judge Adalian. This scene is proleptic in nature in that it is an example of typical foreshadowing. As Adalian pulls through the green light, the narrator describes how unsuspecting he is of how in just a few weeks this memory of "crossing paths with the faded actor [the defendant] and the Mexican woman with the two 'white' boys on the same ordinary day would win him an appearance on cable television" (175). Besides indicating the extent to which Araceli's former domestic quandary will soon implicate her in the legal system, the reader is alerted to large scale, societal-wide affective implications of this trip, which will include passionate activism by those who care about Araceli's case as well as right-wing fear mongering by those who'd like to see her deported at all costs. Through the proleptic suspense, the reader is alerted to, even implicated in, how the uncertainty that Araceli feels will play out into the mediatized theatricalization of her trip to Los Angeles. One might suspect that because Robert Adalian's daily rhythms of commuting were interrupted that he might seek to retaliate or hold a grudge, but instead, he stands up for her. Notably, 200 pages later, Judge Adalian will support Araceli's innocence by reporting how he saw her and the two boys on a very specific date—a date, the memory of which sticks in his mind *because* it was anchored by the memory of his *own* precariousness and uncertainty about his age in relation to the defendant's.[6] Fear, anxiety, uncertainty: these are the emotions that individuals feel, but are also the affects that travel between individuals and through society. They collect thematically within the text, moving freely between the characters, even breaking up patterns and rhythms of individual experience. But these affects, and fear in particular, engage with the text on a formal level here through a transtemporal narrative structure, and it is on this level that Tobar offers a striking riposte to the ontogenesis of fear. Massumi writes that fear "can only be fought on the same affective, ontogenetic ground on which it itself operates"; by layering the clashing rhythms of narrative time with the clashing rhythms of the characters' memories, Tobar at once creates a slow motion effect in the narrative for Judge Adalian—who is prompted to think of his youth and his dotage—as well as rapid, proleptic speeding up for the reader. The result of such temporal see-sawing is the defamiliarization of fear, both for Adalian and for the reader. By having Adalian's fear and uncertainty contribute to his empathy, Tobar attempts to critique the ontogenesis of fear on the level of form. Because that formal critique is motivated through prolepsis, he even implicates the reader in the situation's affective contours.

A fourth scene that makes fear palpable at the level of theme but also deconstructs it at the level of form is the scene of Araceli's capture. It's a tense scene—Araceli has seen herself on TV in the home Mr. Salomón Luján, a successful naturalized *Mexicano* who also serves on the Huntington Park Council, and she decides to make an escape. She walks briskly through Huntington Park, especially upon hearing the helicopters and numerous pedestrians recognizing her. She hops a fence and begins to make a run for it. The narrator compares the chase to a playground game, but as she begins to make a run for it, her fear presents through an italicized self-talk that reveals Tobar's authorial critique:

> *There are other, easier ways of returning to Mexico. They will grab me and drag me across the dirt like a calf in the rodeo, and then cage me. We must endure these rituals of humiliation: this is our Mexican glory, to be pursued and apprehended in public places for bystanders to see.* (261; emphasis in original)

The critique of "illegality" and "deportability" is at its most apparent in this scene, particularly as it calls attention to juvenility and theatricality of deportation. In a manner similar to the bus scene, in which spectators look on at the dying boy with a passive stare, Araceli feels that now *she* is the humiliated object of public spectatorship. The affect of fear is caught up with the rituals of public shaming and humiliation that Araceli sees as part of her "Mexican glory."

Though the free indirect discourse provides a glimpse, what Araceli doesn't see is how this ritual of humiliation is caught up with the fear mongering of a much larger mediascape. When Araceli jumps the fence and makes a run for it, she runs right into the cross hairs of an Estonian cinematographer's viewfinder and the set of a $3.1 million budget indie film. What starts as a distraction to their filming of an actor in the distance becomes part of their cinematic diegesis:

> "They're going to beat her," a crew member said breathlessly. "They're going to beat her to a pulp."
> Take a step toward them. Just one step.
> The actor moved hesitatingly toward the running woman, as if he wanted to help her but was not sure he could.
> Good. Now one more. Just one. Are we getting this?
> "Yes, I'm on a tiny f-stop," the cinematographer said. "The depth of field is magnificent."
> Beautiful.
> Weeks later in the editing room, the director and his editor would incorporate about seventy-five seconds of this footage into their final version of the film. (260–261)

This metaleptic shift dramatizes how the narrative of Araceli's journey is theatricalized and emplotted into a larger narrative of modern media. The novel calls attention to its own readership here, dramatizing how all spectators can't receive certain forms of reality *without* the media. As the narrator describes the scene through the dialog of director and cinematographer, violence and fear are estheticized ("Beautiful.") so much so that they are confused and dematerialized ("Is this real?") (260–261). Through metalepsis—the shifting of narrative levels—Tobar reveals the fiction that is "illegality" and "deportability." The reader witnesses Araceli's capture through her voice in italics, but these italics appear at the end of the same paragraph in which Araceli's capture is reviewed visually on a screen later in the "editing room" (261). Whereas De Genova suggests that the border is "a theatre for staging the spectacle of the illegal alien," Tobar calls attention to how the media itself acts as border between reality and fiction—a border with the same theatrical impetus for staging spectacle (De Genova 436). Araceli's voice is a riposte to this mediatization, as it exposes the humiliation of this mediatized public ritual of humiliation.

It might be enough to say that *The Barbarian Nurseries* simply reflects contemporary issues surrounding human mobility. The logic and terminology of "crises" used to explain migratory uncertainty across the world today also stir the plot of this novel into action.[7] There are also typical fear mongering villains in *The Barbarian Nurseries,* who seem to parody both right-wing antagonism and passively liberal inaction to these perennial crises. Both Ian Goller, the opportunist Assistant District Attorney, and Janet Bryson, the angry single mother and activist, lead their own assault on Araceli's case and against the Mexican "outsiders," who seem to reproduce with a kind of "mathematical inevitability" and squander precious American resources.

But Tobar's fiction can tell us something about contemporary notions of mobility that may not be self-evident or merely reflected by literature. Tobar's most biting criticism of neoliberalism's culture of fear happens not only through typical villains, but through a deep engagement with how fear works. Araceli, as well as numerous characters, is thoroughly affected by fear and its sibling affects of anxiety, irritation, worry, and precarity. Tobar often cues up the affective characteristics of fear at the level of theme but deconstructs its pervasive power at the level of form. The emplotment of fear's transtemporality in the narrative diegesis—through paralepis, analepsis, prolepsis, and metelepsis—heightens the reader's awareness to the media's role in perpetuating fear within the "illegal" immigration debate in America. Thus, employing fear as both a thematic trait and a formal structuring device, Tobar uses fiction to show how economic forces and the media perpetuate notions of "illegality"; yet at the same time, he renders the individual voice and personal story of mobility to expose the fiction that is "illegality." In this way, *The Barbarian Nurseries* is a work of meta-fiction that publishes, unravels, and exposes the fictions that ontogenetic fear naturalizes. The novel demands readers involvement in fear's deconstruction; it demands that we challenge fear with attention to the voice of the migrant worker. It is through this narratological lens that Tobar's critique of "illegality" and "deportability" works against, but on the same terms as, its object: fear.

Notes

1. The COVID-19 crisis obviously has complicated the exceptionalism of the Great Depression as a time of "unparalleled economic uncertainty."
2. A version of this essay was written in the spring of 2016 for a course on "Latin American Literary Theory" taught by Juan Poblete at UC Santa Cruz. Many thanks to him for his comments and support. The essay was also partially inspired by a "listo.gov" billboard just outside my apartment in Daly City, CA: it featured a winged, older Latino man holding his arm across his body in fear, looking up at the sky. Next to him were the words: "¿Terrorismo? La ayuda no te va a caer del cielo." (Terrorism? Help will not fall from the sky). Though imagined in the pre-Trump era, the readings and claims of this essay have only been made more relevant by the Trump administration, whose xenophobic rhetoric and racist policies, according to the Pew Research Center, have caused devastating increases in border apprehensions, ICE arrests, deportations, human rights violations, and social stress (Gramlich 1).
3. Joanna Dreby's ethnographic work suggests that the condition of "deportability" and public promulgation of the term "illegal" contributes to the snowball effect of fear's ontogenesis, causing even some immigrant children to equate *any immigration at all* with illegality (Dreby 22).
4. See Hardt at 21:00 mins. Sianne Ngai's notion of "stuplimity," which she uses to describe "boredom…intertwined with the contemporary experience of aesthetic awe," is also a useful concept to understand the blasé response of the observers (Ngai 8).
5. Freud makes the interesting, albeit pre-Massumian, distinction between fear and anxiety: "'Anxiety' describes a particular state of expecting the danger or preparing for it, even though it may be an unknown one. 'Fear' requires a definite object of which to be afraid" (Freud 11).
6. In this example, the novel offers empathetic connection as a possible outcome of the (perceived) shared precarity between Adalian and Araceli. However, as Juan Poblete rightly points out, this is obviously not the outcome often produced by what he calls the shared "post-social" condition of whites and Latin American domestic workers (Poblete 114).
7. Naomi Klein describes the essential role that fear plays in neoliberalism's success in the late 20th and early 21st centuries. An economics of "shock" or "crises" accompanies massive increases in interest rates, deregulation, and market volatility in the name of what Milton Friedman called a "necessary medicine" to economic restructuring (196). The most comprehensive analysis of crises to date is "Europe/Crises: New Keywords of 'the Crises' in and of 'Europe'," where De Genova and Martina Tazzioli describe crises as a "fixture" of modern "social and political life."

Works cited

De Genova, Nicholas P. "Migrant 'Illegality' and Deportability in Everyday Life." *Annual Review of Anthropology*, vol. 31, Annual Reviews, 2002, p. 419.

De Genova, Nicholas P. "Europe/Crisis: New Keywords of 'the Crisis' in and of 'Europe.'" *Near Futures Online*, no. 1, Mar. 2016. *nearfuturesonline.org*, http://nearfuturesonline.org/europecrisis-new-keywords-of-crisis-in-and-of-europe/.

Dreby, Joanna. *Everyday Illegal: When Policies Undermine Immigrant Families.* University of California Press, 2015.

Freud, Sigmund. *Beyond the Pleasure Principle*, translated by James Strachey. Norton, 1961.
Gramlich, John, and Pew Research Center. "How Border Apprehensions, ICE Arrests and Deportations Have Changed under Trump," *FactTank: News in the Numbers*, 2 Mar. 2020. www.pewresearch.org, https://www.pewresearch.org/fact-tank/2020/03/02/how-border-apprehensions-ice-arrests-and-deportations-have-changed-under-trump/.
Hardt, Michael. *What to Do in a Crisis?*, 2012. *YouTube*, https://www.youtube.com/watch?v=66_W9h5dqy4.
Klein, Naomi. *The Shock Doctrine: The Rise of Disaster Capitalism*. 1st edition. Metropolitan Books/Henry Holt, 2007.
Massumi, Brian. "Fear (The Spectrum Said)." *Positions*, vol. 13, no. 1, 2005, pp. 31–48. Duke University Press, Feb.
Ngai, Sianne. *Ugly Feelings*. 1st edition. Harvard University Press, 2007.
Poblete, Juan. "Americanismo y migrancia: *The Barbarian Nurseries* de Héctor Tobar." *Dimensiones del latinoamericanismo*, edited by Mabel Moraña. Iberoamericana Vervuert, 2018, pp. 113–126.
Roosevelt, Franklin D. "Inaugural Address, March 4, 1933." *The Public Papers and Addresses of Franklin D. Roosevelt: With a Special Introduction and Explanatory Notes by President Roosevelt*, edited by Samuel I. Rosenman, vol. 2. Random House, 1938.
Saint-Amour, Paul K. *Tense Future: Modernism, Total War, Encyclopedic Form*. Oxford University Press, 2015.
Sassen, Saskia. "Incompleteness and the Possibility of Making: Towards Denationalized Citizenship." *Cultural Dynamics*, vol. 21, no. 3, Nov. 2009, pp. 227–254.
Tobar, Héctor. *The Barbarian Nurseries*. 1st edition. Farrar, Straus and Giroux, 2011.

Part V
Human rights: Afro-Brazilians and Afro-Latinas/os

12 Brazilian *quilombos*
Castaínho and its struggle for human rights

Wellington Marinho de Lira

Quilombos: resistance and a new model of society

In the context of colonial Brazil, *quilombos* were political, social, and military structures formed by Black men and women who had escaped slavery that, according to Moura, emerged in the Portuguese colony throughout the regions dedicated to sugarcane production depending on slave labor (*Quilombos* 69). The large number of these well-organized communities grew to the extent that, as Moura observes, they were perceived as a serious threat to the status quo by landlords and slave owners (69).

According to Kabengele Munanga, the word *Quilombo/Kilombo* is of Bantu origin and was used by the people from the southern African continent, especially in the current territories of Angola and Zaire, to designate a very specific type of sociopolitical and military settlement (60). The term *quilombo* seems to have appeared in the region to nominate a kind of society of warriors, which had its origins during the internal disputes in the continent (60). Munanga further explains that *quilombos* were extensive sociocultural structures that could bring together a large number of unrelated peoples from different ethnic groups, joined together by discipline and military might powerful enough to defeat more powerful kingdoms (60). *Quilombos* were further referred to as associations of men open to members from different ethnicities, fundamentally functioning as cross-cultural organizations that acknowledged contributions from diverse cultures (60).

For the purpose of this essay, it is necessary to be mindful that precisely because of these intrinsic features of the *quilombo*, it is not surprising that its social structure and cultural importance crossed the Atlantic and reached the Americas in the hearts and minds of enslaved African peoples. Separated from their families and their respective ethnic groups before entering the slave ships, it is not difficult to understand that once in the Americas, multi-ethnic enslaved people fought for their freedom by returning to the experience and the structural makeup they had known in their homelands. This fact also explains why societies, such as *quilombos*, existed wherever there was slavery: in Brazil, Colombia, the Antilles (Cuba, Jamaica, Haiti, etc.), and even in the United States.

In what follows, this chapter first provides some historical background on *quilombos* from Brazil to then focus on *Quilombo dos Palmares*, the most famous colonial quilombo in the southern part of the State of Pernambuco. By first concentrating on *Palmares* (based on a field project coordinated by the author of this chapter at the Federal Rural University of Pernambuco), the next area of focus examines the community of Castaínho that for a long time was a hidden and an isolated remnant of *Palmares*. This helps reveal their ongoing struggle for human rights, their claim for justice, and the ownership of their ancestral lands. Under the supervision of the author, in 2010 the project initially involved first-year exchange students from Sheridan College in Canada, subsequently continued by local students at our university, UFRPE.

In Brazil, the first *quilombos* appeared in Pernambuco and Bahia around the year 1550. From the beginning, these communities were always organized as a challenge and a result of the colonial system. Even if common sense may dictate that *quilombos* were sporadic manifestations of marginal slaves without social conscience, the truth is, as Moura claims, it was a movement deeply engrained at the core of the national system (*Quilombos* 31). *Quilombos*, however, were not uniform structures. The inner working of these communities depended on the characteristics of their specific contexts, but in general terms, the fugitives were organized to attack travelers, towns, and villages looking for supplies, weapons, and ammunition, often invading farms and setting slaves free, especially liberating women in order to bring a balance in the predominantly male population in the *quilombos*. The oftentimes varied production inside the *quilombos* offered opportunities to trade with nearby populations. In exchange for weapons, gunpowder, and salt, they offered agricultural products, such as chicken, fish, and even clothes and tools for agriculture. This type of trade, in some ways, was encouraged by the structure and characteristics of the colonial economy based on monoculture (sugarcane, for example) and the means of production (tools and raw materials, in particular) that were concentrated in the hands of farm owners and operators of mines, etc. This issue forced neighboring populations to rely on the *quilombos* to obtain the goods they needed.

In social terms, their population built a network of support and interests involving slaves and free Blacks, Indigenous peoples, poor and persecuted whites (for religious, social, or economic reasons), thus not only trading with them but also maintaining emotional and even family ties. In many cases, the settlers rented lands for planting crops within the *quilombo* areas to avoid control and Portuguese taxes. In the same manner, they worked and had small jobs (such as free men and women) in the villages and surrounding areas in order to strengthen the *quilombo* economy. All over Brazil *quilombos* also fulfilled the role of expansion and occupation of the territory to the extent that, according to Edison Carneiro, the Black settlements also helped to conquer forests beyond the areas already conquered by whites, as well as a way to find new sources of natural wealth (25).

Aware of the permanent threat that the *quilombos* represented, the Overseas Council of the Portuguese Crown considered them a strategic danger to the colonial project. It was known that these communities permanently stimulated the escape of slaves, and served as a base and shelter for expeditions that attacked farms, mills, and towns and, worst of all, pointed to the permanent possibility of setting up Black troops able to dominate militarily, with the support of rebellious slaves, other cities in their surroundings.

Quilombo dos Palmares

Among the many *quilombos* of colonial Brazil, the most famous was the *Quilombo dos Palmares* that resisted for more than a 100 years and covered an area ranging from the São Francisco river in Alagoas up north to the town of Cabo de Santo Agostinho in Pernambuco. At the height of *Quilombo dos Palmares*, between 1624 and 1654, its mere existence was perceived as a threat similar to the Dutch invasion in the north and northeast parts of the country; also, a risk to the maintenance of the unity of the territory and the preservation of slavery itself. It is true that the political and economic disruption and the administrative chaos that resulted from the imperial disputes between the Portuguese and the Dutch contributed to the growth of *Palmares* during this period. However, records also show that, although very much aware of the danger that emanated from the powerful structure, even as they were at war with each other, both the Portuguese and the Dutch continued to attack the communities of the *Quilombo dos Palmares*.

In 1695 after the assassination of its main leader, Zumbi *dos Palmares*, the whole community was dispersed. It is necessary to understand that *Palmares* was not just a mere "haven for fugitives" or a "village" because it resembled more a republic formed by a confederation of *mocambos* (or population centers) who had different roles in the *quilombo* structure. The mocambo called *Macaco*, for example, was the capital of *Palmares* and its political and administrative center. The *Mocambo Subupira* served as a military training camp. Besides them, and beyond them, there were other *mocambos* like Tabocas, Oranga, Zumbi, Amaro, Odenga, Aqualtume, Andalquituxe, and Dambragança.

Despite the scarcity of documents and the fact that such documents always reflect the vision of colonizers, we know that, together, the *mocambos* occupied more than 300 km in parallel from Cabo de Santo Agostinho to the São Francisco River, including Serra da Barriga, in the current town called União dos Palmares, state of Alagoas, which was at that time a part of the State of Pernambuco. Estimates suggest that the number of inhabitants ranged from 20,000 and 30,000 people, which made *Palmares* one of the largest population concentrations in Brazil during the colonial times. Through the mappings made by the Portuguese in the numerous attempts of invasion, it is known that the Mocambo Macaco, the main village, had about 1500 houses, and in Subupira, the second largest village, this number was about 800 houses.

The origin of *Palmares* dates back to the late 1500s (the first documented reference is from 1597), and we must emphasize that Black women strengthened the roots and structures of *Palmares*. According to tradition, it is believed that one of its first leaders was Acotirene (or Arotirene), and in the mid-1600s, the *Quilombo* was commanded by Aqualtune, daughter of the King of Congo, who led a force of 10,000 men against Portugal and slave traffickers (the so-called Battle of Mbwila in 1665). The princess was later captured during the battle and brought to Brazil as a "reproductive slave" (rape transformed into economic project) in the region of Porto Calvo, Alagoas, where she led an escape and founded a *mocambo* that had her name. According to oral tradition, Aqualtune would be the mother of Ganga Zumba and Ganga Zona, military chiefs of *Palmares*, and also the mother of Sabina, which was Zumbi's mother.

The importance of *Quilombo dos Palmares*, however, lies not only in its duration and extent, but, above all, the fact that, as Moura explains, it was the greatest attempt at self-government of Blacks out of Africa (*Rebeliões* 110). The location of *Palmares* was strategic. It was far from the coast (where most settlers lived) in a fertile region and at the same time protected by the rainforest nearby (which provided all necessary wood for buildings), possessing an area of rugged and mountainous topography. The *quilombo* also happened to be crossed by nine rivers, which greatly contributed to the mobility and transportation of goods inside the community.

As far as we know, the population of *quilombos* lived under a political and social system, the rigidity of which was proportional to the dangers that surrounded them and their daily life was based on the traditions of many different peoples gathered together inside its borders. Reports document that the most important decisions (such as the agreement signed by Ganga Zumba) were considered collectively by a board made up of representatives chosen in each *mocambo*, thereby convening in Macaco mocambo in order to discuss issues and approve or not such decisions. Not surprisingly, the prosperity and the organizational capacity of this massive *quilombo* was a serious threat to the colonial slave system, provoking a number of governments to control the region by routinely organizing expeditions that aimed to achieve the definitive destruction of *Palmares*. However, their inhabitants effectively resisted their attacks and for over 8 years, these communities managed to defeat around 30 military expeditions organized by the Portuguese and local farmers.

Because of the strength and resistance of the *Palmares* population, and exhausted with the continuous defeats, the governor of Pernambuco, Aires Sousa e Castro, and Ganga Zumba, an important *Palmares* leader, signed the so-called 1678 Agreement or Recife Agreement. By means of this treaty, the Pernambuco government recognized the freedom of all Blacks born in *Palmares* and gave them the permission to use the land located north of Alagoas. Ironically, the agreement took away the autonomy from the *quilombo* communities since now they came under law and religion of Portugal. Some members of the *Quilombo* did not accept the agreement and terms established by Ganga Zumba, which ended up being poisoned by his opponents inside the *quilombo*. After that, *Palmares'* control passed to the new leader named Zumbi who did not consent to negotiations with the colony authorities, preferring instead to sustain the conflictive situation. Unwittingly, by choosing this option, the *Palmares* communities started to pave the way that would culminate in their destruction.

In early Colonial Brazil, *Bandeirantes*, literally "flag-carriers," were explorers, adventurers, slavers, and fortune hunters. They led expeditions carrying the Portuguese flag, the *bandeira*, claiming, by planting the flag, new lands for the Crown of Portugal. In 1694, under the leadership of *Bandeirante* Domingos Jorge Velho from São Paulo, official forces began executing the dismantling of *Palmares*. Initially, even provoking definitive destruction, Zumbi and some of his resistors followers fled, got organized, and continued fighting. In the following year, on November 20, 1695, Zumbi was killed and beheaded by the *Bandeirantes*, who sent his head to Recife as a major symbol of victory against the *Quilombo dos Palmares*. After this tragic event, the inhabitants of *Palmares* disbanded and fled to different areas and formed a nexus of smaller communities. Some of them became increasingly isolated and have continued to resist until the present day while in the process of managing to preserve their traditions. Those surviving communities are known nowadays as "*comunidades quilombolas*" (quilombolas communities) and are spread all over Brazil. One of those surviving communities is the "Comunidade Quilombola de Castainho" in Pernambuco.

The situation of Afro-Brazilians after *Palmares*

From the mid-19th century, England contested slavery in Brazil. Keen to expand its consumer market in Brazil and the world, the English Parliament passed Law Bill Aberdeen (1845), which prohibited the slave trade, giving the power to the English navy to approach and imprison ships of countries that continued with this practice. In 1850, Brazil gave in to British pressure and approved the Eusébio de Queiroz Law that ended the slave trade. On September 28, 1871, the Ventre Livre Law that freed the children of slaves born after that date was approved. Furthermore, in 1885, the Law of Sexagenarian that guaranteed freedom to slaves who were 60 years old or older was enacted. Only in the late 19th century was slavery prohibited worldwide. In Brazil, its abolition occurred on May 13, 1888 with the enactment of Lei Áurea, signed by Princess Isabel.

If the law gave legal freedom to the slaves, the reality of the daily free life was nonetheless cruel to many of them. Without housing and facing dire economic conditions in the absence of government assistance, many Blacks went through tremendous suffering after having gained their freedom. Many could not find jobs. Prejudice and racial discrimination made their lives unnecessarily difficult. The vast majority went to live in terrible housing conditions to survive on informal and temporary jobs, especially those who stayed in big cities. After the fall of *Palmares*, some Afro-Brazilians were captured as slaves, while others fled and took shelter in remote mountainous regions far away from sugar mills and plantations. As already explained, these communities remained hidden and isolated for many years preserving their culture and traditions. After the emancipation of slaves in 1888, people from these quilombola communities felt encouraged to contact small towns around them. It is necessary to understand that despite the prevalent poverty, for those who lived in such communities, the difficulties were not at the same level of those living in the slums of big cities. Yet, as time passed, problems related to the right of the land gradually started to emerge as groups of African descendants got together in communities all over Brazil and tried to strengthen their culture and claim for their rights. Unsurprisingly, many of these communities are located in the Brazilian northeast for the simple reason that this was the very region where in the past plantation owners brought large numbers of Africans to work in their sugarcane plantations.

The context of the state of Pernambuco

Since colonial times, Pernambuco has experienced a history of resistance to slavery as manifested under different models of organization, formation, and strategy, thus revealing the range of solutions found by its population. By occupying places that were not accessible at all, near villages, farms, or mills, some groups grew and managed to establish their own communities. These enclaves had their own rules, their own religion, different approaches to the economy, alliances, networks of protection, and sociability. Those differences would define the ethnic and political difference of these groups. Among these groups, it is worth mentioning *Palmares*, Onze Negras, Conceição da Crioulas, Catucá, and Castaínho that are internationally known for their struggle for human rights. These communities constitute what we call "quilombola communities" or legally known as *quilombos* reminiscent communities. Quilombolas also represent a powerful symbol of a pioneering spirit and collective resistance in their fight for autonomy and land rights. Following the example of these communities, based on the Federal Constitution and the Decree 4.887/2003, some other African-Brazilian communities have been inspired to demand the guarantee to have access and use of their own lands claiming their identity as a *quilombo*. Nowadays, according to the Palmares foundation, there are about 1228 quilombola communities all over Brazil. Among them 83 of these communities are located in the State of Pernambuco.

It is not an easy task to establish an accurate number of the communities that are trying to obtain the official recognition as quilombolas. The official acknowledgment could guarantee them the constitutional right of property over their lands in their struggles for human rights. One of the reasons for this impasse is the difficulty connected to the ethnogenesis of the process itself; some other challenges are related to conceptual and practical issues since the current state of affairs reveals that ethnic and territorial recognition under the notion *"quilombo"* is not an easy one. Unfortunately, the term *quilombo* is far from being well defined. It is indeed an open concept that can vary in form and depends much on the numbers of new communities that apply for having their identities recognized as a *quilombo*. According to the commission of quilombola communities of the State of Pernambuco, there are about 120 quilombola communities inside Pernambuco. Politically, this confirms the importance of these quilombola communities in the history and formation within Pernambuco. Most of these communities are located in the countryside in the region called Sertão where around 80 communities are established, which accounts for more than double of the communities registered in the state. The history of these communities is, in many cases, connected to the history of the municipality they are located in. In many cases, they can also influence the history of the local regions where they once shared the same historical processes of land occupation with the colonizers, such as religious missionaries, farmers, colonial government, Indigenous peoples, and African slaves.

Aside from their own particularities, these quilombola communities have many things in common that pertain to the violation of their human and land rights. It is relatively easy to recognize the struggle for their own land as a unifying factor of the ethnic identity of quilombola communities in Pernambuco. Indeed, movements seeking social transformation affirm a collective ethnic identity that is directly connected to the struggle for the lands in order to establish a more effective dialog with the state and the federal government. Regarding *quilombo* communities, the ownership of the territory has led to discussions that aim to standardize the conceptualization of the term *quilombo* by putting some legal pressure on administrative departments in the government to be aware of the demands of the Black communities (Schmitt) historically excluded from social, political, and cultural participatory processes because of racism. This action, however, has not been an effective mechanism for guaranteeing land ownership for these communities.

Nowadays there are 21 quilombola communities in the process of legalizing their lands in the State of Pernambuco. This represents 3.8% of the national total. From these 21 communities, 43% are in the region of Sertão. The invasions and expropriations of the quilombola territories, however, remain. The communities also have to come to terms with *"grileiros"* (land grabbers and dealers) while INCRA (National Institute for Colonization and Land Reform), their official representative, does not defend their rights the way it should. We also need to be aware that Pernambuco is a state with a high concentration of land reform settlements, and, especially in the regions of the countryside, the CHESF (electricity company) has enforced resettlements as a means to make available territory for the construction of the Itaparica and Sobradinho Dams in the São Francisco River.

In this land dispute, the quilombolas see part, if not all, of their territory being transformed into settlements and resettlements. If territorial loss in this complex context can be baffling, the recovery of these lands seems to be an unattainable right. For instance, there are numerous and varied cases where the land has been declared unproductive by INCRA and proposed for agrarian reform. We can of course also mention cases in which the population has not resisted the new territorial organization and given in to the other settlers, but there are also some cases in which the quilombola territory has been divided by settlements resulting in the separation of families. In the meantime, it is clear that the practices by INCRA, rather than safeguarding the territoriality for the ethnic groups it is supposed to protect, they tend to permit and regularize misappropriations that deeply affect the communities. This situation becomes more alarming when we think about the current situation of the Sertão of São Francisco River, which is facing the implementation of the São Francisco River Transposition project and the imminence of the construction of two hydroelectric plants, namely, Pedra Branca and Riacho. The region encompasses several quilombola communities—of which only one is legally acknowledged—that may be displaced by the project, remaining without their rights over their territory and losing fundamental elements that define their ethnicity. We know of the losses, for instance, of the communities of the Sertão of Itaparica that had their lands flooded by the construction of the dam. In order to survive the process, these communities have been forced to reorganize socially and politically, thus creating new productive practices and reworking their religiosity and history.

Another recurrent situation of territorial loss is caused by the failure of public agencies to deal with communities located in an area of geopolitical division. In the Sertão do Pajeú—but not only in this area—there are emblematic cases of communities that were fragmented by this division, which responds to a logic that overlaps the social and territorial organization of quilombola communities, undersizing the territory and compromising the territoriality of the groups. Finally, it is worth emphasizing that the very procedure for the regularization of the territory is unknown to many communities, becoming another obstacle to the attainment of their rights. In this sense, the relationship with other ethnic populations has been a factor in strengthening the struggle for lands, either by political support or by embracing such a little known and often feared strategy. The same can be said about the construction of a quilombola identity, which is something very sturdy in the Castaínho community. Among quilombola communities in Pernambuco, Castaínho is known for preserving its culture and traditions as well as being aware of its rights.

Castaínho and the Struggle for Human Rights

As already explained, Castaínho is a remnant *quilombo* community of *Quilombo dos Palmares* located in the countryside of Pernambuco in the southeast of the city of Garanhuns. Though formally recognized, its members still strive to achieve the recognition of a basic right for land and housing. About 200 families live in this community. In some homes, however, it is common to find more than one family. In general, they are sons and daughters of that family who get married and continue to live with their parents.

The Castaínho site is located in a rugged region of small hills, set on three levels. On the first level is located the Catholic chapel, some houses, the flourmill, and a shop, as well as the community school. This level is called "Chã," which means plateau. On the second level, there are also some residences, a flourmill, and a shop. This level is called slope. The third level is where the Cajueiro stream is located. In this area, there are some houses, a flourmill and a locale for pottery (a site for the production of objects using clay or clay as raw material). This site is called floodplains.

Castaínho has a council that deliberates political and economic issues for themselves and for the other surrounding quilombola communities. The council of the community has a representative, José Carlos Lopes da Silva. Most of the community income comes from farming. They produce beans, corn, and a large amount of cassava and manioc—used to make flour in a processing house installed in the community. Besides, there are various fruit trees in the locality, such as mango and cashew trees. Part of the production in agriculture is sold in public fairs and markets. In terms of religion, Christianity is predominant and a few still practice religions of African origin, known in Brazil, as African-Brazilian religions. The community exhibits a most significant historical and cultural expression, namely, a dance called *Samba de Coco* that is played annually in May during the Feast of the Black Mother.

Research on the Internet discloses a dearth of information about the community Castaínho. The scarcity of information consequently allows for people from outside the community to be little aware about its existence. This minimal knowledge contributes to an imprecise understanding of the "Feast of the Black Mother," including depictions of the community that characterize it as "people descendant of slaves." The scant information disseminated about the community has contributed to the perpetuation of clichés that only reveal a limited perception about the people from Castaínho as "black people, belonging to a remnant community *quilombo*, who live in the rural area, fighting for their rights, which are remembered at the Day of Black Consciousness, and are mentioned in textbooks as the people trafficked in ships coming from Africa" (Lopes da Silva).

Working in the town of Garanhuns since 2009, the author of this chapter heard about this quilombola community and their struggle to legalize their land. The first contact with Castaínho took place in 2010 when nine exchange students of Social Work from Sheridan College in Canada arrived at the local institution UFRPE (Federal Rural University of Pernambuco). Two of these students worked with media and showed interest in developing some field work in a local community. As we had very limited information written in Portuguese and almost none in English about Castaínho, we decided that two of these students would spend their field work helping the community create a homepage in English so that they could show the world who they are. Two months later when the students left, the community had its own homepage in English, but then another problem emerged: they did not know how to update the homepage because they had no fluency in English. As a means to compensate for the linguistic deficiency, we organized an extension project by offering intensive English and Portuguese courses for the community in the following years (2011/2015), conducted exclusively by students of the university (UFRPE).

Besides the linguistic work, we have made contacts with local leaders and interviewed them to obtain information about their background and history of the community. According to the local leader José Carlos Lopes da Silva, Castaínho was founded right after the end of "*Quilombo dos Palmares*," and since then the history of the community has been defined by the ongoing fight to legalize the possession of their land, as Lopes da Silva explains. When we asked him what the land means to him, emphazising the link between territory and identity, his answer was, "Everything. This is the land where I was born, where my ancestors were born and died, so it is like a part of me, and this is a general feeling inside the community. We think that together we are stronger to fight for what belongs to us."[1] His answer brings to mind Bauman's terms when he writes, "community produces a good feeling because that word brings the feeling of togetherness. It is a warm place, a comfortable and cozy place" (221). Yet, Lopes da Silva's words and interactions with other members of the community also confirm that such characteristics of quilombola strategies, the centrality of Internet support, and social association are crucial elements of their collective resistance.

According to Lopes da Silva, in 1995 they again embarked on a struggle for the legalization of their territory. He concedes that back then they were somehow successful, thanks to the support of the Federation of Agricultural Workers of the State of Pernambuco, the Commission called "*Pastoral da Terra*," the Unified Black Movement (MNU), and the Luiz Freire Cultural Center. On July 14, 2000, the Palmares Cultural Foundation indeed gave the Castaínho community the title of ownership of their land, amounting to 187 hectares. The agency of the federal government responsible for giving the title of land ownership to *quilombos*, however, was the Palmares Cultural Foundation and not the INCRA as it is today. More importantly, the property title had been granted to Castaínho without adopting necessary measures to resettle people that had also been occupying the area. In other words, the communities received the title of ownership without the resolution of disputes involving their land. This oversight affected not only the Castaínho community but also eight other quilombola communities during the administration of Brazilian President Fernando Henrique Cardoso. Currently, under the presidency of the far-right-wing President Jair Bolsonaro, the struggle for land property has become even more precarious as his government actively terminates social movements and human rights organizations.

Since the imperfect official recognition of the rights held by quilombola Castaínho to own the land was dispensed, it is true that INCRA has reopened new processes to attempt to complete the settlement of the area, while conducting some actions necessary to legalize the ownership of quilombas territory, such as registration of families from the *quilombo* and other families that share the same area. However, the initiatives have generated litigations sparked by individuals who process valid property titles and similarly assert their rights to the land in Castaínho. In 2002, for instance, three individuals (two of them related to real estate companies) claimed to be part owners of those lands and filed lawsuits in the federal court against the Palmares Cultural Foundation, which initially issued the ownership title to the community and demanded compensation for the loss of their land.

Nowadays the process of regularization of the lands in Castaínho has the support of the National Geospatial Infrastructure Project (PIGN), a partnership between the Federal University of Pernambuco (UFPE) and the University of New Brunswick, Canada. The Department of Cartographic Engineering (UFPE) has conducted the identification and demarcation of the territory. No provision has been given, however, for the date of completion of the regularization process of the territory in Castaínho. Nevertheless, Lopes da Silva asserts that it is imperative to continue the struggle for the land where he and his ancestors have lived. This can be achieved, as he explains, "only with the community working together towards our main objective that is the well-being of the whole community."[2]

Looking at the example of Castaínho and its struggles for land rights, it is worth alluding to Néstor García Canclini in *Hybrid Cultures* (1995) when he mentions that at the same time that deterritorialization processes take place, "... there are strong reterritorialization movements represented by social movements that reinforce the local...in order to engender local differences and the feelings of belonging to a place" (García Canclini 128). With regard to the concept of belonging to a place, Castaínho's quest for survival is embodied in its spirit of struggle, justice, and the love of its inhabitants for the land of their ancestors and their own land. As Frantz Fanon (1963) once claimed in *The Wretched of the Earth* (1963), "For a colonized people the most essential value, and the most concrete, is first and foremost the land: the land which will bring them bread and, above all, dignity" (67).

Notes

1. This comes from a personal interview in May 2010.
2. See a personal interview conducted in May 2010.

Works cited

Bauman, Zygmunt. *Liquid Love: On the Frailty of Human Bonds.* Polity, 2003.
Carneiro, Edison. "Singularidades dos *Quilombos.*" *Os Quilombos na Dinâmica Social do Brasil*, edited by Clóvis Moura, Maceió/AL, EDUFAL, 2001, pp. 11–18.
Fanon, Frantz. *The Wretched of the Earth.* Grove Press, 1963.
García Canclini, Néstor. *Hybrid Cultures.* University of Minnesota Press, 1995.
Lopes da Silva, José Carlos. Personal Interview in May 2010.
Moura, Clóvis Steiger. *Rebeliões da Senzala: insurreições, quilombos e guerrilhas.* 4th edition. Edições, Mercado Aberto, 1988.
Moura, Clóvis. *Quilombos: resistência ao escravismo.* 3rd edition. Ática, 1993.
Munanga, Kabengele. "Origem e histórico do *quilombo* na África." *Revista USP*, São Paulo, vol. 28, Dezembro 1995-Fevereiro 1996, pp. 56–63.
Schmitt, Alessandra, et al. "A atualização do conceito de *quilombo*: identidade e território nas definições teóricas." *Ambiente & Sociedade*, vol. 10, issue 1, 2002, pp. 1–8. https://www.scielo.br/scielo.php?pid=S1414-753X2002000100008&script=sci_abstract&tlng=pt.

13 *Capá Prieto* and the decolonial Afro-Latin(a/o) American imagination

Luz Angélica Kirschner

The semiautobiographical collection of short stories *Capá Prieto* (2009) by the Afro-Puerto Rican Yvonne Denis Rosario complicates broad ideas about an African diasporic consciousness in the Americas often posited under the assumption that people of African descent have been mainly located in the United States, the Caribbean former colonies of England, and, to a lesser extent, of France.[1] By writing in Puerto Rico, a nation that historically has subdued the sociocultural contribution of people of African descent to the creation of the nation, Denis Rosario's accounts insert the Spanish-speaking Caribbean to enlarge the wide range of struggles for human rights and self-affirmation of peoples of African descent in the American continent, both in historical and contemporary terms. Her inclusion of the Spanish Black Atlantic similarly problematizes reductive approaches to the African diaspora that have precluded a better understanding of the multiple manifestations of Blackness and racialization in the Western hemisphere in general, and the Spanish-speaking Caribbean and Latin America in particular, variegated regions that, despite new developments, traditionally have received less attention in the study of the African diaspora. After all, during the conquest and colonization of the Americas, these were the very regions where people were first heavily shipped at a historical juncture in which a "massive number of people began to lose their equality, their humanness and their rights" (Mignolo 45). We also need to know that despite the proclamation of democratic *mestizaje* (the modern ideology of harmonious racial intermixing) in Spanish-speaking Caribbean and Latin America contexts, manifestations of racism are "not any less profound or real than in other social context of the Americas" (Sánchez González, "Arturo Alfonso Schombug" 143).[2] Despite an unequivocal predilection of racial and cultural Western European "whiteness," the obstinate belief in harmonious *mestiza/o* national identities, indeed, disqualifies expressions of race consciousness and demands for basic human rights as atavistic or unpatriotic acts that threaten the unity of the colorblind nation (Helg 261; Adams, Jr. 3). Though slowly changing, traditionally sociopolitical histories of the regions have privileged class as well as macroeconomic studies over specific analyses of race with the result that scholars have repeatedly missed to make this variable a determining factor in the development of national self-understandings and, most important, contributed to obfuscate the racial determinants so clearly at work in these contexts.[3] From a sociohistorical perspective, I study Denis Rosario's narratives "El silenciamiento" (Silencing), "Periódicos de ayer" (Newspapers of Yesteryear), "Desaucio desde el palmar" (Eviction), and "Ama de leche" (Wet Nurse) to propose that the stories do more than make visible heterogeneous histories of people in the Spanish Black Atlantic. Writing at the intersection of U.S. Latina/o and Latin American narratives of national identity and culture, to different extents, the stories engage Eurocentric national identity discourses in Latin America and the United States whose hegemonic approaches to history, memory, race, ethnicity, and gender perpetuate the marginalization of Black Puerto Ricans on the island and the mainland. By performing a critique of colonial/patriarchal practices that continue to organize contemporary regimes of power in the Americas, this study shows how the narratives simultaneously engage in two projects. On the one hand, the accounts question the ongoing colonial relationship between the United States and Puerto Rico. On the other, the stories frame a common diasporic ground for people of African descent in the Americas to promote the creation of new narratives, while contributing toward the discourses of reparation and human rights in terms of the outrages and long-term damages caused by the trans-Atlantic trade of enslaved Africans and their descendants. In this sense, the study shows how her stories ultimately disclose a decolonizing project in which historical recovery, recuperation, dissemination, and self-pride are crucial to end the ethno-racial segregation of Afro-Puerto Ricans on the island and the U.S. diaspora where white supremacist *mestiza/o* history and the colonial divide between Anglos and Latinos have dominated.

Countering silence and expanding the historical imagination

Capá Prieto, 2009, (*Capá Prieto Stories*, 2010) by Denis Rosario consists of 12 short stories that characterize distinguished Black and mixed race Puerto Rican women and men such as Pura Belpré, Rafael Cordero and his sister Celestina Cordero, Ángela María Dávila, Arturo Alfonso Schomburg, Adolfina Villanueva Osorio, and others whose lives remain largely unknown and/or their sociocultural influence on Puerto Rico unacknowledged. The narratives characterize Puerto Rico as a "'translocal nation' whose boundaries shift between the archipelago of Puerto Rico and its U.S. diaspora" (Duany 187) by displaying their daily struggles in neighborhoods and diverse rural and urban settings located on the island and New York. Testifying to the significant contributions of African descendants to the history of Puerto Rico's and U.S.'s cultural intellectual traditions, the narratives likewise illustrate the characters' commitment to diverse fields such as the military, education, politics, bibliotecology, poetry, and history. Set in the historical moment between the 18th and 20th centuries while interweaving history and fiction, the accounts contribute to right Puerto Rico's nationalist historical record, which under the spell of the *mestizaje* myth highlights a primary Spanish-Indigenous heritage in the figure of the *jíbaro*, the whitened mountain dweller, as the bearer of a nascent Puerto Rican identity and culture. Although in many regions *jíbaros* "vary in phenotype from brown to black" (Whitten, Jr. and Torres 14), the *mestizaje* discourse fails to capture how people of African descent have engaged in cultural practices and transformed Puerto Rican culture, the nation, and its people.[4] To this day, the ongoing institutional commitment "to the notion of a single Puerto Rican culture (with blended racial heritages)" (Godreau 9) significantly limits the spaces to engage expressions of Puerto Rican Blackness and legitimize the African component of Puerto Rican culture.

Capá Prieto opens with the story entitled "El silenciamiento" (Silencing), a subject of Black invisibility that is deeply "inscribed both in the scholarship on the region and in the discourse of black intellectuals and activists" (Andrews, *Afro-Latin America, Black Lives* 2). By revealing the central role that Blacks played in the 1797 British attack of Puerto Rico in the Loíza area, the narrative problematizes the generalized neglect of the contributions of Blacks in the history of the island as agents and actors. The title brings to mind Michel-Rolph Trouillot's oeuvre on history and power, *Silencing the Past: Power and the Production of History*, complicating Puerto Rican national discourse that underscores "the white, Hispanic experience as the main thread that provides coherence to the history of the Puerto Rican people" (Rodríguez-Silva 3). By naturalizing the position of white Creole men as indispensable sociopolitical movers and shakers (3–4), the practice has resulted in the marginalization of "the struggles and aspirations of those deemed or self-identified as black" (4) thus minimizing their participation in the making of the island. In "The Silence of the Black Militia: Socio-Historical Analysis of the British Attack to Puerto Rico of 1797," historian Milagros Denis-Rosario questions the perplexing process of history production on the island that diminishes the relevance of a crisis, in which Puerto Ricans were victorious over British invaders while foregrounding the U.S. American invasion of the island in 1898. Pointing at a historical moment regularly highlighted in the annals of Puerto Rican historiography by way of symposiums, activities, and publications, Denis-Rosario challenges the acumen of the official version of the history of the nation considering that the commemoration of the U.S. aggression actually celebrates the "people's failure on defending their homeland" (70).

In analyzing the British attack on the island through Trouillot's theoretical lens, Milagros Denis-Rosario identifies the marginalization of the event (the result of territorial rivalries between the Spanish and the British empires) in Puerto Rican historiography as a consequence of "the impact of the Haitian Revolution" (50). With the Revolution (1791–1804) underway, she proposes, the validation of the role of Blacks during the British attack could have lighted "the spirit of the colored population" and added "fuel to the fire" (69) of feared Black power and antislavery movements not only in Puerto Rico but also all over the Americas.[5] Archival research reveals that the Spanish Crown largely attributed the victory to high-rank officers, while on the island Governor Don Juan Ramón de Castro, his officials, and the clergy asserted that the "people" made the victory possible (64). Black Puerto Ricans and the non-white men battalions who participated in the resistance, however, were not recognized as integral "to the people" (64) who actively fought the English in Boca de Cangrejos, in the Loíza area. Their performance went mostly unacknowledged or deemed irrelevant despite historical documents confirm the centrality of the Black Militia's resistance in the successful defense of the island.[6] Similar to the silencing of Sans Souci's role in the defeat of Napoleon's troops on Saint Dominique, Denis-Rosario writes, the Black Militia "were silenced by their superiors back then, by society and historians" (65).

In order to prevent the repetition of what Trouillot has called the "onesidedness" (22) of history, "El silenciamiento" revisits a historical event not easily accepted by uncomfortable authorities, institutions, and scholars fearful of slave rebellions thus condemning it to silence. Through a narrative flashback, the story breaks the pattern of concealment by changing the narrator of the historical event. The story focuses on Francisco Lanzos, the Captain and Archivist of the Black Militia, instead of the prejudiced Governor De Castro, who eventually lowers the military ranks of the Black Militia. De Castro devalues their triumph by referring to its members as "esta clase de gente" ("Periódicos de ayer" 70; this kind of people), a derogatory expression (Denis-Rosario 66) used to signify the inferiority and lack of talent of a group of persons. The story follows Lanzos as the free-Black leader whose narrative affirms African religious traditions as central to community life of Black Puerto Ricans in particular and integral to the island in general. His account concurrently evokes not only the brutality of slavery, the inhuman living conditions, the ongoing uprisings against masters and oppressors, the merciless retaliation of owners and colonizers, the depth of violence that spawned the history of Blackness in the Caribbean but also the central role of his men in the defense of the island (15–17). And yet, in 1797, Black and non-white Puerto Ricans were not newcomers or, as it were, diasporic "lost souls" from a distant and fetishized African homeland protecting an alien land. By this time, their culture and Puerto Rico's were rooted in the enslaved and free people of African descent who inhabited the island shortly after the arrival of the Spanish to the Caribbean.[7] In fact, Black Puerto Ricans had defended the island of Vieques from the attacks of the British Army in 1718 (Denis-Rosario 67). During the successful resistance in the Loíza region, non-white Puerto Ricans, who in the eyes of the ruling elites at the time represented a "dangerously" (Chinea, "Fissures" 174) growing populace on the island, were instead outraged "nativos" ("El silenciamiento" 18; natives) fighting "invasores" (18; invaders). Although Black Puerto Ricans honored their African religious traditions, in "El silenciamiento" they do not participate in the Western project of a required "celebration of origins" that objectifies "Africa" (Palmié 60) nor diminish the experiences of the Black experience by failing to recognize particular and creative transformation of cultures on both sides of the Atlantic (Sue and Goash-Boza). Problematizing any reductive ideas about the African diaspora, Lanzos' men bravely defended their Puerto Rican homeland, whose geography (unlike the assaulting British) they intimately knew (18). This occurs in an episode that historians recognize as an example of "the evolution of the national sentiment that was already rooting among Puerto Ricans" (M. Denis-Rosario 67). Besides, Lanzos' account also reveals the contradictions and tensions that plagued the Spanish colonialist enterprise. The colonizers had to recruit free Black men like Lanzos, who could potentially become problematic for the Spanish authorities because of the possibility of Puerto Ricans rebelling to obtain their freedom, that is, unleashing the insurrection of self-liberation by enslaved peoples against masters and oppressors in need of a slave labor force.[8] By taking advantage of the ambiguities of the colonial system, Captain Lanzos explains that the military was one of the few options available to free Blacks in order to improve their socioeconomic position (17) in a pyramidal society based on class and color "which stipulated that both Spaniards and Creoles would derive all privileges from the system" (M. Denis-Rosario 53).[9]

It is important to remember that as early as 1514, rebellious Blacks had launched "the beginning of the maroon in Puerto Rico" (Whitten, Jr. and Torres 16). On the island, other areas of the Caribbean and mainland South and Central America, Norman E. Whitten, Jr. and Arlene Torres write, sovereign maroons capable of maintaining their territoriality were often models for slaves to emulate as they embodied the desires of most enslaved people (16). These earliest acts of resistance in the initial period of the Spanish conquest of the Americas, however, most notably disclose that, despite brutal subordination, "self-liberation," called "*cimarronaje* (run-awayism) in Spanish, *marronage* (same meaning) in French, has been a core feature in the development of African diaspora awareness in the Americas" (Whitten, Jr. and Torres 21). It is thus crucial to recognize, as West and Martin propose, that the antislavery and anti-colonial Haitian Revolution "did not emerge in a historical void" (82), but rather, has to be understood in relation to the longstanding antislavery revolt tradition of the Western hemisphere. In theorizing about Haiti's symbolic value to Black internationalism as "a primary reason" (73) for the hostility and isolation that the Haitian Revolution faced, West and Martin contend that this "had a prehistory of black resistance" (82). The event in fact "represented a culmination of decades of armed struggle by enslaved Africans in the Atlantic world" (72–73) in their quest for freedom and equality even if colonial authorities and white settlers colluded that the conflict "did not represent a commendable model for the future" (Fischer 361). Not only did the majority of the colony's whites remain incredulous of the "humanity" of the partisan mulattos of the French Revolution in Saint Dominique (West and Martin 74), but also they put national interest first as pragmatic French revolutionaries, concluding that "enslaved Africans" were not covered by the Rights of Man and Citizen (74). Such events reflect the masculinist, colonial, and racist philosophical foundations of the Western discourse of human rights. This produced the imperial category of the modern, enlightened, European white "Man" who had the privilege to monologically speak for the human and rights while presupposing "the non-subjectivity, reification, objectification or abjection" (Barreto, "Introduction" 27) of the colonized and the slave but also of women. "Humanity," Mignolo reminds us, "has been created upon philosophical and anthropological categories of Western thought and based on epistemic and ontological colonial differences" (17).

Furthermore, through the experience of Professor Francisco Santaella in the General Archive of the Indies in Sevilla, "El silenciamiento" examines the role that archives have played in the silencing of the history of African and African-descent people from the Spanish Black Atlantic. Not by coincidence, the secretary of the reputed archive informs Santanella, "aquí el espacio es limitado" (19; here space is limited) as a means to rationalize the careless handling of recently arrived old documents from Puerto Rico. The narrative thereby reveals, as Michel-Rolph Trouillot has observed, that the presence and absence that permeate archives "are neither neutral nor natural" but rather "created" (48). Since sources "imply choices" (48), Trouillot claims, they also contribute to determine the boundaries of the event, thus creating silences in historical records (49). The scarcity of documents recording the history of Black Puerto Ricans, in particular and Afro-Latin(a/o) Americans in general, can partly be explained by the thoughtless treatment of sources that often lead not only to the eradication of documents—but also to their banalization in the archives. As the narrative alludes to the ongoing colonial status of the island since 1898 (19), it also unveils the underprivileged treatment of recently arrived documents, such as the 210-year-old manuscript hidden in the walls of the Castillo San Felipe del Morro by Captain and Archivist Francisco Lanzos in 1797 that records Puerto Rico's Spanish colonial history ("El silenciamiento" 15; 21). The account suggests that the colonial histories of non-white Africans and their descendants in Puerto Rico and the Americas remain overlooked in canonical "*Eurocreole*" scholarship (Chinea, "In the Royal Service of Spain" 316; original emphasis). At the same time, the narrative endorses the idea offered by the historian Jorge L. Chinea who proposes that this underrated history likewise "may be found buried in the mass of documents housed in governmental, business, and private repositories" (315) and not exclusively in mainstream archives.[10]

The narrative closes with the silencing of the distinguished history professor from the University of Seville. Santaella, who considers the recovery of Lanzos' manuscript from oblivion his ethical responsibility (22), is arrested in Puerto Rico as he is about to board a plane to the United States after returning the manuscript to a group of Black men among which "Lanzos" belongs (23). Charged by the Spanish authorities with stealing materials from the archive that houses historical documents on the Spanish empire in the Americas and the Philippines, "Las Autoridades Españolas" (23; The Spanish Authorities) ask Santaella to return the documents. The circumstances surrounding his silencing show how such institutions not only assemble but also organize facts and sources, thereby conditioning "the possibility of existence of historical statements" (Trouillot 52). Santaella as a professional is not seen as an independent historian, thus highlighting how the act of collecting is not just the passive act of accumulation of information. Echoing Trouillot once again, "El silenciamiento" reveals the extent to which archives set the rules and "help to select the stories that matter" (Trouillot 52). The incident indeed exposes how power operates in the making and recording of history, that is, how archival supremacy contributes to determine what is historically significant/desirable/appropriate or regulates "the difference between a historian, amateur or professional, ... a charlatan" (52) or a criminal, as in the case of Professor Santaella. His silencing by Spanish authorities suggests the degree to which the production of mainstream European and Spanish history mutes references to events in the colonies (read: colonialism and modern racial slavery) as well as their centrality in the making of capitalist European modernity.[11] The banishment of the Spanish professor for breaking away from the Eurocentric provincialism with his indicting actions illustrates, borrowing Trouillot's terms, how historiography of countries from the so-called Third World continues to be shaped by neocolonial Western practices and conventions in the second decade of the 21st century.[12]

From this perspective, it is not surprising that in the story "Periódicos de ayer" (Newspapers of Yesteryear), *Capá Prieto* honors the lifework of the distinguished, diasporic Afro-Puerto Rican historian, autodidact, archivist, Freemason, and social reformer Arthur A. (Arturo Alfonso) Schomburg (1874–1938). His widely disseminated essay—originally written for people of African descent in the United States, "The Negro Digs Up His Past" (1925)—urges peoples of African ancestry to preserve a sense of their history and consciousness of race (read: racial essentialism, stigmatization, stereotyping, folklorization) by recognizing that official historical accounts have silenced evidence of Black achievement. Apparently told by a dismissive history teacher that Black people had no history, the transnational and transcultural Schomburg spent his life assembling a counter-archive of a global scope by recovering the history of Black peoples to prevent the repetition of unsophisticated misstatements about their humanity, history, and cultures. With the stories of land dispossession and displacement of Afro-Puerto Ricans as a backdrop, "Periódicos de ayer" is narrated from the perspective of the Freemason Uncle Luis who meets Schomburg at the Masonic Logia. Uncle Luis initially assists his masonic brother by storing numerous articles, books, journals, artifacts, manuscripts, and photographs that Schomburg sent from Europe, Latin America, and others places in his effort to recover and preserve the African heritage (65). The practice continues until 1937 when Uncle Luis receives a letter from Schomburg that requests the return of all assembled items and informs him about the $10,000 (66)[13] that the Andrew Carnegie Corporation paid for Schomburg's monumental collection on behalf of the New York Public Library. As history has shown, the transaction gave birth to the Schomburg Center for Research in Black Culture in New York City, the largest public repository of cultural and intellectual artifacts of the African diaspora worldwide.

More importantly, thanks to Uncle Luis the narrative valorizes the life-work of the antiquarian and curator Schomburg. In other words, the uncle's willingness to transmit Schomburg's inspiring tradition of "racial vindication" (Meehan 63) through research, collecting, and networking to his niece ("Periódicos de ayer" 67), a trained historian and professor, can be read as a vindication of Schomburg's legacy at a historical juncture when, as Sánchez González writes, the eminent intellectual "has not yet been moved from margin to center" in Puerto Rican studies on the island (141). Notwithstanding his achievements and affiliations, Schomburg similarly remains "an important though neglected figure in twentieth-century African American and Caribbean cultural history" (Meehan 55).[14] The historian's diasporic race consciousness, which is viewed as not *"really"* a Puerto Rican "aberration" (Sánchez González 143; original emphasis) by sectors of fellow Puerto Ricans who fail to engage race critically, Sánchez González advances, is partly responsible for his marginalization.[15] The scholar continues:

> Within francophone and anglophone Caribbean studies, this complex revision has been duly evaluated as a core episteme for twentieth-century cultural intellectual history. But we have yet to see similar comparative and more comprehensive scholarship concerning the hispanophone Caribbean; until we do, it would be premature to cast judgement on race consciousness among Puerto Rican, Dominican, and Cuban populations collectively. Within the next generation of scholars, racial subjectivity in the reevaluation of social history may very well be the most compelling concern. (144)

By honoring Schomburg's race mindfulness and pride, *Capá Prieto* not only contributes to the revitalization of a marginalized Puerto Rican cultural intellectual tradition that has prioritized "the study of racial subjectivity" (Sánchez González 144) but also to which some Puerto Rican and Latina/o scholars, on the island and the mainland, have belonged. The celebration of a transnational intellectual such as Schomburg, who has been marginalized in Caribbean studies and sidelined by restrictive identity politics, racism, and class prejudice in the African American intellectual tradition of the United States (despite his commitment and intellectual contributions to this community), can similarly be interpreted as an invitation to begin the necessary conversation between Afro-Latinidad and hegemonic narratives of Latinidad, Puerto Ricanness, the Black Atlantic, Africanity,

African Americanness, Blackness, Hispanicity, Caribbeanness, and Latin Americanness. This would enable more progressive and plural perspectives of the history of the peoples who inhabit the Western hemisphere.[16] Finally, the recognition of the diasporic intellectual Schomburg can also be taken as a critique to the nationalist intellectual tradition in Puerto Rico. As Isar P. Godreau contends, the elitist discourse tends to view "the formation of the Puerto Rican nation-state as the cure to all problems" (7) and to largely ignore "the Puerto Rican diaspora" (7), which outnumbers the community on the island, and their contributions to the nation's culture and politics.[17] As we return to Puerto Rico and turn to the analysis of "Desahucio desde el palmar" (Eviction), *Capá Prieto* joins Puerto Rican intellectuals that have expressed their disapproval of an insular discourse that has excluded "'others' from the nation's 'imagined' boundaries" (7).[18] These scholars have also addressed its failure to address tenacious "class, racial, and gender hierarchies" (7) that can be aggravated by "nationalism as a political strategy" while ignoring "to consider the impact of U.S. colonialism on Puerto Rico" (7).

Puerto Rican Blackness and the folklorization of culture

With "Desahucio desde el palmar," *Capá Prieto* returns to the Loíza region that points to Puerto Rican ongoing predicaments of race, culture, gender, and place as it deconstructs the patriarchal discourse of "racial democracy," which ultimately manipulates histories of mixture to promote a whitened national identity by tying "'blackness' to particular places" (Godreau 5). The story that narrates the brutal killing of Adolfina Villanueva Osorio on February 6, 1980 can be read as an act of remembrance that credits the life of a resisting Black woman who was murdered with impunity by the police while she was trying to avoid the eviction of her family, her husband Agustín Carrasquillo, and her six children. The narrative goes beyond challenging the police attempts to portray her as a dangerous woman and a criminal who deserved to be murdered. It also depicts the protracted struggle of Adolfina and her family against wealthy landowners, the Catholic church, the State, and the police to avoid their removal from the land that had been in the family's possession for more than 60 years ("Desahucio desde el palmar" 95). The short story is also a case in point that counters patriarchal traditions reflected in Puerto Rican textbooks of Spanish for public schools, as Marie Ramos Rosado discloses, that reproduce restricted representations of women in general and Black and mixed race women in particular—the latter exponentially characterized negatively in national literary texts (14–15). Yet, the publication of the account in *Capá Prieto* almost 30 years after its occurrence can also be understood as a reminder of the unending silencing and victimization of Afro-Puerto Rican communities, such as Loíza, as well as their historical struggles for recognition. Taking "Desahucio desde el palmar" as a point of departure, I propose that their current discrimination results from the same colonial politics of the State, even as racialized discourses have changed over time, and the utilization of state-sanctioned violence that ended the life of Adolfina Villanueva Osorio and crushed the lives of her husband and her surviving children.

As Rivera Lassén et al. affirm, at a macro-social level institutional racism in Puerto Rico "tends to render invisible the contributions of *negritude* and stigmatize its representations, occlude the denunciation of white supremacy, highlight *hispanidad*, promote the myth of diversity, and legitimate cultural degradation by folklorizing Afro-Caribbean roots" (Rivera Lassén 58). Unlike other Latin American nations that in the past three decades have introduced constitutional changes and developed policies that have transformed the political landscapes within which the political activism of Afro-descendant peoples operate, Puerto Rico has not experienced the resurgence of "Afro-descendant militancy or the resulting antiracist or multicultural affirmative-action policies" (Godreau 9) as established in some Latin American countries. While in those Latin American contexts the ideology of "racial harmony" or *mestizaje* that implies the adherence to a single, though hybrid, national culture has evolved into proclamations of "multiculturalism" that explicitly acknowledge "cultural, ethnic, and racial diversity" (Rahier 1), Puerto Rico remains committed to "the notion of a single Puerto Rican culture" (Godreau 9). Yet, much in line with neoliberal multicultural discourses in Latin American settings where the ideological use of culture, ethnicity, and racial diversity contributes to perpetuate the exploitation of and racism against people of African descent, Puerto Rico has also instrumentalized cultural difference (read: Black Heritage) "as a tool for development and marketing (specially in tourism)" (9). Along these lines, similar to other Latin American countries, notably Colombia (Cárdenas 118), Puerto Ricans too tend to identify coastal regions of the island with Blackness and African traditions. We need to know that Loíza, also called "La Capital de la Tradición" (The Capital of Tradition), has been well known for its large Black population and the preponderance of African traditions, or in Rivera-Rideau's terms, as a site of "folkloric blackness" ("From Carolina" 616). This benevolent kind of Blackness is opposed to stereotypical "urban blackness" of crime, hypersexuality and delinquency located in places associated with urban crime (618). Homogenous folkloric Blackness is deemed traditional, cheerful, spiritual, frugal, friendly and often "gendered as female and old" (Godreau 17–18) and is nostalgically celebrated as the quintessential "construction of blackness" (Rivera Rideau, "From Carolina" 618) of the nation. Unlike urban Blackness that is disruptive of Puerto Rican egalitarian identity, folkloric Blackness safely circumscribed to the coasts affirms Puerto Rican national identity "as defined by racial democracy discourses" (618) and as representative of the African influence in Puerto Rico.

Interestingly, Rivera-Rideau likewise elucidates, how scholarly discourses have supported the perception of Loíza as "the primary signifier of Puerto Rico's African heritage" ("From Carolina" 621). Particularly the investigation of the archeologist Ricardo Alegría from 1948 until 1951 has been responsible for turning Loíza into a weirdly ahistorical "isolated place" (620) exclusively inhabited by Afro-descendants who have "maintained a 'traditional' way of life" unlike other "modern" areas of the island (620). In his position of director of the Instituto de Cultura Puertorriqueña and as a devotee to the notion of "racial democracy" that erases processes of racialization, Alegría greatly assisted in the creation of what today is accepted as "Puerto Rican national culture" (620). The elitist national initiative that sought to establish the parameters of autochthonous Puerto Ricanness aimed to counter "the United States's rationale regarding the occupation" that promulgated notions of Puerto Ricans incapability of "self-government" and their lack of "a definite cultural identity" (Hernández Hiraldo 68) hence confirming how the United States has shaped local discourses of Puerto Rican cultural identity. To this day, the intersection of Loíza and folkloristic Blackness, as Rivera-Rideau observes, solidifies the perception of the town as "the 'natural' place of Otherness within Puerto Rico" (621) irrespective of historical records that contradict its alleged isolation from the rest of the island. Loíza's ostensible historical isolation and the confinement of Blackness within concise geographical boundaries "implies that blackness has limited influence in the development of Puerto Rican culture, thus perpetuating the privileging of whiteness as a norm" ("From Carolina" 621) of the nation, as Rivera-Rideau explains. Moreover, denying racial integration or social assimilation of Afro-Puerto Rican heritage, Godreau illuminates, circumscribed Blackness "conveys the sense that blackness is different or exceptional from the context of the larger 'mixed' nation [while] the broader national context remains unmarked, implicitly represented as mixed and 'non-black'" (5).

Under these circumstances, it may not be surprising that the experience of *loiceños* (inhabitants of Loíza) as residents of, or rather, *Black commodities* in 'The Capital of Tradition' and the (self-) promotion of the area's folkloristic Blackness have not necessarily enhanced the community's prosperity. The hope that the neoliberal development of tourism in the region would rise life standards of *loiceños* and secure their economic survival has remained largely unfulfilled (Hernández Hiraldo 75–76; 78). Studies rather reveal that, for instance, some people in Loíza resent the association of the town, which is also called "Loíza Aldea" (Loíza village), with "a primitive lifestyle" (73). Some have argued that in the name of Puerto Rican national culture, *loiceños* have been subjected to further victimization (read: the perpetuation of poverty) and encountered "kind of governmental discrimination" (75) since "it is easier for them to receive money for cultural purposes than for basic services such as a medical building" (75).[19]

Residents of the Loíza area have articulated how the construction of tourist facilities and exclusive housing projects have been "prioritized over housing for the poor and the locals" (75). The destruction of ecosystems and residential areas for the sake of "development" have aggravated water supply (75), while strict security measures adopted by the state police aim to control increased crime rates (76) incidentally portraying how dehumanizing notions of Blackness (read: folkloric and urban Blackness) are not antithetical, as some may think, but rather coexist in the Puerto Rican context.

In the meantime, it is true that the development of some touristic projects has been successfully challenged particularly by the Asociación de Residentes de Piñones (Residents Association of Piñones) ("Tribunal Supremo"). However, in the context of neoliberal multicultural discourses, the exotization and folklorization of the area with the support of anthropologists continues (*Fundación Nacional*). Poverty and violence afflict socioeconomic struggles of *loiceños,* as according to the census statistics of 2010, "Forty-five percent of the community is estimated to live below the poverty line [and] [f]ifty-five percent of children under 18 years of age live in poverty" (Pitts 1). It is also true that for years, police brutality and excessive or lethal force has affected the life of Puerto Ricans in general. But according to *Island of Impunity: Puerto Rico's Outlaw Police Force,* like in the case of Adolfina Villanueva Osorio, impunity, harassment, intimidation, and "unjustified police violence" continue to affect more severely low-income and Black communities such as Loíza, a municipality "with nearly 65 percent of residents identifying as Black" (51). More recently, Hurricane Maria has caused severe damage in Puerto Rico further deteriorating the existing dire situation caused by over a century of colonial mismanagement as well as recent debt and austerity measures that disrupt job creation, salaries, quality of education, maintenance of basic infrastructure, human and food security, etc.

"Even before Hurricane Maria struck, Puerto Rico's human rights were already being massively undermined by the economic and financial crisis and austerity policies" (Bohoslavsky qtd. in Barron, "U.S. Emergency Response"). After the deadly storm hit the island, like the rest of the country, the municipality of Loíza faced problems with housing, flooding, water supplies, sanitation, food supply, electricity, and medical services. "Puerto Rico is in crisis," writes Agustín Laó-Montes, "[m]ade unimaginably worse by hurricane Maria" ("Afro-Boricua Agency" 12). The hurricane has not only devastated the island. Reminiscent of New Orleans after the devastation caused by Hurricane Katrina in 2005, the slow response of the federal government of one of the richest nations in the history of the world has also underscored the dehumanizing "racial character" of the island's colonial condition (12). Currently, Puerto Ricans, who regardless of skin color are racialized as non-white U.S. citizens, face a profound and complex humanitarian crisis (12) propelled by the general indifference to the value of human life and racism.[20] Unsurprisingly, Afro-Puerto Ricans who have suffered historical structural marginalization and racial discrimination on the island are "overrepresented among those who have suffered the most from the crisis, before and after the storms" (12). As Puerto Ricans on the island struggle to come to terms with the devastation, organize, and move forward the solidarity of the Puerto Rican diaspora has delivered momentous assistance (Martínez). More recently, in reference to the long history of the Puerto Rican colonial experiment, concerned activists and scholars point to the "exodus" (Klein 58) of desperate Puerto Ricans to propose that the current emptying out of the nation "provides a rationale to justify and render neoliberal colonial-capitalist policies as 'natural'" (Negrón-Muntaner par. 34): "If the land is said to be empty, imagining and carrying out its occupation, repurposing, or even abandoning [it] is easier" (Negrón-Muntaner par. 34).

Decolonizing colonial power legacies: a continuing project

Writing about Afro in/exclusion and the new visibility of Afro-descendants in Latin American settings, Walsh reflects on the extent "to which political and legal advances and attention to social inclusion transform the colonial models of power that organize and authorize the state and determine and regulate the politics and policies of rights" (28). Taking Ecuador as a demonstrative example, Walsh ponders the vocabulary that President Rafael Correa frequently adopted when engaging the progressive Ecuadorian state in its endeavor to eradicate poverty and modernize the nation. The scholar draws attention to Correa's frequent use of the elusive term "new beginning" (28) which "can be perceived as a necessity to erase the past" (Ocles qtd. in Walsh 28). However, speaking from the perspective of marginalized peoples the Afro-Ecuadorian leader Alexandra Ocles asserts, "it is necessary to go back and look at this past when we consider new ways of doing politics in relation to historically discriminated groups and if we want to generate mechanisms of reparation" (qtd. in Walsh 28). Another Afro-Ecuadorian leading figure, Juan García, further unravels the composite position of Afro-descendants in the Ecuadorian context:

> I don't believe that this government, the Ecuadorian State, or any other government for that matter, wants or knows how to confront the historic debt it has with the Afro-Ecuadorian community. I say that it does not know how because it does not know history or the perspective of the Afro-community. It knows a national history where we Afros form a very small part, if at all, but supposedly we have done nothing, we have given nothing. And because they have not measured the debt as a contribution to a people that against its will had to give much work to this state and national construction, *it is assumed that there is no debt, or need for reparation.* (qtd. in Walsh 28–29; added emphasis)

In line with Ocles's and García's perspectives, *Capá Prieto* embodies Afro-Puerto Rican history, consequently pivoting the work against the erasure of memory on the part of people of African descent in the Spanish-speaking Caribbean and Latin America. The stories deconstruct the discourse of "racial democracy" that has sought to encapsulate *negritud*, commodify it, and render it invisible while undoing it in the nation's pursuit of whiteness and *hispanidad*. By promoting Black self-affirmation, Denis Rosario's decolonizing project of historically grounded research, recovery, dissemination, and self-pride seeks to end the ethno-racial segregation of Afro-Puerto Ricans on the island and the diaspora that white supremacist *mestiza/o* history and "the civilizational/racial divide between *Anglos* and *Latinos*" (Laó-Montes "Afro-Boricua Agency" 12; emphasis in original) have colluded to enact at sociocultural and political levels. More importantly, her work reverses the dispossession of Black and non-white Puerto Ricans of the cultivation of their history and cultural past that, similar to other Latin American nations, have shaped the Puerto Rican sociocultural landscape. With this context as a backdrop, "Ama de leche" (Wet Nurse) displays the awareness of the crucial link between historical memory and the creation of new narratives that become part of the public imagination as a means to confront colonial structural legacies, achieve recognition of historical injustice, and address the necessity of reparation in the struggle for basic human rights.

Pointing at "una deuda que nunca se pagó" (40; a debt that was never paid), through the portrayal of the life of the slave Maíta (Josefa Osorio Villarán), who was the wet nurse of the four children of wealthy Mr. José Dolores Gorrión and his sickly wife, Mrs. Gorrión, the narrative does more than document the achievements of Afro-Puerto Ricans. The story serves as a metaphor not only to demonstrate the central role of Afro-Puerto Rican Black women and their children in the economic and sociocultural fabric of Puerto Rico but also to reveal the expendable nature of their labor since they are viewed as mere commodities. At a more general level, Maíta reminds us of the experiences of enslaved people of African descent and the generalized lack of knowledge about and acknowledgement of the significant roles they played in the creation of the modern world ushered by the first trans-Atlantic voyage of Christopher Columbus. "Discussions of the origins of the modern economies of the Atlantic world," Walker states, "have simply neglected to mention that it was Africans and their descendants who paid with their lives the high price of this development by providing the involuntary and unremunerated labor, both skilled and unskilled, that made it possible" (4).

In this sense, "Ama de leche" circuitously indicates the tangled relationship between slavery in the Americas and the acceleration of the modern capitalist world. In reference to Schomburg, Adalaine Holton proposes that "the economy of the West was largely built on the labor of Afrodiasporic peoples under the institutions of slavery and colonialism" (235). Rather than viewing the slave trade as a peripheral event, Howard Dodson couches it as

> central to the development of Europe and the Americas. ... [I]t was through the slave trade and its related economic activities that Europe; Africa; North, Central, and South America; and the Caribbean were knit into a system of mutual interdependency, with Europe and the United States as the dominant, controlling influences that they are today. (121)

In order to advocate for the compensation of a historical debt that remains unpaid scholars interested in decolonializing knowledge need to be aware of the 500-year-old legacy "of epistemic and ontological racism constructed by imperial discourses" (Mignolo 23) that has dehumanized colonized peoples in the Americas and other parts of the world. The current humanitarian crisis that Puerto Ricans, as non-white U.S. citizens, and Afro-Puerto Ricans go through painfully reminds us of a colonial inheritance that continues to pervade world history. Such developments have influenced the treatment that peoples/communities receive in the Western hemisphere and many parts of the modern world. From this perspective, the racialization at work in the current socioeconomic Puerto Rican crisis, borrowing Roosbelinda Cárdenas' words from another context, is not "an unexplainable calamity" but rather "a historical continuity" (131). In the wake of the declaration of the Durban conference in 2001 that "condemned slavery as a crime against humanity" (Rauhut 137), a decolonial, rehumanizing project certainly has the responsibility

> to set the record straight about the nature of African experience in the Western hemisphere, and to rewrite in a fundamental way the history of the Americas to include the impact of the African presence, an African economic, political, and socio-cultural activity, on the shaping of the Americas and the modern world. (Dodson 120)

Yet, a project of justice through reparations, as suggested in "Ama de leche," similarly seeks to reconceptualize the "Western human" and deter the ranking of humanity to justify relations of domination and exploitation as we strive to reach the point where "there is no need for someone specific to talk about the human, because human is what we are talking about" (Mignolo 23).

Notes

1. Capá prieto is the name of a tree native of the Antilles, Central America, and regions of northern Latin America. It was also the name of the abolitionist and pro-independence secret society involved in the Lares Revolt of 1868. See also Jossianna Arroyo 69–70.
2. By no means has the ideology of mestizaje been experienced uniformly; every single nation developed its own version of the peculiar ideology that became the "symbol of [the region's] racial harmony" (Wade 263).

3. For the ideological entanglements of Puerto Rican racism, see Ileana M. Rodríguez-Silva, *Silencing Race: Disentangling Blackness, Colonialism, and National Identities in Puerto Rico*.
4. See also Arlene Torres, "La gran familia puertorriqueña 'Ej prieta de beldá'."
5. In *Slave Revolts in Puerto Rico*, Guillermo A. Baralt for instance reports how after the slave insurgence in Partido de Aguadilla on October 15, 1795, governor De Castro linked the occurrence with the struggle in Saint Dominique and stipulated a number of measures that sought "to counter the propaganda of the supreme French libertarians" (7).
6. For more history of "Milicianos Morenos" and their historical banishment from mainstream narratives of the 'New World' see also Jorge L. Chinea, "In the Royal Service of Spain."
7. See also Torres and Whitten for the arrival of freed and free Black men with the Spanish conquerors 44–46.
8. For the delicate balance that Spain had to strike between exploitation; the defense of imperial interests from European rivals; the recruitment of Caribbean free colored, enslaved Africans, runaways, misplaced Europeans, etc. in Puerto Rico see, Jorge L. Chinea, Race and Labor in the Hispanic Caribbean.
9. Milagros Denis-Rosario similarly expounds that (a) the absence of white men, (b) the belief that Blacks were more resistant to tropical illnesses, (c) the fact that many of those slaves were already trained for combat in Africa, and (d) the need to rely on military units in case of an emergency, were some of the most common reasons that encouraged the recruitment of both free colored men and slaves in the colonial system (55).
10. The groundbreaking research in the volume *Afro-Latino Voices: Narratives from the Early Modern Ibero-Atlantic World*, 1550–1812 confirms Chinea's assertion. The editors and authors of the anthology study historical sources such as testaments, letters, petitions, trial proceedings, and wills to reveal everyday existences of Africans in the Spanish Atlantic that present them as independent actors that often managed to build remarkable existences against all odds, create support communities, and prevail in the face of marginalization and oppression.
11. Only recently has Spain started to acknowledge the African elements present in cultures of Andalusia and the centrality of Spain in the enslavement of black peoples from Africa between the 14th and 19th centuries. See Ángeles Lucas, "La huella cultural de los esclavos negros en España es indeleble."
12. It is relevant to mention that in "El turbante del Maestro" (The Teacher's Turban), *Capá Prieto* similarly problematize the marginalization of Black women in Puerto Rican archives. The story reveals the ongoing historical silencing of the Black teacher and educator Celestina Cordero Molina (1787–1862), one of the sisters of the celebrated teacher Rafael Cordero (1790–1868) acknowledged as "The Father of Public Education" in Puerto Rico. Ignoring the existence of official documents that confirm Celestina as the initiator of the school where her brother taught, to this day, her presence in history books consists of brief references in her brother's biography (Alverio-Ramos).
13. Library officials actually received the $10,000 grant in March 1926 (Meehan 65).
14. According to Agustin Laó-Montes, a redefinition of Schomburg seems to have taken place among U.S. Puerto Ricans ("Decolonial Moves" 173).
15. For the persistent denial of racialized marginalization on the island, see also Rodríguez-Silva 1–17.
16. For resistance among some members of the African American intellectual community to the racially "suspicions" Schomburg see Lisa Sánchez González, *Boricua Literature* 56–66.

17. With the story "La cucaracha y el ratón en la biblioteca" (The Roach and the Mouse at the Library), *Capá Prieto* similarly celebrates the legacy of Pura Teresa Belpré (1902–1982), the first certified Afro-Puerto Rican librarian in the New York Public System. Belpré was a contemporary of Schomburg in the 135th Street Branch Library that eventually became the Schomburg Center. The title of the story brings to mind Belpré's first storybook *Perez and Martina* published in 1932.
18. Petra R. Rivera-Rideau elucidates, Neuyoricans are more strongly affected by the exclusionary discourse due to the nation's complicated politics of Blackness. Their "racial identities and perceived connections to blackness (especially U.S. African American culture) become the primary source of contention regarding their incorporation into the island" (*Remixing Reggaetón* 25).
19. In the context of this discussion, it is necessary to mention that supporters of the PNP (New Progressive Party) that advocates the statehood of Puerto Rico argued that environmentalists and critical voices of the construction of expensive hotels and housing were acting out of "racism" (75). According to their reasoning, these constituencies sought to prevent the economic progress of Loíza and its community. Incidentally the PNP intervention, Isar P. Godreau illustrates, reveals how capitalist interests and "the enduring imperial legacy of the United States shape local discourses of 'race' in the region" (13).
20. To understand the racialization of Puerto Ricans, see Laó-Montes who elucidates the three factors that converge to effect the complicated racialization of Puerto Rico and Puerto Ricans in the U.S. context (12).

Works cited

ACLU American Civil Liberties Union. *Island of Impunity: Puerto Rico's Outlaw Police Force.* June 2012, aclu.org/report/island-impunity-puerto-ricos-outlaw-police-force.

Adams, Jr., Robert Lee, editor. "Rewriting the African Diaspora in Latin American and the Caribbean: Beyond Disciplinary and National Boundaries." *Rewriting the African Diaspora in Latin American and the Caribbean: Beyond Disciplinary and National Boundaries.* Routledge, 2013, pp. 1–18.

Alverio-Ramos, Zulmarie. *Biografía de Celestina Cordero Molina.* Monografias.com. 2005, www.monografias.com/trabajos85/biografia-celestina-cordero-molina/biografia-celestina-cordero-molina.shtml#justiciapa.

Andrews, George Reid. *Afro-Latin America, Black Lives, 1600-2000.* Harvard University Press, 2016.

Baralt, Guillermo A. *Slave Revolts in Puerto Rico: Conspiracies and Uprisings, 1795-1873*, translated by Christine Ayorinde. Markus Wiener Publishers, 2007.

Barreto, José-Manuel, editor. "Introduction: Decolonial Strategies and Dialogue in the Human Rights Field." *Human Rights from A Third World Perspective: Critique, History and International Law.* Cambridge Scholars Publishing, 2013, pp. 1–42.

Barron, Laignee. "U.S. Emergency Response Efforts in Puerto Rico Aren't Good Enough, U.N. Experts Say," *TIME*, October 31, 2017, time.com/5003470/united-nations-puerto-rico-hurricane-response/.

Cárdenas, Roosbelinda. "Multicultural Politics for Afro-Colombians: An Articulation 'Without Guarantees'." *Black Social Movements in Latin America:*

From Monocultural Mestizaje to Multiculturalism, edited by Jean Muteba Rahier. Palgrave, 2012, pp. 113–133.

Chinea, Jorge L. *Race and Labor in the Hispanic Caribbean: The West Indian Immigrant Worker Experience in Puerto Rico, 1880–1850*. University Press of Florida, 2005.

Chinea, Jorge L., "In the Royal Service of Spain: The *Milicianos Morenos* Manuel and Antonio Pérez during the Napoleonic Invasion, 1808-1812." *Afro-Latino Voices: Narratives from the Early Modern Ibero-Atlantic World, 1550-1812*, edited by Kathryn Joy McKnight and Leo J. Garofalo. Hackett Publishing Company, 2009, pp. 315–325.

Denis Rosario, Yvonne. *Capá Prieto*. Editorial Isla Negra, 2009.

Denis-Rosario, Milagros. "The Silence of the Black Militia: Socio-Historical Analysis of the British Attack to Puerto Rico of 1797." *MEMORIAS Revista digital de Historia y Arqueología desde el Caribe colombiano*, vol. 8, issue 14, junio 2011, pp. 48–74.

Dodson, Howard. "The Transatlantic Slave Trade and the Making of the Modern World." *African Roots/American Cultures: Africa in the Creation of the Americas*, edited by Sheila S. Walker. Rowman & Littlefield, 2001, pp.118–122.

Duany, Jorge. "The Rough Edges of Puerto Rican Identities: Race, Gender, and Transnationalism." *Latin American Research Review*, vol. 40, issue 3, 2005, pp. 177–190.

Fischer, Sibylle. "Unthinkable History? The Haitian Revolution, Historiography, and Modernity on the Periphery." *A Companion to African-American Studies*, edited by Lewis R. Gordon and Jane Ann Gordon. Blackwell, 2006, pp. 361–376.

Fundación Nacional para la Cultura Popular. "Abren parque histórico en Loíza." 7 Feb. 2018, prpop.org/2018/02/abren-parque-historico-en-loiza/.

Helg, Aline. "Abolition and Afro-Latin Americans." *A Companion to Latin American History*, edited by Thomas E. Holloway. Blackwell, pp. 247–263.

Hernández Hiraldo, Samiri and Mariana Ortega-Brena. "'If God were Black and from Loíza': Managing Identities in a Puerto Rican Seaside Town." *Latin American Perspectives*, vol. 33, issue 1, 2006, pp. 66–82.

Holton, Adalaine. "Decolonizing History: Arthur Schomburg's Afrodiasporic Archive." *The Journal of African American History*, vol. 92, issue 2, spring 2007, pp. 218–238.

Klein, Naomi. *The Battle for Paradise: Puerto Rico Takes On the Disaster Capitalists*. Haymarket Books, 2018.

Laó-Montes, Agustin. "Afro-Boricua Agency: Against the Myth of the Whitest of the Antilles." *ReVista Harvard Review of Latin America, Afro-Latin Americans*, vol. 16, issue 2, winter 2018, pp. 12–15.

Laó-Montes, Agustin. "Decolonial Moves: Trans-Locating African Diaspora Spaces." *Globalization and the Decolonial Option*, edited by Walter Mignolo and Arturo Escobar. Routledge, 2010, pp. 163–192.

Lucas, Ángeles. "La huella cultural de los esclavos negros en España es indeleble." *El País*, 01 Oct. 2016. elpais.com/cultura/2016/09/29/actualidad/1475145150_732138.html.

Martínez, Victor. "The Diaspora Helps Rebuild Puerto Rico." Centro: Center for Puerto Rican Studies, centropr.hunter.cuny.edu/events-news/rebuild-puerto-rico/policy/diaspora-helps-rebuild-puerto-rico.

Meehan, Kevin. *People Get Ready: African American and Caribbean Cultural Exchange.* University Press of Mississippi, 2009.
Mignolo, Walter. "Who Speaks for the 'Human' in Human Rights?." *Human Rights from A Third World Perspective: Critique, History and International Law,* edited by José-Manuel Barreto. Cambridge Scholars Publishing, 2013, pp. 44–64.
Negrón-Muntaner, Frances. "The Emptying Island: Puerto Rican Expulsion in Post-Maria Time." Columbia University: Hemispheric Institute, December 19, 2019, hemisphericinstitute.org/en/emisferica-14-1-expulsion/14-1-essays/the-emptying-island-puerto-rican-expulsion-in-post-maria-time.html.
Palmié, Stephan. "On Talking Past Each Other, Productively: Anthropology and the Black Atlantic, Twenty Years On." *Transatlantic Caribbean: Dialogues of Peoples, Practices, Ideas,* edited by Ingrid Kummels et al. Transcript, 2014, pp. 57–75.
Pitts, Terrance. "The Leaders of Loíza, Afro-Puerto Ricans Struggle for Change." *Open Society Foundations,* 18 Aug. 2012, opensocietyfoundations.org/voices/leaders-lo-za-afro-puerto-ricans-struggle-change.
Rahier, Jean Muteba, editor. "Introduction: Black Social Movements in Latin America: From Monocultural Mestizaje and 'Invisibility' to Multiculturalism and State Corporatism/Co-optation." *Black Social Movements in Latin America: From Monocultural Mestizaje to Multiculturalism.* Palgrave, 2012, pp. 1–12.
Ramos Rosado, Marie. *Destellos de la negritud: investigaciones caribeñas.* Isla Negra Editores, 2011.
Rauhut, Claudia. "Caribbean Activism for Slavery Reparations: An Overview." *Practices of Resistance in the Caribbean: Narratives, Aesthetics, Politics,* edited by Wiebke Beuhausen et al. Routledge, 2018, pp. 137–150.
Rivera Lassén, Ana Irma. "Afrodescendant Women: A Race and Gender Intersectional Spiderweb." *Meridians: Feminism, Race, Transnationalism,* vol. 14, issue 2, 2016, pp. 56–70.
Rivera-Rideau, Petra R. "From Carolina to Loiza: Race, Place, and Puerto Rican Racial Democracy." *Identities: Global Studies in Culture and Power,* vol. 20, issue 5, 2012, pp. 616–632.
Rivera-Rideau, Petra R. *Remixing Reggaetón: The Cultural Politics of Race in Puerto Rico.* Duke University Press, 2015.
Rodríguez-Silva, Ileana M. *Silencing Race: Disentangling Blackness, Colonialism, and National Identities in Puerto Rico.* Palgrave, 2012.
Sánchez González, Lisa. "Arturo Alfonso Schombug: A Transamerican Intellectual." *African Roots/American Cultures: Africa in the Creation of the Americas,* edited by Sheila S. Walker. Rowman & Littlefield, 2001, pp. 139–151.
Sánchez-González, Lisa. *Boricua Literature: A Literary History of the Puerto Rican Diaspora.* New York University Press, 2001.
Sue, Christina A. and Tanya Golash-Boza. "Blackness in Mestizo America: The Cases of Mexico and Peru." *Latino(a) Research Review,* vol. 7, issue 1–2, 2008–09, pp. 30–56.
Torres, Arlene and Norman E. Whitten, Jr., editors. "Introduction to Volume Two: Eastern South America and the Caribbean." *Blackness in Latin America and the Caribbean: Eastern South America. Vol. II.* Indiana University Press, 1998, pp. 34–71.

Torres, Arlene. "La gran familia puertorriqueña 'Ej prieta de beldá' (The Great Puerto Rican Familiy is Really Really Black)." *Blackness in Latin America and the Caribbean: Eastern South America.* Vol., edited by Arlene Torres and Norman E. Whitten, Jr. Indiana University Press, 1998, pp. 285–306.

TRIBUNA - Puerto Rico. "Tribunal Supremo detiene Proyecto Costa Serena." *TRIBUNA Puerto Rico*, 12 Julio 2012, /tribunapr.com/2012/07/12/tribunal-supremo-detiene-proyecto-costa-serena.html.

Trouillot, Michel-Rolph. *Silencing the Past: Power and the Production of History.* Beacon Press, 1995.

Wade, Peter. "Race and Nation: An Anthropological View." *Race and Nation in the Modern Latin America*, edited by Anne S. Appelbaum et al. University of North Caroline Press, 2003, pp. 263–281.

Walker, Sheila S., editor. "Introduction: Are You Hip to the Jive? (Re) Writing/ Righting the Pan-American Discourse." *African Roots/American Cultures: Africa in the Creation of the Americas.* Rowman & Littlefield, 2001, pp. 1–44.

Walsh, Catherine. "Afro In/Exclusion, Resistance, and the 'Progressive State:' (De)Colonial Struggles, Questions, and Reflections." *Black Social Movements in Latin America: From Monocultural Mestizaje to Multiculturalism*, edited by Jean Muteba Rahier. Palgrave, 2012, pp.15–34.

West, Michael O. and William G. Martin, editors. "Haiti, I'm Sorry: The Haitian Revolution and the Forging of the Black International." *From Toussaint to Tupac: The Black International since the Age of Revolution.* The University of North Carolina Press, 2009, pp. 72–104.

Whitten, Jr., Norman E. and Arlene Torres, editors. "General Introduction: To Forge the Future in the Fires of the Past. An Interpretative Essay on Racism, Resistance, and Liberation." *Blackness in Latin America and the Caribbean: Social Dynamics and Cultural Transformations.* Vol I. Indiana University Press, 1998, pp. 3–33.

14 "We got Latin soul!"

Transbarrio dialogs and Afro-Latin identity formation in New York's Puerto Rican community during the age of Black Power (1966–1972)

Matti Steinitz

In his text "Before People Called Me a Spic,[1] They Called Me a N...," Pablo "Yoruba" Guzmán—a founding member of the Black Panther-inspired Puerto Rican revolutionary organization Young Lords Party—recalls his youth as a child of Afro-Puerto Rican immigrants in the 1960s:

> In New York, Puerto Ricans were growing up alongside African-Americans in the same barrios, and only the fools among us [...] could not see that we had a heck of a lot in common. And it began, of course, with rhythm and dance. [...] After the conga, the rest followed pretty quickly: 'Chitlins,' 'Cuchifritos.' 'Soul.' 'Salsa.' At least half the Puerto Rican family had to pick up on having the same nappy hair as their African–American cousins. (240)

Concluding his thoughts on the close relations between African Americans and Puerto Ricans and the significance of the Black Freedom Struggle for the emergence of the Young Lords in the late 1960s, Guzmán writes, "We did this while we danced at parties after a day of fighting the police, just to get basic rights, with the Panthers. Blasting James Brown and Tito Puente" (243).

Guzman's evocation of rhythm and dance, Soul and Salsa, as points of departure for cross-cultural dialogs between African Americans and Nuyoricans (New York-born Puerto Ricans) in the 1960s, as well as his memories of Young Lords dancing with Black Panthers to the sounds of James Brown *and* Tito Puente, the kings of Black and Latin music, respectively, speak for the outstanding role of popular music in the forging of interethnic alliances between two marginalized communities who struggled for empowerment in the streets of New York. Along these lines, there is some logic to the fact that the founding of a New York chapter of the Young Lords in 1969—an organization that embodied the aspirations of young Nuyoricans to follow the model of the Black Panther Party in organizing their community—was preceded by the emergence of a crossover genre named Latin Boogaloo in 1966. Latin Boogaloo gained huge popularity among New York's Puerto Rican and Black youth while causing the outrage of *música latina* purists and traditionalists who rejected the fusion of Hispano-Caribbean styles as Mambo, Cha-Cha, and Son Montuno with African American Rhythm and Blues (R'n'B) and Soul influences as a form of contamination.

Crossing borders: hemispheric dialogs in the Black Americas

The significance of Latin Boogaloo goes well beyond that of a short-lived New York City dance craze: its emergence epitomizes the rise of Black-Latino alliances and the strong interethnic appeal of African American culture and politics in the era of Civil Rights and Black Power. It also marks the first manifestation of Latin Soul as a new transcultural and transnational genre that would become an important platform for dialogs between African Americans and Afro-Latinos in hemispheric sites of transculturation as distant as New York, Colón (Panamá), or Rio de Janeiro. This study focuses on New York's African American and Puerto Rican communities and the manner they bridged racialized boundaries. In addition, this study specifically addresses how these border-crossings materialized in the intertwined creation of new sounds and radical political movements in the Black Power era. By translating messages, esthetic representations, and symbols of African American defiance into Latin contexts, Latin Soul, and the related Puerto Rican engagement with African American culture in New York played a significant role in the construction of Afro-Latino identity discourses and the creation of radical interethnic alliances that had strong repercussions throughout the Americas. Parting from the assumption that African American Soul music was a decisive factor for Black Power's transnational appeal, we examine how appropriations of the genre in Latin American contexts contributed to the trans-local dissemination of Black Power-inspired discourses and symbols and the emergence of Afro-Latino social movements in the 1970s.

These issues often collided with dominant nationalist ideologies of *mestizaje* and *democracia racial* that neglected the existence of racial prejudice and tabooed the affirmation of Blackness. As an effective message carrier and key medium for the creation of networks of solidarity and connectedness between Afro-diasporic groups, Soul music played a significant role for human rights struggles in the Western Hemisphere. It gave voice to shared experiences of exclusion and dissent while encouraging border-crossing alliances against the diverse manifestations of anti-Black racism that have shaped the Americas throughout the 20th century. By assessing the impact of the African American freedom struggle on Afro-Latino communities, this study aims to shed light on a chapter of U.S.-Latin American relations that has remained somewhat under-explored until now.

One obvious explanation for the scarcity of academic work on the numerous and meaningful hemispheric exchanges and flows between these diverse

Afro populations is found in the conflictive and unequal relations between the United States and Latin America. For a long time, interventionist and imperial U.S. policies in Latin America have dominated discussions on inter-American relations in ways that apparently left little space for counter-hegemonic North-South dialogs. Evidently these dialogs would not fit into ideological agendas of academics and anti-imperialist activists alike, leading to what Ifeoma Nwankwo called a "dearth of critical scholarship on relations between U.S. African Americans and the rest of the Americas" (Nwankwo 188). Throughout the 20th century, anti-imperialism and anti-U.S.-Americanism had become common ground for Latin America's nationalist and populist movements, and there was a strong impulse against any cultural and political influences from the United States (Ostendorf 25). Clearly, there was also a racial dimension to the rejection of U.S. African American influences: Latin America's nationalist elites, left-wing activists, and academics alike met the Black Power-related ideas, slogans, and sounds of the 1960s and 1970s with hostility as they challenged the dominant ideologies of *mestizaje* and *democracia racial* (Stam and Shohat 51–53). Hence, the significance of the African American freedom struggle for the formation of Afro-Latino identity discourses and social movements has been downplayed or ignored.

Despite this hostile environment and official repudiation, the Black struggle in the United States had a deep impact on Afro-Latino communities (Laó-Montes 300). The 1970s and 1980s witnessed the rise of Afro-Latino cultural and political movements—a process that George Reid Andrews described as "blackening" in his landmark study *Afro-Latin America*. These were clearly inspired by the powerful influences of the U.S. Civil Rights and Black Power movements. Addressing these often silenced dialogs and furthering a truly transnational and hemispheric perspective on the Black Americas will contribute to the increased efforts to overcome methodological nationalism that defines the field of inter-American Studies.

"Say it loud": Black music and human rights struggles

Studying the history of human rights struggles in the Americas through the lens of popular music proves to be a very fruitful endeavor, as many of these struggles have found their most vivid expressions in diverse musical genres. This was especially the case in the 1960s and 1970s, when diverse musical forms accompanied and inspired the rebellions of youth movements across the hemisphere against persisting inequalities, the Vietnam War, state violence, authoritarianism, and racial discrimination. In the United States, predominantly African American genres like Jazz, R'n'B, Soul, and Funk gave voice to a new era of Black consciousness which inspired the emergence of other styles as Reggae and Hip Hop, thus becoming key manifestations of border-crossing youth cultures that have defied racial discrimination in its varied forms. Simultaneously, the emergence of Salsa resulting from hemispheric transculturation between Afro-Caribbean forms in New York reflected the construction of a new Afro-diasporic Latino identity. Black musical expressions accompanied, and often encouraged, Afro-diasporic struggles against oppression in the Americas from the days of slavery until the 21st century. While all of these genres reflected specific sociopolitical realities and consumer tastes in the local contexts of their origin, it was their mobility, their outstanding ability to transcend geographical borders, and cultural boundaries that made them conduits of transnational movements for human rights and social justice. Musical expression constituted a core medium for the articulation of new identity constructions and racial solidarity in these contexts and in many circumstances, music was "strategically employed to develop identification between people who otherwise may be culturally, ideologically, or spatially separate or distinct from one another," as Shana Redmond puts it (1f). According to Redmond, the collective consumption of music functions as a method of participation within the border-crossing liberation projects is characteristic of the African diaspora.

Knowledge of the Black movement in the United States "was transmitted into Black ghettos and communities all over the world by Afro-American music" (Union Jack 171), as Paul Gilroy points out. The adaptation of these styles often went hand-in-hand with an implicit protest against the status quo that was shaped by colonial legacies and white supremacy in most of the sites in question. The emergence of Soul music in the 1960s not only coincided with the rise of the African American freedom struggle but also with a dramatic expansion of the record industry and radio stations. These two entities, the record industry and radio stations, made the dynamic sounds of Black America available to new audiences beyond U.S. borders. Soul songs like Sam Cooke's "A Change is Gonna Come" (1964), Aretha Franklin's "Respect" (1967), The Impressions' "Keep on Pushing" (1967), James Brown's "Say It Loud, I'm Black and I'm Proud" (1968), or Nina Simone's "To Be Young, Gifted, and Black" (1969) reflected the growing sense of Black self-affirmation and assertiveness in the face of white supremacy related to the Black Power movement. The synchronism of the movement's and the genre's peak phase between 1965 and 1975 underscores the close interrelation between both: Soul musicians answered the demand for unapologetically Black sounds *and* encouraged the emergence of Black pride among African Americans. These acts of self-affirmation turned Soul music into one of the most important cultural expressions of the Black Power era which has been widely perceived as soundtrack of the movement in the United States as well as abroad (Steinitz 2019, Van DeBurg, Ward). The transnational diffusion of Soul music conditioned by its commodification and the expansion of the music industry in the 1960s and 1970s constituted a key chapter in what Brazilian investigator Livio Sansone labeled the "globalization of blackness" (1). This was an ongoing process of cultural transfers between highly mobile Afro-diasporic communities in which Black popular culture from the United States occupied a prominent position as a major focus of identification. Referring to the related emergence of Funk in Brazilian contexts, George Yúdice discerns a "transbarrio sampling from one subaltern group to another" (131), in which the translation of U.S. Black music to Latin American contexts provides a way to articulate opposition with the local racial hierarchies.

"Alliance of survival": African American—Puerto Rican interactions in New York

The emergence of Latin Soul and the Young Lords in New York is closely connected with the city's role as a key site of hemispheric transculturation and breeding ground for the emergence of interethnic alliances and diasporic exchanges between African Americans and Afro-Latinos. In his insightful essay on "overlapping diasporas," Earl Lewis describes the role of U.S. cities like New York, "where African-descended immigrants encountered American Blacks, creating in the encounter what has been called a trans–geographical America" (786). Regarding the impact of U.S. Black politics and culture in Latino contexts, New York is of special interest, as it has been the site of an intense cross-cultural dialog between African Americans and Puerto Rican migrants (many of whom are Afro-descendants). These cross-cultural dialogs manifested themselves to the fullest during the era of Civil Rights and Black Power movements. The movements and sounds that emerged from these interactions between African Americans and Puerto Ricans resulted from coexistence in the streets of the Bronx and Harlem, the undisputed capital of Black America. The Eastern section would become known as El Barrio or Spanish Harlem due to the large congregation of Puerto Ricans who settled there upon arrival on the U.S. mainland. Like no other Spanish-speaking migrant community in the United States, New York Puerto Ricans were exposed to African American language, music, customs, and culture, which makes Ramón Grosfoguel and Chloé S. Georas conclude: "Puerto Ricans were African Americanized in New York City, the new contact zone of colonial encounter" (106).

How did the interethnic "alliance of survival" (Torres 3) between African Americans and Puerto Ricans come into being despite contrasting historical and cultural backgrounds and the widespread tendency among Hispanic migrant communities to distance themselves sharply from African Americans? Despite their manifold differences, both communities shared legacies of slavery, colonialism, racism, and capitalist exploitation. Between the 1920s and the 1950s, New York became the main destination of two parallel Great Migrations: African American rural workers from the Deep South, striving for a new life without Jim Crow and extreme poverty, and immigrants from the island of Puerto Rico. The Island was a U.S. territory with colonial status since the Spanish-American war of 1898, inhabitants of which were granted U.S. citizenship through the Jones-Shafroth Act of 1917. Many migrants from Puerto Rico had followed specific recruitment measures by the U.S. Labor Department that tried to compensate the labor scarcity that was caused by a sharp decrease in European immigration after the enactment of more restrictive immigration laws. By 1970, African Americans and Puerto Ricans comprised about 30% of the city's population (Torres 65). Relegated to the bottom of New York's social hierarchies as "a submerged, exploited, and very possibly permanent proletariat" (qtd in Torres 61), living in the same neighborhoods under extremely precarious conditions with high rates of poverty and unemployment, both communities shared experiences of race- and class-based exclusion from the white world on a daily basis. Hinting at African Americans' and Puerto Ricans' common status as New York's racialized and most exploited labor force, Grosfoguel and Georas state that both communities shared "their respective long historical relationships as colonial/racial subjects within the U.S. empire and their subordinated location in the reproduction of those hierarchies today" (104).

Against the backdrop of the rebellious 1960s, many African Americans and Puerto Ricans stood up against their common status of second class-citizenship. One hundred years after the abolition of slavery, African Americans were still struggling to attain full equality and emancipation, while Puerto Ricans on the island and in the United States remained in a colonial status with only limited citizenship rights (Torres 65). Despite existing tensions between Puerto Ricans and African Americans who were competing for the same housing and jobs and the fact that some Puerto Ricans did not want to socialize with African Americans (Glasser), the overall sentiment was one of solidarity and connectedness. As African American activist Denise Oliver-Vélez, founding member of the Young Lords Party, recalls: "We were facing the same kind of oppression and after a couple of years living in the U.S. many Puerto Ricans would realize that African Americans were their natural allies" (Oliver-Vélez). Situating themselves in a context of worldwide anti-colonial struggles, Black and Puerto Rican radicals agreed in their analysis that both communities constituted "internal colonies" destined to provide white America with cheap labor force. In January 1967, SNCC leader Stokely Carmichael travelled to Puerto Rico as part of his efforts to internationalize the U.S. Black struggle and met with Juan Mari Bras, leader of the Movement for Puerto Rican independence. They issued a joint statement, stating that African-Americans constituted the "vanguard of a common struggle against U.S. imperialism." Furthermore, they continued: "[J]ust as 'Black Power' signifies a struggle for liberation and control of African American communities by Black people, the independence struggle in Puerto Rico is for control by Puerto Ricans of their own lives and the wealth of the country. Black people constitute a colony within the U.S. Puerto Rico is a colony outside the U.S." (Rivero 67).

Embracing Blackness: Nuyoricans between U.S. and Puerto Rican racisms

When Black Power and Black nationalism gained increased popularity in the mid-to-late 1960s—while realizing a large portion of Puerto Rican migrants to New York happened to be of African descent—this started to play a decisive role in the forging of African American/Puerto Rican alliances and the related emergence of Nuyorican and Afro-Latino identity constructions. Deeply inspired by African American mass mobilizations against segregation and the defiance of white supremacy, many young Nuyoricans—Black, Brown, and white—identified with the Black Freedom Struggle and started to address the multiple levels of racial oppression they experienced. Not only did they begin to confront the racism extant in the U.S. mainland but also began questioning the neglect of Blackness on the Puerto Rican island. Embracing U.S. Black identity and challenging Puerto Rican anti-Black racism, as prominently discussed in Piri Thomas' autobiography *Down These Mean Streets* (1967), became a recurrent theme for young Nuyoricans. Jeffrey Ogbar notes:

> There was a particular appeal that made Black Power a model for young people of color longing for an end to the racial oppression they had endured. It allowed many to affirm themselves without concern for white scrutiny or hostility. Puerto Rican baby boomers in the mainland grew Afros, celebrated African and Taíno ancestry, and less identified as 'white', instead making references to themselves as brown people." ("Puerto Rico" 163)

Hailing from an island where the existence of racism was neglected and the prevalent stigmatization of Blackness disguised behind the veils of multiethnic *mestizaje* discourse, Afro-Puerto Rican migrants who arrived in New York City were confronted with the U.S. "one-drop rule" binary racial discourse, which often classified them as Black for the first time in their lives (Zentella 27). While Puerto Rican anti-Black racial discourses on the island had the effect of "whitening" its population, migration to the mainland and the related processes of racialization tended to produce a "browning effect" among Puerto Ricans, as Jorge Duany contends (256). While Chicanos on the West Coast also forged alliances with African Americans in the 1960s, no other Hispanic migrant communities in the United States developed ties of connectedness with African Americans as intense as New York Puerto Ricans. As Adrián Burgos Jr. points out, "Settlement in New York City not only influenced community formation but also kindled a shared sense of Blackness based on consciousness of race and diaspora" (75).

Alongside Afro-Cubans, Afro-Puerto Rican immigrants constituted the first large Afro-Latino community in the United States, their presence in

Harlem as the global hub of Black transnationalism reinforcing the often-neglected condition of the Hispanic Caribbean as part of the African diaspora. Many Afro-Puerto Ricans found themselves caught between conflicting modes of racialization: not only did their identities as Black *and* Hispanic jeopardize dominant U.S. racial categorizations and delineations according to which the label "Hispanic" was constructed in sharp contrast to "Black." In addition, by identifying with African Americans and affirming their Black identity, many of them challenged homogenizing identity discourses from their homelands in which Blackness was consistently stigmatized. The close relations that developed between African Americans and Afro-Latino immigrants due to their common racial exclusion in the United States were regarded with deep suspicion, "muted or even drowned out by the naturalizing call of panlatinidad," as Raquel Rivera observes (250). This was especially the case for Nuyoricans, who "have often found themselves excluded or have even excluded themselves from the generally accepted bounds of latinidad, given the constitutional urban Afro-diasporicity of their cultural identity" (255).

"Cha-cha with a backbeat": the rise of Latin Boogaloo

"Cornbread, hog maw, and chitterlings," goes the refrain in Joe Cuba's 1966 hit recording "Bang, Bang," referencing some typical elements of African American "soul food" from the Deep South. "*Comiendo cuchifritos,*" another voice exclaims in Spanish, alluding to a classic of Puerto Rican street food in New York City. The song celebrated the fusion of African American and Latin American cultures, not only in terms of lyrical allusions to food but also by combining rhythms and sonic elements from both traditions. As singer Jimmy Sabater recalls, "Bang, Bang" was born out of an on stage-improvisation, when the Joe Cuba Sextet—a group that consisted mostly of young Puerto Rican musicians—played a gig at the Palm Gardens Ballroom in New York for a predominantly African American audience: "The place was packed, but when we were playing all those mambos and cha-chas, nobody was dancing. So at the end of the first set, I went over to Joe Cuba and said, 'Look, Sonny, I have an idea for a tune that I think might get them up" (qtd in Flores 79). According to Sabater, the African American audience instantly began to dance when the band added a funky backbeat to their usual Latin repertoire. Latin Boogaloo was born, not only taking New York's Latin dance floors and airwaves by storm, but also gaining considerable popularity among African American audiences. As "first Nuyorican music," the new sound symbolized the "guiding, exemplary role of African American culture and politics for that generation of Puerto Ricans growing up in New York" (82), as Juan Flores has insightfully observed in his landmark book *From Bomba to Hip-Hop* (2000).

Boogaloo did not come out of the blue. The advent of the new sound, described as "cha-cha with a backbeat" by Pucho of the Latin Soul Brothers

(Flores), was preceded by decades of sonic dialogs between both communities which started to take place since the first migration waves in the 1920s, ever since "Afro-American and Puerto Rican cultures have co-existed in Harlem. As a result, these Harlemites could not help being influenced by each other's way of life and music," (239) as Max Salazar points out in his essay on "Afro-American Latinized Rhythms." Prior to the emergence of Latin Soul, New York's Puerto Rican migrants had passionately listened and adapted Jazz, R'n'B, and Doo-Wop. The Harlem encounters of African American Jazz pioneers such as Dizzy Gillespie and Max Roach with Afro-Cuban musicians like Mario Bauzá, Machito, and Mongo Santamaría resulted in the emergence of Bebop and Latin Jazz in the 1940s. It had a long-lasting influence on first-generation Nuyoricans like Tito Puente, Ray Barretto, and Eddie Palmieri who would become superstars of New York's Latino scene in the 1950s, 1960s, and 1970s. All three of them were born and raised in Spanish Harlem to Puerto Rican immigrants who had arrived with the first migration wave after 1917. In the 1950s, timbales-player Tito Puente became known as "El Rey del Mambo," a popular genre that blended big band Jazz with Afro-Cuban rhythms and, much like the later Boogaloo, was criticized for its "[B]lack American vulgarity" (qtd in Raussert 10). Like Mongo Santamaría, who arguably released one of the first Latin Soul songs with his version of Herbie Hancock's "Watermelon Man" (1961), percussionist Ray Barretto and pianist Eddie Palmieri, all would become protagonists of Salsa music for the Fania label in the late 1960s and 1970s. They also successfully experimented with African American influences in recordings like "El Watusi" (1962) and "Azúcar" (1965), respectively. In 1965, the Joe Cuba Sextet had released "El Pito" (1966), an R&B-inspired Latino song in which a chorus repeated the line "I'll never go back to Georgia"—a clear allusion to the African American Great Migration experience, sung by Puerto Ricans who had never entered the Deep South. Despite these harbingers of successful Black-Latino fusion, most established Latino musicians were caught by surprise by the success of "Bang, Bang" and the subsequent Latin Boogaloo craze during which a new generation of Nuyorican teens and twens turned the established hierarchies of New York's music scene upside down. The rise of Latin Boogaloo in the summer of 1966 reflected the strong cross-cultural appeal of African American Soul music among young Nuyoricans, In Black and Spanish Harlem, Soul music had been all over the airwaves, coinciding with daily news of Civil Rights struggles in the South, urban rebellions in the North, and anticolonial movements in the Third World. To many, the dynamic and uplifting sounds of Soul music as well as the national and international success of African American musicians like James Brown, Etta James, Marvin Gaye, Otis Redding, Ray Charles, Aretha Franklin, or Wilson Pickett became synonymous with the dawning of a new era. This new era allowed them to engage in a positive reevaluation of formerly stigmatized identities, bringing about freedom from the devastating effects of white supremacy and colonialism. Though Soul would become a signifier for Blackness, a quality which "soul brothers" and "soul sisters" had, and whites did not (Neal 94), the empowering message of Soul music to "keep on pushing" (Curtis Mayfield) in the face of the most adverse conditions, also resonated heavily among non-African American people of color in general, and Puerto Ricans in particular.

Latin Boogaloo answered demands among Puerto Rican and African American audiences and promoters "to add a little soul to [Latin] music," as songwriter and trumpet player Tony Pabón recalls (Salazar 243). Clearly oriented at expanding audiences of Latin music, Latin Boogaloo experienced a short-lived but intense period of success and popularity in the mid-to-late 1960s. Its protagonists were young Nuyorican musicians such as Pete Rodríguez ("I Like It Like That," 1966), Johnny Colón ("Boogaloo Blues," 1966), Bobby "Mr. Soul" Valentin ("Use It Before You Lose It," 1967), Héctor Rivera ("At the Party," 1966), and Afro-Cuban singer La Lupe ("Fever," 1967), who earned a reputation as "Queen of Latin Soul." She was one of the very few female artists of the male-dominated genre.[2] Most of these musicians had grown up in Spanish Harlem, exposed to the sounds of Black America and the Hispanic Caribbean alike. To them, the "Swinging Combination" (Orquesta Olivieri) of Latin and Soul music represented the possibility of creating a sound that connected their Latin heritage and the day-to-day interactions with their African Americans peers. As Juan Flores observes, "It was both a bridge and a break, for with all the continuities and influences in terms of musical style, the Boogaloo diverged from the prevailing models of Latin music in significant ways" (80).

While immensely successful among Puerto Rican and African American youngsters, Latin Boogaloo was held in disdain for its lack of sophistication by New York's established Latino music bandleaders. These older musicians felt relegated to the sidelines by a couple of "kids [who] were off clave" (Flores 109), and "didn't even know what side of the instrument to play out of" (95), as Eddie Palmieri put it. Ironically, some of the most emblematic Latin Soul tracks were recorded by representatives of the "old guard" who had to cede to pressure by promoters and labels to answer to the public demand for crossover sounds.

"We Got Latin Soul" (1969), a Latin adaptation of Dyke and the Blazers' Black pride anthem "We Got More Soul" (1969) by Mongo Santamaria; "The Soul Drummers," "Boogaloo con Soul" (released on the album "Latino con Soul," 1967), and "Right On" (1970) by Ray Barretto; "The African Twist" (1968) by Eddie Palmieri; and "Black Brothers" (1973) by Tito Puente are only some examples for songs, musical approaches and titles of which gave voice to the era-defining spirit of African American-Latino connectedness. Considering the acknowledged connotation of the term "Soul" as a marker for assertive Black identity in the Black Power era, its continued usage in

Latin music contexts testifies to the construction of new Afro-Latin ethnicities related to the emergence of Latin Boogaloo in 1960s New York. By appropriating R'n'B and Soul and departing from sophisticated Latin Jazz-inspired traditions, Boogaloo musicians created a style whose popularity transcended the Nuyorican community, reaching out to African American audiences and showing "the greatest potential that we had to really cross over in terms of music" (qtd in Flores 89), as Latin music promoter Izzy Sanabria put it. Due to the cross-cultural success of the new sound, Latin Boogaloo musicians were signed to perform and tour with Soul music superstars as James Brown, The Drifters, and The Temptations (83). Inspired by Latin Soul, many African American Soul and Funk bands of the era started to include Latino-oriented percussion in their repertoires. Showing its non-essentialist and transcultural qualities, the genre also became a platform for non-Latino musicians like Pucho and the Latin Soul Brothers, a band comprising entirely African Americans. Pucho was born as Henry Brown in Harlem in 1938. Like many of his African American contemporaries in the 1940s and 1950s, he was fascinated with Latino percussion as performed by New York-residents Machito, Mongo Santamaría, and Tito Puente. And in the 1960s, he became one of the leading *timbaleros* of the era, confusing the audiences, as he recalls: "When I became successful as a bandleader and started to play with the big shots of Latin music, people were really surprised when they learned that I was a black guy from Harlem who didn't speak a word of Spanish 'Pucho' was just a name I picked from a poster in my room" (Brown 2018).

There is probably no other musician who testifies more to the condition of New York as hemispheric capital of "overlapping diasporas" more than Joe Bataan—the widely acknowledged "King of Latin Soul," born and raised in Spanish Harlem: "My father was Filipino, my mother was African-American, and my culture is Puerto Rican" (Flores 106). With his 1967 release of "Gypsy Woman," a Latino cover version of a 1961 recording by Curtis Mayfield and the Impressions, he became very popular among Black and Puerto Rican audiences. In songs like "Ordinary Guy" (1968), "Poor Boy" (1969), and the Latino pride anthem "Young, Gifted, and Brown" (1970)—an adaptation of Nina Simone's "Young, Gifted, and Black"—Bataan reflected the social realities of the period in a much more explicit way than most other Latin Soul releases. Reflecting on his relations with the movement, Bataan said,

> Strictly speaking, I was not an activist. But it seems like many activists liked my music and my ability to unite the black and Puerto Rican ghetto youth on the dancefloor by speaking about what was going on. So I played on a fundraiser for the Young Lords at the Apollo Theater and in 1973 I was invited by Angela Davis to join her with my band on a trip to a socialist World Youth Festival in East Berlin!" (Bataan 2018)

As a protagonist of the Latin Soul movement, Bataan's trajectory transcends the short-lived Latin Boogaloo era in many ways and testifies to the long-lasting legacy of the genre. In the early 1970s, Bataan conceived the term "SalSoul"—a combination of Salsa and Soul—that would become the name of a successful Latin and Disco label on which he released "Rap-O Clap-O" (1979), one of the very first Hip Hop songs ever recorded.

While older generations of established Latin musicians like Tito Puente had despised Latin Boogaloo for musical and commercial reasons, between 1966 and 1969, many Latin musicians who refused to play Boogaloo or Latin Soul had problems being signed on for gigs. There were also racial implications regarding its rejection on behalf of nationalist Puerto Rican elites from the island who spoke out against the genre, condemning it as a betrayal of the community (Lipsitz 79), because it "violated the bounds that kept distinct what was Black and what was Latino" (244), as Raquel Rivera stated. Traditionalists and advocates of Eurocentric *mestizaje* discourse found that African American influences in style, language, and music, as represented in Nuyorican culture and Latin Soul, constituted a contamination of the explicitly non-Black Puerto Rican Latino heritage they propagated.

This attitude, fearful of the impact of Black Power on Puerto Ricans, was reflected in an extremely hostile stance toward Nuyorican expressions of identification with African American culture, which dominated the public discourse in Puerto Rico, as Yeidy Rivero demonstrates in her discussion of the Afro hairstyle on the island. According to Rivero, the popularization of the Afro as a symbol of Black empowerment among Afro-Puerto Ricans constituted a "direct affront to the island's racist ideologies and practices [...], an in-your-face resistance to hegemonic racial discourse" (83) which "[...] symbolically connected Puerto Ricans on the island with the African American-Puerto Rican-Afro Puerto Rican radical mobilizations that had taken place in the United States since the early 1960s" (84). The dissemination of African American influences in Puerto Rico was aided in great measure by the overwhelming success of New York-style Latin Boogaloo on the island, which could not be prevented by the local guardians of *mestizaje* discourse who saw the translation of U.S. Blackness into Puerto Rican contexts as an imminent threat to their racial hegemony.

To the relief of its numerous adversaries in New York and on the island, the era of Latin Boogaloo was abruptly terminated in 1969. Allegedly following a concerted move by old bandleaders and the burgeoning Fania label, New York's promoters suddenly refrained from hiring Boogaloo musicians for gigs and radio stations stopped playing their records (Flores 107ff). The demise of Latin Boogaloo and the subsequent commercial success of Salsa reflected the widespread tendency to return to "pure" and "authentic" Latino music, without English lyrics and overexplicit references to African American music and culture. Based on Afro-Cuban musical traditions and encompassing a variety of Afro-diasporic genres from the Hispanic Caribbean, Salsa emerged as the product of a market strategy by Fania Records, founders of which Johnny Pacheco and Jerry Masucci had pushed aggressively to monopolize New York's Latino scene. With Salsa acquiring an unrivaled status as the ultimate trans-Latino sound in the 1970s, Fania became the hemisphere's leading Latino music label, also referred to as "Latin Motown." While established musicians like Mongo Santamaría, Tito Puente, Eddie Palmieri, Ray Barretto, Cheo Feliciano, Larry Harlow, and Celia Cruz, who were all members of the Fania All-Stars, benefitted heavily from Salsa's triumphal march to world success, most protagonists of the Boogaloo generation were not part of the show, many of them leaving the music business. Nevertheless, the long-lasting impulses and contributions of the Latin Boogaloo era to subsequent Afro-diasporic genres throughout the Americas confirm the accuracy of a statement by Max Salazar: "The Boogaloo might have been killed off, but Latin Soul lived on" (247).

"Rainbow radicalism": Young Lords and Black power in the barrio

By bridging musical traditions, celebrating common cultural practices, and blending African American slang and Spanish lyrics, Latin Soul/Boogaloo accompanied, intonated, and sometimes maybe even encouraged the building of political alliances between Puerto Ricans and African Americans. Still, with notable exceptions like some of the Joe Bataan songs or Jimmy Sabater's "Times Are Changing" (1969)—in which the Afro-Puerto Rican singer refers to his assuming of Black identity, exclaiming that the time to claim Black rights in the United States has come.

There are very few Latin Soul recordings that would qualify as classical message songs with an explicit reference to the social and political movements that were defining the period. New York Latin Soul's emancipatory potential is likely not to be found in the lyrics, but rather, a Hispanic migrant community adapting African American forms in contexts that were shaped by a deep-rooted stigmatization of Blackness (this holds true for the U.S. mainland *and* Puerto Rico). This in itself constitutes a defiant act with deeply political connotations. The appropriation of African American Soul by Puerto Rican migrants as featured in Latin Boogaloo is interpreted as "strategic anti-essentialism" by George Lipsitz.

> [Nuyoricans] found that performing an identity that was not entirely their own brought them closer to their [African] roots. [...] [T]his

anti-essentialist strategy revealed the heterogeneity and complexity of their group's identity sufficiently to position them to take part in subsequent national and international fusion musics [...] that enabled them to imagine and enact alliances with other groups. (79)

In this light, the embracing of U.S. Black culture by a young generation of Nuyoricans as manifested in Latin Boogaloo might be interpreted not only as a means of showing solidarity and identification with the African American struggle, but also as a way of affirming Puerto Rico's neglected African heritage and challenging the Puerto Rican elites' racism and denial.

Examining the relations between the successive emergences of Latin Soul and the Young Lords as related expressions of Black-Latino solidarity, we find it remarkable how changes in popular music reflected and heralded social and political developments. The Latin Boogaloo hype started in the summer of 1966—just in between Stokely Carmichael's initial call for Black Power on a civil rights demonstration in Mississippi and the foundation of the Black Panther Party in Oakland. The rise of the Black Power movement and the simultaneous anticolonial liberation struggles in the Third World appealed to Puerto Rican nationalists who advocated for independence from the United States and were gaining currency in the Nuyorican community. Committed to an agenda of revolutionary internationalism and the building of interethnic alliances with other oppressed groups, the Black Panther Party "[...] represented the model for revolutionary struggle, resistance, and radical chic," to Puerto Ricans and other non-African American groups as Chicanos/as, Asian Americans, Native Americans, and even poor whites, as Jeffrey Ogbar describes in his essay "Rainbow Radicalism" (194). Corresponding with the border-crossing spirit of the Latin Boogaloo, the invitation of the Black Panthers to other marginalized communities to become part of interethnic "rainbow coalitions" with the common goal of overcoming white supremacy and capitalism resonated heavily among young Nuyoricans, who had grown up facing the same forms of discrimination as their African American peers.

Inspired by his conversations with BPP leader Fred Hampton, former gang leader José "Cha Cha" Jiménez founded the Young Lords in 1968 to mobilize Chicago's Puerto Rican gang members against racism and for Puerto Rican independence—creating a month of Soul dances as one of their first social activities to collect funds (Flores-Rodríguez 62). In 1969, a small group of students founded in New York a Young Lords chapter. Those involved in this endeavor included Afro-Puerto Ricans Pablo "Yoruba" Guzmán and Felipe Luciano and the African American Denise Oliver-Vélez; they attracted many young Puerto Ricans not only from Spanish Harlem and the Bronx, but also African Americans, as Johana Fernández emphasizes:

With a formal leadership largely composed of afro-Latinos (especially in the New York chapter) and with one-quarter of its membership comprised of African Americans, YLP members launched one of the first Latino formations that saw itself as part of the African Diaspora; that was instrumental in theorizing and identifying the structures of racism embedded in the culture, language, and history of Latin America and its institutions; and that would commit itself to the struggle against racism in the United States and insist that poor African Americans and Latinos shared common political and economic interests. (Fernández 1)

Following the example of the BPP, Young Lords organized free breakfast programs for children, led grassroots campaigns for better access to health care, and educated members in Black and Puerto Rican history, among many other things. Pablo "Yoruba" Guzmán, whose nickname allegedly is related to the pride he took in his African ancestry, confirms the exemplary role of the African American freedom struggle for the Young Lords efforts to organize Puerto Ricans:

We know that the number-one group that's leading that struggle [for liberation] are Black people, 'cause Black people – if we remember the rule that says the most oppressed will take the vanguard role in the struggle – Black people, man, have gone through the most shit. Black people, along with Chicanos and Native Americans, are the greatest allies we can have. So we must build the Puerto Rican-Black alliance. That is the basis for the American Revolution for us. (237)

Embodying the intimate relations between New York's African American and Puerto Rican radical activists and artists, Young Lords cofounder Felipe Luciano also became known as a member of The Last Poets—a Black nationalist spoken word group that had emerged from the Black Arts Movement in the late 1960s and gained popularity with incendiary poems for Black revolution and against white supremacy. In several poems, as the bilingual English-Spanish "Jíbaro, My Pretty N..." (*The Last Poets* 1971), Luciano addressed the specific situation of being Black and Puerto Rican, adding a genuinely Nuyorican perspective to these emblematic expressions of socially conscious poetry in times of Black Power radicalism. Being the only Puerto Rican in an African American group, Luciano played an important role for interethnic dialogs as a transcultural communicator between both communities and a voice for uniting Latino and Black struggles, which was heard in Spanish *and* Black Harlem. With their specific style of rapping, their politically charged lyrics in the language of New York's ghettos and barrios, and their successful blending of Black and Puerto Rican voices, The Last Poets are considered by many to be the legitimate forefathers of Hip Hop, to which Puerto Ricans have also contributed significantly. In the spirit of transbarrio solidarity that defined the era of Latin Boogaloo and its aftermath Felipe Luciano's participation in The Last Poets underlines the role of New York's role as key site for cross-cultural Black-Latino joint-ventures (Wilkinson 2006).

Hemispheric impact: Soul and Black power beyond borders

Since the Harlem Renaissance of the 1920s and 1930s, New York has underscored its condition as a fertile breeding ground for cross-cultural Afro-diasporic genres and movements and focal point of political and cultural currents associated with Black transnationalism. The emergence of Latin Boogaloo and the Young Lords in the 1960s constitutes another significant chapter of that history, illustrating the prominent role of Black popular music in the making of transcultural and transnational movements for human rights. The rise of Latin Soul/Boogaloo and the Young Lords was a manifestation of Nuyorican counter-culture, which was informed by the interactions between African Americans and Puerto Ricans in New York and encouraged young Latinos to embrace and affirm often neglected Afro-diasporic identities, challenging hegemonic *mestizaje* discourses that dominated Latin American societies. The resulting Afro-Latino identity constructions and interethnic alliances transcended the boundaries of communities, cultures, ethnicities, neighborhoods, and nations, appealing to Afro-descendants throughout the Americas. Latin Soul/Boogaloo and Young Lords translated African American sounds, expressions, and symbols, making them accessible to new audiences in Latin American contexts. Soul-inspired Latino sounds from Spanish Harlem became extremely popular in countries such as Puerto Rico, Venezuela, Colombia, Panamá, Perú, and the Dominican Republic, as Israel Sánchez-Coll and Ian Seda confirm: "La radio en Sur América se ve invadida por el Boogaloo, los programas estelares especializados en música caribeña pronto se tomarían literalmente por este nuevo sonido." (The radio in South America found itself invaded by Boogaloo, while stellar programs specialized in Caribbean music would soon be overtaken literally by this new sound; l.)

Underlining the significance of New York as hemispheric gateway for the circulation of African American influences in Afro-Latin America, the emergence of *combos nacionales* in Panama and the Black Rio movement in Brazil in the late 1960s and 1970s, arguably Latin America's two most vibrant local Soul scenes, were partly inspired by musicians like Earnie King and Ralph Weeks from Colón and Toni Tornado and Tim Maia from Rio de Janeiro, all of whom had lived as migrants in 1960s New York before becoming trailblazers of Soul music in their home countries. Throughout the hemisphere, the popularization of Soul music and the Afro hairstyle was linked to an identification with the Black Power movement and the defiance of local forms of anti-Black racism among Afro-Latino youth, which became manifest through increased political mobilizations and the rise of Black movements in the late 1970s and 1980s (Steinitz 2017).

As the genesis of Latin Boogaloo and the subsequent hemispheric diffusion of Soul music demonstrate, the genre was a decisive factor for Black Power's transnational appeal that allowed for the bridging of political, cultural, and linguistic barriers between formerly separated Afro-diasporic communities and the emergence of border-crossing alliances between them. In Latin America, where Black Power was demonized and feared for its inflammatory effects on local Black communities, the symbolic appropriation of U.S. forms of Blackness as manifested in the consumption and translation of Soul music constituted a rupture with dominant *mestizaje* and *democracia racial* ideologies and the related traditionalist stereotypes. Soul music displayed an extraordinary potential to spread political messages of Black empowerment across the Hemisphere, providing young Afro-Latinos with a means to break with dominant paternalistic and folkloristic identity concepts—and to articulate dissent against the neglected forms of Latin American racism. The empowering impulse of Soul was significant for the formation of anti-racist movements and the emergence of inter-American networks of solidarity which connected formerly isolated Afro-Latino communities with other sites of the African diaspora in their struggles for human rights.

Notes

1. "Spic" is a derogatory term for Puerto Ricans in the United States.
2. Even by the anything but progressive standards of the U.S. popular music industry in the 1960s and 1970s, it is striking how much the patriarchal structures of Latin American societies were reflected in the extreme scarcity of female performers in New York's Latin music scene. While the female contingent in Soul music is quite impressive (represented by international stars like Aretha Franklin, Nina Simone, Etta James, Tina Turner, Diana Ross, Lyn Collins, Marva Whitney, only to name a few), Afro-Cuban singers La Lupe and Celia Cruz were virtually the only Latina performers to get some kind of recognition in the 1960s and 1970s, the golden eras of Boogaloo and Salsa, respectively. See: Aparicio, F. R. (2003): "La India, La Lupe and Celia: Toward a Feminist Genealogy of Salsa Music." In: A. J. Cruz, R. Hernández-Pecoraro, & J. Tolliver (Eds.), *Disciplines in the Line: Feminist Research on Spanish, Latin American, and U.S. Latina Women* (pp. 37–57). Newark, DE: Juan de la Cuesta.

Works cited

Bataan, Joe. Personal Interview. 18 Sep. 2018.
Brown, David-Luis. *Waves of Decolonization – Discourses of Race and Hemispheric Citizenship in Cuba, Mexico, and the United States.* Duke UP, 2008.
Brown, Henry "Pucho". Personal Interview. 20 Sep. 2018.

Burgos, Adrián, Jr. "'The Latins from Manhattan' – Confronting Race and Building Community in Jim Crow Baseball, 1906–1950." *Mambo Montage – The Latinization of New York*, edited by Agustín Laó-Montes and Arlene Dávila. Columbia UP, 2001, pp. 73–95.

Cuba, Joe. *Bang, Bang*. New York: Tico Records, 1966.

Duany, Jorge. *The Puerto Rican Nation on the Move – Identities on the Island and in the United States*. The U of North Carolina P, 2002.

Dzidzienyo, Anani and Suzanne Oboler, editors. *Neither Enemies nor Friends: Latinos, Blacks, Afro-Latinos*. Palgrave, 2005.

Fernández, Johanna. "The Young Lords: Its Origins and Convergences with the Black Panther Party." Ibiblio – The Public's Library and Digital Archive. Web. 15 Jan. 2018.

Flores, Juan. *From Bomba to Hip-Hop: Puerto Rican Culture and Latino Identity*. Columbia UP, 2000.

Flores-Rodríguez, Ángel G. "The Young Lords, Puerto Rican Liberation, and the Black Freedom Struggle – Interview with José "Cha Cha" Jiménez." *OAH Magazine of History*, vol. 26, issue 1, 2012, pp. 61–64.

Gilroy, Paul. *There Ain't No Black in the Union Jack*. Routledge, 1987.

Gilroy, Paul. *The Black Atlantic – Modernity and Double Consciousness*. Verso, 1993.

Glasser, Ruth. *My Music Is My Flag: Puerto Rican Musicians and Their New York Communities, 1917–1940*. U of California P, 1995.

Grosfoguel, Ramón, and Chloé Georas. "Latino Caribbean Diasporas in New York." *Mambo Montage – The Latinization of New York*, edited by Agustín Laó-Montes and Arlene Dávila. Columbia UP, 2001, pp. 97–118.

Guzmán, Pablo. "Yoruba: Before People Called Me a Spic, They Called Me a Nigger." *The Afro-Latin@ Reader – History and Culture in the United States*, edited by Miriam Jiménez and Juan Flores. Duke UP, 2010, pp. 235–243.

Jiménez, Miriam and Juan Flores, editors. *The Afro-Latin@ Reader – History and Culture in the United States*. Duke UP, 2010.

King, Earnie. Personal Interview. 6 Apr. 2017.

Laó-Montes, Agustín and Arlene Dávila, editors. *Mambo Montage – The Latinization of New York*. Columbia UP, 2001.

Laó-Montes, Agustín. "Cartografía del campo político afrodescendiente en América Latina." *Debates sobre ciudadanía y políticas raciales en las Américas Negras*, edited by Claudia Rosero-Labbé, et al. Universidad Nacional de Colombia, 2010, pp. 279–316.

Lewis, Earl. "To Turn As on A Pivot: Writing African American History into a History of Overlapping Diasporas." *The American Historical Review*, vol. 100, issue 3, 1995, pp. 765–787.

Lipsitz, George. *Dangerous Crossroads – Popular Music, Postmodernism and the Politics of Place*. Verso, 1994.

Maloney, Gerardo. Personal Interview. 4 Apr. 2017.

Neal, Mark Anthony. *What the Music Said – Black Popular Music and Black Popular Culture*. Routledge, 1999.

Nwankwo, Ifeoma Kiddoe. "The Promises and Perils of US African-American Hemispherism: Latin America in Martin Delany's Blake and Gayl Jones's Mosquito." *Hemispheric American Studies: Essays Beyond the Nation*, edited by Caroline Levander and Robert Levine. Rutgers University Press, 2008, pp. 187–204.

Ogbar, Jeffrey. "Puerto Rico en Mi Corazón, The Young Lords, Black Power and Puerto Rican Nationalism in the U.S., 1966–1972." *Centro Journal*, vol. 1, 2006, pp. 67–74.

Ogbar, Jeffrey. "Rainbow Radicalism. The Rise of the Radical Ethnic Nationalism." *The Black Power Movement – Rethinking the Civil Rights-Black Power Era*, edited by Peniel E. Joseph. Routledge, 2006, pp. 193–228.

Oliver-Vélez, Denise. Personal Interview. 21 Sep. 2018.

Ostendorf, Berndt. "Americanization and Anti-Americanism in the Age of Globalization." *North-Americanization of Latin America? Culture, Gender, and Nation in the Americas*, edited by Hans-Joachim König and Stefan Rinke. Verlag Hans-Dieter Heinz, 2004, pp. 19–45.

Raussert, Wilfried and Michelle Habell-Pallán, editors. *Cornbread and Cuchifritos – Ethnic Identity Politics, Transnationalization, and Transculturation in American Urban Popular Music*. Wissenschaftlicher Verlag Trier, 2011.

Redmond, Shana L. *Anthem – Social Movements and the Sound of Solidarity in the African Diaspora*. New York University Press, 2014.

Reid Andrews, George. *Afro-Latin America, 1800–2000*. Oxford UP, 2004.

Rivera, Raquel Z. "Hip-Hop, Puerto Ricans, and Ethnoracial Identities in New York." *Mambo Montage – The Latinization of New York*, edited by Agustín Laó-Montes and Arlene Dávila. Columbia UP, 2001, pp. 235–262.

Rivero, Yeidy. *Tuning Out Blackness: Race and Nation in the History of Puerto Rican Television*. Duke UP Books, 2005.

Sabater, Jimmy. *Times are Changin*. New York: Tico Records, 1969.

Salazar, Max. "Afro-American Latinized Rhythms." *Salsiology – Afro-Cuban Music and the Evolution of Salsa in New York City*, edited by Vernon Boggs. Greenwood Press, 1992, pp. 237–248.

Sánchez-Coll, Israel, and Ian Seda. "Boogaloo y Sing – A – Ling. Un repaso histórico en sus 40 años." Herencia Latina Feb 2005. Web. 15 Jan. 2018.

Sansone, Livio. *Blackness without Ethnicity: Constructing Race in Brazil*. Palgrave Macmillan, 2003.

Stam, Robert, and Ella Shohat. *Race in Translation – Culture Wars Around the Postcolonial Atlantic*. New York UP, 2012.

Steinitz, Matti. "Black Power in a paraíso racial? The Black Rio Movement, U.S. Soul Music, and Afro-Brazilian Mobilizations under Military Rule (1970–1976)." *Politics of Entanglement in the Americas: Connecting Transnational Flows and Local Perspectives*, edited by Lukas Rehm, Jochen Kemner, and Olaf Kaltmeier. WVT Wissenschaftlicher Verlag, 2017, pp. 13–30.

Steinitz, Matti. "'Calling Out Around the World' – How Soul Music Transnationalized the African-American Freedom Struggle." *Sonic Politics. Music and Social Movements in the Americas from the 1960s to the Present*, edited by Wilfried Raussert and Olaf Kaltmeier. Routledge, 2019.

The Last Poets. "Jíbaro, My Pretty Nigger." Right On! Original Soundtrack. Juggernaut Records, 1971.

Thomas, Piri. *Down These Mean Streets*. Knopf, 1967.

Torres, Andrés. *Between Melting Pot and Mosaic – African Americans and Puerto Ricans in the New York Political Economy*. Temple UP, 1995.

Van Deburg, William. *New Day in Babylon – The Black Power Movement and American Culture*. The U of Chicago P, 1992.

Ward, Brian. *Just My Soul Responding – Rhythm and Blues, Black Consciousness and Race Relations.* Routledge, 1998.

Wilkinson, Michelle Joan. "'To Make a Poet Black': Canonizing Puerto Rican Poets in the Black Arts Movement." *New Thoughts on the Black Arts Movement*, edited by Lisa Gail Collins and Margo Natalie Crawford. Rutgers UP, 2006, pp. 317–332.

Yúdice, George. *The Expediency of Culture – Uses of Culture in the Global Era.* Duke, 2003.

Zentella, Ana Celia. "A Nuyorican's View of Our History and Language(s) in New York, 1945–1965." *Boricuas in Gotham – Puerto Ricans in the Making of New York City*, edited by Gabriel Haslip-Viera, et al. Markus Wiener Publishers, 2004, pp. 21–34.

Part VI
Human right, animals rights, and posthuman rights

15 From racism to speciesism
The question of freedom of the other in the works of J. M. Coetzee and Jure Detela

Marjetka Golež Kaučič

Introduction

The purpose of this contribution is to present a thematized critique of the human–human relationship and the human–animal relationship through an analysis of selected prose works by the South African writer and Nobel laureate J. M. Coetzee and poems and writings by the Slovenian poet Jure Detela.[1] This analysis will be conducted on the basis of contemporary anthropological, ecocritical, and non-speciesist critical animal studies and philosophical thinking about concepts of racism and speciesism as discriminatory practices and will describe their thematization by the abovementioned authors.[2] The two concepts are discursively connected movements for animal rights having emerged from movements for human rights, following in the footsteps of abolitionism as the fundamental model of a new world in which all living creatures would be equal.[3] I will attempt to show that literature, as a tangible reality, enables the thematization of racism and speciesism and their consequences. In the words of Theodor W. Adorno, literature is virtually the only place where "suffering [can] still find its own voice" (Adorno 252; see also Schweizer), or as Mario Ortiz-Robles puts it, "Literature helps us imagine alternative ways to live with animals, and animals help us imagine a new role for literature in a world where our animal future is uncertain" (5).

Literature is capable of revealing the close links between racial and species-based discrimination and allows us to understand the equality of two existential entities: that is, humanity and nonhuman subjectivity, which are both vulnerable to neglect, suffering, and even killing on the basis of not only racial marginalization but also "cultural marginalization" (Zapf 4, Čeh Steger, "Ekološko" 57). Literature can give a voice to the Other, or as Kari Weil states, it may enable us "to understand and give voice to others" (*Thinking Animals* 7) and, according to Rosi Braidotti, can help us establish a "neoliteral relation to animals" (528). Consequently, literature has the responsibility to address situations when human beings, as apparent subjects defined by their skin color, ethnicity, or any other element that makes them different from the majority, become objects of discrimination, as well as situations when animals, a priori excluded from subjectification, become objects not only of discrimination but also torture, suffering, and killing, as they represent objects of human use. In this sense, literature is needed so "the experience of animals can be integrated into the mind" (Detela, "Sporočilo" 2). In what follows, I will explore whether the shift from a racist to a speciesist perspective can be based on the transition from the desubjectification of human beings to the desubjectification of animals and can thus draw an equation between animals and human beings on the same objective level. After all, in the history of humanity, the thematization of the Other is manifested in the use of linguistic discrimination. People of color or of other ethnicities are frequently given names that equate them with animals, which has arguably resulted in the mass genocide of individual ethnicities and the enslavement of people on the basis of the enslavement and genocide of animals as an excuse for the discriminatory relationship to people. For this reason, it is necessary to reexamine the underlying principles of human rights, and, taking them as our basis, determine whether the same moral status is assured to everyone, while simultaneously assigning the status of persons also to animals. The transition from the category of human property (slaves) to not being human property is also possible with regard to the animal world, namely, by viewing the abolitionist orientation of the human world as applicable to the animal world. The anthropologist Tim Ingold emphasizes that animals are not *like* persons, they *are* persons: "Now the ontological equivalence of humans and animals, as organism-persons and as fellow participants in a life process, carries a corollary of capital importance" (xxiv).

It is precisely through literary thematization that "a leap in consciousness" can occur, namely, by influencing changes in the understanding of our relationship to animals, with human beings shifting their worldview from anthropocentric to eco- (or bio-)centric. According to Lawrence Buell, "eco-literature, in which human interest is not the sole legitimate interest, can generate empathy for animals" (qtd. in Starre 23). In Stefan Hofer's view, art is based on observing the observed and makes possible the particular potential of ecological communication, inasmuch as increased perception (the esthetic function) is characteristic of artistic communication. Because art is not bound to the accurate and truthful mediation of truth, its ecological communication is particular and unobtrusive. It is precisely in this quality that its particular power resides (Hofer 181). Literature thematizes the human and nonhuman position in society, as well as human relations to the Other and the different, and can lead the reader to reconsider assumptions regarding the non-hierarchy of dominant perspectives on human beings, the world, nature, and animals. It attempts to sharpen the critical viewpoint of harmful societal and cultural practices, especially racism, speciesism, and any other kind of discrimination and demonization of the Other and to enable the creative energy of literature to participate in the formation of these processes.

The lawyer and animal rights advocate Steven M. Wise once wrote a book about a slave in London in 1771, who was named James Somerset (*Though the Heavens May Fall*). In a separate article, Wise describes Somerset as "an invisible man" and explains, "He wasn't literally invisible, but legally invisible" (Wise, "The Basic Rights" par. 1). And this was because he was a property. Wise goes on to discuss how, for three centuries, the legal system in the United States allowed human beings to be "formally sold, bred, and distributed like beasts, as Judge John T. Noonan noted" (Wise par. 3). Today animals are treated similar to property all over the world without any rights or freedoms, which means they have no autonomy or self-determination: they are things, and things do not behave autonomously; persons do. This is the very basis on which the sharp division between human beings and animals has developed.[4] The categories that both connect and distinguish humans from can be structured as follows:

Table 15.1 Traditional comparison of the human being and the non-human being or animal

Human being	Nonhuman being or animal
Racism and apartheid/apartness of human beings: discrimination on the basis of race, skin, color, culture, or religion	Speciesism and apartheid/apartness of animals: discrimination on the basis of species, and also between animal species
(Non)freedom of the human being or slavery, property, the human being as object and not as person	(Non)freedom of the animal or slavery, the animal as property, as object, and not as person
Human rights	Animal rights
Abolitionism or the emancipation of humans, which is legally formalized	Abolitionism or the emancipation of animals, which is still only a theory and a movement
Human life is inviolable	Animal life can be transformed into food, shoes, clothing, etc.

The starting point of the present contribution, therefore, is rejection of the conception of animals as the invisible Other who are not equal to us. In fact, the way most people today perceive animals is similar to the way most white people in the past perceived Blacks, Indians, and other socially ostracized groups as inferior to themselves or socially excluded (Piekarski 707). As Matthew Calarco notes, the status and nature of who is the Other cannot be decided or settled once and for all (71). At the same time, I reject Emmanuel Levinas's notion that the Other must have a human face, that we must encounter the Other, and that the Other must speak to us (96–97). In this view, the Other can be a human being with a different skin color, but not an animal that belongs to another species and cannot speak to us, even if their communication is on a level we do not understand. If an animal spoke our language, it would no longer be invisible and inaudible. But we all know the language of suffering, the response to violence; even if it is inaudible, we are aware of it. Therefore, we are the ones who should give animals a voice so they can speak through us, as Kari Weil believes; she understands "the animal question" as a liminal issue of language, epistemology, and ethics, such as has already been treated in women's and postcolonial studies (Weil, "Report" 4). Michał Piekarski ponders the question of what would happen if a duck that was about to be shot spoke and cried out not to be shot, saying that it was no different from the hunter. The reaction would probably be entirely different. Piekarski writes, "The animal is the remote Other, which cannot be included in our 'rational' ethics of speaking beings" (712).

According to Judith Butler, there will always be a subject that will not be seen as a completely real subject and a life that will not be seen as a completely real life (4), which means that it is some form of legally codified and normal social acceptance that determines whether people of color are something less than persons and animals merely objects. But people act the way they think, so literature should change their thinking and thus their actions. John Berger argues that animals have disappeared from human awareness and sight, becoming invisible and without meaning (3–28), while Akira Mizuta Lippit notes that people have developed a cultural blindness regarding animals (1–26). Hence, we can understand the thematization of "the animal question" in literature as an ethical reversal that allows us *to see* an animal as an individual, a moral subject, and *to know* what the animal is experiencing. Only in this way is the ontological reversal possible.

J. M. Coetzee: human and animal apartheid

Without a doubt, one of the most perfidious systems of racial discrimination has been apartheid (the word means "apartness"), which was the political doctrine and system of racial segregation, oppression, and exploitation through which the government of the Republic of South Africa ruled from 1948 to 1994. It was also the foundation of the South African economic and political structure, with Black workers receiving low wages and living in poverty under the authority of the white minority (see Mattos 9–11). The foundation of apartheid law was the colonial status of the South African republic through the conquest of the Khoikhoi and San peoples, as well as the importation of Black slaves, who were considered to represent a lower developmental stage of civilization. We find a similar perspective on Blacks in the slavery system in the United States, and after the abolition of slavery in the discrimination of the African American population.

The works of J. M. Coetzee emerged from the environment of a country under colonialism, postcolonialism, apartheid, and postapartheid and were influenced by the predominant sociopolitical situation. Coetzee thus brought the consequences of apartheid and colonialism into his writing. This is an important point because his attitude toward animals is closely connected with the racial discrimination of the majority Black population and the subsequent guilt of the white population, both of which he clearly thematizes in all of his works. In two allegorical texts—*Foe* (1986) and *Life & Times of Michael K* (1983)—Coetzee depicts a well-planned racist crime in which the human relationship to animals is implicit. In *Foe*, a reworking of Daniel Defoe's classic novel *Robinson Crusoe*, the principal character, Susan Barton, states, "Hitherto I had found Friday a shadowy creature and paid him little more attention than I would have given any house-slave in Brazil" (22), whereby Coetzee makes direct reference to racism and the unequal treatment of Blacks. *Foe* was written during the apartheid period in South Africa. Friday is different: he is Black, and when he comes to England, people look at him as if he is a cannibal. Additionally, Friday has no tongue (presumably, it was cut out by slave hunters) and so is a mute creature, more similar to animals than people. Susan Barton had been a castaway with Cruso (as Coetzee spells the name), who compared Friday to a dog (21)—just as Black people in Africa have often been compared to animals. Silence, the inability to speak, devotion, and non-activeness combine in Coetzee's work to form the majority's view of the Other, in which the Other can be an ostracized white person, an oppressed Black person, or animals who "confront us with silence" as we read in a later work (*Elizabeth Costello* 70). But Friday is at least able to make murmuring sounds, whereupon Cruso suddenly announces, "The voice of man" (*Foe* 22).

In all his literary works, Coetzee attempts to thematize his home country, in which politics is intertwined with the fate of individuals trapped in the colonial, apartheid, and postapartheid community, a setting where the oppression of the Other was built into the law and racism was part of the intentional exploitation of the Other. In his later works, Coetzee makes the jump from racism to speciesism, the oppression of the Other shifting from the human to the animal world. Torture and killing were permitted by apartheid—the division between Black from white—because of the division between human and animal. In the book *Disgrace* (1999), and especially in *The Lives of Animals* (1999), which was later incorporated into *Elizabeth Costello* (2003), colonialism, which introduced the exploitation of the Other and the superiority of white over Black through apartheid, develops into a postapartheid perspective on the situation in a country where the division between people still lingers and animals are subject to eradication. Here the issue is the liberation of the oppressed.

In *Life & Times of Michael K.*, Coetzee thematizes the life of the individual in South Africa in a time of "fictional" civil war, where an individual is discriminated against and stigmatized because of poverty and Otherness, as he does not want to participate in a crime against the Other. Thus, he too becomes Other and lives a life apart from other people. Coetzee often compares the ostracized to animals (68). The desperate struggle for freedom, for individual freedom, which is more powerful than hunger, is also thematized in the work (106).

In the autobiographical narrative, *Boyhood: Scenes from Provincial Life* (1997), Coetzee describes how his mother cut out the tongue of a live chicken, an act that marked him for life although he turned his gaze away (1–2). This direct cruelty to animals, this "blindness of the soul," as Stanley Cavell calls it (92–94), and the human response of "deflection" as Ian Hacking terms it (Hacking 146)—the turning of the gaze away from what people do to animals—are present as a theme in *Disgrace*, in which the closing of the eyes toward the everyday slaughter of animals is verbalized (see Golež Kauč ič, "Thematization"). *Disgrace*, an extremely complex work written only 5 years after the end of apartheid, was received in very different ways: from some people accusing Coetzee of racism to others finding that the thematizing of animal suffering gave the novel its ethical power (Willet). Coetzee himself expressed the opinion that the reaction of the authorities to the publication of the book was understandable and related to the idea of deflection: "The response of South Africa's legislators to what disturbs their white electorate is usually to order it out of sight. If people are starving, let them starve far away in the bush, where their bodies will not be a reproach" ("Into" 361).

In the view of both Derek Attridge and Jen Poyner, *Disgrace* is a postcolonial text with ethical and political elements (Attridge, Poyner 13; see also Attwell), yet it is also an artistic text that addresses not only the past but also the destructive consequences of racial segregation on the future of South Africa (see Vovk, "Sramota"; Vovk, *Res neznosna resnobnost*). It is a work that thematizes the shame of the individual, of the white man, as well as the increasingly powerful division between the unreality of accepting people of all different races in the same way and the struggle for racial equality. In this work, we can also see the connection between racial and species-based inequality. The protagonist, Professor David Lurie, who has seduced a Black student and subsequently been disgraced and banished from academic life, compares her with animals, first with a mole and a rabbit (Coetzee, *Disgrace* 25)—and later with a bird (32).

For Coetzee, vulnerability is what connects the animal and human world (Taylor 60–72). After he is disgraced because of his sexual relationship with the student, Lurie compares his situation with the suffering of a dog in the community of Kenilworth, where he had lived as a child. The dog had been beaten each time he wanted to pursue a female dog that lived nearby; as a result, each time he smelled the female, he pressed his ears to his head and tried to hide (89–90). In *Disgrace*, Coetzee depicts the changed position of the white minority at the end of apartheid and the revenge of the Black majority in an episode in which three Black men rape a white woman and kill the dogs that were in her care. The rapists shoot the animals "in a country where dogs are bred to snarl at the mere smell of a black man" (110). This is, in a way, a form of concealed and legalized revenge for historical injustice, but it is, as always, taken against innocent victims. This is a country where organizations against cruelty to animals close their doors and only volunteers provide help, sometimes euthanizing dogs, of which there are too many according to the criteria of a human society that decides whether animals live or die, animals that are not considered equal to the directives of the human society.[5] Or as Lucy says about one of the female dogs are nothing more than the furniture or the alarm system. (91). After the slaughter of the animals, Lucy stops eating meat (121).[6] Coetzee merges human suffering with the suffering of animals and also thematizes the guilt of the white person, in this case Lucy, who becomes pregnant as a result of the rape and even decides to marry one of her Black rapists,[7] as if this would expiate the collective guilt. Maria Teresa Segarra Costaguta Mattos believes that, "Lucy's silence over the violence imposed on her may be understood as solidarity over the long lived silence of the colonized, depicted in Coetzee's other books such as *Foe* (1986) and *In the Heart of the Country* (1977)" (Mattos 29).

Although Lurie did not previously have an empathic attitude toward animals, he develops one, helping two sheep that are tied up in the sun, even though he knows they will soon be slaughtered. He would like to turn his gaze away from their suffering (124). The dialog between David and Lucy reveals the humiliation of a person to the level of a dog, unneeded, cast off, the Other that, in the situation as Lucy experiences it, is closest to her (230). Later Lurie comes to feel a powerful compassion for the dogs in the shelter, even though he has to put them to sleep. He decides that he will be an angel of death and help euthanize dogs, that they will get rid of them because nobody wants them. He concludes that the dogs know what is going to happen to them and that they feel "the disgrace of dying" (143). *Disgrace* concludes with a final sequence depicting the shame of a man's killing of a living creature (a lame dog) that has expressed nothing but love for the man (220). It is quite evident that in his work Coetzee combines a criticism of racism and speciesism, believing that the two discriminatory practices are closely connected. We relate to animals as meat rather than as sentient beings (see Dunayer 139–149), an idea that receives literary treatment in Coetzee's novella *The Lives of Animals*.

Gary Francione, a leading thinker in critical animal studies, emphasizes the point that the fundamental rights of humans and nonhuman animals are treated very differently, which is a form of speciesism, and that there are no real differences between racism and speciesism (*Introduction*). It follows, then, that we must transfer the fundamental freedoms that are at least formally enjoyed by human beings to animals. Steven M. Wise puts it this way:

> Today virtually no legal scholar or moral philosopher seriously contends that rational arguments support a claim that all and not only human beings ought to possess fundamental liberties. Yet there most fundamental liberties are denied to every nonhuman animal. This not only inflicts grave injustice upon its victims, but underlines the arbitrariness of claiming fundamental liberties only for human beings. ("Argument" 134–135)

Wise agrees with David Brion Davis that economic interests are what prevent people from giving freedom and autonomy to animals. And yet if economic interests could be overcome when human slavery was abolished, they can also be overcome with regard to the exploitation of animals (qtd. in Wise "Argument" 137; see also Haraway).

In *The Lives of Animals*,[8] Coetzee sharpens his criticism of the view that humankind is the crown of creation and that people can legally kill animals for a variety of reasons that are embedded in people's consciousness as "normal." This shorter work comprises two fictional lectures by the main character, a novelist named Elizabeth Costello: "The Philosophers and the Animals" and "The Poets and the Animals." In the text, Costello takes the position that vegetarianism is the only diet possible if we want to end the constant massacre of animals. Coetzee introduces the character of Costello's daughter-in-law, Norma, a doctor of the philosophy of mind, to present the counter-argument. She is, of course, a stubborn advocate of meat-eating. Through the character of Costello, Coetzee avers that we are all incarnate beings, animals no less than people, or as Costello knows what it is like to be a corpse (*Elizabeth Costello* 74).[9] But because we place humans above animals, the killing of human beings is considered murder, while the killing of animals is not, because they are not the same species—not human beings. Costello cannot accept what she calls a "holocaust" (77)—the daily murder of animals. Others may be able to get used to it, but she cannot.

Coetzee's use of the word "holocaust"[10] is legitimate precisely because, just as the world failed to respond to the Nazis behavior toward the Jews, so does the world today fails to respond to the mass killing of animals, and what is more, people blot out the daily horror of this killing from their consciousness (see Diamond, "Difficulty" 49). Coetzee connects the horror of the daily slaughter of animals to events at Treblinka (compare Adorno) and metaphorically and linguistically compares the animals to the massacred Jews (*Elisabeth Costello* 64–65). Jacques Derrida also speaks of the animal holocaust in his essay "The Animal That Therefore I Am (More to Follow)," in which he describes how in the last two centuries we have been confronted with the horror of animal exploitation: "Everybody knows what the production, breeding, transport, and slaughter of these animals has become" (26). Although he believes that it is precisely because of the animal holocaust that we have arrived at a new "experience of this compassion" (28), this does not necessarily lead to animal rights but rather to a heightened sense of responsibility and justice toward animals through the fundamentals of empathy (26–27). Francione, however, rejects the notion of mere ethical justice in the use of animals, that is, of handling them with compassion; rather, he believes it is imperative to immediately stop using animals and their parts (*Introduction* 165). Coetzee does not go that far. He believes that vegetarianism offers the possibility of at least removing from sight the daily corpses wrapped in cellophane. The philosopher Stanley Cavell believes that Coetzee's character Elizabeth Costello uses her words to assuage her guilty conscience about the day-to-day murder of millions of animals (115). Costello reflects on the question of being a bat or a human being and concludes that it is all the same: we all are full of life and are all living souls. And it is this conclusion that reveals to us that it is all the same, too, whether we possess a human mind or an animal mind (*Elisabeth Costello* 78).

Throughout *The Lives of Animals*, Coetzee poses explicit questions about the meaning of vegetarianism and the decision to adopt it. He cites Plutarch's discourse "On the Eating of Flesh," which he refers to as "The Plutarch Response." This is Costello's most forceful response to the question of why she is a vegetarian; it is her way of "throwing down a gauntlet." Costello cites this response in the first person and not as it is found in Plutarch's discourse. She is astonished that someone can put in his mouth the corpse of a dead animal and not find it nasty to chew hacked flesh and swallow the juices of death-wounds (*Elizabeth Costello* 83). In the second part of *The Lives of Animals*, titled "The Poets and the Animals," Coetzee again through his alter ego Costello, now drawing on Rainer Maria Rilke, Ted Hughes, and Jonathan Swift, presents quite a few questions about human relationships to animals—and quite a few poetic images about the way animals see the world from their cages and whether they even realize that they are not free. Costello goes on to underscore the question of whether a jaguar could survive without meat and whether a human being could do the same and concludes that the jaguar would not survive but the human being could live on a vegetarian diet. Then she puts forward the claim that people like to eat meat precisely for the reason that they are destroying animals that cannot defend themselves against humans. Costello believes that we treat animals as prisoners of war, as herds and slave populations that propagate for our own use (104). She concludes that literature can speak about human and animal rights more poetically, and even more zooethically, than the philosopher or anthropologist.

The work ends with three questions posed to Costello by a philosophy professor and her responses to them. They touch on how we understand the world and death, the speech of animals in contrast to human speech, animals' lack of awareness of death, and the fact that they possess no intellectual horror. In terms of the lack of speech and the interest in life, Costello cites two examples from history and real life: that of Albert Camus witnessing the decapitation of a chicken and the mortal cry of the slaughtered animal. This scene led Camus to write an attack on the guillotine in 1958, which in turn was a factor in the decision to end the death penalty in France. Thus, the chicken spoke. The other thesis that Costello rejects is that animals have no interest in living, which is based on the anthropocentric view that no matter how much an animal fights for life, it does not have the intellectual experience of terror before death (109). Through Costello's words, Coetzee recommends the reading of the poets, but if the poets do not move you, just walk beside the animal to the slaughter house (111). But sadly, poetry does not possess this power, and Costello is left feeling that she is witness to a crime of inconceivable proportions, as people offer her slices of corpses, which they bought for money. She illustrates the enormous divide between human and nonhuman subjectivity by saying that it is like visiting friends and finding soap in the bathroom that is made from human fat from Treblinka (115). The idea horrifies us, but we are not horrified if someone shows us a rug made from the skin of a cow, because this is socially acceptable (see Golež Kaučič "Thematization").

Jure Detela: zooethical poetry and animal rights

While Coetzee's novels are famous and researched throughout the world, the poetry, essays, and scholarly writings of Jure Detela are known mostly to Slovenian readers. For this reason, it is necessary to begin with an overview of Detela and his work. Jure Detela was a Slovenian poet, art historian, and intellectual who dedicated his life and poetry to reflecting on the transformation of human attitudes toward animals. He was born in Ljubljana in 1951 and died there in 1992 when he decided to depart this life because of his love for animals. Detela lived and worked under socialism, when animal rights was barely part of the public discourse in Slovenia. His poems, essays, and scholarly texts were revolutionary for the time. His views on the relationship between human beings and animals are very contemporary, falling in the abolitionist approach to animal rights; his poetry, meanwhile, belongs to what is known as literary ecology and zooethical poetics. But Detela did not fight only for the rights of animals. He also agitated for an end to the death penalty in Yugoslavia. He was thus both a poet and an activist. He opened up the cages in the Ljubljana zoo, since he believed that deer, hares, foxes, and wolves, which are able to live in the forest in Slovenia, did not belong in cages. He was a sharp critic of repressive political systems that exploited animals even as they disseminated false images of the animal world in the form of kitsch and counterfeit reality. He wrote,

> Animals are more powerful in our inner lives than repressive systems. This is why repressive systems must resort to deceit. Repressive systems establish false asylums of children's love toward animals (for example, Disney's Bambi), the a priori purpose of which is to draw their attention away from facts such as the abattoir and the hunt. ("Poezija" 524)

Detela was thus not only engaged in Slovenian life, but was also connected through his poetry to the world. In the poem "Docile Eyes" ("Krotke oči," no. 11: *Pesmi* 163), he thematizes the horrific crime—a crime of global proportions—that was perpetrated against the American buffalo, against thousands of docile eyes, when William Cody (Buffalo Bill) slaughtered 4282 of these animals in 1867 and 1868. At the time this happened, the worldwide public was not upset because the victims were animals; quite the contrary, Cody became a hero. Detela did not conceive of animals as symbols or metaphors. Through poetry and literal meaning, he wanted poetry to define real relationships in both the material and internal worlds. Detela resisted symbolization and subjectification in his poetry because he believed that the messages in his poems that dealt with the problem of violence against animals should not be reduced to "an attribute of the poet's subjectivity" ("Ker noč em" 207). He was firmly convinced that poetry must thematize real animals, their position as objects, which also makes it structurally possible for people to become objects of production in exploitative systems.

Detela argued unconditionally for the rights of individuals within a genus or species, which means that he went farther than those who advocate for the rights for individual (and usually endangered) animal species. Detela advocated for the protection of animals in Slovenia and Yugoslavia as early as the 1970s and 1980s, a period when a philosophical interest in the idea of animal equality was on the rise around the world. This came out of a period that witnessed a variety of social movements supporting marginalized social groups—women, gays and lesbians, and ethnic minorities. As a result, it became necessary to address the issue of the final discrimination, the one human beings make between themselves and animals. Once again, the moral status of animals was examined, in particular the transformation of our traditional relationship to them, which was constituted as the fruit of wider philosophical reflection about the equality of animals and man (see Singer; Regan; Golež Kaučič "Zoofolkloristics").

In theory, we protect animals from unnecessary suffering, but we do not take this obligation seriously, or rather we do not fulfill it legally or formally. The discourse on animal rights itself came in for criticism precisely because it did not take into account their position in the world. One early critique came from Cora Diamond, who argued persuasively that the question of whether animals have rights is misguided and "a totally wrong way of beginning the discussion." What is at stake, she said, was not whether animals have rights, but whether animals are considered food (Diamond, "Eating Meat" 467–468; see also Suen 9).

The same idea—that animals are considered food and that this is wrong—is treated by Detela in his essay "Ekologija, ekonomija preživetja in živalske pravice" ("Ecology, the Economy of Survival, and Animal Rights," 1988). In Detela's opinion, only adherence to a ban on the killing of protected beings for food would mitigate the guilt of killing and allow us to exit the economy of survival, so that at the very least we could renounce our most violent practices toward animals: the wearing of skins, meat eating, hunting, visiting zoos, etc. The abolishment of all use of animals, and especially the elimination of the meat and food industries (a commerce in corpses and the processing or their parts into food products), is the most important step in the shift from human rights alone to animal rights as well, and it must be unconditional; he stressed as his manifesto the need to abandon the horizon of thought that represents the authority of human beings over animals and nature and relinquish the crown of rule over all living things in the world.

Detela was against any kind of use of animals, and so re-examined anything that bore the prefix *eco-*; thus, he is also critical of ecologists who are indifferent to the fate of the countless domestic animals that are part of the food industry and no longer living beings. Detela offers the solution of shifting agriculture from the breeding of livestock to crop cultivation. In his treatise, he also draws attention to the sanctity of animal life, and not just human life, but he does this in terms of practical morality. Discussing unconditional values and the laws people write, whether in relation to human or animal rights, Detela notes sharp discrepancies in the enforcement of individual laws:

> In an ethics that exists only beneath the firmament of empirical knowledge, there can be no ethics. In an ethics that exists only beneath the firmament of the empirical, the following law, for instance, would be entirely consistent: One must not kill a three-year old child with torments that last more than three days and three nights, except in cases where… (here readers may use their own imaginations to complete the law with anything empirical: because many things can happen, oh, so many things…). (Detela, "Ekologija" 1473)

Detela's ethics toward animals are closely connected to his ethics toward people. He believes that people are among the most sensitive animals, which is why he interprets animal rights as a continuation of the struggle against slavery and the death penalty. As early as 1977, Detela wrote,

> In short, these facts prove that aggression toward animals is one of the fundamental problems of our civilization and that the first step ecology must take if it wants to be effective is to actively appreciate the fact that animals live for themselves and for that purpose, on earth and in the universe, which they themselves choose, not for human benefit. (Detela, "Poezija" 524)

Detela brings these views into his poetry as well. In his best known work, "Poem for Deer" ("Pesem za jelene"), he expresses his conviction in the inherent value of animals and the barbarity of humans who kill them. His opposition to the killing of animals, in this case the deer that are killed in large numbers by members of the so-called nature conservation organizations—that is to say, hunters—leads him to confess his admiration for the free and innocent deer (*Pesmi* 119–120; see also Golež Kaučič "Thematization").[11] Branislava Vičar believes that through this poem Detela "expands the borders of our sensitivity to violence, to ensure that violence against animals and the suffering of animals do not fall outside its horizon" (Vičar 38). The poet himself, in an unpublished note, said of this: "I don't understand why we don't look at violence against people and violence against animals from the same perspective" ("Želja").

Detela occasionally expresses the desire to be indifferent to the deaths of animals (*Pesmi* 66, Pesem za angela [Poem for Angel, no. 55]), but he realizes that his body is connected to other living beings, so ignorance and indifference are not possible. It is precisely the ability to feel pain that most closely connects human beings to animals. As Detela once wrote, the screams of rabbits and deer that have been shot and the weeping of murdered seals are surprisingly similar to human screams and human weeping ("Poezija" 523). Later, in the essay "Ecology, the Economy of Survival and Animal Rights," he wrote, "the claim that the chamois that tears up and destroys the mountain greenery is as cruel as the hunter who kills it is almost insane in its fanatic determination to deny, in the name of some generalizing idea, any respect for the feelings that form specific experiences" (1477).

Detela also uses the image of the killing of chamois in the poem "zakaj zvok puške" ("Why the sound of the gun shot") (no. 4, *Pesmi* 156) and expresses the desire to die with these animals in the early summer (no. 1, *Pesmi,* 153). Detela's poetry, then, is also a witness that calls for the establishment of "a total metaphor" ("Sporočilo" 1), one that would make it possible for nonhuman subjectivity to no longer be relegated to the margins of the social and political spheres but instead be autonomous in its existence and treated as equal to human beings—and vegetarianism is the first step in this process. In the essay "V svojih pesmih" ("In my poems"), Detela admits that poetry cannot solve the problem of violence against animals, but it can confront the reader with facts and awaken a desire to stop the violence. It is not poetry that can stop the violence; only action can do that (19; see also Jovanovski 89).

Conclusion

Coetzee and Detela represent two different peoples—one of a colonizing nation, the other of a nation that did not have its own sovereign state until 1991, having spent most of its existence under foreign powers. One would expect, then, that they would write about racism and speciesism in completely differently ways. In many aspects, this is true, as racism did not exist in its most primary form in Slovenia or Yugoslavia—as it did in South Africa—although a negative attitude toward difference, the Other, and people from a different cultural background was always present. And yet both authors have a very similar relationship to animals: to their lives and moral status and to questions of freedom and equal treatment. Coetzee was a world-famous writer, Detela was a Slovenian visionary who unfortunately never achieved international acclaim because he did not write in a 'world language.' Both writers realized that the two discriminatory practices, speciesism and racism, and indeed any valuation of a living creature on the basis of imaginary constructs, are more powerfully connected than they seem. Both supported the abolition of any kind of slavery or non-freedom of races or species and the individuals within them. Both believed that we must respect animals as moral subjects that, like people, have their own interests, the first of which is that no one takes their lives. This is only possible if we do not characterize animal subjectivity as an object, as food, or as property. One step in this process is the decision to eat only plants (to be vegan). The authors express their relationship to the Other, one in which nonhuman subjectivity is based on the perspective that the animal is a living being, a being from an alien world, a person, a moral subject; in short, the animal is not marginalized but central to the human perspective. If racism is now recognized as inappropriate discrimination in the human world (although it is still covertly practiced), speciesism is a form of discrimination that remains unrecognized, since it effects "second-class beings" who appear in forms that no longer have anything to do with existence or life and so deflect the gaze away from a daily massacre of unimaginable proportions. The animal rights movement, or welfarism, is merely one of the first wobbly steps toward the realization of abolitionism, which must be the serious foundation for any real paradigmatic change in both spheres, human and animal, which are still viewed separately. The power of literature to affect these issues can be exceptional, as it delivers signals that can change human thinking and perhaps lead us to active resistance.

Notes

1. The author acknowledges the financial support from the Slovenian Research Agency (research core funding No. P6-0111). The chapter has been translated by Erica Johnson Debeljak.
2. Speciesism is discrimination that takes place on the basis of species. Richard Ryder, who coined the term, supports the thesis that to be a member of a certain species does not infer moral values in and of itself ("Experiments" 81; see also Ryder, "Speciesism").
3. The basic principle of the abolitionist approach to animal rights is as follows: that all human and nonhuman sentient beings have the right not be treated as the property of others. Veganism is the moral foundation of abolitionism and the rejection of speciesism, and all other forms of discrimination including racism and sexism (Francione *Animals*).
4. In Toronto in November 2016, a trial began against a Slovenian woman named Anita Kranjc, who was accused of damaging property that belonged to another: she had given water to pigs destined for the slaughterhouse. In the courtroom, her attorney claimed that the pigs were persons, not things. If the judge upholds this definition, it will set an important precedent for later trials of this kind (Prijatelj Videmšek 16).
5. Haraway writes about the many mongrel dogs that became homeless at the end of apartheid, which were ignored by the new regime: "The new state could not care less what happens to these animate tools of a former racist regime. [...] The sanctuary practices are private charity directed to nonhumans whom many people would see as better killed (euthanized? Is there any 'good death' here?) in a nation where unaddressed human economic misery remains immense" (37).

6. It is worth noting that an enormous amount of meat is eaten in South Africa, a fact that Coetzee emphasizes in *Disgrace* when he has Bev, the owner of the shelter for abandoned dogs, say that the large amount of meat people eat only does them harm and she does not know how human beings can make amends before animals (84).
7. At this time, the law that forbids Blacks from owning property—the Native Land Act, Act no. 27, of 1913—was no longer in force, and the Land Bank could offer Black farmers assistance to become landowners.
8. In Roman Bartosch's view, this is the most analyzed text with regard to the animal rights issue and the most influential work in the field of human/animal studies and ecocriticism (36).
9. As noted earlier, Coetzee later incorporated *The Lives of Animals* into the novel *Elizabeth Costello*. The citations refer to this later novel.
10. Brett Ashley Kaplan also discusses references to the Holocaust in Coetzee's novels (186–188, 192–193).
11. The poem was first published in 1977 in the journal *Problemi Literatura* (Ljubljana).

Works cited

Adorno, Theodore W. *Can One Live after Auschwitz?: A Philosophical Reader*, edited by Rolf Tiedemann, Stanford University Press, 2003.

Adorno, Theodore, W. et al. *Estetika in politika* [*Aesthetics and Politics*]. 1977. Translated by Jaš a Drnovš ek and Rok Benč in. Ljubljana, Studia Humanitatis, 2013.

Attridge, Derek. "Age of Bronze, State of Grace: Music and Dogs in Coetzee's Disgrace." *Novel: A Forum on Fiction*, vol. 34, no.1, 2000, pp. 98–121.

Attwell, David. *J. M. Coetzee: South Africa and the Politics of Writing*. University of California Press, 1993.

Bartosch, Roman. "A Poet Is a Nightingale: An Introduction to Animal Poetics." *Anglistik: International Journal of English Studies*, vol. 27, no. 2, 2016, pp. 35–46.

Berger, John. "Why Look at Animals?" 1980. *About Looking*. Vintage International, 1991, pp. 3–28.

Braidotti, Rosi. "Animals, Anomalies, and Inorganic Others." *PMLA*, vol. 124, no. 2, 2009, pp. 526–532.

Buell, Lawrence. *The Environmental Imagination: Thoreau, Nature Writing, and the Formation of American Culture*. Belknap Press of Harvard University Press, 1995.

Butler, Judith. *Frames of War: When is Life Grievable?* Verso, 2009.

Čeh Steger, Jožica. "Ekologizacija literarne vede in ekokritika" ["The Ecologization of Literary Studies and Eco-Criticism"]. *Slavistična revija*, vol. 60, no. 2, 2012, pp. 199–212.

———. "Ekološko usmerjena literarna veda in Prež ihove samorastniške novele" ["Ecologically Oriented Literary Studies and Prež ihov's Self-Sown Novellas"]. *Jezik in slovstvo*, vol. 55, nos. 3–4, 2010, pp. 53–62.

Calarco, Matthew. *Zoographies: The Question of the Animal from Heidegger to Derrida*. Columbia University Press, 2008.

Cavell, Stanley. "Companionable Thinking." Cavell et al., pp. 91–126. Cavell, Stanley, et al. *Philosophy & Animal Life*. Columbia University Press, 2008.

Coetzee, John Maxwell *Boyhood: Scenes from Provincial Life*. 1997. Penguin, 1998.

———. *Disgrace*. Secker & Warburg, 1999.

———. "Into the Dark Chamber: The Writer and the South African State." 1986. *Doubling the Point*, edited by David Attwell, Harvard University Press, 1992, pp. 361–68.
———. *Elizabeth Costello: Eight Lessons*. Secker & Warburg, 2003.
———. *Foe*. Penguin Books, 1987.
———. *Life & Times of Michael K*. 1983. Vintage, 1998.
Davis, David Brion. "Free at Last; The Enduring Legacy of the South's Civil War Victory." *New York Times*, 26 August 2001.
Derrida, Jaques. "The Animal That Therefore I Am (More to Follow)." *The Animal That Therefore I Am*, edited by Marie-Louise Mallet, translated by David Wills, Fordham University Press, 2008, pp. 1–51.
Detela, Jure. "Ekologija, ekonomija prež ivetja in ž ivalske pravice" ["Ecology, the Economy of Survival and Animal Rights"]. *Nova revija*, no. 77, 1988, pp. 1473–1484.
———. "Kernočem, da bi bralci mojih pesmi…" ["Because I do not want readers of my poems…"]. Detela, *Orfič ni dokumenti*, vol. 1, 2011, pp. 206–207.
———. "Poezija znanega liberalca in podoficirja Jurija Detele na témo: Čebelarstvo in prevzgoja bobrov na Slovaš kem in pa č ebelarstvo in prevzgoja bobrov pri nas na Slovenskem z ozirom" ["The Poetry of the Well-Known Liberal and Sub-Officer Jurij Detela on the Topic: Beekeeping and the Re-Education of Beavers in Slovakia and Beekeeping and the Re-Education of Beavers Here in Slovenia, Respectively"]. *Sredica, Problemi Literatura*, nos. 170–71 (vol. 16, nos. 3–4), 1977, pp. 521–524. Digitalna knjiž nica Slovenije, https://www.dlib.si/details/URN:NBN:SI:DOC-WWO82RNH. Accessed 23 May 2016.
———. "Sporoč ilo" ["Message"]. *Tribuna*, no. 2, vol. 25, 1975–1976, pp. 1–3.
———. "V svojih pesmih" ["In my poems"]. *Zapisi o umetnosti: eseji [Writings on art: Essays]*, edited by Miklavž Komelj, Koper, Hyperion, 2005, 17–24.
———. "Želja po zvestobi dobesednemu pomenu…" ["The desire to be faithful to the literal meaning…"]. Detela, *Orfič ni dokumenti*, vol. 1, 2011, p. 203.
———. Orfični dokumenti: Teksti in fragmenti iz zapuš č ine [Orphic Documents: Unpublished texts and Fragments]., edited by Miklavž Komelj, Koper, Hyperion, 2011.
———. *Pesmi [Poems]*. Salzburg, Wieser, 1992.
Diamond, Cora. "Eating Meat and Eating People." *Philosophy*, vol. 53, no. 206, 1978, pp. 465–479.
———. "The Difficulty of Reality and the Difficulty of Philosophy." *Philosophy & Animal Life*, edited by Stanley Cavell et al., Columbia University Press, 2008, pp. 43–89.
Dunayer, Joan. *Animal Equality: Language and Liberation*. Ryce Publishing, 2001.
Francione, Gary L. Introduction to Animal Rights: Your Child or the Dog? Temple University Press, 2000.
———. *Animals as Persons: Essays on the Abolition of Animal Exploitation*. Columbia University Press, 2008.
———. *Animals as Persons: Essays on the Abolition of Animal Exploitation*. Columbia University Press, 2008.
Golež Kaučič, Marjetka. "Thematization of Nonhuman Subjectivity in Folklore, Philosophical, and Literary Texts." *Cosmos*, vol. 27, 2011, pp. 121–154.
———. "Zoofolkloristics: First Insights Towards the New Discipline." *Narodna umjetnost*, vol. 52, no. 1, 2015, pp. 7–30.
Hacking, Ian. "Deflection." Cavell et al., *Philosophy & Animal Life*, 2008, pp. 139–172.

Haraway, Donna. *When Species Meet*. University of Minnesota Press, 2008.
Hofer, Stefan. *Die Ökologie der Literatur [The Ecology of Literature]*. Transcript Verlag, 2007.
Ingold, Tim, editor. *What Is an Animal?* Routledge, 1994.
Jovanovski, Alenka. "Violence, Animal Rights and Ecopoetry in the Work of Jure Detela." *Ecology through Poetry: The Right to Live*, edited by Jelka Kernev Štrajn et al., Calcutta, Sampark, 2013, pp. 86–119.
Kaplan, Brett Ashley. *Landscapes of Holocaust Memory*. Routledge, 2010.
Levinas, Emmanuel. *Totality and Infinity. An Essay on Exteriority*. Translated by Alphonso Lingis. Martinus Nijhoff Publishers, 1979.
Lippit, Akira Mizuta. *Electric Animal: Toward a Rhetoric of Wild Life*. University of Minnesota Press, 2008.
Mattos, Maria Teresa Segarra Costaguta. "Racial Tension in Post-Apartheid South Africa: A Reading of Disgrace." 2012. LUME: Universidade Federal do Rio Grande do Sul Digital Repository, http://hdl.handle.net/10183/70626. Accessed 22 May 2016. Graduation thesis.
Ortiz-Robles, Mario. *Literature and Animal Studies*. Routledge, 2016.
Piekarski, Michal. "The Problem of the Question About Animal Ethics: Discussion with Mark Coeckelbergh and David Gunkel." *Journal of Agricultural and Environmental Ethics*, vol. 29, no. 4, 2016, pp. 705–715.
Poyner, Jane. *J. M. Coetzee and the Paradox of Postcolonial Authorship*. Ashgate Publishing, 2009.
Prijatelj Videmšek, Maja. "Če ljubite svoje otroke, postanite vegani" ["If you love your children, become vegans"]. *Delo*, 30 November 2016, p. 16.
Regan, Tom. *The Case for Animal Rights*. University of California Press, 1983.
Ryder, Richard D. "Experiments on Animals." *Animals, Men and Morals: An Enquiry into the Maltreatment of Non-Humans*, edited by Stanley Godlovitch et al. Grove Press, 1971.
———. "Speciesism." 1998. *Encyclopedia of Animal Rights and Animal Welfare*, edited by Marc Bekoff, 2nd edition, Greenwood Press, 2009, vol. 2, p. 320.
Schweizer, Harold. *Suffering and the Remedy of Art*. State University of New York Press, 1997.
Singer, Peter. *Animal Liberation: A New Ethics for Our Treatment of Animals*. New York Review, 1975.
Starre, Aleksander. "Always Already Green: Zur Entwicklung und den literatur theoretischen Prämisen des amerikanischen Ecocriticism." *Ökologische Transformationen und literarische Repräsentationen [Ecological Transformations and Literary Representations]*, edited by Maren Ermisch et al., Göttingen, 2010, pp. 13–34.
Suen, Alison. *The Speaking Animal: Ethics, Language and the Human-Animal Divide*. Rowman & Littlefield International, 2015.
Taylor, Chloe. "The Precarious Lives of Animals: Butler, Coetzee, and Animal Ethics." *Philosophy Today*, vol. 52, no. 1, 2008, pp. 60–72.
Vičar, Branislava. "Si kdaj videl svobodnega konja?: Filozofski kontekst animalističně etike v poeziji Jureta Detele in Miklavž a Komelja" ["Did You Ever See a Free Horse?: The Philosophical Context of the Animalist Ethics in the Poetry of Jure Detela and Miklavž Komelj"]. *Etika v slovenskem jeziku, literaturi in kulturi* [Ethics in Slovenian Language, Literature, and Culture], edited by Aleksander Bjelčevič et al., Ljubljana, Znanstvena založ ba Filozofske fakultete, 2013, pp. 35–45.

Vovk, Urban. *Res neznosna resnobnost!?: Trije eseji o Kuciju [A Truly Unbearable Seriousness!?: Three Essays on Coetzee]*. Ljubljana, LUD Literatura, 2011.

———. "Sramota kot stanje: Sramota, ki nima konca" ["Shame as a Condition: Shame That Has No End"]. Afterword J. M. Coetzee, *Sramota [Disgrace]*, translated by Alenka Moder Saje, Radovljica, Didakta, 2004, pp. 247–251.

Weil, Kari. "A Report on the Animal Turn." *Differences: A Journal of Feminist Cultural Studies*, vol. 21, no. 2, 2010, pp. 1–23.

———. *Thinking Animals: Why Animal Studies Now?* Columbia University Press, 2012.

Willet, Cynthia. "Ground zero for a post-moral ethics in J.M. Coetzee's *Disgrace* and Julia Kristeva's *melancholic*." *Continental Philosophy Review*, vol. 45, no. 1, 2012, pp. 1–22.

Wise, Steven M. "An Argument for the Basic Legal Rights of Farmed Animals." *Michigan Law Review First Impressions*, vol. 106, no. 1, 2008, pp. 133–37. Michigan Law Scholarship Repository, http://repository.law.umich.edu/mlr_fi/vol106/iss1/4. Accessed 12 April 2016.

———. "The Basic Rights of Some Non-Human Animals Under the Common Law." *Reform*, no. 91, Summer 2007–2008, pp. 11–13. Australasian Legal Information Institute database, http://www.austlii.edu.au/au/journals/ALRCRefJl/2007/3.html. Accessed 11 April 2016.

———. *Though the Heavens May Fall: The Landmark Trial That Led to the End of Human Slavery*. Da Capo Press, 2006.

Zapf, Hubert. *Literatur als kulturelle Ökologie: Zur kulturellen Funktion imaginativer Texte an Beispielen des amerikanischen Romans [Literature as Cultural Ecology: On the Cultural Function of Imaginative Texts with Examples from the American Novel]*. Max Niemeyer, 2002.

16 To be or not to be human
The plasticity of posthuman rights

Nicole Sparling Barco

In the context of our contemporary brave new world, any debates surrounding posthuman rights must first grapple with the question of whether posthuman subjects have the rights to be or not to be *human*. We are also faced with the dilemma that ontological doubts about the status, definition, and shifting boundary of the human in a posthuman era could undermine the stability of the liberal humanist subject, to whom rights have been historically attached. In "Posthuman Rights," Steen Christiansen characterizes human rights as an "an anthropological machine embedded in discourses of the human as much as the discourses of rights" and raises the important question of what our hierarchy of values will be: "we do need to ask ourselves if the rights of the human trumps the rights to be human and what this will mean for the human rights to come" (112). Such a question urges us to be cautious not to disappear the liberal humanist subject, to whom rights have been historically attached, and careful not to sacrifice the critical work that human rights theory, advocacy, discourse, and law have accomplished as we continue to mold and shape the subject of rights in emerging posthuman frontiers, and as we embrace the plasticity and possibility of posthuman rights.

Clearly, posthumanism is a multivalent term that describes several trains of thought that are somehow *after* humanism, in that they operate under the guise of attacking, opposing, and subsuming humanism and its critiques.[1] The process of reading through a critical posthumanist lens, which Stefan Herbrechter and Ivan Callus demonstrate, may in fact lend itself to a clearer articulation of human rights. Most importantly, they argue that "terror" of "dehumanisation and annihilation" causes us to be wary of what lies in humanism's shadows and the real human cost (and the cost *other*wise) of sustaining it ("What is a Posthumanist Reading?" 101). Herbrechter and Callus provocatively propose that "humans might be critical posthumanists out of humanitarian interest" (101).

In this chapter, I use Karen Tei Yamashita's *Through the Arc of the Rain Forest* to argue that the theoretical framework of critical posthumanism and the concept of the critical posthuman subject could be used to develop a theory of posthuman rights. Particularly relevant to this purpose is Pramod K. Nayar's definition of critical posthumanism as a "*radical decentering of* the traditional sovereign, coherent and autonomous human in order to demonstrate how the human is always already evolving with, constituted by and constitutive of multiple forms of life and machines" (2; original emphasis). Nayar concludes that this brand of critical posthumanism creates a hybrid human subject, in which the posthuman is already imbricated and foundational, being and becoming with the human (10).

Nayar's crticial posthumanism with its concepts of *"natureculture"* as the interface of *"materials"* and *"immaterials"* via *"hybrid dynamics"* (10; original emphasis) could be, perhaps, illuminated by Rosi Braidotti's vitalist materialist vision of critical posthumanism: "I define the critical posthuman subject within an eco-philosophy of multiple belongings, as a relational subject constituted in and by multiplicity, that is to say a subject that works across differences and is also internally differentiated, but still grounded and accountable" (49). Braidotti's critical posthuman subject is constantly in dialogue with, simultaneously, "vital and self-organizing matter" and "a non-Human definition of Life as *zoe*, or a dynamic and generative force" (86). Braidotti situates the posthuman as a mode of "becoming-animal, becoming-earth, becoming-machine" (66), to which I would suggest a shift in directionality, inspired by object-oriented ontology, the notion of animal-becoming-human, earth-becoming-human, and machine-becoming-human.

If, as Begoña Simal argues, "we are indeed living in a 'transnatural' world where nothing remains 'untouched,' everything has been directly or indirectly 'contaminated' by human actions, and culture and technology have invaded what used to be the inviolable realm of 'nature'" (15), then the process of "becoming-earth" in a transnatural world is always already interpolated with a human subject rendered posthuman. By dramatizing this interconnectivity between human, animal, and earth and the processes of becoming—even as those processes are mediated by technology and globalization—Karen Tei Yamashita's *Through the Arc of the Rain Forest* can help us visualize, under a critical posthumanist lens, the creation of a transnatural world filled with posthuman subjects and the destructive impacts of an unfettered, unsustainable global capitalism, including its real effects on material bodies—human, posthuman, and otherwise.

As a transnational novel that follows the migration patterns of its characters between Japan, the United States, Europe, and Brazil, the novel's primary setting, *Through the Arc of the Rain Forest* has perplexed readers, scholars, and critics alike with the precise ontological status of its narrator, which we learn is, materially, a plastic ball forged of nonbiodegradable waste. Virtually indestructible, with both magnetic and malleable properties, the ball orbits Kazumasa Ishimaru, and, together, they become the hero of the story.[2] Although the ball represents an alien and alienating figure in the novel, especially as it intersects with Kazumasa's Asian migrant identity, it also creates an endearing affect/effect when it is rendered, by prophecy, a sign of Kazumasa's good fortune.[3] The ball revolves around Kazumasa, who is the center of its universe, which would suggest that he holds some magnetic force in relation to this "foreign" object that becomes assimilated to his own identity. Although we could read this particular constellation as a reinforcement of humanist principles,[4] Kazumasa's ball uses its elemental force to propel Kazumasa's movements as it also obstructs his vision, for the ball has the power to change the trajectory of Kazumasa's life, as in his immigration from Japan to Brazil, and propels the narrative itself.[5] For instance, the ball has the ability to sense the stability of other metals and assists Kazumasa in saving lives by acting as a safety calibration system. At times, the ball jerks Kazumasa and redirects him toward material with like properties, such as the Matacão (Yamashita's fictional invention located in the Amazon region of Brazil); indeed, because Kazumasa understands the Matacão to be the ball's "true mother," he dutifully supports the ball's inherent right to "join" like material (106).

The ball, as narrator, possesses an intuition resembling omniscience, or an "artificial" intelligence that it cannot communicate verbally with the other characters in the novel.[6] The fact that the ball compares itself to a pet and situates Kazumasa as its master not only suggests undying loyalty on its part and the presumption of mutual care and affection but also a certain interspecies hierarchy (24). The ball's description of their relation(ship) juxtaposed with Kazumasa's presumption of their kinship is quite revealing, as it not only upholds the hierarchy but also assumes that he is biologically linked with the ball, as if the ball is his own progeny (106). Kazumasa's feeling of human responsibility for and accountability to the ball as his own creation is justified, and also grounded in the origin story of the Matacão, and its associated myths (202, 95–96). The very existence of the Matacão redefines what we mean by "raw" materials and "natural" resources by imagining a material created by nonbiodegradable waste as a new organic posthuman superproduct, which becomes the very substance of a capitalist globalized modernity and its eventual downfall.[7]

In this vein, the Matacão could be categorized as a hyperobject, which, according to Timothy Morton, "force[s] us into an intimacy with our own death (because they are toxic), with others (because everyone is affected by them), and with the future (because they are massively distributed in time)" (139). The Matacão performs all of these functions by forcing us to come to terms with the possibility of our own annihilation through the rendering of ourselves as toxic waste; by allowing us to see the way that the material of the Matacão interfaces with the organic and inorganic, the living and nonliving, the human and its others; and by enabling us to see, in a deeper sense, the ecological time of its past and its future. Morton also suggests that "[a] hyperobject could be the very long-lasting product of direct human manufacture, such as Styrofoam or plastic bags, or the sum of all the whirring machinery of capitalism," characterizing hyperobjects as *"viscous,* which means that they 'stick' to beings that are involved with them" (1). Kazumasa's ball could be one agential materiality that allows us to physically see the impact of this hyperobject, but it does not allow us to observe the hyperobject in its totality, as it "massively outscale[s] us" (12). But, what would it mean for a hyperobject to narrate? Is it possible for the hyperobject to also be integral to and speak for a posthuman subject?

For me, at the heart of this "shiny mercuric matter" (Yamashita 180) is where the magical realism of Yamashita's text resides and the Matacão plastic is also, as Simal describes, "ambiguously construed as either (postmodern) virtual or (premodern) magical" (11). What is more, Yamashita's narrator claims that Matacão plastic was the stuff of simulacra, and that it captured "the very sensation of life" (143). A fictional U.S. corporation, GGG, has this living, magical material scientifically tested, mined, and completely transformed into a global commodity,[8] so much so that it becomes the "technological" discovery of what historians would call The Plastics Age (here we see a reference to the author's contemporary reality, aka 1990) (143). The "infinite mutability," to borrow from Heise (144), and the materiality of this metaphor allow us to imagine what I would call "a more posthuman ecology." Not only is this plastic integral to the earth and ubiquitous in human culture, but it also becomes bodily incorporated as ingested plastic food. According to Herbrechter and Callus, "A posthumanist reading is enabled by the deconstruction of the integrity of the human and the other, of the natural and the alienable" ("What is a Posthumanist Reading?" 96). Within the framework of critical posthumanism, then, the integrity of the human is compromised at the same time that human integrity becomes the overarching ethical imperative in a posthuman ecology, where we imagine all entities "should act towards one another in a spirit of brotherhood" (United Nations General Assembly, art. 1).

The process of human-becoming-earth and earth-becoming-human is very clearly represented in the Matacão. This plastic material was the result of nonbiodegradable waste, which places its origins in human industry.[9] However, "nature" has also acted upon this material and altered its properties, so that its deposits are found throughout the world and become part of the earth's surface. Then, in turn, human beings have used it to manufacture their own reality and become consumers of their own industrial waste in its modified form. The Matacão plastic also changes the makeup of the human body by functioning as a prosthetic, a surgical enhancement, and a food source; and when it becomes infected by Rickettsia, an all-consuming pathogen that is vector borne and causes typhus,[10] this material collapses and disintegrates, leaving scars of devastation on posthuman subjects and making visible the impact of the hyperobject. The death and disappearance of Kazumasa's ball (205–206), which was formerly imperceptible as a subject, becomes now visible, haunting the space it once occupied with the memory of its violent removal. Compared to "radical plastic surgery," we can more clearly understand that such a loss could account for the resultant, permanent "tropical tilt of his head" (211).[11] Only by giving shape and subjectivity to the material, through Kazumasa's ball, can the reader really understand what it would mean to "become earth" and, conversely, how earth could "become human." At the same time, Kazumasa's ball reminds us of the permanent marks that hyperobjects can leave on posthuman subjects.

Here, we can read Braidotti's definition of the critical posthuman subject onto the hybrid figure of Kazumasa and his ball. Yamashita imbues the ball—literally, as a self-organizing material subject and, figuratively, as a vital narrator—with an agency, omniscience, and intelligence that directs the action of the *novela* at the same time that she invokes empathy for Kazumasa and the ball itself. What is more, Kazumasa's ball takes for granted that we understand that the narrative perspective belongs to it until we are already invested in the story (8). If we are to continue reading after that moment, we must suspend our disbelief and accept the marvelous fact of a plastic narrator, a fact that object-oriented ontology helps us to understand.

In truth, the "nature" of this dynamic duo creates more questions than answers. Why, for instance, does the ball attach itself to Kazumasa? If we know that the ball has magnetic attraction to like material, do we then assume that Kazumasa is made of similar essence? Is there some portion of him that resonates with and understands the ball on a metaphysical level? If so, what does that mean? Is Yamashita getting at what Braidotti considers to be "a *zoe*-centred embodied subject" that is "becoming-posthuman" (193)? Considering that the distant origin of the ball is industrial waste, which is a byproduct of our own technological creation, could the ball be feeding us "a bunch of garbage" or a "load of crap," asking us to incorporate it into ourselves under the guise of digesting something shiny and new?

Regardless of how we try to explain it, the relation between Kazumasa and his ball is a material reality with which we have to come to terms. And yet, the ball undermines any simple reading of its ontology by insisting that it is a reproduction that relies on a distant origin, as if it were "reborn like any other dead spirit in the Afro-Brazilian syncretic religious rite of Candomblé" and "brought back by a memory, I have become a memory" (3). What strikes me as interesting here is the concept that Kazumasa's ball could be read as an *egum* (a spirit reborn), but the question of why the reader must keep the memory of Kazumasa's ball alive remains. Our marvelous plastic narrator is presumably an *egum* (a spirit reborn), but could also be an *antepassado egungum* (ancestor) or even an *orixá* (orisha, or deity), depending on the extent to which the spirit is memorialized by the entire community.[12] The fact that we remain ignorant of who the spirit was in life and why they should be memorialized leaves us with nostalgia for someone we can no longer remember, with *saudades*, but for whom? These questions remain unanswered as the *novela* concludes with the narrating ball's refusal to identify its precise origins (mythical or otherwise) or ontological status.

Projecting this memory onto the future, Caroline Rody signals a posthumanism haunted by the death of the human subject: "Perhaps, located in a moment after environmental disaster when humankind is a memory, we are addressed by a post-rain forest omniscience with nobody to know; 'Whose memory?'—I can't imagine anyone's" (637). Here, Rody's interpretation amplifies the feeling of *saudades* invoked by the novel by imagining a future in which we cannot remember our own existence on earth, a vaster time that encompasses the past and future of the hyperobject. Although the tendency to emphasize the material aspects of the narrator and, by extension, the Matacão plastic is understandable given the global capitalist context of Yamashita's future world, I would contend that these spiritual explanations add something vital to a critical posthumanist reading of Yamashita's narrative project.

Callus and Herbrechter remind us that "as a critical discourse, posthumanism does not necessarily seek emancipation from humanism, philosophy, modernity or postmodernity, but remains rooted in their cultural memory even while aware of the specificities of the present and of the various changes it heralds" ("Posthumanist Subjectivities" 241–242). Taken as a metaphor of posthumanism, the cultural memory of the conjured narrator rendered spirited ball and the *saudades* that it evokes through its absence recalls Callus and Herbrechter's discussion of Jean-Luc Nancy in relation to the "haunted" subject, which "always has someone or something else, an other, *coming after it*, in the punned senses in that phrase of succession and pursuit, and in the disjunctive times and spaces of hauntology" ("Posthumanist Subjectivities" 246). Tellingly, Yamashita's rain forest haunts us with reflections and refractions of humans, human others, nonhuman others, posthuman subjects, posthuman others, so that they all, in the end, begin to resemble ourselves, as always already embodied and embedded in a transnatural world.

For me, the living attachment between Kazumasa and the ball, which propels their immigration to Brazil, represents what Braidotti refers to as "a *zoe*-centred embodied subject" that is "becoming-posthuman," a process she describes as "redefining one's sense of attachment and connection to a shared world, a territorial space" (193). In this case, "the subject is a transversal entity, fully immersed in and immanent to a network of non-human (animal, vegetable, viral) relations" and "shot through with relational linkages of the contaminating/viral kind which inter-connect it to a variety of others, starting from the environmental or eco-others and includ[ing] the technological apparatus" (193). As such, the animated presence of the ball obfuscates Kazumasa's view, influences how people read him, alters the trajectory of his life, and is a constant reminder of his interface with animal, earth, and machine, so much so that it becomes difficult to define the "nature" of such a figure.

In Yamashita's novel, the problem remains that "life itself" is reduced to material, which becomes commodified within a globalized economy that relies on limitless supplies and unbridled growth, thus raising the question of which other versions of "life itself" have undergone, undergo, or will undergo the same process. I would argue that magical realism, as a generic form, enables us to perceive "life itself" in Kazumasa's ball where modern science or global capitalism might render it an object to be classified, measured, and sold. Moreover, the novel allows us to imagine what a vitalist materialist vision of the critical posthuman subject might look like and reminds us that this embodied and embedded subject is *zoe*-centered and animated, forever impacted by hyperobjects. As Braidotti proposes, "A posthuman ethics for a non-unitary subject proposes an enlarged sense of inter-connection between self and others, including the non-human or 'earth' others, by removing the obstacle of self-centred individualism," and *zoe* is at the heart of the matter (49–50). When we keep the question "what are we made of?" at the forefront, we can imagine a more ethical notion of human rights in a posthuman era, where the right to be human is integral to human rights.

What can we learn, then, from Yamashita's text that will help us to understand the way that the Amazon rainforest has been rendered a site of human rights violations, genocide of Indigenous peoples, ecological devastation, and cultural annihilation? Julia Bittencourt Costa Moreira's timely thesis exposes how "violations to indigenous rights and environmental degradation in Brazil share a history of violence" (29). Under the military regime (1964–1985), the Amazon was considered a threat to national sovereignty, security, and unity, constituted by a war on three fronts: political, economic, and international (15). If unmanaged, the Amazon could potentially harbor political subversives, i.e., socialists, its natural resources could be exploited by foreign capital and international interests, and Brazilian sovereignty could be undermined by human rights advocates and conservationists (15). Also, given that the Amazon was rhetorically configured as empty, the mere presence of Indigenous peoples contradicted that logic, so the perception of "indigenous peoples as enemies of the nation" was "reflected in discourses that advocated for the reduction of indigenous reserves to enable development and the settlement of 'Brazilian citizens'" (15). Such discourses legitimized violence against Indigenous peoples, as *The Figueiredo Report* (1967) demonstrates by providing substantial evidence confirming the genocide and other atrocities committed against Indigenous peoples of the Amazon by the SPI (Serviço de Proteção aos Índios), a government agency meant to "protect" Indigenous peoples.

In Bittencourt's view, President Jair Bolsonaro echoes in his populist rhetoric the former military regime with his "integrationist perspective towards indigenous peoples" and in the way environmentalism is perceived as a foreign ploy to restrict Brazil's development and control over its own resources (39). Bolsonaro has also made the controversial decision to shift key responsibilities from the Environment Ministry to the Agriculture Ministry, in support of the ruralist agenda. The president has declared publicly "that not a single centimeter of land will be demarcated for indigenous peoples and that both 'conservation units' (protected areas for natural ecosystems) and indigenous lands should be open to agriculture and mining" (Fearnside and Ferrante 261).

In response to foreign criticism of the deterioration of Indigenous rights under his government, Bolsonaro often shifts attention to what he thinks should be the "real" human rights agenda, namely, an integrationist one characterized by modernization, development, and assimilation of Indigenous peoples into a dominant Brazilian national culture. However, Bittencourt concludes that "recognizing and ensuring indigenous rights and ownership over land represents a double necessity," namely, "it is crucial to guaranteeing indigenous safety and the respect of basic human rights, as well as to advancing ecological protection and efforts to tackle climate changes" (49). As stewards of the rainforest and, our planet, such human rights violations not only represent the active annihilation of a people and a culture, but perhaps also our home planet and world.

Narratives of environmental degradation and Indigenous human rights violations have now forced us to come to terms with an apocalyptic posthuman world, in this case, a world *without* humans. Upendra Baxi suggests that we could forge a new kind of "resistance" to "apocalyptic visions of the posthuman" inspired by "human rights norms and standards, and even values" (238). Baxi provocatively asks us to consider the future of human rights where the "'biosphere' may thus overall be conceived as entitling some new personification of, and for, the future of human rights" or the possibility of a "collective species (even planetary) envisagement of human rights" (237). If we are to survive at all, I would argue, we must adopt a more expansive theoretical framework, at once transnatural and planetary, for understanding what is at stake in the right to *be* human. This, in turn, reveals the dire necessity of becoming "critical posthumanists out of humanitarian interest" (Herbrechter and Callus 101) and "critical posthuman subject[s]" who are both "grounded and accountable" (Braidotti 49).

Notes

1. See Ivan Callus in "Reclusiveness and posthuman subjectivity" on the "post" in posthumanism as "both in the sense of successiveness but also in the sense of pursuing and harrying, of not letting alone" (308).
2. Begoña Simal, in "The Junkyard in the Jungle: Transnational, Transnatural Nature in Karen Tei Yamashita's *Through the Arc of the Rain Forest*," refers to this collective character as "the person-cum-ball known as Kazumasa" (12).
3. Interesting here is Stephen Hong Sohn's observation that "the alien stands as a convenient metaphor for the experiences of Asian Americans, which range from the extraterrestrial being who seems to speak in a strange, yet familiar, accented English to the migrant subject excluded from legislative enfranchisement. In this respect the Alien/Asian does invoke conceptions of its homonymic counterparts, alienation and alien-nation. Indeed, the notion of the Alien/Asian centrally is concerned with Asian American spatial subjectivities and temporal heterogeneities, especially as various cultural productions imagine futures and alternative realities in which issues of racial marginality are often encrypted, reconfigured, and/or transformed" (6). Aimee Bahng also reads Yamashita's text very fruitfully as "postcolonial science fiction," which "intervenes in a genre that has often imagined Asians as alien" (124),

and, instead, "manifestations of the alien in the Asian American fabulation take the shape of mutant agents of empire such as Mabelle and her lover J. B. Tweep" (125).
4. For example, Ursula K. Heise observes that the ball "functions rather obviously as a miniature replica of the Earth itself, the voice that emerges from the depths of geology" and "it orbits around a human head as if to signal the inevitability of anthropocentrism in even so fantastic a narrative strategy" (147).
5. Incredible work on framing Yamashita's novel within the context of Asian American, Latin American, and the Asian Diaspora in the New World has already been done, and should be acknowledged here, although it is not the focus of my essay. Bahng's archival work, for example, in "Extrapolating Transnational Arcs, Excavating Imperial Legacies: The Speculative Acts of Karen Tei Yamashita's *Through the Arc of the Rainforest*" has contextualized the novel within the framework of the transnational histories "of multiple, intertwined, and flexible empires" that have shaped its narrative (125). Also invoked in Yamashita's text, according to Bahng, are narratives representing "a century of transpacific passages" (137), not only for the purposes of labor or investing capital (129), but also forced migration and restrictions on mobility, as in "Asian exclusion and immigration restriction" in the United States and Brazil, relocation in the wake of World War II, and movement of labor of Japanese Brazilians, in particular, from the Americas to Japan (138). According to Rachel C. Lee, in *The Americas of Asian American Literature: Gendered Fictions of Nation and Transnation*, "Its divergence from an East-West emphasis—its diminishment of both Asia and America by the presence of a third location, Brazil—requires a rethinking of the orientalist and counterorientalist dualism undergirding much of Asian American criticism" and "*Through the Arc* shatters the space-time of Asian America through its choice of a fantastical projection of a 21st-century world without boundaries, thereby urging Asian Americanists to frame their analyses not only in terms of national politics but in terms of transnational or global conditions" (97, 111). Also significant is Heise's contribution in "Local Rock and Global Plastic: World Ecology and the Experience of Place," which situates Yamashita's work within the larger framework of Latin American magical realist fiction and North American multicultural writing.
6. Ironically, the whole narrative is based on the presupposition that the ball *does* speak, and that the *novela* itself will in the future become a memory for the reader, who is many times removed from its original source, which we can only get access to obliquely, that is, through another person's memory. Heise also argues that "Yamashita's text reaches beyond its own boundaries to include the reader into the ritual, since the sphere and its story have now become part of the reader's memory as well" (148).
7. Lee also reads the entire novel as an extensive critique of the way that globalization and capitalism shape modern lives: "Therefore, though Yamashita's novel may be responding to the new world (dis)order brought on by the spread of capitalism, her critique of globalization exceeds, or is not confined to, a critique of global capital. She also scrutinizes the forms of life and social relations that are altered by global communications networks, technologies of high-speed travel, world cultural organizations, and ecological movements that are not reducible to capital's effects" (112). For Bahng, the relation between Kazumasa and his ball as "Japan's sometimes contradictory connections to the expansive logics of late capitalism" (129). In Bahng's reading, "[t]he rubbery and plastic properties of the Matacão allude to the resilience and flexibility of empire, which continues to resurface in mutated form in

Yamashita's extrapolation of this near-future that emerges from an excavated history of U.S. and European empire in the South American tropics" (127). Although I find this an insightful possibility, I do not think we can fully comprehend Yamashita's metaphor of the Matacão without considering, at the same time, the perspective of Kazumasa's ball. Why, then, does Yamashita choose to narrate from the perspective of empire and also, to imagine a filial relation between Kazumasa and his ball, one that shapes both of their identities? I would proffer that posthumanism helps us to think through this particular conundrum.

8. Among the historical references that the Matacão makes—together with its surrounding economy, adjacency to "a metal cemetery" (99), and the amusement park, Chicolándia—according to Bahng, is to *Fordlándia*, a rubber plantation set up by the Ford corporation, which "strived to be an all-inclusive neo-colonial system, extending the plantation infrastructure" (123). According to Bahng's investigation into the company's archives, "the Ford rubber plantations in Brazil worked to fulfill a Fordist fantasy of bringing 'modernity' and 'progress' to the 'almost impenetrable tropical jungle.'" (123). For an in-depth analysis of the metal cemetery, and its symbolic implications, see Simal.

9. In *Vibrant Matter: A Political Ecology of Things*, Jane Bennett poses the question: "How, for example, would patterns of consumption change if we faced not litter, rubbish, trash, or 'the recycling,' but an accumulating pile of lively and potentially dangerous matter?" (Preface). Here, Bennett gets at the core of what Yamashita's narrative project does, which is to imagine the Matacão as vibrant matter.

10. According to Joel Henrique Ellwanger et al., the impact of deforestation in the Amazon is of planetary proportions: "The Amazon rainforest is also crucial for maintaining planetary health due to its pivotal role in regulating the Earth's climate. In a broader perspective, protecting Amazon ecosystems is essential for biodiversity preservation, climate regulation, energy production, food and water security; it is also important for pollination, natural/biological control of pests, the region's economy and human health, not forgetting to mention its aesthetic and cultural value. Amazon ecosystems have an important role for the dynamics and control of zoonotic diseases and vector-borne infections, a very important, although sometimes neglected, point" (1–2), so this overgrowth of Rickettsia in Yamashita's text becomes a symptom of disrupted local and planetary ecosystems.

11. Bahng reads this moment as "Kazumasa suffer[ing] and mourn[ing] the loss of his attachment to that which marked him as alien" (130). Caroline Rody interprets the "tropical tilt" as a sign that "the immigrant has become a Brazilian" (629).

12. See Reginaldo Prandi's "O Candomblé e o tempo: Concepções de tempo, saber e autoridade da África para as religiões afro-brasileiras" for an in-depth discussion of the concept of time in Candomblé.

Works cited

Badmington, Neil. "Theorizing Posthumanism." *Posthumanism,* special issue of *Cultural Critique*, vol. 53, Winter 2003, pp.10–27.

Bahng, Aimee. "Extrapolating Transnational Arcs, Excavating Imperial Legacies: The Speculative Acts of Karen Tei Yamashita's *Through the Arc of the Rain Forest.*" *Alien/Asian,* special issue of *MELUS*, vol. 33, issue 4, Winter 2008, pp. 123–144.

Baxi, Upendra. "The Posthuman and Human Rights." *Human Rights in a Posthuman World: Critical Essays*. Oxford University Press, 2007, pp. 197–239.
Bennett, Jane. *Vibrant Matter: A Political Ecology of Things*. Duke University Press, 2010.
Bittencourt Costa Moreira, Julia. *Brazilian Indigenous Peoples' Rights and Natural Environment Under Threat: Reflections on the Possible Impacts of Far-Right Populism's Empowerment in Brazil*. 2019. Lunds Universitet. http://lup.lub.lu.se/student-papers/record/8983690.
Braidotti, Rosi. *The Posthuman*. Polity Press, 2013.
Callus, Ivan. "Reclusiveness and Posthuman Subjectivity." *Subjectivity*, vol. 5, issue 3, 2012, pp. 290–311. https://doi.org/10.1057/sub.2012.12.
Callus, Ivan, and Stefan Herbrechter. "Introduction: Posthumanist Subjectivities, or, Coming After the Subject ..." *Subjectivity*, vol. 5, issue 3, 2012, pp. 241–264. https://doi.org/10.1057/sub.2012.17.
Christiansen, Steen. "Posthuman Rights." *Academic Quarter*, vol. 5, Autumn 2012, pp. 101–112. https://doi.org/10.5278/ojs.academicquarter.v0i5.2875.
Ellwanger, Joel Henrique et al. "Beyond Diversity Loss and Climate Change: Impacts of Amazon Deforestation on Infectious Diseases and Public Health." *Anais da Academia Brasileira de Ciências/Annals of the Brazilian Academy of Sciences*, vol. 92, issue 1, 2020, pp. 1–33. www.scielo.br/aabc.
Ferrante, Lucas and Philip M. Fearnside. "Brazil's New President and 'Ruralists' Threaten Amazonia's Environment, Traditional Peoples and the Global Climate." *Environmental Conservation*, vol. 46, issue 4, 2019, pp. 261–263. https://doi.org/10.1017/S0376892919000213.
Heise, Ursula K. "Local Rock and Global Plastic: World Ecology and the Experience of Place."*Comparative Literature Studies*, vol. 41, issue 1, 2004, pp. 126–152.
Herbrechter, Stefan, and Ivan Callus. "What is a Posthumanist Reading?" *Angelaki: Journal of Theoretical Humanities*, vol. 13, issue 1, 2008, pp. 95–111. https://doi.org/10.1080/09697250802156091.
Lee, Rachel C. "Global-Local Discourse and Gendered Screen Fictions in Karen Tei Yamashita's *Through the Arc of the Rain Forest*." *The Americas of Asian American Literature: Gendered Fictions of Nation and Transnation*. Princeton University Press, 1999. *ProQuest Ebook Central*. https://ebookcentral-proquest-com.cmich.idm.oclc.org/lib/cmich-ebooks/detail.action?docID=617314.
Morton, Timothy. *Hyperobjects: Philosophy and Ecology after the End of the World*. University of Minnesota Press, 2013.
Nayar, Pramod K. *Posthumanism*. Polity Press, 2014.
Prandi, Reginaldo. "O Candomblé e o tempo: Concepções de tempo, saber e autoridade da África para as religiões brasileiros." *Revista Brasileira de Ciências Sociais*, vol. 16, issue 47, Oct. 2001, pp. 43–58. https://doi.org/10.1590/S0102-69092001000300003.
Rody, Caroline. "Impossible Voices: Ethnic Postmodern Narration in Toni Morrison's *Jazz* and Karen Tei Yamashita's *Through the Arc of the Rain Forest*." *Contemporary Literature*, vol. 41, issue 4, Winter 2000, pp. 618–641.
Simal, Begoña. "The Junkyard in the Jungle: Transnational, Transnatural Nature in Karen Tei Yamashita's *Through the Arc of the Rain Forest*." *Journal of Transnational American Studies*, vol. 2, issue 1, 2010, pp. 1–25. https://escholarship.org/uc/item/4567j2n1.

Sohn, Stephen Hong. "Introduction: Alien/Asian: Imagining the Racialized Future." *Alien/Asian, a special issue of MELUS*, vol. 33, issue 4, Winter 2008, pp. 5–22. *JSTOR* https://www.jstor.org/stable/20343505.

United Nations General Assembly. "The Universal Declaration of Human Rights." *United Nations, 217 (III) A, 1948, Paris, art. 1,* http://www.un.org/en/universal-declaration-human-rights/.

Yamashita, Karen Tei. *Through the Arc of the Rain Forest.* Coffee House Press, 1990.

Index

Note: Page numbers in *italics* indicate figures, **bold** indicate tables and with "n" indicates endnotes in the text.

9/11 150–153; *see also* trauma
24 (television show) 151

Abarca, J. L. 12
Abarca, M. 12
abduction 31
Aberdeen, B. 215
"aberrations of affect" 64
abolitionism 265, **267**, 278, 278n3
abolitionist approach to animal rights 278n3
Abramson, J. 155
Abruna, L. 136
abuse: colonial 4; domestic 125; human rights 13, 16, 32, 40–41, 64; sexual 17, 35, 128; women 125
abusive colonial power 17
accountability 14, 17, 285
activism: critique and 181; democratic 181–182; human rights 10, 184; legal 194n4; passionate 203; politics and 132, 183, 232; research and 168
Adalian, R. 202–203
Adamic, L. 184
Adorno, T. W. 265
affective geography 66–67
Africa 7, 14, 34, 68, 128, 214, 227, 238n11, 269
African Americans 36, 41; Afro-Latino immigrants and 250; Black pride among 246; class prejudice 230; culture 254; embarrassing international criticism 9; equality and emancipation 248; female dominance in 124; firefighters 149; freedom struggle 244, 257; fundamental rights of enslaved 10; genres 245; humanity and rights of 10; intra-racial gender-based violence 125; language 247; Latin heritage 252; mass mobilizations 249; music and culture 255; musicians 251; politics 125; population 268; Puerto Ricans and 243; racial injustice 11; rural workers 247; slang and Spanish lyrics 255; Soul music 244; struggle 256; unprovoked killing of 41; *see also* Asian Americans
African Charter on Human and Peoples' Rights 119
Afro-Brazilians 215–216, 287
Afro-Caribbean 232, 246
Afro-Cuban 249, 251–252, 255, 259n2
Afro-descendants 14, 232–233, 235, 247
Afro-Latin(a/o) 247; Americans 9, 228, 258; communities 244–245; identity 249; identity discourse 245; immigrants 250; social movements 244
Afro-Latinidades 14
Afro-Puerto Rican: Black women 236; colonial inheritance 237; ethno-racial segregation 224, 236; heritage 233; immigrants 243, 249; migrants 249; racialization 250; silencing and victimization 231; structural marginalization and racial discrimination 234; *see also* African Americans
"Age of Migration" 6
Age of Revolution 6
Agreement or Recife Agreement (1678) 214

Index

Ain't I a Woman (hooks) 124
Alarcón, F. 72
Alarcón, N. 61
Alegría, R. 232–233
alienation 65, 68, 70, 73, 136–137, 290n3
Allen, C. 155
Allen, G. 122
Allende, I. 38
alliance of survival 247–248
allyship 167–171
almoners *see* polymaths
Alta Mira 102
Amazon 285, 289, 292n10
American Blacks 247; *see also* African Americans
American Convention on Human Rights 12, 42, 119; *see also* human rights
América Negra (Ferreira) 64
American Evangelicalism 50
American hero 150–153
American Indian Movement 37
American Indians 51; *see also* African Americans
American Monomyth, The 152, 155, 157; *see also* Classical Monomyth
American Revolution 36, 257
American Sniper (Eastwood) 155–157
Amin, S. 72
Amnesty International Report 2017/18 61, 74n4, 75n7
Among Flowers – A Walk in the Himalayas (Kincaid) 134
Anáhuac 51
Anaya, R. 69
Andalusia 238n11
Andes 72
Andrews, G. R. 245
Andros, E. 50
Angel of Bethesda, The (Mather) 49
Anglos 188, 224, 236
Angola 211
animal apartheid 268–274
animal rights: abolitionist approach to 278n3; discourse 275; inherent systematic violation 73; movement 278; racism and speciesism 265; zooethical poetry and 274–277
Annie John (Kincaid) 136–137
annihilation 7, 283, 285, 290
anti-colonialism 1
anti-Communist 15–16, 186
Antigone (Sophocles) 87, 89
anti-immigrant policies 11
anti-imperialism 1, 245

Antilles 211, 237n1
antiterrorism 16
anxiety 206n5; of castration 68; fear and 197, 201–203; feelings of 200; parental absence 200; stress and 200
Anzaldúa, G. A. 10, 122, 129n5
apartheid *see* animal apartheid
Apologetic History (de las Casas) 34
Aquinas, T. 33
Arab Jews 7
Arabs 7, 11, 16, 156
Aranda-Alvarado, B. 149
arbitrary detention 31
archetypal tales 85–88
Arendt, H. 42–43
Argentina 14, 38–39
Arias, D. 97–100, 103
Armstrong, J. 66
army of occupation (1917–1920) 103–106, *104*
artificial intelligence 285
Ashkenazim 7
Ashley's War (movie) 157
Asia 3, 7, 121–122, 291
Asian Americans 10, 256, 290n3, 291n5; *see also* African Americans
Asociación de Residentes de Piñones (Residents Association of Piñones) 234
Asturias, M. Á. 38–39
Atahualpa (Inca emperor) 34
Atlantic Charter 37
Atlantic Ocean 3
atrocities 4–5, 7, 34, 39, 109, 289
At the Bottom of the River (Kincaid) 134
"At the Party" (Rivera) 252
Attridge, D. 270
Autobiography of My Mother, The (Kincaid) 134–136
autonomy 63, 163–167, 169, 172–173, 215–216, 267, 272
Ayres, E. D. 185–186

backlash against feminism 147–148
Baelo-Allué, S. 158n1
Bahía 212
Balkan 7
Banana Trilogy (Asturias) 39
Bandeirantes (flag-carriers) 215
"Bang, Bang" (Sextet) 250–251
Baralt, G. A. 238n5
Barbarian Nurseries, The (Tobar) 196–205; deportability 204–205; fear 197, 203; human mobility 205; illegality 197–198, 202, 204–205; indebtedness 198

Barnett, G. 108
Barreto, J.-M. 1
Barretto, R. 251, 255
Bartosch, R. 279n8
basic human rights 10–11, 61, 64, 193, 223, 236, 243, 290; *see also* human rights
Bataan, J. 253–254
Batman (movie) 151
Bauzá, M. 251
Baxi, U. 290
Beamer, L. 154
Beamer, T. 154
Bearss, H. 100, 102
Beauvois, J. 17
Beckles, H. 15
Beginning and End of Rape: Confronting Sexual Violence in Native America, The (Deer) 16–17
Belli, G. 62, 64
Beloved (Morrison) 129
Belpré, P. 224
Bendix, R. F. 166
Benítez-Rojo, A. 67
Bennett, J. 292n9
Berger, J. 268
Berkman, B. 152–153
Between the World and Me (Coates) 142
biases 47, 55, 61
Biblia Americana (Smolinski and Stievermann) 45, 51
biological dimorphism 120
Black(s) 8–11, 212; diaspora 64; ghettos and communities 246; invisibility 225; music 245–247; people 75n8, 219, 229, 238n11, 248, 257, 269; populations 14, 232, 268; Puerto Rico 225; slaves 268; *see also* African Americans
Black Americas 244–247, 252
Black Atlantic 69, 223–224, 228, 230
blackening 245
Black Freedom Struggle 243
Black-Latino alliances 244
#BlackLivesMatter 11, 41
Black Macho and the Myth of the Super Woman (Wallace) 124
Black Militia 226
Blackness 124, 140, 223, 226, 231–234, 239n18, 244, 249–250, 252, 254–255, 259
Black Panther Party (BPP) 243, 256–257
Black Panthers 243, 256
Black Power 226, 244–249, 252, 255–259
Black Puerto Ricans 224, 226, 228

Black women writers 117–129; gender production 119–123; intersectional sensitization 119–123; literature as instrument of decoloniality 125–129; as targets of violence 123–125
Blake, W. 85–86
blanqueamiento (whitening) 13
Boca de Cangrejos 226
Bolivia 39
Bolsonaro, J. 221, 289–290
Bonetti, K. 134
"Boogaloo Blues" (Colón) 252
Book of Genesis 85
Boot, M. 97
Borderlands/La Frontera: The New Mestiza (Anzaldúa) 10
Borgwardt, E. 37
Boston, Massachusetts 46, 52–53
Boukman, D. 35–36, 41
Boyhood: Scenes from Provincial Life (Coetzee) 269
Boyle, T. C. 70–71, 75n10
Braidotti, R. 265, 284, 286, 288–289
Brand, D. 64, 74n2
Bras, J. M. 248
Brazil 2, 34–35, 39, 41, 106, 284, 288; development 289; military dictatorship 13; Potiguaras 63; racial discrimination 64
Brazilian *quilombos* 211–221; Afro-Brazilians 215–216; Castaínho (remnant quilombo community) 219–221; *Palmares* 215–216; Pernambuco 216–218; *Quilombo dos Palmares* (community) 213–215; resistance 211–213
Breath, Eyes, Memory (Danticat) 126
Breitwieser, M. R. 50
British Army 226
British North America 50
Broeck, S. 4
Brown, J. 243, 246, 253
Brown, M. 142
Brownmiller, S. 123
Brown v. Board of Education 190
brutalization 66–67, 73, 75n6
Bryson, J. 205
Buckalew, C. 107
Buell, L. 266
Bulosan, C. 10
Burgos, A. Jr. 249
Bush, G. W. 150–151, 156, 197
Bush, L. 150
Butler, J. 268

Index

Cabrera, M. E. 38
Cáceres, R. 96–97
Cakchiquel (ethnic group) 89
Cakchiquel Indians 89
Calarco, M. 267
Caldeira, I. 133
Calder, B. 107
California 11, 183; Channel Islands 70–71; cultural conflict 184; ethnic migrants 185; Mexicans 188; racial riots 186; racist legislation 189
Callus, I. 283, 286, 288, 290n1
Caminero-Santangelo, M. 11
Campbell, C. 101
Campbell, J. 151
Camus, A. 273
Canada 2, 11, 14, 16, 38, 41, 63–64; Aboriginal population 63; economic integration 12; engagement in United States 12; Indigenous peoples 12
Canclini, N. G. 221
Canto General (Neruda) 62
Capá Prieto (Rosario) 223–237, 237n1, 238n12, 239n17; countering silence 224–231; decolonizing colonial power legacies 235–237; "El silenciamiento" (Silencing) 225–226, 228–229; folklorization of culture 231–235; Puerto Rican Blackness 231–235
Caperton, A. W. 99
capitalism 6, 15, 41–42, 121, 256, 284–285, 289, 291n7
captivity narratives 45, 145–147, 151–152, 157
Cárdenas, R. 237
Cardenas, S. 16, 40
Cardoso, F, H. 221
Caribbean 2–4, 34, 41, 75n7, 95–96, 105–106, 134, 178n23, 223, 226–227, 230, 236, 238n8
Carmichael, S. 256
Carneiro, E. 212
Carney, T. 101
Carter, J. 38
Caruth, C. 67
Castaínho (remnant quilombo community) 219–221
Castilian Mariology 52
Castillo, P. 107–108
Castillo San Felipe del Morro 228
Catholic Christianity 49; *see also* Protestant Christianity
Catholic Church 47, 52, 54, 83, 86

Catholic Cosmopolitanism and Human Rights (Taylor) 54
Catholicism 50, 54–55
"Catholicization" 47, 49–50
Catholics 47, 49
Catwoman (movie) 151
Caucasus 121
caudillos 97–98
Cavell, S. 269, 272
Center of Mental Health and Human Rights (CINTRAS) 14
Central America 41–42, 51–52, 74n4, 81–92, 227; archetypal tales 85–88; framework 82–84; *friccionalidad* (stylistic game) 87–88; genocide 81; Guatemalan 85–88; historical pretexts 82–84; human rights in 85; literary representation of violence 88–91; senselessness 82–84
Central Asia 121
Ceremony (Silko) 74
Cha-Cha 244
"Cha-cha with a backbeat" (Flores) 250–255
Chaim 51
Chang, M. M. 88
Channel Islands 70–71
Charen, M. 147
Chávez, C. 10
Cheney, D. 151
CHESF (electricity company) 218
Chiapas 12–13, 15, 72
Chicanos/as 10, 256
Chicomuselo 12
Chile 14, 37–39, 41, 63
China 7
Chinea, J. L. 228
Chinese-Canadians 11
Christian European 33
Christiansen, S. 283
Churchill, W. 37
cimarronaje (run-awayism) 227
cimarrones (runaway African slaves in Latin America) 13
Civil Rights 10, 244, 247
Civil Rights Act of 1964 9
Civil Rights Movement 124, 181
Clapham, A. 32
Classical Monomyth 151; *see also* American Monomyth, The
Coates, T.-N. 142
Cody, W. 274
Coetzee, J. M. 265, 268–274, 279n6
Cold War 13, 15, 38

Coleridge, S. T. 90
collective trauma 144–145; *see also* trauma
Collins, P. H. 117
Colombia 16, 41, 106, 211, 232
Colón (Panamá) 244
Colón, J. 252
colonialism 2, 4, 10, 16–17, 36; Conquest and 33; ethics 4; human rights violations 12; racism and 10; slavery and 6, 139
coloniality 71, 158n1; of gender 117, 124; of heritage thinking 166; of knowledge 117, 119, 129; of power 3, 65, 117, 119, 129n2; *see also* decoloniality
colonization 10, 75n8, 139; conquest and 4, 6; history 17; imperialism and 7; New World 3; oppression and 15
Colt-Browning Model 1895 machine gun 102
Columbian Exchange 2
Columbus, C. 3, 33, 39, 236
Commission for Historical Clarification (CEH) 92
Commission for Historical Clarification of the Guatemalan Civil War 88
communism 38, 40
"concrete utopia" 72
Condé, M. 62, 64
Congress 103
conquest and colonization 4, 6
Consejo de Indias 34
Convention for the Safeguarding of the Intangible Cultural Heritage 174
Convention on the Elimination of All Forms of Discrimination Against Women (CEDAW) 119
Convention on the Elimination of All Forms of Race Discrimination (CERD) 119
Coolitude 15
Cordero, C. 224
Cordero, R. 224
Cornejo-Polar, A. 65
Correa, R. 235
Corregidora (Jones) 127–128
"cosmopolitan Catholicism" 54
Costello, E. 272–273
Cotton Mather and Benjamin Franklin: The Price of Representative Personality (Breitwieser) 50
countering silence 224–231
COVID-19 18, 206n1

Crahan, M. E. 54
Crenshaw, K. 125
Creole identity 53
crimes against humanity 7
Criminal Injuries Compensation Fund 149
criminality 70, 186
criollo (person of Spanish ancestry born in the Latin American countries) 12, 53
crossing borders 244–245
Crossing the Mangrove (Condé) 62
Crow, J. 247
Cruz, C. 255
Cuban revolution 13
culture/cultural: denigration 70; discrimination 187; folklorization of 231–235; heritage 166, 193; identity 193; in-betweenness 63, 65; marginalization 265; national identity and 224; Puerto Rican 225; trauma and 145
Curtin, D. 75n9

dance and music 165; cultural heritage 166; Indigenous peoples in Mexico 167; postrevolutionary political and ideological processes 169; P'urhépecha 167, 173; self-determination and management 171
Dance of the Old Men 163, *165*, 165–168, 170–174, *175*, 176, 177n11, 178n15
Daniels, J. 108
Danticat, E. 38, 125–126
Daredevil (movie) 151
da Silva, L. 220–221
Dávila, Á. M. 224
Davis, D. B. 34–35, 272
Day of Black Consciousness 219
de Castro, J. R. 226, 238n5
Declaration of OAS Human Rights 74n4
Declaration of the Rights of Man 5
decoloniality 7, 125–129; *see also* coloniality
decolonization 64, 66, 70, 72–73, 235–237
Deer, S. 16–17
Defoe, D. 269
deforestation 292n10
De Genova, N. 197–198, 205
dehumanization/dehumanisation 10, 120, 122–123, 128, 142, 156, 185, 283

de Las Casas, B. 4–7, 33–34, 41
Delgado, R. 184, 189
democracia racial 244–245, 259
democratic activism 181–182; *see also* activism
de Montesinos, A. 4, 33, 41
Denis-Rosario, M. 225–226, 238n9
Department of Cartographic Engineering 221
deportability 198, 204–205, 206n3
deprivation 16, 70, 169, 189
Derrida, J. 272
desaparecidos (disappeared) 32
de Sepúlveda, J. G. 33
DeShazer, M. 118
Detela, J. 265, 274–277
deterritorialization 63, 65, 70, 72
developing countries 8
developing democratic tradition of human rights 182–184
de Vitoria, F. 4–5, 7, 84
Dew Breaker, The (Danticat) 38
Díaz, P. 38, 169
difference 184–187; biotic 71; confessional 49; epochal 52; equal 192; gender 120; racial and sexual 119, 158n1
Different Mirror: A History of Multicultural America, A (Takaki) 10
dimorphism *see* biological dimorphism
disaster capitalism 70; *see also* capitalism
discrimination: class 139; combat 132; cultural 187; legislative 11; linguistic 266; marginalization and 170, 234; oppression and 11; prejudice and 142, 216; racial and species-based 64, 70, 139, 184, 216, 234, 245–246, 265, 268; racist 9; structural 8, 14
Disgrace (Coetzee) 269–271, 279n6
dispossession 31, 63, 189, 229, 236
dis/translocation 61
"Docile Eyes" (Detela) 274
Doctrine of Discovery 33
Documenting the Undocumented: Latinola Narratives and Social Justice in the Era of Operation Gatekeeper (Caminero-Santangelo) 11
Dodson, H. 237
dollar diplomacy 97
domestic abuse 125; *see also* abuse
Domestic Abuse in the Novels of African American Women (Humann) 125

Dominican Republic 95–111; army of occupation (1917–1920) 103–106, *104*; march on Santiago de los Caballeros 99–103, *100*; protecting "America's lake" 96–99; protest in United States 106–109; withdrawal 109–111
Don Carlos de Sigüenza y Góngora (Leonard) 51
Doo-Wop 251
Douglass, F. 10
Down These Mean Streets (Thomas) 249
Dreby, J. 206n3
Drew, D. 134–135
Drifters, The 253
D. R. Office of Human Rights by the Archbishop of Guatemala, The 83
drug trafficking 61
Drums and Colours (Walcott) 67
Duany, J. 249
Dubón, E. G. 88
Dunlap, R. 101
Dussel, E. 3, 7, 64
Duvaliers 38
Dzidzienyo, A. 8–9

Eastern Europe 13
Eastwood, C. 155–157
eco-literature 266
economic growth 8, 70
economic integration 12
economic oppression 9; *see also* oppression
economic refugees 8
Ecuador 235
egalitarian multiculturalism 64
El arte de ficcionar (Wallner) 82
Elizabeth Costello, The (Coetzee) 269
Ellison, R. 64, 75n11
Ellwanger, J. H. 292n10
"El Pito" (Sextet) 251
El Portalito (bar) 87
El Salvador 39, 88
El Señor Presidente (Asturias) 38
"El silenciamiento" (Silencing) 225–226, 228–229
embracing Blackness 249–250; *see also* Blackness
EMP 88
England 223
enslaved Africans 224, 227–228
environmental degradation 69
environmental disasters 8
environmental racism 75n9

Environment Ministry to the
  Agriculture Ministry 289
epistemic violence 64
equality 12; of Africans 34;
  functional 191–193; human rights
  132; juridical 36; mankind 6; racial
  22; rights 10, 43; social contract
  based on 36; socioeconomic 8;
  women 20
Erdrich, L. 63–64
Erikson, K. 144
eschatology 53–54
ethical avoidance 4
ethics 167–171; colonialism 4; toward
  animals 276
ethnic migrants 185
Euro-American imperialism 8
Eurocentric Human 17
Europe 4, 9, 14, 105, 229, 284
European-American 146
European Convention for the
  Protection of Human Rights and
  Fundamental Freedoms 119
European Enlightenment 4, 12
European Renaissance 4
Evangelicalization 55
Eva's Man (Jones) 127–128
exclusivism 17
exploitation 3–4, 15, 20, 31, 33–36, 39,
  41–42, 66, 68, 71, 73, 84, 119, 121, 125,
  127, 272
Esquivel, L. 62

Fair Employment Practices
  Committee 191
Fair Employment Practices
  legislation 188
Fair Racial Practices Act 188, 190
Faludi, S. 144, 147–151, 154–155,
  157–158
Falwell, J. 147–148
Fania Records 255
Fanon, F. 64, 221
Faulkner, W. 75n6
Federal Rural University of
  Pernambuco (UFRPE) 220
Federal University of Pernambuco
  (UFPE) 221
Feliciano, C. 255
female survivors 153–154
femicide 16–17
femicidios (the murder of women with
  impunity) 16
feminism 117–118, 147–148

Fente, R. M. 1
Ferguson, M. 135
Fernández, J. 256
Ferreira, E 64
"Fever" (Lupe) 252
Fiallo, F. 108
Figueiredo Report, The 289
Filipinos 186
Fire Department of New York
  (FDNY) 152, 155
First Nations 41, 63, 74n3
Fischer, S. 6
Flores, J. 250–251
Foe (Coetzee) 268–269, 271
folklorization of culture 231–235
forced migration 31
Forcinito, A. 1
*For Colored Girls Who Have Considered
  Suicide/When the Rainbow is Enuf*
  (Shange) 126n126
Foreign Miners License
  Tax 189
Formicola, J. R. 54
Fortson, E. 102
Fourteenth Amendment 189
France 6, 223
Francione, G. 271–272
Franklin, A. 246
Fray Bartolomé de las Casas Center for
  Human Rights 13
free trade 12
*French Declaration on the Rights of
  Man and Citizen* 12
French Revolution 1, 4–6, 36, 227
Frente Farabundo Martí de Liberación
  Nacional (FMLN) 88
Freud, S. 206n5
friccionalidad (stylistic game of
  combining fiction and reality) 82,
  87–88
From Bomba to Hip-Hop
  (Flores) 250
functional equality 191–193; *see also*
  equality
Funk music 245, 247; *see also specific
  music*

Galeano, E. 73
game *see friccionalidad* (game)
gang criminality 70
Gannett, L. S. 107
Ganzevoort, R. R. 145
García, J. 235–236
Garner, E. 142

gender 2, 150; coloniality 20, 117, 124–125; colonial/modern 121–123, 125, 127; concrete utopia 72; conflicts 61, 124; differences 120; discourses 122; gap 155; hierarchies 231; identity 132; inequality among journalists 155; legitimize war and national security 150; marginalization 224; power preclude 125; production 119–123; race and 119, 124–125; relations 17, 122; representation 155; roles/heteronormativity 16, 127; self-worth 124
gender-based crime 16
genderization of labor 121
Genealogy of Resistance, A (Philip) 126
General Pinochet 14
genocide 31, 33, 62, 65; Central America 81; human rights and 81; against the Indigenous people 81
geographic violence 64; *see also* violence
Georas, C. S. 247
George, R. 149
Gerardi, M. J. J. 88
Ghost Dance Movement 37
Gibbs, N. 145
Gillespie, D. 251
Gilmore, L. 135–136, 138
Gilroy, P. 246
Giuliani, R. 151
Glissant, É 65
global inequality 8
globalization 11, 247
Glorious Revolution 50
Glowin, J. 102
Godreau, I. P. 231, 233
Goldberg, D. T. 4
Gold Rush 189
Goller, I. 205
González, D. J. 10
González, S. 230
Good Neighbor Policy 111n2
Gorrión, J. D. 236
Grandmothers of the Plaza de Mayo *(Asociacion Civil Abuelas de la Plaza de Mayo)* 14
Graúna, G. 63, 74
Great Awakenings 55
Great Britain 9
Great Depression 186, 196, 206n1
Grosfoguel, R. 247

"Grotian tradition" 54
guadalupanismo 52
Guadeloupeans 67, 69
Guardian, The 148
Guardia Nacional Dominicana 105, 109
Guatemala 39, 41; civil war 81–82, 85, 91; Guatemalan 85–88; human rights in 83
Guatemala: Memory of Silence (Guatemala: memoria del silencio) – Report of the Commission for Historical Clarification 83
Guatemalan Civil War 39
Guatemala: Never Again, Report of the Interdiocesan Project; Recovery of Historical Memory—REMHI 83
Guatemalan National Revolutionary Unity (URNG) 83
Guggenheims 38
Guilitraro, D. A. 63
Gunn, P. A. 121
Guzmán, P. 41, 243, 256–257

Habermas, J. 4
Hacking, I. 270
Haiti 4, 38–39, 97–99, 105, 107, 109
Haitian Constitution 6
Haitian immigrants 64; *see also* immigrants
Haitian Revolution (1791-1804) 5–6, 35–36, 227
Hall, N. 99
Hampton, F. 256
Hancock, H. 251
Haraway, D. 278n5
Harding, W. G. 95–96, 107–109
Harlee, W. 106
Harlow, L. 255
Harris, B. 48
Harris, W. 70
Hato Mayor 106
Hatuey *(Taíno* Cacique) 4–6
Hearsts 38
Hegel, G. W. F. 4
Hein, S. 149
Heise, U. K. 291n4
Henríquez y Carbajal, F. 103
Herbrechter, S. 283, 286, 288
Hernández-Truyol, B. E. 118–119
Hernton, C. C. 123–125, 127, 129n7, 130n8
Heroes (television show) 151
heterosexual patriarchy 120
Hin-mahtoo-yah-lat-kekht, N. P. 71
Hip Hop music 245, 257

Hispanic Caribbean 250, 255
hispanidad 232, 236
Hispaniola 33, 103, 106–109
Hofer, S. 266
Hollywood 146
Holocaust 91–92, 140, 147
Holton, A. 236
homelessness 62–63
hommes de lettres 54
hooks, bell 124
hopelessness 145
horacistas 97
Hospital del Amor de Dios 50
House of Spirits, The (Allende) 38
Huerta, D. 10
Hughes, C. E. 109
Hughes, T. 273
human–animal relationship 265
human apartheid 268–274
human being **267**
human–human relationship 265
humanism 17, 283, 288; *see also* posthumanism
humanitarian paternalism 98
Humann, H. D. 125
human relationships to animals 273
human rights: during 18th century 46; abuses 13, 40–41; activism 10, 184; activists 16; advocacy for 9; in Central America 85; codification of 48; complaints 16; dance and music 165; Dance of the Old Men 176; developing democratic tradition of 182–184; discourse 54; Eurocentric approaches 4; evolution of 11–12; free trade and 12; genocide and 81; in Guatemala 83; history of 47, 54; inclusionary approaches 5; inter-American 12; international 11; internationalize 42; interpretations of 48; narrating and castigating 32; preservation of 37; research 48; retrogression in 75n7; retrogression of 68; sexual identities 117; struggle for 219–221; struggles 245–247; trials 14; United States 8–18, 54; violations 12–13, 15–16, 18, 31, 34, 36, 38–39, 41, 61–62, 66, 173–177; of women 36
Human Rights and United States Policy toward Latin America (Schoultz) 38–39
Human Rights from the Third World Perspective: Critique, History and International Law (Barreto) 1

Human Rights in Latin America and Iberian Cultures (Forcinito, Fente and McDonough) 1
Human Rights in Latin America: A Politics of Terror and Hope (Cárdenas) 16
human suffering 271
hunger 31, 39, 269
Hurricane Katrina 10, 234
Hurricane Maria 234
Hybrid Cultures (Canclini) 221

I, Rigoberta Menchú (Menchú) 39
identitarian in-betweenness 66
identity *see* national identity
"I Like It Like That" (Rodríguez) 252
Ill Fares the Land (McWilliams) 185
immigrants 17, 36; Afro-Puerto Rican 243; Haitian 64; hostility toward 11; labor of 9; racialized stratification of 9; undocumented 11
immigration 191, 205, 248, 285, 288
imperialism 1–2, 7–8, 111, 137, 187, 192
Impressions, The 246
in-betweenness 66
indemnification 64
Independent School District v. Salvatierra 189, 194n8
Indian captivity narratives 146; *see also* captivity narratives
Indian Removal Act of 1830 37
Indian Spring (Primavera indiana, poema sacrohistórico, idea de María Santíssima de Guadalupe) (Sigüenza y Góngora) 52
Indigenous communities 5, 15, 39
Indigenousness 170
Indigenous people 4, 11–15, 32, 34, 51, 63, 81, 173, 212
Indigenous populations 4–5, 17, 33–34, 36–37
Indigenous P'urhépecha Autonomous National 165
Indigenous P'urhépecha people 170, 177n1
Indigenous Response to #Me Too, An (film) 17
Indigenous women 15–17, 122
indios amigos 37
Indo-Canadians 11
Industrial Revolution 4
inequality 8, 13, 31, 33, 36, 67, 117, 119, 155, 186–188, 270; *see also* equality
infringements 31
Ingold, T. 266

Inhuman Bondage: The Rise and Fall of Slavery in the New World (Davis) 34
inhumanity 34
Insensatez (Senselessness) (Moya) 81–89
Institute for Ethnic Democracy 191
Intangible Cultural Heritage of Humanity 165–168, 174, *175*, 178n31
Inteligencia Militar 88
interactions in New York 247–248
Inter-American Court of Human Rights 16
inter-American human rights 12
Inter Caetera 33
internalization 65, 75n8
International Association of Inter-American Studies 43
International Covenant on Economic, Social and Cultural Rights 181
international human rights 11
International Journal of Intangible Heritage 177n7
International Organization of Migration 75n4
Internet 11
Internment Program of Japanese Americans 186
intersectionality 20, 117, 120–121, 125, 127
intersectional sensitization 119–123
Interstellar (movie) 155, 157
In the Heart of the Country (Coetzee) 271
Invention of Women, The (Oyewùmí) 122
Iraq war 156
Iser, W. 90
Ishimaru, K. 284–285
Island of Hispaniola 4
Island of Impunity: Puerto Rico's Outlaw Police Force 234
Island of Janitzio 170
Island of Jarácuaro 170–171
Ismene 87
Itzá (Nahua warrior) 62

Jamaica 127
Japan 284
Japanese-Canadians 11
Java 7
Jazz music 245, 251, 253
Jewett, R. 152
Jewish Holocaust 7
Jewish refugees 11
jíbaro 225
Jiménez, J. I. 97–99, 256
jimenistas 97
Johnson, J. W. 107

Jones, G. 125, 127–128
Jones-Shafroth Act of 1917 248
Journal of International Relations 106
Joy, D. L. 71
Juárez, B. 177n11, 177n13
juridical equality 36; *see also* equality
Justice and Accountability Project (JCAP) 12

Karzai, H. 150
Kazumasa's ball 23, 284–289, 290n2, 291n7, 292n7
"Keep on Pushing" (Impressions) 246
Keller, H. A. 10
Kelly, R. W. 155
Khoikhoi people 268
Kincaid, J. 125, 132–142
King, E. 258
King, M. L. Jr. 41
Klein, N. 70, 206n7
Knapp, H. 105
Kochiyama, Y. 10
Kohut, K. 90
Kolhatkar, S. 156
Kranjc, A. 278n4
Kyle, C. 155–156
Kyle, T. 157
Kymlicka, W. 192

La Batalla de Chile (Guzmán) 41
labor unions 39
La Brûlerie (Ollivier) 64
La Cumbre 102
LaDuke, W. 10
Lake Pátzcuaro 167–171
La mujer habitada (Belli) 62
land ownership inequality 67
land tenure 61, 67, 72, 74n2
Lanzos, F. 226–228
Lassén, R. 232
Las Trencheras 101
Latin America 6, 12–13, 15–17, 37–39, 54, 74n2, 108, 128, 223–224, 229, 236, 291n5; Afro-descendants 14; countries 14; debt repayment 96; human rights violation 15; societies 14; unequal relations between United States and 245; women 14
Latin American Literary Theory 206n2
Latina/o 10, 14, 224, 230
Latin Boogaloo 243–244, 250–256, 258–259
Latin Motown *see* Fania Records
Latin Soul 244, 247, 251, 253–254, 258–259

Lawrence, J. S. 152
League of Nations 95
Lee, H. 109–110, *110*, 291n7
Lefebvre, H. 75n10
legal activism 194n4; *see also* activism
legislative discrimination 11
Lejeune, P. 136
Leonard, I. A. 51–52
lesbian, gay, bisexual, transgender, queer, intersexual, and asexual (LGBTQIA+) 11, 15
L'espérance-macadam (Pineau) 67
Levinas, E. 267
Levy, A. 155
Life & Times of Michael K (Coetzee) 268–269
Limits of Autobiography–Trauma and Testimony, The (Gilmore) 136
Lippit, A. M. 268
Lipsitz, G. 255
literary representation of violence 88–91
literature as instrument of decoloniality 125–129
Little, A. M. 33
Lives of Animals, The (Coetzee) 269, 271–273
loiceños 233–234
lo mexicano 170
London Tate Gallery 85
López, G. 170–172, 178n14
Los Angeles 186, 202
Lost (television show) 151
Lucas, L. 75n15
Luciano, F. 256–258
Lucy (Kincaid) 134, 136–137
Lugones, M. 3, 117, 119–120, 122
Lupe, L. 252
Lurie, D. 270

Macaco 213
Machito 251, 253
Mackenbach, W. 90
Madres de la Plaza de Mayo 41
Magnalia Christi Americana (Mather) 52
Maia, T. 258
Maldonado-Torres, N. 121, 123
male heroes 153–154
Malinche (Esquivel) 62
Mambo 244
"Manifesto I" (Graúna) 63
Map to the Door of No Return, A (Brand) 64
Mapuches 63
Mara Salva Trucha (gang) 92

march on Santiago de los Caballeros 99–103, *100*
marginalization 70, 224–225, 234
Mariategui, J. C. 74n2
Marine Corps 95–96, 99, 103, 105, 107, 109, 111
Marix, A. 101
Marquis, C. 135
marronage 227
Martin, T. 11
masculinity 123
massacres 62, 89
mass migration 3, 7
Massumi, B. 197
Masucci, J. 255
Matacão 285–286, 288, 291n7, 292n8
Mather, C.: about 45; American Evangelical 49; *Angel of Bethesda, The* 49; Catholicism 55; as historians 51; impact on the publication landscapes 48; interpretations of human rights 48; involvement in Glorious Revolution 50; life and work 47, 52; literary figures 46; *Magnalia Christi Americana* 52; marginalized social groups 54; polymaths 45; posthumous receptions 50; "Puritan gargoyle" 51; "Puritan Saints" 51; reception history 46, 49, 52–53; reformation/enlightenment 50, 54; roles in early modern publishing 48; theologian 51
Mathers: Three Generations of Puritan Intellectuals, 1596–1728, The (Middlekauff) 50
Mattos, M. T. S. C. 271
Mayer, A. 45
Mazza, K. 153
McClennen, S. A. 2, 8
McDonough, K. 1
McWilliams, C. 181–194; activism 183; developing democratic tradition of human rights 182–184; difference 184–187; functional equality 191–193; race and law 187–191; worldwide nationality and citizenship code 193–194
Medal of Honor 104
Medals of Honor 102
Menchú, R. 39–40
Mendez v. Westminster 189–190
Mendoza, L. M. 149
mental violence 64
Mercado, G. F. 168, 174–175, 178n31
Mercy, A (Morrison) 35, 62

Merino, Y. 153
Merkel, C. 106
mestizaje 237n2
mestizaje/mestiza/o 12–13, 14, 36, 223–225, 232, 244–245, 249, 254, 258–259
Methodism 47
#*Me Too Movement* 17
Mexican Americans 182–183, 185–186, 188, 190
Mexican–American War 188
mexicanidad 170
Mexicanness 170, 173
Mexico 15, 37, 41, 52, 63, 163, 178n23, 193; *see also* P'urhépecha
Mexico City 45
Mezrain 51
Michoacán 169–170
microaggressions 141
Middle East 7, 13, 16
Middlekauff, R. L. 50
Mignolo, W. 3–5, 7, 228
migrants 7, 74n4, 185; communities 8; ethnic 185; workers 63
migration: mass 3, 7; migrant workers 63; (trans)national 61; United States 134
Miller, C. 111
Miller, J. R. 12
minority groups 9
misery 64
Missouri Review 134
Mizrahim 7
mocambo 213–214
Mocambo Macaco 213
Mocambo Subupira 213
modern/colonial gender system 121–123, 125, 127
modern colonialism 5; *see also* colonialism
modernity 47–48; Euro-American myth of 64; reformation and enlightenment 50
Modernity Disavowed: Haiti and the Cultures of Slavery in the Age of Revolution (Fischer) 6
modernization 290
Monroe Doctrine 96
Monte Cristi 98, 100, *100*, 102
Montes, A. L. 234
Montesinos 33
Morales, J. 81–82
Moravcsik, A. 42
Moreira, J. B. C. 289–290
Morne Câpresse (Pineau) 67–68

Morrison, T. 35, 62–64, 71–72, 129, 133, 139, 142
Morton, T. 285
Moura, C. S. 211–212
Movimento Tortura Nunca Mais (MTNM) 14
Moya, H. C. 81–88, 90–91
Mr. Potter (Kincaid) 134
Mrs. Dalloway (Woolf) 137
mixed race 224, 231
Munanga, K. 211
music *see specific music*
música latina 244
Muslims 11, 16–17, 145
My Brother (Kincaid) 134
My Garden Book (Kincaid) 134
myth *see* rebirth of myth
mythopoetic articulation 66

Nahua peoples 62
Naphtuhim 51
Napoleon 226
narratives *see* captivity narratives
Nation, The 106–107, 183, 189
National Convergence Front, The (political party) 82
"national gargoyle" 51
National Geospatial Infrastructure Project (PIGN) 221
national identity 224
National Institute for Colonization and Land Reform (INCRA) 217–218, 221
National Labor Relations Board 191
(trans)national migration 61
national minority 9
national security 8
Native Americans 10, 17, 36–37, 256
naturalization 191
natural law 5
Navarette 102
Nayar, P. K. 283–284
Nazi Germany 7, 9, 11, 37
Neff, P. 149
negritud/e 232, 236
Negro Family: The Case for National Action, The 124
neocolonial violence 61–74; affective geography 66–67; alienation 68, 70; *América Negra* (Ferreira) 64; basic rights 61; *Canto General* (Neruda) 62; *Ceremony* (Silko) 74; *Crossing the Mangrove* (Condé) 62; cultural in-betweenness 63, 65; decolonization 64; deterritorialization 63, 65, 70, 72;

dis/translocation 61; *Drums and Colours* (Walcott) 67; homelessness 63; identitarian in-betweenness 66; *La Brûlerie* (Ollivier) 64; *La mujer habitada* (Belli) 62; land ownership inequality 67; *L'espérance-macadam* (Pineau) 67; *Malinche* (Esquivel) 62; Manifesto I (Graúna) 63; *Map to the Door of No Return, A* (Brand) 64; massacres 62; *Mercy, A* (Morrison) 62; *Morne Câpresse* (Pineau) 67–68; Nahua peoples 62; (trans)national migration 61; otherization 64–65; *Paradise* (Morrison) 71–72; rootless people 69; *Round House, The* (Erdrich) 63; *Slash* (Armstrong) 66; Spanish colonizers 62; "Temporada Apologica" (Guilitraro) 63; *Their Dogs Came With Them* (Viramontes) 70; *When the Killing's Done* (Boyle) 70–71; ...*Y no se lo tragó la tierra/... And the Earth Did Not Part* (Rivera) 63; *see also* violence
neoliberal globalization 8
neoliberalism 16
Nepal 134
Neruda, P. 62, 64
New England 46, 48–50, 53, 137
New England Protestantism 55
New Federal Civil Rights Act 191
Newfoundland 37
New Jersey (battleship) 102
New Jerusalem 46, 52–53
New Orleans, Louisiana 10
New Progressive Party (PNP) 239n19
New Spain 46, 47, 53
New Spanish Mariology 54
New World 4, 34–35
New York 224, 243–244, 246–247
New York City 244, 249–250
New Yorker, The 134, 148
New York Police Department (NYPD) 152, 155
New York Times, The 108
Nicaragua 39
Ni Una Más (Not One More) 16
Noche de Muertos of the Island of Janitzio 168
nongovernmental organizations 42
nonhuman being or animal **267**
nonhuman rights violations 61–62
non-P'urhépecha 172
Noonan, J. T. 267
North Africa 7

North America 35, 41, 47, 49–50, 63, 178n23
North American Trade Agreement (NAFTA) 15
Nuremberg Trial 9
Nuyoricans (New York-born Puerto Ricans) 243, 249–250, 256
Nwankwo, I. 245

Oakes, U. 53
Obama, B. 150, 197
Oboler, S. 8–10
Ocles, A. 235–236
Oedipus 87
Ogbar, J. 249, 255–258
Old Betonie 74
Oliver-Vélez, D. 248, 256
Ollivier, É 64
Olson, C. 182
Omi, M. 190
oppression: colonization and 15; discrimination and 11; Europe 4; exploitation and 4
organ harvesting 61
Organization of American States (OAS) 12, 42
organ trafficking 32
Origin of Others (Morrison) 133, 139
Ortega, J. 149
Ortiz-Robles, M. 265
Osorio, A. V. 224, 231–232, 234
otherization 62, 64–65
Ottawa 12
Ottoman Empire 7
Overseas Council of the Portuguese Crown 213
Oxford Encyclopedia of Latinos & Latinas in Contemporary Politics, Law, and Social Movements, The (Oboler and González) 10
Oyewùmí, O. 121–122

Pabón, T. 252
Pacheco, J. 255
Pachuco zoot-suiters 186
Paine, T. 36
Palmares 213, 215–216
Palmares Cultural Foundation 220–221
Palmieri, E. 251, 255
Palumbo-Liu, D. 41
Panama Canal 96
Papal Bull of 1452 33
paradigm shift 49
Paradise (Morrison) 71–72

Paraguay 37, 39
Paredes, J. 129n4
passionate activism 203; *see also* activism
Pastoral da Terra 220
patriarchal discourse 231
PATRIOT Act 11
Pedra Branca (hydroelectric plant) 218
Pendleton, J. 99–102, *100*
Pentagon 147, 149, 152
People (magazine) 153
people of color 8, 24, 141, 249, 252, 266, 268
Pérez, J. 103, 112n5
Pernambuco 212, 216–218
persecution 7, 45
Peru 16
Philip, M. N. 125–126, 128
Philippines 229
physical violence 64; *see also* violence
Piekarski, M. 268
Pietist Protestant missionary movement 53
Pineau, G. 67–69, 72–73, 75n8
Pinochet, A. 38
Pipes, C. L. 124
Pirekuas 170
Pizarro, F. 34
Plessy v. Fergusson 190
Plutarch 273
Poblete, J. 206n2, 206n6
"Poem for Deer" (Detela) 276
political oppression 9
political refugees 8
pollution 31
polymaths 45
Polyneikes 87
Pope Alexander VI 33
popular music 243
Portugal 4, 34
Portuguese 4
postapartheid 268
postcolonialism 268
posthumanism 17, 23, 284, 286–288, 290n1
posthuman rights 283–290; *see also* human rights
Potiguaras 63
poverty 7, 16, 40, 64, 70, 111, 141, 216, 234–235, 247–248, 268–269
powerlessness 145
Poyner, J. 270
prejudice 41, 140, 142, 147, 158, 182–184, 187–188, 190, 192, 216, 226, 230, 244

primavera del mundo (the spring of the world) 53
progressive organizations 11
protecting "America's lake" 96–99
Protestant Christianity 49
Protestantism 54
Protestant New England Christianity 50
Protestants 47, 49, 54
protest in United States 106–109
Publick Occurrences Both Forreign and Domestick (newspaper) 48
Puente, T. 243, 251, 253, 255
Puerto Plata 100, 102
Puerto Rican Blackness 225, 231–235
Puerto Rico 223, 243–259; African American 247–248; alliance of survival 247–248; Black Americas 244–245; Black music 245–247; Black power beyond borders 258–259; Black power in the barrio 255–258; Blacks 225; "cha-cha with a backbeat" 250–255; crossing borders 244–245; culture 225; embracing Blackness 249–250; historiography 225; human rights struggles 245–247; Hurricane Maria 234; immigrants 251; interactions in New York 247–248; Latin Boogaloo 250–255; Latin Soul 258–259; migrants 247; national identity 232; nationalist historical record 225; nationalist intellectual tradition in 231; Nuyoricans 249–250; racisms 249–250; rainbow radicalism 255–258; resurgence 232; sociocultural landscape 236; Spanish colonial history 228; translocal nation 224; United States 249–250; women 224; Young Lords 255–258; *see also* African American; Afro-Latin(a/o)
P'urhépecha: celebration of Noche de Muertos 170; communities 169, 171, 176; dance and music 167, 172–173; empire 169; ensembles 172; highlands 171; islands 170; language 178n29; musicians 177n13; people 170–176; performers 170; practitioners 173; rights and power 171; self-control 172
P'urhépecha Nation 163–167
Puritan America 145–146, 157
"Puritan errand" 54
Puritanism 51
"Puritan Saints" (Mather) 51
Puritan society 146

Quetzalcóatl (Aztec god) 51
Quijano, A. 3, 7, 65, 117, 119–120
quilombos see Brazilian *quilombos*
Quilombo dos Palmares (community) 213–215, 220

race: Blacks and 11; dehumanization 142; democracy 231; discourses 9; discrimination 9, 64, 70, 139, 216, 234, 245, 246, 268; diversity 232; harmony 232; injustice 11; and law 187–191; legislation 189; marginality 265, 290n3; persecution 7; prejudice 192, 244; revolution 181; riots 186; segregation 268; vindication 230
racial/ethnic divide 61
racialization 223
racisms: colonialism and 10; expression 8; humanitarian paternalism and 98; physicality of 142; Puerto Rican 249–250
racism to speciesism 265–278; animal rights 274–277; human and animal apartheid 268–274; zooethical poetry 274–277
radical feminism 154; *see also* feminism
Raffestin, C. 75n10
"Rainbow Radicalism" (Ogbar) 255–258
rape and sexual abuse 35; *see also* abuse
rapprochement 55
"ready.gov" ad campaign 197
reappropriation 171–173
rebirth of myth 144–158; 9/11 150–153; American hero 150–153; backlash against feminism 147–148; captivity narratives 145–147; current scenario 154–157; female survivors 153–154; male heroes 153–154; silencing of female voices 148–150; trauma 144–145, 150–153; Wayne, J. 145–147
Redmond, S. 246
Reforma Social 106
Reggae music 245
religious fundamentalism 16
religious minorities 11
religious persecution 7
Rematriation Magazine 17
Republic of South Africa 268
research: human rights 48; positionality 167–171
resistance 171–173, 211–213
Respect (Franklin) 246
restorative justice 14
Revolution (1791–1804) 225

Rhode Island (battleship) 102
Rhythm and Blues (R'n'B) 244–245, 251, 253
rhythm and dance 243
Riacho (hydroelectric plant) 218
Ribeiro, M. 118–119
Rich, A. 66
Richter, D. K. 36
rights and empires 45–55; during 18th century 46–47; Evangelicalization 55; marginalized social groups 54; paradigm shift 49; Puritanism 51
Rights of Man, The (Paine) 36
Rights of Man and Citizen 228
Rilke, R. M. 273
Rio de Janeiro 244
Rivera, R. 250, 252
Rivera, T. 63 (see ...*Y no se lo tragó la tierra*/...AND THE EARTH DID NOT PART)
Rivera-Rideau, P. R. 232–233, 239n18
Rivero, Y. 254
Roach, M. 251
Robbins, K. 107
Robinson Crusoe (Defoe) 269
Robinson, S. 109
Rockefellers 38
Rodríguez, P 252
Rody, C. 287–288
Roosevelt, F. D. 37, 95–96, 108, 111n2, 112n3, 188, 196
Roosevelt, T. 37
rootless people 69
Rosado, M. R. 231
Rosario, D. 223–237
Rosas, J. M. 37
Round House, The (Erdrich) 63
Royal Convent of Jesus Mary of Mexico City (Sigüenza y Góngora) 51
Royster, J. J. 118
Rumsfeld, D. 151
Rushforth, T. 105
Russell, W. W. 97–98, 103
Ryder, R. 278n2

Sabater, J. 250, 255
Sacralization 47
Saint-Amour, P. 201
Saint-Domingue 6, 35
Salazar, M. 251, 255
Salem, Massachusetts 45
Salsa music 251
SalSoul 254
Samba de Coco (dance) 219

Sandoval, C. 117–118
San people 268
Sansone, L. 247
Santaella, F. 228
Santamaría, M. 251, 253, 255
Santiago 99–103, *100*
Santiago de los Caballeros 99–103, *100*
Santo Domingo *see* Dominican Republic
São Francisco River 213, 218
Sassafras, Cypress & Indigo (Shange) 126–127
Sassen, S. 198
Sawyer, M. 14
Sayer, D. 177n10
"Say It Loud, I'm Black and I'm Proud" (Brown) 246
Schenandoah, M. 17
Schomburg, A. A. 224, 229–230
Schoultz, L. 38–39
Scott, W. 142
Searchers, The (Wayne) 146
Second Reconstruction 183
Second World War (1939–1945) 7, 9, 47, 181
See Now Then (Kincaid) 132–142; autobiography and fiction 133–138, 142; creative processes 134; inferiority 140; microaggressions 141; racism 142; shaping of memory 138; truth-telling 136–137
Sephardim 7
Sertão do Pajeú 218
Serviço de Proteção aos Índios (SPI) 289
Sextet, J. C. 250, 251
sexual abuse 17, 35, 128; Indigenous women 17; rape and 35; *see also* abuse
sexual exploitation 31
sexual harassment 17
sexual identities 117
Sexual Mountain and Black Women Writers, The (Hernton) 124–125
Shange, N. 125–127
shared heritage 166
Shulock, E. 148–149
Sigüenza y Góngora, Carlos de: about 45; Catholicism 55; *criollo* 53; as historians 51; impact on the publication landscapes 48; *Indian Spring (Primavera indiana, poema sacrohistórico, idea de María Santíssima de Guadalupe)* 52; interpretations of human rights 48; life and work 47, 52; literary figures 46; marginalized social groups 54; mathematician 51; national politics 53; New Spanish collective conscience 49; polymaths 45; posthumous receptions 50; printing output 48; reception history 46, 52–53; reformation/enlightenment 50, 54; roles in early modern publishing 48; Royal Convent of Jesus Mary of Mexico City 51
silencing of female voices 148–150
Silencing the Past: Power and the Production of History (Trouillot) 6, 225
Silko, L. M. 74
Simal, B. 284, 290n2
Simone, N. 246, 253
Sisters in Spirit 16
Slash (Armstrong) 66
Slaughter, J. R. 2, 8
slavery 31; colonialism and 6, 139; inhumanity and 34
Sleepy Lagoon 183, 185, 188
Slotkin, R. 146
Slovenia 274–275, 277
Small Place (Kincaid) 134
Smith, M. 153
Smolinski, R. 45
Snowden, T. 109
Soare, A. 149
social marginalization 70
Society of Jesus 47, 52
socioeconomic inequality 13
Sohn, S. H. 290n3
Soja, E. 66, 75n10
Somerset, J. 267
Songs of Innocence and Experience (Blake) 85
Son Montuno 244
Sontag, S. 148
Sophocles 87
Souci, S. 226
Soul 245
Soul and Salsa 243
Soul music 246, 258
Soul musicians 246
Sousa e Castro, A. 214
South Africa 269, 279n6
South America 35, 41–42, 50–52, 227
South American Indians 51
South Carolina 127
Southern California 190
Southern United States 11
Spain 4, 106, 193, 238n8, 238n11
Spaniards 4–5, 84

Spanish-American War of 1898 248
Spanish Black Atlantic 224, 228
Spanish colonizers 62
Spanish Conquest 84
Spanish-European invasion 168
Spanish-speaking Caribbean 223
speciesism 278n2–3
Spic 259n1; *see also* Puerto Rico
Spider-Man (movie) 151
Sri Lanka 7
State Department 9, 96–98, 103, 109
state-sponsored terrorism 14
Stefancic, J. 184, 189
Stievermann, J. 45
struggle for human rights 219–221
suffering of animals 271
Supreme Indigenous Council of Michoacán 163, *164*, 169
survival alliance *see* alliance of survival
Swift, J. 273
systemic sexual feminicide 16

Takaki, R. 10
Takesue, A. B. 71
Talk Stories (Kincaid) 134
Taylor, L. F. 54
"Temporada Apologika" (Guilitraro) 63
Temptations, The 253
Tendencias (magazine) 88
Tense Future: Modernism, Total War, Encyclopedic Form (Saint-Amour) 201
terrenos baldíos (vacant lands) 37
Terror Dream: What 9/11 Revealed about America, The (Faludi) 144
Their Dogs Came With Them (Viramontes) 70
Thomas, A. 51
Thomas, P. 249
Thompson, T. L. 36
Though the Heavens May Fall (Wise) 267
Through the Arc of the Rain Forest (Yamashita) 283–284, 290n2, 291n5
Time 149
"Times Are Changing" (Sabater) 255
Tlostanova, M. 121–122
Tobar, H. 196–205
"To Be Young, Gifted, and Black" (Simone) 246
Torfs, R. 54
Tornado, T. 258
Toronto Star 149

Torres, E. 227
To the Lighthouse (Woolf) 137
Traister, R. 155, 157
transfrontera contact zone 71
trauma 144–145, 150–153
traumatic experiences 67
Treaty of Guadalupe Hidalgo 188
Treitler, V. B. 9
Trouillot, M.-R. 3, 6–7, 225, 228–229
Truth Commission on the Historical Clarification of the Armed Conflict in Guatemala 89–90
Tully, J. 181–184, 187

UN Declaration of Human Rights 33, 36
undocumented immigrants 11
"unfinished revolutions" 6
Unified Black Movement (MNU) 220
United Fruit Company 38
United Nations 9, 31–32, 42, 89–90, 132; *Guatemala: Memory of Silence (Guatemala: memoria del silencio) – Report of the Commission for Historical Clarification* 83; *International Covenant on Economic, Social and Cultural Rights* 181
United Nations Declaration on the Rights of Indigenous Peoples 74n3
United Nations Educational, Scientific and Cultural Organization (UNESCO): *pirekua* as Intangible Cultural Heritage of 168; Representative List of the Intangible Cultural Heritage of Humanity 173; research and activism 168; song as world heritage 173–177
United States 284; African descent 223; agriculture 185; Canada engagement in 12; Catholicism 55; cultural intellectual traditions 224; foreign policies 148; foreign policy 147, 151; human rights 8–18, 54; land ownership inequality 67; Latina/o 224; migrant workers 63; military actions in the Caribbean 95; national history 47; national security 96, 106; popular music industry 259n2; protest in 106–109; Puerto Rican 249–250; racial categorizations 250; Spanish-speaking migrant community 247; unequal relations between Latin America and 245; warships 99

Universal Declaration of Human Rights (UDHR) 7, 31–32, 36, 42, 61, 118, 174, 181
University of New Brunswick 221
University of Seville 228
UN Secretary General 83
unwarranted interference 95
urban blackness 232
Uruguay 37–39, 106
U.S. Constitution 12
U.S. Declaration of Independence of 1776 6
"Use It Before You Lose It" (Valentin) 252
U.S. Labor Department 248
U.S. Marines 98–106, *104*, 110
U.S. Navy 96
U.S. Senate 96

Valentin, B. 252
van der Kroef, J. M. 84
Vásquez, H. 97
Veerman, A. L. 145
veganism 278n3
Venezuela 41
Vibrant Matter: A Political Ecology of Things (Bennett) 292n9
Vičar (this name is one word), B. 276
Vick, W. 103
Videla, J. R. 38
Vietnam War 38, 245
Villarán, J. O. 236
Villard, O. G. 107
violations of human rights 12–13, 15–16, 18, 31, 34, 36, 38–39, 41, 61–62, 66, 173–177
violence: Black women writers 123–125; deprivation and 16; geographic 64; literary representation of 88–91; poverty and 234; *see also* neocolonial violence
Viramontes, H. M. 70–71, 75n10
Virginia 149
Virgin of Guadalupe 46, 52
virility 123

Walcott, D. 67
Wallace, M. 124
Wallerstein, I. 3, 7
Wallner, A. O. 82, 88
Wall Street 196
Walsh, C. 235
War on Terror 10, 16

"Watermelon Man" (Hancock) 251
Wayne, J. 145–147, 151, 157
Weeks, R. 258
Weil, K. 265, 267
welfarism 278
What We All Long For (Brand) 74n2
When the Killing's Done (Boyle) 70–71
White, H. 86
white bourgeois womanhood 120
white Creole men 225 should not be capitalized
White House 150
whiteness 223, 236
white War for Independence 6
Whitten, N. E. Jr. 227
"Why the sound of the gun shot" (Detela) 277
Williams, E. 103–104
willing suspension of disbelief 90
Wilson, W. 95, 97
Winans, R. 102
Winant, H. 190
Wise, F. 98–99
Wise, S. M. 267, 271–272
withdrawal 109–111
Witte, J. 54
Women's Media Center 155
women writers *see* Black women writers
Woodcock, B. 85
Woolf, V. 137
"world Christianity" 53
World Peace Begins With Human Dignity 73, 75n15
World Trade Center 147, 149, 152–153; *see also* 9/11
World War I 96, 105–107, 111
worldwide nationality and citizenship code 193–194
Wretched of the Earth, The (Fanon) 221
WWII 146
Wynter, S. 3

Xantippe 62
XLV Artistic Contest of the P'urhépecha People 163, *164–165*
X-Men (movie) 151

Yamashita, K. T. 283–284, 286, 288, 290n2, 291n5
…Y no se lo tragó la tierra/…AND THE EARTH DID NOT PART (Rivera) 63
Yoruba 122

Young, C. 147–148
Young, I. M. 192
Young Lords Party 243, 247, 255–258
YouTube 41
Yugoslavia 274–275, 277

Zacán P'urhépecha Concurso 165, 168, 171–173, *176*

Zaire 211
Zapatista 15, 72, 169
Zimmerman, G. 11
Zinn, H. 10
"zone of nonbeing" 64
zooethical poetry 274–277
Zoot Suit Riots 183, 186
Zumba, G. 214–215

Printed in the United States
by Baker & Taylor Publisher Services